BROADWAY'S BEAUTIFUL LOSERS

BROADWAY'S BEAUTIFUL LOSERS

BY MARILYN STASIO

Delacorte Press / New York

DESIGN BY BEN BIRNBAUM

Library of Congress Cataloging in Publication Data

Stasio, Marilyn, 1940–   comp.
Broadway's beautiful losers.

CONTENTS: Look: we've come through, by H. Wheeler.—
The beauty part, by S. J. Perelman.—The last analysis,
by S. Bellow. [etc.]
1. American drama—20th century. 2. American drama
—20th century—History and criticism. 3. Theater—New
York (City). I. Title.
PS634.S83   812'.5'408   76-178723

To my parents, who believe in me,
and
To my husband, in whom I believe.

ACKNOWLEDGMENTS

That this book exists at all is a tribute to the dedication, generosity, and pure guts of theatre people—specifically, of the many writers, directors, producers, actors, and other creative people who suffered me to interview them, raking over old wounds and picking over old regrets. These are the real "winners," and I hope I have honored their trust in me. Special thanks go to my colleague, author and critic John Lahr, who graciously made available to me several invaluable private tapes, of which I made extensive use in the chapter on *The Beauty Part*. My deepest thanks go to my amazing husband, who not only handed me this project on a silver platter, but cared enough to keep the spark alive. My gratitude, too, to: Phyllis Westberg, my gem of an agent; and Stanley Newman, my understanding editor at *Cue* magazine.

Contents

INTRODUCTION

LAMENT FOR FAILURES

by Howard Dietz

Sing a lament for the plays that fail—
A dirge for the shows that fold.
A tear on the bier of the flops of the year
And the tickets that couldn't be sold.
Requiem sound for the overly ribald—
The "ball in the air" that was faultily dribbled—
And the play that had little to say.
Wringing of hands for the major fiascos,
The Saturday sundown of would-be Belascos
And the scenery carted away.
Sing a lament.
Sing for the actors who practiced in vain
Lines that were labeled inept and inane.
Sing for the orchestra down in the pits
Playing the numbers that sounded like hits.
Sing for the authors who wrote in the dawn,
The "doctors" who came when the patient was gone.
Sing for the backers who put up the dough—
One for the backer and two for the show.
Sing with your faces way down to the floor
The dancers, directors, the deans of decor.
Sing a lament.
Sing a lament for the plays that fail
For Sullivan and McBride
But make it a wake for the critics' mistake—
The Beautiful One that died.

Requesting that his dirge be "accompanied on a grass harp," lyricist-playwright Howard Dietz wrote this lament in 1952, right after Truman Capote's *The Grass Harp* folded on Broadway. It first appeared in the drama section of *The New York Times*, and is here reprinted with the author's permission.

xiii

Nobody loves a loser. Ours is an upwardly mobile culture in a success-oriented age, a civilization in which failure is embarrassing, threatening, and, in a metaphorical sense, even vaguely anti-American. The American theater is no less a reflection of its success-culture orientation than the American Stock Exchange or the National Football League. Psychologically as much as economically, the commercial theater is rigidly gripped by the success syndrome. Structured as an industry, it is therefore subject to the same economic laws which determine any other business venture functioning within our free-enterprise system. Its productions are not works of dramatic art judged on artistic grounds, but industrial commodities evaluated on an open commercial market.

Since commercial success is not always synonymous with artistic merit, it does not necessarily follow that a "hit" is a "good" show, while a "flop" is a "bad" show—although, that is, indeed, the system of aesthetics under which the Broadway theater functions. If we apply the more appropriate commercial criteria of evaluation, it is far more justifiable to qualify the "hit" as a commercially successful commodity. Judged by the same economically determined value system, the "flop" thus becomes nothing more than an unmarketable commodity, something which deviates in one fashion or another from the product demanded by its consumer-audience.

The elements which determine the commercial failure of a play are frequently the same factors which flaw it on artistic grounds—but not always. All too often a play flops on grounds only peripherally related to dramatic art, but essentially determined by the theater's current function, as a purveyor of commercial merchandise.

These are Broadway's "beautiful losers," the plays with which this book is concerned. These are the plays that are victimized by a system whose structure and values automatically pronounce them failures. These are the plays that pass into oblivion as theater art because they have failed as commercial products. They have had no influence on the development of dramatic literature; they have earned neither recognition nor reward for their creators; they have brought no joy to the audiences who might have loved them.

All five plays in this collection have three things in common: they all possess distinct merit as theater art; they were all failures on Broadway's commercial market; and, therefore, they all illustrate the diverse and often arbitrary factors which predetermine a play's failure as a commercial commodity without seriously affecting its quality as a work of dramatic art. While it is hoped that a close analysis of these five plays will lead to a reevaluation of their artistic merits, it is the complementary intention of this study to isolate and examine some of the many and complex nonartistic factors, inherent in Broadway's commercial structure, which each season send more "beautiful losers" into oblivion.

Under the economic dictates of Broadway's system of production, anything less than a hit is a flop. Since a "hit," technically speaking, is a show which recovers its investment and returns a profit, any show which fails to do so automatically becomes a "flop." So, while it is possible for a show to achieve an extended run, by meeting its operating costs on a week-to-week basis from its box office returns, such a show is surviving, not flourishing. And to the trade, if not to the uninitiated public, the show remains a flop. Operating under these stringent economic conditions, the commercial theater simply cannot support any production that is flawed, or of limited audience appeal, or that in any one of a variety of ways deviates from the Broadway market's pattern of formularized success. Thus, if a single element contributing to a play's total production is the slightest bit askew, the show can become an instant failure.

Assuming that a play has a script with artistic merit, it can still become a "beautiful loser" by virtue of its production flaws. Any number of factors can mutilate a decent script in production: the casting is poor; the show is underfinanced; a director is inexperienced or inept; an individual element like music or choreography may be inadequate to the rest of the production; the second act is poorly written; the show has been overproduced; etc. Sometimes, a more arbitrary reason determines a flop—shows have succeeded and failed because of their *titles*.

Very often, a show is confounded by its mere placement in time: it opens in the wake of a political assassination or a transit or newspaper strike, or in a season, a decade, or even a century that can't accommodate its theatrical viewpoint. *Pal Joey* is a perfect example of a show that opened out of its time. When it was produced originally in 1940 it was almost universally loathed for its then-shocking plot about the tawdry love affair of its two unsavory principals; but twelve years later, in revival, it was hailed as a classic of the musical genre. Similarly, *Awake and Sing*, opening in the early 1930's in the depths of the Depression, was much too discomforting for depressed America, although by the late

1930's when it was revived, the climate had changed sufficiently to afford it a far warmer reception.

Sometimes—and this is even more of a heartbreaker—a play flops because it has been misplaced. Some shows, regardless of their merits of script or production, simply don't belong on Broadway, under the current structure, because of their nonformula subject matter or unconventional production approaches. If a play is too much of a maverick, the Broadway audience just won't support it. Among such misguided and misplaced productions of the 1968–69 season were John Guare's *Cop-Out* and the Terrence McNally/Israel Horovitz/Leonard Melfi venture, *Morning, Noon, and Night.* One wonders how *Borstal Boy, Sheep on the Runway,* and *Inquest,* which were all casualties of the following season, would have fared had they been produced off Broadway instead of on Broadway. In 1971, *The Trial of the Catonsville Nine* was a smash off Broadway, but flopped a few days after it was transferred to a Broadway house. At the start of the 1971–72 season, Truman Capote's *The Grass Harp* was revived, in musical version, in an overproduced Broadway mounting which summarily flopped.

Jules Feiffer's macabre satire, *Little Murders,* is the most obvious example, in recent seasons, of a play that lost its way on Broadway. After an open-and-shut disaster of a production during the 1966–67 Broadway season, the play was revived the following season *off* Broadway, and was a solid success. Although some would have it that the Broadway production was a shambles, and that the play didn't come alive until Alan Arkin took it under his arm off Broadway, this is largely cant. Arkin's casting and his directorial interpretation were much more compatible with the play's unusual black-comedy vision, but even in its Broadway production the lethal humor of Feiffer's play came across loud and clear, if reviewers and audiences had wanted to listen. The play was simply too nonconformist for the success machine of Broadway, in which hits are manufactured according to fixed patterns, for consumption by an audience whose tastes have been determined on the same rigid principles.

As false a system of "aesthetics" as Broadway's economically determined structure of "hits" and "flops" has proved, and as harmful as it has been for individual plays of distinguished but uncommon merit, one can only speculate on the full extent of its effect on the contemporary American theater. On the most basic level, it has contributed to the general stagnation currently undermining the *living* aspect of the theater.

Spiraling costs for producing and operating theatrical ventures have made this the age of the "super hit"—the blockbuster "smasheroo" which alone can reach the huge number of theatergoers whose mass support is crucial if a play is to recover its enormous investment and return a profit to its investors. A play must run for years to be successful on these terms (unless it is lucky enough to secure a movie deal for its producers), and given the still-swelling costs of theater economics, there are indications that the present three- and four- and even seven-year runs of the "super hits" will be extended even longer in the future.

The result is a theater composed of museum pieces—shows running for years and years, constantly going through cast turnovers, changing subtly or even in great leaps from their original dramatic conception, and eventually going to seed. There are thousands of theatergoers who never view these hoary "super hits" until after they have gone to pot. And since many of them believe in all innocence that they are experiencing the same theatrical event which five or six years ago brought a cheering opening-night audience to its feet, they can only conclude that this sodden object before them indeed represents the legendary "magic" of the theater. When one considers the potential theater lovers alienated by such dismal experiences, and what this could mean for the future of the American theater, one begins to sense the insidious nature of Broadway as the onetime repository of a "living" art form now debased into a mechanized factory of commodities known as "hits" and "flops."

In addition to having forced Broadway into its current position as the breeding ground of "super hits" and "instant flops," the economically determined structure of the commercial theater has wielded a crippling influence on the kind of theater art written and produced each season. Intimidated by imposing production costs, and not a little wary of the diminishing law of returns, the canny theatrical producer grows ever more cautious. As a businessman functioning in a high-risk industry, his tendency is to produce shows securely within the safe tradition of past successes. This production principle of the "formula hit" has led to a numbing number of repetitive play productions, as well as to a general leveling of theatrical standards about what constitutes a "good" (i.e., "potential hit") show. Each season, there is a deadening carbon-copy sameness about most of the entries, and a resultant hesitancy to experiment, to take chances, to be adventuresome, to grow.

These aspects of the functioning, living art of the theater have been increasingly relegated to areas outside of Broadway proper—to off and off-off Broadway, regional theaters, and repertory companies, primarily— where the financial risks against success are not as stringent. The result has been Broadway's growing tendency to become a "showcase" for productions conceived and nurtured elsewhere. In recent seasons, *Vivat! Vivat Regina!, Old Times, Home, Sleuth, Conduct Unbecoming, The Philanthropist, Hadrian VII,* and several other Broadway offerings came out of London, while *The Great White Hope, Indians, Story Theatre, We Bombed in New Haven,* and other productions originated in regional theaters within the United States.

Since safety has become such an important aspect of theatrical production on Broadway, there is a clear tendency on the part of the commercial producer to mount shows with the greatest margin for success—revivals, lavish spectacle-musicals, light comedies featuring major stars, plays "pretested" in London, in stock, or in regional theater fields, and dramas by "safe" name writers like Arthur Miller and Edward Albee. By their very nature, certain kinds of theater art have automatically become high risks, potential flops before they are even written.

The most conspicuous casualty is the straight drama. Each season, fewer and fewer serious plays are produced, and following the hit/flop scoreboard each season, it does seem as if the straight play is being phased out of existence on Broadway. Every producer knows that straight dramatic fare must be produced and promoted with special care if it is to succeed. But few producers choose to take that care. The economics of mainstem producing being what they are, straight plays are often brought in "on the cheap," without major stars and without sufficient financial backing to keep them open until their special audience finds them. Under the hit/flop stranglehold, the drama—which takes a much longer time to capture the interest of its smaller audience segment— must endure the same quickie do-or-die ordeal as the musical and the comedy, to which audiences respond immediately. And even if a drama does succeed, the returns are much less lucrative than those for some superspectacle. So, the savvy producer finds himself backing fewer chancy dramas, and concentrating more and more on the hit-formula show.

What the existing system has done, therefore, is effectively elbow off the legitimate stage certain forms of theater art. Any show that speaks to a splinter segment of the audience, rather than to the middle-brow common denominator, stands a poor chance of success in the open market. Although the most obvious and appalling casualty is the serious dramatic play, shows that are experimental in either form or content are also extremely risky for Broadway production, as are one-act plays, political satire, verse drama, and any play whose thematic point of view is openly critical of the way of life pursued by the very audience which makes up the bulk of the theater-supporting Broadway public.

The producer who chooses to challenge this analysis of Broadway's production structure might well argue that he is simply supplying the public with what it wants—a variation on the supply-and-demand principle of economics. The obvious retort is that supply-and-demand is a two-way street of reciprocal influence; that audiences nurtured on one-dimensional theater art soon learn to demand it. Nevertheless, the producer's argument has a certain validity. The theatergoer does indeed exert an influence on the type of theater presented on Broadway, so the forces which shape his needs and determine his desires are thus indirectly influencing the state of the American theater. Theatergoing habits are defined by the totality of our contemporary life experience. However one isolates and analyzes the component parts of modern-day life, it does appear that there are forces at work which have blunted our capacity for certain kinds of pleasure, and created in us the need for more bomb-blasting forms of stimulation, both in art and in life.

Today's theatergoer demands of his theatrical experience something a bit more sensational, a bit more spectacular than the theatergoer of an earlier age. While at the moment this means nothing more than super-lavish musical extravaganzas, it is possible to foresee a day in which Broadway will accommodate the public's desire for "something special" with sensual treats of such splendor that they are no longer theater at all but in the same stimulation category as a bear-baiting or a hanging.

Along with this public demand for more voluptuous theatrical experiences comes the theatergoer's greater need of assurance that he is getting his money's worth from the theater. In recent years this has led to an almost fanatical dependence on professional critical opinion. Certainly this became evident during New York City's many and diverse newspaper strikes, when Broadway reached a state of hysterical crisis. Show after show flopped because the theatergoer, deprived of the voice of the critics during the news blackout, declined to take the chance of making his own judgments.

And yet, like everybody else in the legitimate theater, the critics themselves are strangled in the prevalent hit-or-flop syndrome. Burdened by the uncompromising, win-or-lose nature of Broadway, a good many well-intentioned critics are seduced into overpraising shows of limited merit, rather than feel responsible for their failure. Besides fostering mediocrity, this policy turns the critic into a good-natured, but frankly immoral, camp follower. On the other hand, more scrupulous critics can hold fast to their principles and watch some perfectly admirable productions get wiped out because their restrained and heavily qualified admiration failed to ignite public support.

While the critic's dilemma remains a special one, the theatergoer's indecisiveness engenders scorn from the theater people who experience it firsthand. James Coco, the star of Neil Simon's comedy *Last of the Red Hot Lovers,* told an interviewer of a familiar phenomenon. During previews of the show, audiences laughed easily and unaffectedly, Coco said. But once the reviewers had "officially" told people in print that the show was a laff-riot, subsequent audiences roared, screamed, and literally shouted with the laughter that seemed to be called for.

The most undermining result of this dependent audience attitude is in the development of a "herd instinct" among theatergoers. An audience which has relinquished independent thought and judgment is hardly the inquiring, aware, *vital* audience which the theater must have in order to grow. Just as the shows themselves level off into soporific sameness, under the hit/flop system, so too does the audience. Since a hit *must* run forever in order to pay off its big-budget investment and make a sizable profit, it follows that shows must appeal to the lowest common denominator—the vast middle-ground audience.

One would like to believe that this audience is less reality than myth. But if indeed it actually does exist, it has been created and perpetuated by the Broadway system itself, with its tendency to appeal primarily to those specific but insubstantial needs for light relaxation and sensual stimulation which exist in all of us. Since the audience is offered little beyond this limited satisfaction, this is the limited pleasure which we have come to associate with theatergoing, and which we demand of all theatrical experience. The middlebrow audience does exist, then, but in the sense that it has been created out of the middlebrow in each of us. The larger part of our intellectual sensibilities, meanwhile, experiences a vague, unexpressed desire for the theater which could satisfy other, deeper needs. Consistently deprived of it, our theatrical tastes become blunted, and after a while we don't even know what we're missing because we've been so long without it.

From time to time there are hopeful indications that theatergoers themselves are chaffing with dissatisfaction within the "bland behemoth" role to which they've been consigned. *Cue* magazine initiated two surveys on the nature of the theatergoing animal and discovered that a clear majority of readers deplored the standardization of the hit shows which are the staple of theater fare available on Broadway. They indicated a belief that the theater is not addressing the issues of our society, and professed a strong dissatisfaction with the general direction in which the theater seems to be developing. Interestingly, too, when asked to recall their most satisfying theatrical experiences, they named plays by such authors as Eugene O'Neill, William Shakespeare, Tennessee Williams, Arthur Miller, and Edward Albee.

One would like to believe in the sincerity of those responses; to feel them to be the honest, fed-up-to-here protestations of a vital and articulate segment of the theatergoing public—and not merely the conscience-balming platitudes which readers thought were *expected* of them. And yet, these loftily idealistic responses are difficult to reconcile with the stunning apathy which invariably greets nonformula shows and turns them into instant flops whenever they do appear on Broadway.

It could hardly be denied that the audience is also in some measure responsible for the debilitating and self-perpetuating system of the Broadway theater. But the fixing of culpability is not strictly the aim of this book. Rather, it is to awaken recognition of the general malaise gripping the contemporary theater, and to relate it to the economically based structure of the Broadway production system itself. Until such time as this system is forced into substantial and far-reaching change, the American theater will continue its decline as a living art. Thus, the phenomenon of the "beautiful loser" becomes both a symptom of the theater's malaise and, within the context of this book, a means of provoking theater lovers to search out radical ways to thrust our medievally structured theater into a kind of revolutionary renaissance.

LOOK: WE'VE COME THROUGH

---

by Hugh Wheeler

CAST OF CHARACTERS

BELLE DORT

JENNIFER LEWISON

WAIN DUMKE

MILTIE MIZER

BOBBY KRAWEIG

SKIP

Act One

SCENE I

The living room of an apartment in the Chelsea section of New York, high-ceilinged with the seediness of an unrestored brownstone. The furniture is haphazard and gimcrack with a few bits of "amusing" Victoriana from junk stores. The atmosphere isn't depressing, because there is something young and feminine about the muddle—theater posters on the walls, gay flimsy curtains on the two windows Left. A door Right leads to the bedroom. Another door Rear Right reveals a bit of the kitchenette beyond which is the bathroom. The front door Rear Left leads directly to the landing. A daybed stands in the center of the rear wall between the two doors. There is a table between the windows, a bulky old air-conditioner (which isn't working) is in the window closest to the proscenium. An electric fan is near the other window.

At the rise of the curtain, the window without the air conditioner is open. Its curtains float like a sail in the whirr of the fan. BELLE DORT *is sitting unobtrusively reading, wearing heavy, shell-rimmed glasses. She is nineteen, with no evident prettiness. As she reads,* JENNIFER LEWISON *bursts in from the bedroom, dressed only in panties and a bra.* JENNIFER *is an attractive, struggling actress of twenty-one, whose "sophistication" is her most cherished possession. Now she is distraught and therefore more girlish than she would like to be. She is carrying a nail-polishing kit and is walking in a most peculiar, ducklike manner which she explains by pointing at her feet.*

JENNIFER. Nail polish. Won't dry. (*She dumps the polishing kit on the table, hurries to the phone and dials.*) Mr. Onopolis, *dear,* where the hell is my dress? . . . But you swore. Five o'clock. Look at it now. It's practically midnight. (*Gazes out at the broad daylight outside.*)

3

Mercy, how colorful. But, listen, Mr. O., this is a matter of life or death. Literally. So rush out onto the street and grab a boy—any boy. (*Slams down receiver and turns to* BELLE.) Wouldn't you know? The delivery boy was nabbed last night in an East Side rumble.

BELLE. Is Mr. Onopolis sending the dress anyway?

JENNIFER. He can't leave the store. He's got to find someone.

BELLE. I can go.

JENNIFER. Would you, darling? Would you? Oh no, Miltie'll be here any second and I can't be alone with him stark naked. Oh dear, why do I get so unstrung? It's only my entire career at stake. That's all. (*Closes her eyes and mutters to herself as if in an incantation.*) Keep calm. Be sophisticated at all times. Keep calm. (*In her pacing, she comes up to* BELLE *and notices the glasses.*) Really! (*She snatches the glasses off* BELLE'S *nose.*) Do you want a red band on your nose again? With that boy from Doubleday's taking you to *Ivan the Terrible*, Part Two?

BELLE. He isn't coming.

JENNIFER. What happened this time?

BELLE. I called it off in the lunch hour.

JENNIFER. But why, for heaven's sake?

BELLE. I knew he'd only invited me because he'd had a spat with Gloria. I told him he didn't have to take me if he didn't want to, so he said: All right.

JENNIFER. Angels and ministers of grace defend us.

BELLE. I don't see what's wrong with that.

JENNIFER. Oh well, I suppose it's legitimate at nineteen. You should have seen me when I hit New York. Straws in my hair.

BELLE. Not you. Even at Taylor High you were the most glamorous creature I'd ever laid eyes on.

JENNIFER. (*Pleased.*) Was I really?

BELLE. You and Wain.

JENNIFER (*Less pleased*). We don't have to drag Wain in, do we? (*Noticing.*) Oh damn, I've left a toe out. (*She runs to the table, picks up the nail-polishing kit, squats down on the floor and starts to work.*)

BELLE. I'll always remember the first time I saw you. Coming out of the science lab. Wain had his arm over your shoulder. It was an October morning, all golden and sunny—and you glittered.

JENNIFER. We did look rather divine together, I must admit. I adored showing him off. Almost as good as a mink coat.

BELLE. Later when you got to be friendly with Sally and came to the house, I always hid. Don't you remember?

JENNIFER. It's an appalling admission but I hardly remember you at all.

BELLE. I hid because I was ashamed.

JENNIFER. For pity's sake, of what?

BELLE. Of being skinny and clumsy—but mostly of the braces on my teeth. It was sacrilege, I thought—to confront Beauty with the Beast.

JENNIFER. Rather an odd child, weren't you, dear?

BELLE. According to Mom and Sally, I was a Communist.

JENNIFER. Darling, are you sure it was me you were hiding from? Now I come to think of it, Sally always used to say . . .

BELLE. That idiot sister of mine. As if I had any stupid feeling about Wain. It was the two of you indivisible. The day you eloped, I locked myself into the john with D. H. Lawrence. I wanted to die. Not because you'd gone, exactly, but because it made me realize I'd have to stay in that terrible town forever.

JENNIFER (*The toe is finished. She rises with the kit*). You weren't much of a prophet, were you, dear?

BELLE. You and Wain helped on that too. I swore if you could escape, I could.

JENNIFER (*Taking the polish back to the table*). You can thank your lucky stars you didn't do it by eloping.

BELLE. I would have if anyone had asked me.

JENNIFER. Didn't Leroy Archer? He always asked everyone.

BELLE. Not me. Oh, the bliss of that bus terminal. I'll always remember. Good-bye Groversville. No more Yurkee's drugstore, no more Charlie Doyle's Jaguar honking for Arlene next door. No more Mom reading out loud from the *Reader's Digest*. "Should Teen-agers Go Steady?" "Does Apple Pie Cause Cancer?"

JENNIFER. Darling, does it?

BELLE (*On her hobby horse*). All those elm trees and deep freezes. Gracious living. Play together, pray together. The grass roots of America. Our Town. Conformity. Ugh!

JENNIFER. Listen, sweetie. A tiny word of advice from a struggling actress. You're a dear girl, you're divinely prompt about paying your part of the rent and I cherish you. But if you want boys to take you to *Ivan the Terrible*, Part Two—do try to be just a little less articulate.

BELLE. I do talk, don't I?

JENNIFER. Yes, darling.

BELLE. But what's wrong with talking—with communicating?

JENNIFER. It's just that some people don't like being communicated to *all* the time.

BELLE. If only you and Wain had communicated a little.

JENNIFER. Lack of communication wasn't our problem. We called each other every name in the dictionary. (*Studying her idly, then peering at her hair.*) You never used that hair spray, and I implored you.

BELLE (*Defensive*). What's the point of hair sprays? If you've got stringy hair, you've got stringy hair and it's up to you to become interesting as someone with stringy hair. Look at Collette.

JENNIFER. Yes, darling, I know. . . . Oh, my God, is there anything to drink in the house? (*Makes a dash into the kitchenette.*)

BELLE. There's still some of the vodka you bought yesterday, isn't there? And some tonic water.

JENNIFER (*From kitchen*). But agents drink Scotch. (*Much clattering of bottles in kitchen.*) It's catastrophe, total catastrophe. (*Re-emerges from kitchen, holding up an empty Scotch bottle in one hand and a half full bottle of bourbon in the other.*) Not a whisper of Scotch. But I found this bourbon way back of Wain's guitar in the bathroom. He must have left it when I threw him out. But, gosh, that's over four months ago. Does bourbon go bad?

BELLE. I don't think so. Pour it in the Scotch bottle. He'll never know the difference.

JENNIFER. Won't he?

BELLE. Of course not. Give them the right labels and they're happy. Sheep.

JENNIFER. Oh well, I suppose. . . . (*She starts to transfer the liquor. The front door buzzer rings a loud, jaunty tattoo.* BELLE *gets up.*) Oh God, Miltie! (*Closes her eyes and incants.*) Keep calm, keep calm.

BELLE (*Pressing the door buzzer*). It could be your dress.

JENNIFER. A delivery boy ringing like that? Oh well, why not —if they keep getting nabbed in rumbles. Darling, you don't have any money, do you? I never went to collect my unemployment.

BELLE. That's all right. I was paid today.

JENNIFER. Bright Angel! Then handle it while I hurtle into a robe. (*Scurries into the bedroom, taking the two bottles with her. As she goes into the bedroom, she stumbles on a little step.*) Damn. My polish! (*Exits. There is a knock at the door.* BELLE, *with her glasses on, goes to open it.* WAIN DUMKE *is standing on the threshold.* WAIN, JENNIFER'S *husband, is twenty-two, a big blond, very handsome "hunk of man" of the Hollywood starlet variety. He is wearing a light windbreaker, a sports*

shirt, and tight jeans. He carries an old army duffel bag. The instant
BELLE *sees him, she is transfixed. She gazes at him in astonished pleasure.*
Then, self-conscious, whips off her glasses.)

BELLE. Wain!

WAIN. (*Not recognizing her*). Hi.

BELLE. You don't recognize me, do you?

WAIN. Sure, you're one of the kids from downstairs, Rosalie, Phyllis,
hi.

BELLE. I'm Belle, Sally Dort's sister from Groversville. I'm living
here with Jennifer at the moment.

WAIN (*Studies her, finds her totally uninteresting, smiles with mechanical charm*). Well, little old Sally's sister. What d'you know? (*He
drops his duffel bag on the floor.*) God, it's a sweat box in here. Why
the hell doesn't she have the air-conditioner on?

BELLE. It makes such a terrible noise.

WAIN. Girls! (*He strips off his windbreaker and moves toward the
air-conditioner.*)

BELLE (*Watching him, studying the air-conditioner*). I realize this
is none of my business and I despise nosy people. But have you come
back?

WAIN. I'm not in Kalamazoo, am I?

BELLE. I mean, are you planning to come back to Jennifer, because if
you are . . . Gosh, I don't know. There's a terrible mental block. But I'm
sure we'll be able to get around it if we're clever, with me as a kind of
catalyst.

WAIN (*Barely listening, studying air-conditioner*). Look, Phyllis,
let's just relax a little, eh? I'm just in from the Coast. I'm beat. (*He
turns on a knob. The air-conditioner starts making an appalling racket.*)

BELLE (*Shouting*). You see what I mean?

WAIN (*Fiddling unsuccessfully with the knobs, yelling*). For Christ's
sakes—and it's only six years old.

BELLE (*Shouting*). It's disgusting, isn't it? All this built-in obso-
lescence.

WAIN (*Shouting*). Uh? (*At this moment,* JENNIFER, *in a bathrobe,
terribly sophisticated just in case it is Miltie, sweeps in from the bedroom. She sees* WAIN *and reacts in dismay.*)

JENNIFER. Oh, no! (*This is swallowed up in the noise of the air-
conditioner. She shouts.*) For pity's sake, turn that thing off! (WAIN
shows no sign of moving. BELLE, *leaving her glasses on the table, runs to
the machine, fiddles, mixes up the switches, finally stops the noise.*)

WAIN (*With not quite convincing sexy swagger*). Hi, Jenny.

JENNIFER (*Her composure recovered, very sweet*). Well, well, the return of the breadloser. (*Looks at the duffel bag and points.*) If that revoltingly familiar object means what I think it means—good-bye, darling, ta ta. Divine to have seen you. But no room at the inn.

WAIN. That's a hell of a welcome.

JENNIFER. It isn't meant to be a welcome, dear.

BELLE. But, Jennifer, he's come all the way from the Coast. At least give him a chance to open his mouth.

JENNIFER. What would I want his mouth open for?

WAIN (*To Belle*). Look, kid, how about stepping into the bedroom for a while?

BELLE. Yes, yes, of course, Wain. (*Starts for bedroom.*)

JENNIFER. Dearest Belle, if you move a muscle I'll wring your neck.

BELLE. But you've got to let him . . .

JENNIFER. Communicate? Darling, Wain has only four speeches and I know them by heart. Unless I'm much mistaken, this is the moment for speech number three. We've had our ups and downs, but, gosh, Jenny kid, there's a bond that nothing can sever. Accurately interpreted, this means—he's broke and wants to come crawling home to Mother. Right, Wain?

WAIN. Bitchy as ever, aren't you, baby?

JENNIFER. A tiny bit, dear, but only in self-defense. Poor Wain, how was the Coast? Very unfriendly?

WAIN. For the record, the Coast was fine. I did two Indie Western pilots.

JENNIFER. Well, well.

WAIN. There was an even bigger break building up at Desilu, but I bailed out because . . . (*He breaks off, gesturing with his head at* BELLE. BELLE *starts for the bedroom.*)

JENNIFER (*Commanding*). Belle! (BELLE *stops.*)

WAIN (*Resigned to her presence, sexily hitches up his jeans and moves toward Jennifer, both the conquering hero and the penitent male*). Gosh, Jenny, I don't blame you for being this way. I know what I was like at the end, bumming around, living off you. But it was just that I wasn't getting the breaks and now . . . (*Takes her in his arms.*) Okay, baby. Let's forget the sparring and get down to essentials. Four months. God how I missed you. You missed me too if only you'd stop kidding yourself. (*He embraces her passionately.*) Hi, honey, hiya. How you feel now, honey? (JENNIFER, *completely relaxed in his embrace, lets him kiss her and fondle her, then she moves aside and gives a big, gaping yawn.*)

JENNIFER. Ah me, the flame that was once a fire not even an ember. (*To* BELLE.) Darling, I was wrong. That's speech number four.

WAIN (*Making a rather halfhearted grab at her*). For God's sake, Jenny, lay off.

JENNIFER (*Patting his arm*). Dearest Wain, you're a dear, sweet boy for them that likes that sort of thing and let's have lunch sometime. But it just so happens I'm expecting a very important date and I don't want this dump reeking of withered orange blossom. So—and I say this in the fondest possible way (*Points at duffel bag*), take up your bed, in which, I must admit, I've had my moments—and walk.

BELLE (*Putting her hand protectively on* WAIN's *arm*). But, Jennifer . . .

JENNIFER. Dearest Belle, don't look so agonized. He's used to being talked to this way. Aren't you, dear?

WAIN. She just shoots her mouth off.

BELLE. But whatever you feel, he's your husband. He's trying to make a reconciliation. It's an immensely important moment. You can't possibly leave everything unresolved.

JENNIFER. Name one thing between me and Wain that's unresolved. (*To* WAIN.) Isn't she sweet, darling? And devoted to you.

WAIN. Who's this guy that's coming?

BELLE. He's nothing personal—just a theatrical agent.

JENNIFER. Oh God, now you've told him that, he'll never go. (*The front door buzzer rings.*)

BELLE (*Excited*). It's him. (*Presses door release.*)

JENNIFER. *He*, dear. Don't you learn anything at Doubleday's? Oh dear, disaster again. (*To* Wain.) All right, sweetie, I know when I'm licked. Stick around awhile, spend the evening with Belle if she'll have you. But don't you dare try to steal Miltie. And if you're still here when I get back tonight . . . (*Makes a throat-cutting gesture. Then turns to* BELLE.) Belle dear, get the bourbon—Scotch—out of the bedroom. (BELLE *hurries into the bedroom.* JENNIFER *surveys* WAIN *dispiritedly.*) Wouldn't you know! Oh, well. (*She abbreviates her incantation.*) K.C. K.C. (*There is a knock on the door.* JENNIFER, *at her most sophisticated, sweeps to open it.* MILTIE MIZER, *twenty-eight, enters. He wears an Italian silk suit, very dark sunglasses, and an air of immense cosmopolitan nonchalance which does not entirely camouflage the original Flatbush.*) Miltie—darling!

MILTIE (*Surveys her near-nudity through the dark glasses, then raises them and continues the scrutiny*). Well, this is starting our evening off on the right foot, isn't it?

JENNIFER. This ghastly neighborhood. It's totally impossible to get a dress delivered in time.

MILTIE. My dear child, don't blame the neighborhood. Kate Hepburn, I assure you, has just such a problem in Turtle Bay. Let me look at you. Yes, yes, fine. I don't think I've oversold you.

JENNIFER. Miltie, you don't mean you've got something for me?

MILTIE. Didn't I make a solemn oath over those rather bruised Rob Roys at Virginia's?

JENNIFER. Oh, Miltie angel, tell me. I'm dying.

MILTIE. Patience, my child. Aren't you going to introduce me to your little friends?

JENNIFER. Oh, Miltie, you are a monster. (*Introducing* BELLE.) This is Belle Dort, my roommate. Belle—Mr. Mizer.

BELLE. Hello.

MILTIE. Miss Dort.

JENNIFER (*Turning to* WAIN). And this is Wain Dumke. A husband of mine.

MILTIE. So.

JENNIFER. It was ages ago, of course. Practically in the cradle. Doomed from the altar.

WAIN (*Impressed with agent*). Hi, Mr. Mizer.

BELLE. Wain's an actor too, Mr. Mizer. He's just been doing all sorts of television on the Coast.

MILTIE (*Alert*). Who did you work for?

WAIN. Ost and Raden.

MILTIE (*Patronizing*). Well, well. One has to make a start somewhere.

WAIN. I did a couple of Western pilots for them. A big part in one —the sheriff's kid brother. The show's got a brand-new gimmick. You see, it's the sheriff's kid brother who . . .

JENNIFER (*Annoyed*). Wain darling, not the entire plot, please.

MILTIE (*Inspecting* WAIN). Walk around. (WAIN *starts in a Western slouch.*) Now—the rear view, please. (WAIN *turns and struts away from* MILTIE.) Work on that derriere, kid. Get some expression into it. In the field of TV Westerns, there's only room at the top for a truly triumphant ass. (*Loses all interest in* WAIN, *looks at the bottle in* BELLE's *hand. To* JENNIFER.) Is your roommate carrying that bottle purely as a defensive weapon?

BELLE. Oh, I'm sorry. Would you like a drink? Some Scotch?

MILTIE. Something a little less inevitable, I feel. Bourbon on the rocks, perhaps—if you please.

WAIN (*Unasked*). I'll take Scotch.

BELLE (*Looking down at the bottle with some uncertainty*). All right. (*Goes into kitchenette.*)

JENNIFER. (*Grabs* MILTIE, *who graciously lets her draw him to the daybed, where they sit down together.*) Now, Miltie. Now, now. Tell me, please.

MILTIE (*Very professional*). Can you fly to San Francisco tomorrow?

JENNIFER. I could fly to Baluchistan.

MILTIE. I wouldn't recommend it. Now you did tell me you could sing, didn't you? Not singing singing, thank God. Acting singing.

JENNIFER. Of course. I'm a wonderful acting singer, aren't I, Wain?

WAIN. She's okay.

MILTIE. *Guys and Dolls*, wasn't it, in some sad little tent in the Midwest?

JENNIFER. Oh, Miltie, it was a huge tent. And then I did *I Am a Camera* all through Oklahoma.

MILTIE. I'm surprised you didn't run out of film. Now, listen with both ears. There's a musical opening on the Coast. They've run into trouble. The sad little starlet they exhumed in L.A. for the ingenue— suddenly she's four months pregnant. They need a replacement right away.

JENNIFER. Oh, Miltie darling, and you suggested me?

MILTIE. I stuck my neck out. I'm perfectly conscious of it. But what's a neck for if it isn't stuck out occasionally—in a worthy cause? So it's all set. I fly you out tomorrow for an audition. And if my hunch is right . . . (*He runs one finger down her bare leg.*) What do we see in the making? We see yet another American Dream coming true. Simple, Midwestern child soars to her apotheosis on the cover of *Life* magazine. (BELLE *comes out of the kitchen with the two drinks.*)

JENNIFER. Belle, it's incredible. A big musical on the Coast.

BELLE. Oh, Jennifer, I am glad. (*Takes drink to* MILTIE, *who accepts it with a dazzling smile.*) Bourbon. (*Takes drink to* WAIN.) Scotch. (*The front door buzzer rings.* BELLE *presses the release.*)

JENNIFER. The dress at last. That divine Mr. Onopolis *did* pick up a boy.

MILTIE. In broad daylight? What orgies go on in your neighborhood! Is Mr. Onopolis the local Tiberius?

JENNIFER. Probably. At least he's Greek, and the Greeks invented all that, didn't they?

MILTIE. (*Watching her appreciatively through the sunglasses.*) I *Am a Camera* all through Oklahoma. I like that.

WAIN. I sing folk ballads, Mr. Mizer.

JENNIFER. Shut up, darling. (*There is a knock at the door.* BELLE *opens it.* BOBBY KRAWEIG *enters, carrying* JENNIFER'S *dress on a hanger in a plastic bag. He is nineteen but seems about sixteen, in a sports shirt and slacks. Although there is nothing effeminate about him—in fact he looks like any little tough neighborhood kid—there is a subtle difference, a sensitivity which, not immediately noticeable, is there.*)

BOBBY. Miss Lewison's residence?

BELLE. That's right.

JENNIFER. At long last. Bring it over, please. (BOBBY *takes the dress to her.*)

BOBBY. That's two-sixty-five, he says.

JENNIFER. Belle, darling, be an angel. (BELLE *goes to her purse on the table without her glasses on and pulls out three bills.* BOBBY *stands a little self-consciously.* MILTIE *is watching him keenly.*)

MILTIE. So this is Mr. Onopolis' pick-up. (WAIN *titters.*)

JENNIFER. Really, Miltie! (BELLE, *indignant at* MILTIE, *gives the three bills to* BOBBY, *who is ignoring* MILTIE.)

BELLE. Here you are. (BOBBY *takes the bills and starts to feel in his pocket for change.*) No, no. Keep the change. It was terribly kind of you to bring the dress. You don't work for Mr. Onopolis, do you? You just did it as a favor.

BOBBY. He come out of the store and stopped me.

MILTIE. Wearing a wreath of vine leaves probably and a leopard skin.

BOBBY (*Swinging around on him, glaring*). What's the matter with you? You want to start something?

MILTIE. Nothing personal, kid. Just a rather tired little fantasy we were weaving. (BOBBY *glares at him, then he goes to the door, opens it, turns back, glaring to* MILTIE.)

BOBBY. Slob! (*He exits, slamming the door.*)

WAIN. Slob—what d'you know?

BELLE (*Indignant*). I don't blame him. It's positively . . .

JENNIFER (*Admonishing*). Belle, Belle, Belle. Miltie, darling, you mustn't mind her. She's wracked with a love of the downtrodden. (*Slipping out of the robe, letting it fall on the floor and starting to step into the dress.*) How absolutely divine it all is. When do we start?

MILTIE. Idlewild ten-thirty a.m. A heroic hour, I'm afraid.

JENNIFER (*In dress*). California, here I come. Wain darling—the zipper. Oh God, that's a throwback, isn't it? Miltie dearest, please come and do me up. (MILTIE *crosses and does up the zipper with cerebral lasciviousness.*) Where are we going to dine? Sardi's?

MILTIE. Do you think so? I was planning on something a little cosier. There's a rather amusing Syrian bistro on lower Third Avenue. Of course there isn't actually an El outside but one gets the impression of an El. Okay?

JENNIFER. Darling, whatever you pick, I'm sure it's the dernier cri. (*Runs to* BELLE *and kisses her.*) Dearest Belle. (*Inspects her nose.*) The red band's completely gone. (*Goes to* WAIN *and embraces him.*) Bye, darling. Someday we'll meet again. One always does. Stick around and take Belle to *Ivan the Terrible*, Part Two. She's dying to see it and it's the least you can do. And then . . . (*She points at the duffel bag*) one of those divine cubicles at the Y. I'm sure they'll welcome you with open arms. (*She and* MILTIE *exit.* BELLE, *a little self-conscious, stands looking at* WAIN.)

BELLE. Would you like a little more Scotch?

WAIN (*Quite indifferent to her*). Okay.

BELLE. It isn't Scotch really. It's bourbon. I hate lying to people. Jennifer poured it into the Scotch bottle because she thought Miltie took Scotch.

WAIN. Scotch, bourbon, gin—they hit the same spot, don't they?

BELLE. I suppose so. (*Starts for kitchenette.*) Excuse me. (*Goes in, comes out with bottle.*) What a dreadful man Miltie was, wasn't he? Making fun of that poor little boy.

WAIN. An agent's an agent.

BELLE. I haven't had much experience with them. It's wonderful for Jennifer anyway. Here. This is all there is. (*She puts the Scotch bottle on the table.* WAIN *pours himself a large shot and sits down on the daybed.* BELLE *hovers, rather at a loss.*) You don't have to take me to *Ivan the Terrible* unless you really want to.

WAIN. What's that? Some French movie?

BELLE. Well, no—not exactly. Some boy was going to take me to-night but I put him off because he wasn't really keen. It's so degrading to make people do what they don't want to, just because they promised, isn't it? (*This gets no reaction from* WAIN.) I am so sorry about Jennifer.

WAIN (*Almost admiring*). Threw me out on my ear, didn't she?

BELLE. And when you'd come all the way from the Coast, too! I tried to be a catalyst but, well, even with a catalyst, both the two elements have a bit to want to get together, don't they? I mean, it's all so complicated.

WAIN. Jenny just thinks she's complicated.

BELLE. The trouble is her career really. She's so ambitious. That's good, but it's bad too because it makes you underrate the human equation. You must feel suicidal.

WAIN. Oh well, I thought I'd try it out. You can never tell with Jenny. If she's low, love her up a bit and she melts. It was that goddam agent. Made her think she was Sarah Bernhardt.

BELLE. I suppose with her going to San Francisco and everything, it isn't worth trying any more right now, is it?

WAIN. If a marriage is a bust, I guess it's a bust. It's dumb trying to pick up again.

BELLE. But it seems such a shame. I was always so sure you and Jennifer were made for each other—to live happily ever after.

WAIN. You try living with Jenny.

BELLE. Oh, I understand the difficulties better now I've actually met you. Jennifer's such a strong character. But then I don't really see why it isn't perfectly satisfactory for a strong woman to have a weak husband.

WAIN. Uh?

BELLE. I mean, I'm realistic. I can see how people are. In spite of your looks—and I think looks are terribly important—you're insecure, which is kind of weak, isn't it? You need someone who helps to boost your morale. And there was Jennifer always undermining you.

WAIN. You can say that again.

BELLE. If only she could make that one little adjustment! Oh dear, everything's so difficult, isn't it?

WAIN. You get by.

BELLE. And strange too. Fancy you and me being together like this in Manhattan.

WAIN. Look, kid, there's nothing in the icebox, is there? Like a quick snack.

BELLE. There's some eggs. And I haven't eaten yet. I thought maybe I'd fix us an omelette and some salad—just a little light supper.

WAIN. All that fuss. Isn't there cold cuts or something?

BELLE. I think there's some baloney. But I thought . . .

WAIN. Baloney's okay.

BELLE. Shall I get it now?

WAIN. I don't see what there's to wait for. My gut's shriveling.

BELLE. All right. (*Goes into the kitchen, calls from there.*) You're sure you don't want the omelette? We've got candles.

WAIN (*Sprawled on the daybed*). All that rich stuff's bad when your stomach's acting up.

BELLE (*Coming out of the kitchen with some sliced baloney, a plate, a knife, and a half-opened package loaf*). I'm afraid there isn't any butter so I couldn't have made the omelette anyway. (*She puts the stuff on the table.* WAIN *rises and looks at it.*)

WAIN. Mayonnaise?

BELLE. Yes, yes, I think there is. (*Hurries into the kitchen.* WAIN *starts assembling a sandwich.* BELLE *returns with the mayonnaise.*) Here it is. Mass-produced, I'm afraid. (WAIN *spreads it on a piece of bread, makes a large sandwich with baloney.*) I am glad you were so successful on the Coast.

WAIN (*Interested*). A couple of big shots from CBS saw one of the pilots. Crazy about me.

BELLE. Now, I suppose, you'll go back and pick up that other big opportunity.

WAIN. Maybe. In a way it was kind of vague.

BELLE. So perhaps you'll be staying on in Manhattan awhile?

WAIN. Maybe.

BELLE. Then, with Jennifer away and everything—I mean, I'm sure you know dozens of people in New York. But whenever you're at a loose end . . . New York can be terribly lonely. At least I find it so. Rush, rush, rush, but never the people you really want to see. And after all, there's a sort of bond. Groversville.

WAIN (*Munching*). God, when you look back—what a dump.

BELLE (*Enthusiastic*). Wasn't it terrible? All that smugness, that dreadful conformity.

WAIN. That high school auditorium, couldn't have held more than four, five hundred at most. (*Finishes sandwich.*) Well, I guess I hit the road to the Y.

BELLE. Already?

WAIN. Better to make it early before the mob. (*Starts for the door and his duffel bag, turns back, pours what's left of the bourbon into his glass and drains it.*)

BELLE. Will you be coming back for the movie? Or do you think you're too tired?

WAIN. Gosh, kid, some other time, eh?

BELLE. Of course. Anytime. I'm almost always here.

WAIN (*Picking up duffel bag, turning*). You're a good kid, Sally.

BELLE. I'm Belle, Sally's sister.

WAIN. Go in there and pitch for me with Jenny tonight.

BELLE. Of course.

WAIN. I'll give you a call. See how it pans out. God, she makes me mad sometimes, but Jenny—she's okay. (*Turns to the door, pauses, drops duffel bag, feels in back pocket of his jeans.*) Look, kid, I wonder . . . That bus fare from L.A. I'm kind of low.

BELLE. It's quite all right. I got paid today. (*Goes to table where her purse is, opens it, fumbles, then picks up her glasses and puts them on.*) Oh dear, I thought I had more than this. Is five any good?

WAIN. That's fine. I got a friend I can borrow from tomorrow.

BELLE (*Taking off her glasses, handing him the money*). Then— here.

WAIN (*Taking the five-dollar bill*). See you, kid.

BELLE. The number's in the book. But—how silly of me. You know, don't you? Good-bye, Wain. (WAIN *exits.* BELLE *stands, then puts on her glasses again. She goes to the table, picks up a single piece of baloney and eats it. She goes to the phonograph and puts on a record. It is Dylan Thomas reading his own poems. She goes back to the table, makes a huge sandwich, sits down on the studio couch, munching, listening enraptured. The doorbell rings. In a daze she doesn't hear it. It rings again. She gets up with her glasses on and presses the buzzer. She crosses to the hi-fi and turns the volume down a little, still listening. There is a knock on the door. She opens it.* BOBBY *is standing there.*) Oh, it's you. Is there something . . . ?

BOBBY. The dress was two-sixty-five. Right? You give me three bills. One was a five spot. (*Holds it out.*)

BELLE. Oh God, I didn't have my glasses on.

BOBBY. I figured you pulled the wrong bill.

BELLE (*Taking it*). Oh thanks. Thanks very much. I'll get another dollar. (*She hurries to her purse and searches for a dollar.* BOBBY *listens, rather baffled, to Dylan Thomas. She brings the dollar.*) Thanks terribly.

BOBBY (*Taking the bill*). I figured you just felt in your purse and grabbed the first bill.

BELLE. I'm always doing something like that. It's awfully good of you.

BOBBY. I noticed no sooner I got back to the store. Didn't want you figuring you'd lost five bucks or something. (*Hesitates, then rather shyly.*) Hey—that. What is it?

BELLE. It's Dylan Thomas. He's a poet.

BOBBY. Boy, can he talk fast. What's he talking about?

BELLE. Everything. Life, death.

BOBBY. He must have a real big brain.

BELLE. Oh, he did. He's dead now.

BOBBY. What'd he die from?

BELLE. Beer mostly.

BOBBY. No kidding. (*Makes a little gesture with his hand.*) Well, miss—see yah.

BELLE. Why don't you come in and have a drink, a talk?

BOBBY. Ah, no, no.

BELLE. Why not? There's some vodka.

BOBBY. Thanks, but . . .

BELLE. Maybe you've got a date.

BOBBY. Yes, I mean no. I got a date for later, but . . .

BELLE. Then come on in.

BOBBY. It's just— They still there?

BELLE. Oh no. They've all gone.

BOBBY. Guys like that heavy-set, dark complected guy—they make me puke.

BELLE. He was awful, wasn't he? But you fixed him.

BOBBY. Is he crazy thinking I'd let a guy pick me up on the street?

BELLE. He was trying to be smart. That's all those people care about, trying to be smart.

BOBBY. Queers are okay. They got their rights like anyone else.

BELLE. Oh yes, of course.

BOBBY. But making cracks—like I was a cheap hustler or something.

BELLE. Why don't you just forget all about him and come in and have a drink?

BOBBY (*Hesitates*). Okay. (BELLE *moves for him to pass her into the room and shuts the door.*)

BELLE. Are you hungry?

BOBBY. Gosh, I had me a bite at Chock Full of Nuts.

BELLE. Now I come to think of it, that's just as well. There's no butter for an omelette. I'll turn Dylan Thomas off. It's awful to listen and not to listen. (*She goes to the machine and turns it off.* BOBBY *looks around.*)

BOBBY. Nice place you got here. Them drapes—I like a nice bright color.

BELLE. It isn't me really. Jennifer—my roommate—fixed everything.

BOBBY. You should see my mom's parlor. She don't throw nothing away. Who knows, she says, one day they'll be antiques. Are they antique! Lvov. Year One.

BELLE. Lvov's in Poland, isn't it?

BOBBY. Little old Polack. That's me. Mom and Pop both. Twenty-seven years in this country and know all the English Pop knew? "Unemployment Insurance." Haha.

BELLE. Too bad he didn't go to adult-education classes. Some of them are supposed to be very good.

BOBBY. Pop at night school? That'd be the day. With a can of beer in one hand and his shoes off. Was old Pop a mess!

BELLE. So he's dead then?

BOBBY. Who knows? Mom threw him out when I was nothing more than a kid. Got on her nerves, she said. Mom's nerves. Boy, you'd never think one person got room enough for so many nerves.

BELLE. I'll get you that drink. I'm afraid there's only vodka. (*Starts for kitchen, turns.*) You are old enough, aren't you?

BOBBY. Me? I'm nineteen.

BELLE. You'd never know looking at you.

BOBBY. Wait a coupla years. Old age will creep up.

BELLE. Is vodka and tonic all right?

BOBBY. Just a straight shot, please. (*As* BELLE *goes to kitchen.*) Hey. Look at that air-conditioner. Whyn't you got it on?

BELLE. It makes a noise like Vesuvius erupting. (*Goes into kitchen.* BOBBY *gets up, goes to air-conditioner, turns it on, it works perfectly.* BELLE *comes out of the kitchen with vodka bottle and a glass.*) It's working. What on earth did you do?

BOBBY. Just turned it on.

BELLE. You're wonderful.

BOBBY. Old magic fingers. (*Taking the vodka.*) What about you?

BELLE. I don't drink.

BOBBY. Then no, no, thanks. I don't drink alone.

BELLE. But please.

BOBBY. Drinking when your hostess ain't drinking? That's terrible.

BELLE. Is it? I never know about those things.

BOBBY. That's how I took up the booze. Mr. Millington—Arthur'd say, "Leaving me to drink alone, Bobby? That's terrible manners." So I picked up the habit.

BELLE (*Seeing he is concerned*). All right. I'll take a shot—just to celebrate the five dollars.

BOBBY. That's it. (BELLE *goes into the kitchenette and comes out with an extra glass.*)

BELLE (*Raising her glass*). Well . . .

BOBBY (*Raising his*). Skol. (*Pause.*) How old are you? Twenty-three—four?

BELLE. I'm nineteen, too.

BOBBY. I guess it's them glasses.

BELLE. I don't care how old or young I look. All this emphasis on youth in this country is feeble-minded. It's what you are that matters. Don't you think so?

BOBBY. Things like that I don't think about too much.

BELLE. But you ought to. It's so important. They're trying to turn us all into sheep. You've got to fight all the time for your identity.

BOBBY. Know something? You're awful easy to talk to.

BELLE. That's the first time anyone's said that.

BOBBY. Most girls—giggling, twitching their skirts. Hey, Bobby, how d'ya like the shade of my new fingernail polish? Mom says these days they're all courvés . . .

BELLE. What's that?

BOBBY. Whores. And she should know, I guess. Waiting table with all them broads from the toy factory crowding in lunchtime. You should hear 'em, Mom says. Sodom and Gomorrah. Boy, do they get on her nerves.

BELLE. I can understand that.

BOBBY. Know something? I usta try bringing a couple of girls back home Sunday afternoons sometimes. Was that out of line! My son dragging tramps back to my house! My son, my son. That's Mom's theme song, I guess.

BELLE. Oh, I don't think that's right at all.

BOBBY. Oh, old Mom's okay. If she wants it that way . . . she's the one pays the rent. Yeah, old Mom sure don't go for girls. Arthur's the same way, but that's only natural.

BELLE. Who's Arthur?

BOBBY. Mr. Millington. I go there every Friday night or Saturday lunch, depending.

BELLE. Then he's some sort of a friend?

BOBBY. Mr. Millington's been real good to me. Give me this medal. (*Shows gold medal around his neck.*)

BELLE. It's pretty.

BOBBY. Mr. Millington's been real good to me. Name the people been real good to you. Name them on the fingers of your hand. That bunch in the shipping room at Gimbels—you should see 'em. And it's not much better at upholstery class nights. Those guys—smart! But Mr. Millington's always been a real gentleman. And if he wants something . . . okay. What you got to lose?

BELLE. You mean if—if he wants something . . . (*Making a rather helpless gesture.*)

BOBBY. If he wants—you know—what you got to lose?

BELLE. I don't think I'd like to give an opinion on that off the top of my head. I'd have to think. It isn't something I've quite fitted in yet.

BOBBY. Ain't nothing like hustling. Nothing like that.

BELLE. Oh no.

BOBBY. You know? You're real broadminded.

BELLE (*Almost indignant*). Oh, of course I am.

BOBBY. You finished your vodka. Went down real smooth, didn't it?

BELLE. As a matter of fact, I feel a lot better.

BOBBY. Why? You feeling bad?

BELLE. Things can be disappointing, rather.

BOBBY. That guy was here?

BELLE. It's extraordinary how slowly one matures. Back home where I come from, I always thought of him as a kind of God. But he isn't at all. He's self-centered, terribly crass really, and not very bright, but . . .

BOBBY. You're still hot for him?

BELLE. Oh, nothing like that.

BOBBY. But you kind of hero-worship him?

BELLE. I suppose so.

BOBBY (*Enthusiastic*). Boy, you should meet Skip.

BELLE. Who's he?

BOBBY. Skip? He's my buddy. You should see him. Big, brawny, all the girls crazy about him. Just let him walk down the block and it's: Hi, Skip, Skippy boy. What's new, Skipper? I call him Bro. He calls me Bro. That's for brother.

BELLE. That's very nice.

BOBBY. Old Skip's a hero all right. Football, baseball, everything. Once he got this baseball bat bang on the knee. Had trouble with it ever since and when it hurt real bad I'd fix it for him. Like this. (*Massages his knee.*) Worked like a dream. Like I said—magic fingers.

BELLE. I wish I could do things with my hands. I'm hopeless.

BOBBY. I bet old Skip misses me when that knee acts up. He's in the navy now. A sub. Been gone over two years, but he sends me post cards sometimes one, two a month regular. Is he giving them French and them Jap girls a whirl. Wow, old Skip. But this guy, this blond, he in the service too?

BELLE. No, he's an actor.

BOBBY. Boy, what d'ya know. TV?

BELLE. Yes.

BOBBY. What happen? He stood you up?

BELLE. Oh, no, it's just seeing him again after all this time.

BOBBY. And it didn't go good? Didn't even invite you someplace?

BELLE. There was some talk of going to a movie I want to see very much, but he was too tired.

BOBBY. What movie?

BELLE. *Ivan the Terrible*, Part Two.

BOBBY. What's that?

BELLE. It's a Russian movie.

BOBBY. Good old Khrushchev.

BELLE. It's wonderful, they say. Eisenstein. He was a great genius.

BOBBY. Like that poet who died of beer?

BELLE. In a rather different way.

BOBBY. You like that deep stuff, don't you?

BELLE. It's not just liking. It's much more than that. There isn't anything else really. I mean, artistic achievement, real creative achievement—without it, blow the whole world up with the atom bomb. That's why I work at Doubleday's. It's just a beginning, but so long as you're near books or pictures or music—it's got to be all right.

BOBBY. I kind of liked that poet.

BELLE. I am glad.

BOBBY. He does something to you. Maybe I'd like this movie too.

BELLE. I'm sure you would.

BOBBY (*Getting up*). Then what about it, uh?

BELLE (*Delighted*). You mean we might go?

BOBBY. Why not? I got the dough. Four bucks and the tip you give me.

BELLE. Oh, no, no. I'd pay for myself. But do you really want to? I mean I just hate forcing . . .

BOBBY. Where's it? Up in Broadway? Some two buck show?

BELLE. Oh no, it's 34th Street, I think.

BOBBY. Okay. What we waiting for?

BELLE. But—but what about Mr. Millington?

BOBBY. I'll call him up.

BELLE. But is that all right?

BOBBY. Where's the phone? (*Goes to it, feels in his pocket and puts a dime on the table by the phone.*)

BELLE. But you don't have to pay for the call.

BOBBY. A dime's a dime, ain't it? Who knows when it comes in handy? (*Dials.*) Arthur? . . . It's me. . . . Look, Arthur, trouble with Mother. Her nerves. . . . Gosh, I don't know. . . . Maybe later . . . eleven-thirty, twelve, okay? . . . Okay. (*Puts down receiver.*) He don't mind how late it is.

BELLE. Am I all right like this? I've got a better dress.

BOBBY. We're looking at the movie, ain't we? Using our minds.

BELLE (*Going to air-conditioner*). I think I'd better turn this off. If it starts to act up when we're out, it'd keep the whole house awake. (*Switches off air-conditioner.*) Okay. (*Goes to table and picks up purse.*) Ready?

BOBBY. Know something? You and me such buddies already and I don't know your name.

BELLE. It's Belle.

BOBBY. That's funny.

BELLE. Why?

BOBBY. One of Arthur's friends—they call him Belle. Big, heavy-set guy with a bald head. Can you imagine? (*Holds out his hand.*) Okay, kid. Let's make tracks. That's how old Skip always says it. Okay, bro, let's make tracks. (BELLE *goes toward him, passes a mirror, stops and looks in.*)

BELLE. Oh God.

BOBBY. What is it? (*He goes and stands beside her. They both look in the mirror.*)

BELLE. It's my hair. So goddam stringy.

BOBBY. Know something? So's mine. You should see me mornings. Real bedraggled. But I got a hair spray. A real fine hair spray. Use it sometime. You'd be surprised. (*Grabs her hand and guides her toward the door.*) Wow. You should see Mom's face. *Her* son off to the movies with a girl. (*They reach the door.* BOBBY *opens it. They exit as the curtain falls.*)

SCENE II

The same—the same night. It is almost midnight. The air-conditioner is off. There are the remains of a meal (the omelette) on the table and two candelabra with four candles in each glimmer on it. BELLE *is lying full length on the daybed with her shoes off, a glass of red wine in her hand.* BOBBY *is sitting in the chair with a glass of wine too. The end of César Franck's* Symphonic Variations *is coming from the phonograph. Both* BOBBY *and* BELLE *are listening in silence until the record comes to an end.* BELLE *jumps up, switches it off, and turns eagerly to* BOBBY.

BOBBY. Boy, classical music, poetry, old *Ivan the Terrible* with them beatnik beards. We're living it up, ain't we?

BELLE. I do hope I haven't forced too much. Jennifer's always saying I plunge in and brandish my enthusiasm like some terrible schoolmarm and scare people away.

BOBBY. Scare 'em away with that fancy omelette?

BELLE. I'm glad we got the butter.

BOBBY. How's the vino, Signora?

BELLE. Delicious.

BOBBY. Been better if I'd had more than one-sixty-five left. Old Arthur would say it was lousy—domestic.

BELLE. I expect he's a gourmet.

BOBBY. Sure. Been to Europe with his mom. Twice. Brought me back a leather wallet from Italy someplace. One of the kids at upholstery class pinched it. Say, Belle, is it okay being with me? I mean, you don't feel like it's wasting time or something?

BELLE. Of course not.

BOBBY. But I'm sorry that guy stood you up.

BELLE. Oh, you don't have to be. After all, he hardly knows me. Didn't even recognize me to begin with—and then he's Jennifer's husband.

BOBBY. But she tossed him out, you said. Isn't nothing disloyal about going for him if she's tossed him out.

BELLE. I try to analyze my feelings. It's so important always to try to analyze and I think I know exactly what it is about Wain for me.

BOBBY. What's that?

BELLE. Back home, I used to weave all sorts of romances about him. You know, saving me from Indians and burning planes and things. But even then I think I suspected he wasn't very sensitive or even clever. But that didn't change the feeling and it still doesn't, which proves that what I really want is the body. It's just a virgin mixing up a purely physical feeling with other things.

BOBBY. You're a virgin?

BELLE. Oh yes.

BOBBY. Gosh.

BELLE. Oh, it isn't because I'm prudish. It's just—well, quite a bit of it, I guess, is no opportunity.

BOBBY. Opportunity? You should walk down my block. Half them girls don't know who they had, who they hadn't. Millie Brownlow. Boy! Any night after 9:30—back of Sampson's garage.

BELLE. But it's something about me too—something that deters like an insect repellent. I used to be terribly discouraged but now I'm glad in a way because all that promiscuousness . . . it's so . . . well, where's the warmth? Scrabbling around on couches, in backs of cars.

BOBBY. In telephone booths they do it. Can you imagine? Hello, hello—operator.

BELLE. Not that I disapprove. I mean in this society, sex is everybody's burden and if society's warped them . . . Oh, you've got to be tolerant. All forms of sex—everything. What harm does it do? I mean, the harm's been done. But that isn't how it should be—all that mixing your body up with the mind and guilt and fetishes and things . . . oh, no. Have you read *Lady Chatterley's Lover*?

BOBBY. It's a book, isn't it? I seen it on the table in Arthur's living room.

BELLE. It's quite extraordinary. It was written over thirty years ago but it's all there. The body isn't the slave of the mind. They're both equal. And the body should be completely free. Sex between a man and a woman should be pure, mindless rapture like with animals.

BOBBY (*Vehement*). Animals, yes. That's what it's like—with animals.

BELLE. Oh, I didn't mean it in any bad sense.

BOBBY. You see it in their eyes. You should have seen! My first time. Must have been twelve, thirteen—the guy that run the paper route. Like cats on the back fence or something. But—what you do? You go along with it. If someone's good to you, if you see that look—okay. Half the

time, think of something else—a Coke, maybe, or swimming at Coney. Big deal. (*Pause.*) You and that Wain like a couple of animals—boy.

BELLE. I don't think I expressed myself very well.

BOBBY. Oh well, that's old Skip's way with the girls! Wham, bang. Hey, bring me another beer! Well, well, listen to us. Classical music one minute, talking dirt the next.

BELLE. But you see how that proves my point. It shouldn't be dirt.

BOBBY. Gosh, Belle. I wasn't criticizing you. I was putting me in just the same as you. Look, how about a little music?

BELLE. Oh, would you really like some? Romantic? Or classical?

BOBBY. How about something with a little jump?

BELLE. Jazz? I'm afraid I'm not very good at it yet. But Jennifer's got lots of stuff there.

BOBBY (*Rising and going to inspect the records*). That's my girl. We've given the mind a big break. Now let's give the old body a spin. (*Wriggles unselfconsciously in rhythm.*) You dance?

BELLE (*Quick*). Oh, no, no, not much.

BOBBY (*Anxious*). You don't disapprove, do you?

BELLE. Oh, not at all. I mean, it's a wonderful physical means of expression. But . . . it's awful, isn't it? I'm so musical, but I don't seem to have much rhythm.

BOBBY. Ah, you just think that. (*He picks up a record.*) Hey, cha-cha. What you know? (*Puts it on. The cha-cha rhythm comes out rather loud.*)

BELLE (*Anxious*). A little softer, maybe. It's quite late.

BOBBY. Okay. (*Turns down volume.*)

BELLE (*Looking at watch*). Gosh, it's almost midnight.

BOBBY (*Coming toward her, dancing sinuously and well to the cha-cha-cha*). Señorita? (*He makes a move quite unselfconsciously to receive* BELLE *as a partner.* BELLE, *self-consciously, moves away.*)

BELLE. What about Mr. Millington?

BOBBY. Gosh, old Arthur. I clean forgot.

BELLE. You said you'd be there at twelve.

BOBBY. Seeing old Arthur? He's okay, but all that don't mix.

BELLE. But you did promise.

BOBBY. Look, if I stay awhile, you let me learn you the cha-cha?

BELLE. I'm really awfully clumsy.

BOBBY. That's just nerves. You ain't nervous with me, are you, Belle?

BELLE. Okay. (BOBBY *goes to the phone, feels in his jeans.*)

BOBBY. Gosh, fresh outta dimes.

BELLE. As if that matters! But, Bobby, I don't want . . . I mean if Mr. Millington's going to be disappointed. But . . . oh dear, everything always seems so complicated.

BOBBY. Turn down the cha-cha. Old Arthur hearing that? Boy, would I be in trouble! (BELLE, *rather reluctantly, goes and turns the music off.* BOBBY *dials.*) Hey, Arthur? . . . Look, it's tough. I don't think I can make it. . . . You know how Mom is. . . . Sure, one of her days. . . . Gee, yes, I know. I'm sorry. . . . Sure, Arthur. Real soon. . . . It's just one of those things. . . . So long, Arthur. (*Puts down phone, turns grinning to* BELLE.) Okay, lady—musica. (BELLE *turns on the music again.* BOBBY *comes dancing toward her in rhythm.*) It's a cinch. A real cinch. See the basic step? Old Arthur Murray. Haha. (*He takes her by the waist.*) One . . . dadada. . . . Two . . . dadada. . . . Three dadada . . . Chachacha (*A little lesson starts.* BELLE *is very clumsy at the beginning.*)

BELLE. But doesn't the behind have to do something?

BOBBY. Sure, sure, but later. One . . . ahahah, TWO ahahaha, THREE ahaha—chachacha. Boy, we better turn on the air-conditioner. We're going to sweat it up.

BELLE. No. I don't dare. If it makes that terrible noise . . .

BOBBY. With me? Little old me?

BELLE. No, Bobby, please.

BOBBY. You ain't got no faith. (BOBBY *goes to air-conditioner, turns it on. It's perfectly all right. He makes prize-fighter victory gesture.*)

BELLE. Heavens! (BOBBY *comes dancing back to her.* BELLE *goes to him. They dance with* BELLE *getting the rhythm.*) One aha, two ahaha, three ahaha CHA CHA CHA.

BOBBY. Boy, you're getting it. (*They dance more successfully.*) Yeah, girl. Now the butt—the behind. Look. (*Indicates.* BELLE *tries, doesn't do too badly, then gives up, laughing happily.*)

BOBBY. You ever been to the Palladium? Boy, you should see those colored chicks . . . Porto Ricans, Jamaicans. Man, can they swing it? Hey, gimme that bracelet. (BELLE *gives him the bracelet off her wrist.*) A coupla lessons and this'll be you. (*He puts her bracelet on his wrist and goes into a comedy sexy solo dance. The door opens.* JENNIFER *and* MILTIE *enter.*)

JENNIFER (*Letting them in*). All right, Miltie—just one drink. (*Sees.*) My God, Belshazzar's feast. (BOBBY, *self-conscious, stops dancing.*)

BELLE (*Rather flustered*). Hello, Jennifer.

JENNIFER. What pipes—what timbrels. But, who on earth . . . ?

MILTIE (*Recognizing* BOBBY). Well, well, our little friend. Still at his gay pursuits.

BOBBY (*Putting up his fists like a bantam-weight boxer*). You want something from me? Okay. You gonna get something from me. (*He swings,* MILTIE *dodges.* BELLE *jumps in.*)

JENNIFER. Oh my God, back where we started from. (BOBBY *swings at* MILTIE, *who dodges.*)

BELLE. No, no, Bobby. Ignore him!

BOBBY (*Stopping, but glaring at* MILTIE). Them slobs. Split their skulls. What you find? Crap.

JENNIFER. Oh la, la.

BOBBY. I know where I'm welcome and I know where I'm not welcome and where I'm not welcome I don't stick around. (*Goes to door.*)

BELLE (*Moving toward him*). But, Bobby, please!

BOBBY (*At door, ignoring her, glaring at* MILTIE). You and your eyetalian suit. I got friends make you look like a men's room attendant. (*He opens the door, exits, slamming the door.*)

JENNIFER (*To* BELLE). Darling, I'm desperately sorry. But what an odd way to spend an evening. With Mr. Onopolis' delivery boy.

BELLE (*Fierce*). He isn't a delivery boy. He just delivered the dress as a courtesy.

JENNIFER. Rather a nicety, dear.

BELLE. And—who cares anyway? If he was a delivery boy, what difference does that make? What's wrong with delivery boys? He took me to *Ivan the Terrible* and he honestly enjoyed it. That's more than that pseudo-sophisticated slave of the Hidden Persuaders could do in a million years. I'm going to the bathroom and then I'm going to bed. And to hell with all of you. (*Storms toward the kitchen, then stops, turns.*) Not you, Jennifer. (*Exits to kitchen.*)

MILTIE (*Mildly curious*). Going to the bathroom in the kitchen?

JENNIFER. It's madness, darling. That's how the apartment's constructed.

MILTIE. Rather witty. Spirited child, isn't she? Little or no light touch, though, I'm afraid.

JENNIFER. Darling, she might as well be Goethe.

MILTIE. It's rather refreshing. One forgets how amusing unamusing people can be.

JENNIFER. They make a nice change, don't they? Like those pickled pig's eyes at the Syrian Bistro.

MILTIE (*Slightly discomfited*). No evening can be an unqualified success. (*He becomes conscious of the music, uses it to restore his sophistication.*) If this was an Irene Dunne movie, we'd dance.

JENNIFER (*Instantly picking it up, repairing any damage*). The night away.

MILTIE (*Taking off jacket and carefully draping it on a chair*). Unfortunately, unlike Randolph Scott, I perspire. (*Gets into dancing position. Says with terrible Midwestern twang.*) Voulez-vous danser avec moi, Mademoiselle Carruthers?

JENNIFER. Oh, Buckley, how did you know it was my favorite tune? (*They start to dance a sedate, mock cha-cha. They talk the while, exploiting the movements of the dance,* MILTIE *amorously,* JENNIFER, *as tactfully as possible, non-amorously.*)

MILTIE. Do you know something rather engaging about me?

JENNIFER. What is that, Buckley?

MILTIE. Not only am I as normal as blueberry pie. I am also a cock-eyed optimist (*cha-cha*). And I'm convinced that the noblest of human sentiments—gratitude—is not entirely dead.

JENNIFER. Words can't express my gratitude.

MILTIE. I wasn't planning on your expressing it in *words*.

JENNIFER (*Trying to stop it*). Miltie darling, it's hideously late and there's that early start tomorrow.

MILTIE. But what is pleasanter than to reel onto TWA more dead than alive?

JENNIFER. Cha-cha-cha. My packing, Miltie.

MILTIE (*Leading her in the dance so that he spins her until she immediately faces the bedroom*). That, I presume, is your bedroom? . . .

JENNIFER. Well, yes.

MILTIE. Then how about a little quiet packing together?

JENNIFER. Aren't you forgetting poor, sweet Belle? I'm supposed to be setting her an example (*cha-cha-cha*). I'm practically in the position of a mother.

MILTIE. Then let me appeal to the mother in you. (*Kisses (?) her and then dances her right up to the bedroom door.*) As —dolf Scott would have said, it'll be music, honey. Sheer music.

JENNIFER. Music to pack by. (*They are at the door.* JENNIFER *disengages herself and goes to the chair, from which she picks up his jacket, muttering her incantation to herself.*) K.C. K.C. (*He follows her, grabs her.*)

MILTIE. Little girl. (*He kisses her again while she holds the coat up to prevent it from being crushed.*)

JENNIFER. Oh well, come on, darling. If 'twere done, 'twere well 'twere done quickly.

MILTIE. Sometimes I feel Shakespeare's insight into the human psyche has been grossly overrated. (*He puts his arm around her, beams a moment through his sunglasses, and guides her into the bedroom. During this scene, the music has run down and the needle scratches on the end of the disc. For a moment the stage is empty, then* BELLE *comes in from the kitchen. She is in pajamas and a simple robe. She is carrying her clothes in a neat pile. She is defiant, prepared to make a scene if need be but finds the room empty. She puts her clothes on a chair, notices the scratching phonograph, goes and turns it off. Then, rearranging the coffee table, etc., pulls out the convertible couch revealing her made-up bed. She is just getting into it when there's a quiet tap on the door. She isn't wearing her glasses. She gets up and goes to answer it.* BOBBY *is standing there.*)

BELLE. Bobby.

BOBBY. Your bracelet. (*Holding it out.*) I'm always walking out of here with something, ain't I?

BELLE. Thank you. But how did you get in the downstairs door?

BOBBY. I didn't. I noticed no sooner I walked out. I hung around on the stairs. Come near to walking away with it. Come near to saying, "To hell with her bracelet." Gee, I'm sorry, Belle. But when I get mad!

BELLE. I'm so glad you came back.

BOBBY. No hard feelings?

BELLE. I should be asking you. (*Sound of* MILTIE's *giggling laugh muffled from the bedroom.*)

BOBBY. They in there?

BELLE. Yes.

BOBBY. At it like animals.

BELLE (*Pouring it out*). Oh, why doesn't she see? She doesn't want him. It's just her career. There's nothing, absolutely nothing. And he— he's only getting his money's worth. Oh, it's disgusting. I know I shouldn't say that. But if only she'd understand. It's the death of the body.

BOBBY. You want I should go in and throw him out? That's what old Skip'd do. Throw him out on his ass.

BELLE. No, no. One mustn't interfere. But when you think she turned Wain away.

BOBBY. Gee, you'd better get in bed. You're cold.

BELLE. In all this heat?

BOBBY. With my air-conditioner on? (*They stand looking at each other.*)

BOBBY. Well, I better be making tracks downtown. Better get Mom over.

BELLE. Will she still be awake?

BOBBY. Mom? You kidding?

BELLE. Always? Even—even when you go to Mr. Millington?

BOBBY. Five, six in the morning, it's the same. Lying in bed with the cold cream on her face. "Where you bin? Where you bin?" Takes half an hour, forty-five minutes to calm her down. It's her legs partly too. She suffers terrible from her veins. (*Pause.*) Know something, Belle? I had a real good evening.

BELLE. So did I.

BOBBY. We're buddies, ain't we?

BELLE. Of course we are.

BOBBY. None of that stuff. Nothing dirty. (*Self-consciously holding out hand.*) Shake on that? (BELLE *takes his hand. They stand a moment with their hands gripping each other.* MILTIE's *laughter comes from the bedroom.* BOBBY *takes his hand away.*) Don't you pay 'em no mind.

BELLE. Oh, I don't.

BOBBY. You get your rest.

BELLE. All right. What about your subway fare?

BOBBY. That's okay. I gotta token. Night, Belle.

BELLE. Good night, Bobby. (BOBBY *leaves.* BELLE *shuts the door behind him. She turns off the lights and walks toward the bed. As she is getting into it,* MILTIE's *laugh comes again. She starts to pace. She is obviously infected with it, hating it and also hating her own contrasting loneliness. She goes to the window and looks out. It is the window with the air-conditioner.* MILTIE's *laugh comes again and* JENNIFER's *high giggle. The siren of a distant fire engine sounds.* BELLE *beats with her fists on the air-conditioner. It jumps on, making its terrible racket. She stands rigid by it as the curtain falls.*)

FRIEDMAN-ABELES

Act Two

SCENE I

The same—three weeks later, Saturday, 11:30 a.m. BOBBY, *in blue jeans and sports shirt, is lying sprawled happily on the day-bed, studying a jumbo-sized postcard of a tropical hotel.* BELLE, *her head wrapped in a towel, her glasses on, comes out of the kitchen with one bottle of Coke and one glass of Coke. She is wearing a pretty robe. There is a can of hair spray, comb, brush, et cetera on the table and drawn up to it is a straight-backed chair on which* BOBBY *is in the process of giving* BELLE *a home permanent. The air-conditioner, working, is on.*

BELLE (*Going to daybed*). Here's your Coke.

BOBBY (*Reaching for the bottle*). Right out of the bottle. That's old Skip's way. You got a Coke bottle in your hand, you got a weapon of defense. That's what Skip says. What you suppose old Joan Crawford would think if she knew she was selling weapons? But that's Pepsi, ain't it?

BELLE (*Sitting down quite unselfconsciously on the daybed with him, patting her hair*). Don't you suppose it's dry yet?

BOBBY. He said an hour, din't he? Only called ten, fifteen minutes ago.

BELLE. But you never know with people.

BOBBY. Relax, relax, give it a coupla minutes more. (*Rolling over, presenting postcard.*) Hey, Belle, take another look. Great big helluva hotel, isn't it? (*Reading.*) Hotel Arawak, Ocho Rios, Jamaica. What's Arawak?

BELLE. I'm not quite sure. It could be a tropical flower.

BOBBY. That's it. All them red flowers back of the pool. Boy, old Skip living it up! Sixty-eight bucks a day just for room and food. Of course, he hasn't been living there. He was in the sub tied up to a—a something pier.

BELLE (*Taking postcard*). Bauxite.

BOBBY. What's that?

BELLE. Oh dear, one should know. Some sort of metal. I'll look it up at Doubleday's, shall I?

BOBBY. Sixty-eight bucks a day and old Skip says he was in the coffee shop all the time. Trust old Skip. Gosh, think, Skip hitting town today. Will we be living it up tonight. Wow—watch out, Broadway.

BELLE (*Handing back postcard*). It's strange, isn't it? Skip coming back and Wain calling me out of a clear blue sky on the same day.

BOBBY. Unexpected visitors. Probably in your astrology and mine both. That Wain give you back the five bucks yet?

BELLE. I haven't even seen him.

BOBBY. Uh.

BELLE. I hope he doesn't notice the hair.

BOBBY. You crazy? What you think I'm doing it for but for guys to notice?

BELLE. I mean, I'd hate him to think I did it especially for him. Coquetry's so false. And it's all against my principles anyway. I've always said, if you've got stringy hair . . .

BOBBY. . . . you gotta become interesting with stringy hair. I know. Hey, Belle, know something? Old Arthur's crazy to meet Skip. I dunno.

BELLE. I wouldn't think it's a very good idea, would you?

BOBBY. Old Skip's funny. Anything like that—he sees red.

BELLE. Lots of people do. It's a herd reaction. Probably anal-sadistic I think, but I'm not quite sure. All that conventional morality!

BOBBY. Oh, Skip ain't moral. Nothing like that. But just let someone try something. Boy, does he boss me around. Shape up, Bobby. Hey, kid, a little action. He gets me straightened out, okay. You know, if Skip figured out about me and Arthur I'd feel ashamed. Sometimes I do. I think about old Skip when I'm with Arthur and . . . Hey, Belle, you think it's bad going with queers?

BELLE. You know I'd never dream of criticizing anyone else's way of life.

BOBBY. Mom's crazy about Arthur. He asks her up to the apartment for dinner a coupla times. Boy, does she go for it. A couple of martinis. Her finger all crooked like this, chattering away like she was at the Hotel Ritz, them spike heels on her feet in spite of her veins. You got a good friend in Arthur, she says. A real good friend who might get you some-place.

BELLE. As if that was the point of friendship!

BOBBY. Yeah, Mom's nuts about Arthur! Makes you think, don't it.

Mom crazy about Arthur. Boy, everything's so complicated. That's what you always say.

BELLE. What?

BOBBY. Everything's so complicated. Aw, what the hell. Old Arthur's okay. A coupla hours Friday nights or Saturday lunch. That ain't going to make no world come to no end. Makes a change from upholstery school too. Hey, get on that chair.

BELLE. Ready?

BOBBY. Get on that chair. Your boy friend's coming and old Arthur's already fixing that shrimp cocktail to put in the icebox. He always got a shrimp cocktail ready for me. I go for shrimp cocktails. (BELLE *goes over to the wooden chair by the table and sits down, picking up another towel and wrapping it around her shoulders.* BOBBY *comes to her and starts to take off the towel from her head.*) Princess Margaret unveiling the cornerstone. That's what old Arthur would say.

BELLE. You are clever to be able to do it.

BOBBY. Oh, it don't bother me. Mom had me fixing her hair no sooner I was out of sixth grade. Ironing, housecleaning, fixing supper, too. She got me well trained.

BELLE (*Agitated*). I do hope it'll be all right. (BOBBY *whisks off towel, revealing her hair screwed up in tight curls or pins or whatever the process is.*)

BOBBY. Okay.

BELLE. Bobby, give me the mirror. Let me see the worst.

BOBBY. Hold your horses. Old Antoine's fixing this personal. (*Picks up comb and expertly combs out the curls.*) Boy, are you going to wow that Wain.

BELLE. You know there'll be nothing like that.

BOBBY. Called you, din't he? Asked to come and see you, din't he?

BELLE. Only after three weeks. Probably he just wants news of Jennifer. I almost said on the phone, "Really, there's no need to come because Jennifer never answers my letters." But . . . Maybe I should have said that.

BOBBY. Nervous, ain't you?

BELLE. It's so silly of me.

BOBBY. You—always criticizing yourself. Sometimes I figure you're not gonna be satisfied not until you're one great big brain—like a Martian or something.

BELLE. Oh, that isn't true at all. Is it really coming out all right?

BOBBY. Duchess of Windsor.

BELLE. Perhaps I am too scrupulous.

BOBBY. What's that?

BELLE. Pessimistic, I mean. Always assuming no one will ever want me.

BOBBY. That's crazy.

BELLE. Looking the way I do?

BOBBY. You don't look bad. Sometimes you look real pretty.

BELLE. I don't.

BOBBY. No kidding. Sometimes I look at you and say to myself, "My, she's real pretty." Even with the glasses on sometimes.

BELLE. You think that just because you're my friend.

BOBBY. I'm your friend, okay.

BELLE. And then the sexual element doesn't enter in.

BOBBY (*Defensive*). What you mean?

BELLE. I mean you don't look at girls from that angle.

BOBBY (*Angry, stopping brushing*). What angle? You mean from sex? Just because I don't go for it. Think it's a dirty nothing—all of it, a lousy dirty nothing—for the birds—that don't mean I can't. . . . You think I can't look at girls from sex?

BELLE. Bobby dear, you musn't think I meant any kind of criticism.

BOBBY. Oh yeah, yeah. You know something? You talk a lot.

BELLE. Oh, I know I do.

BOBBY. All that—the body freed from the mind. The body having a life of its own. Rapture and all. Okay, what you doing with your body? There's this Wain. You're crazy about him. You don't think he's too bright, okay, but the body appeals to you and he's coming today. . . . So okay. Talk, talk, talk. Why don't you do something about it?

BELLE. That's logical, I must admit. It's absolutely logical. But . . . (*Twists to look up at him.*)

BOBBY. Hey, don't wriggle. How'm I gonna brush? (*Mollified, starts brushing again.*)

BELLE. I do see what you mean. I do realize the discrepancy. Everything's so— Oh dear, I'm saying that again.

BOBBY. Almost had a fight, din't we?

BELLE. Oh, no, not really.

BOBBY. That'd be the end—me and you fighting really. (*Stops brushing.*) Okay. Fini.

BELLE (*Beginning to jump up*). Oh Bobby.

BOBBY (*Pushing her down again*). Hey, wait, wait. The hair spray. (*He picks it up.* BELLE *looks at it dubiously.*)

BELLE. Won't it get in my eyes?

BOBBY. Maybe. Put the towel up then. (BELLE *lifts the towel up from in front of her and covers her face with it.* BOBBY *applies the spray, quoting commercial.*) The most glamorous women in the world pant for lustrous Folly Hair Spray. No matting oil, no hair-brittling cream . . . (*Stops spraying.*) Okay. (BELLE *lets the towel drop from her face, she sits an instant and then jumps up, sending the towel flopping onto the floor and runs to the mirror. She stands gazing at herself.* BOBBY *goes over to join her. They stand looking at her reflection.*)

BOBBY. Least it ain't bedraggled.

BELLE (*Turning to him*). It does. It does boost the morale! (BOBBY *takes her in his arms and does a few measures with her of the chachacha. Each beat calling out, CHACHACHA. The door buzzer rings.*)

BELLE (*Breaking away, panicked*). Oh God, it's Wain. (BELLE *rushes to pick up the towel off the floor.*)

BOBBY. Hey, hey—relax.

BELLE (*Tossing the towel into the kitchenette*). But I'm in this robe.

BOBBY. Why not? Think Lady Chatterley never entertained that guy in her bathrobe?

BELLE. But . . . (*The buzzer rings again.*)

BOBBY. Ain't you gonna answer it? (BELLE *stands hesitant.* BOBBY *starts for door.*)

BELLE. Bobby! (BOBBY *presses the release buzzer, makes a little farewell wave.*)

BOBBY. Okay, Belle. See ya. (*Opens door.*)

BELLE. Oh, Bobby, please, please, don't go.

BOBBY. You crazy? Old Arthur's tapping his foot. (*Looks at table.*) Keep the hair spray.

BELLE. Oh no, no.

BOBBY. It's a gift. (*Starts out, remembers the postcard on the bed, makes a dive for it.*) Old Arawak. (*Grabs it up, returns to the door, turns.*) The glasses. (*Indicates she should take them off, waves, exits. For a moment* BELLE *stands paralyzed. She glances hopelessly to the bedroom. No time to change. She runs to the table, puts the chair back in place, grabs the hair spray, comb, and brush. The doorbell rings. She drops the spray, etc., back on the table. She hesitates. She runs to the mirror, looks at herself. There is a second ring. She starts toward the door, remembers her glasses, takes them off, puts them on the table, goes back to the door and opens it.* WAIN *in blue jeans and sports shirt is standing there.*)

BELLE. Oh, hello, Wain.

WAIN. Hi, kid.

BELLE. Do come in. (*Indicates stuff on table.*) I do apologize. I was just fixing my hair. (WAIN *comes in.* BELLE *closes the door behind him.*) I didn't exactly expect you quite so soon, so . . . (*Looks down at robe.*) Well.

WAIN. Don't give it a thought, kid.

BELLE. I feel terrible about drinks. I mean I haven't bought any lately. Jennifer hasn't sent her part of the rent yet and . . . (*Thinks of five dollars and is horrified.*) But how stupid of me. I hate people who make excuses. There's beer.

WAIN. Beer's okay.

BELLE. I'll get it. (BELLE *goes into kitchenette.* WAIN *notices that the air-conditioner is working, goes over and inspects it.* BELLE *comes out of the kitchenette with two bottles of beer and two glasses.*)

WAIN. You got this working again.

BELLE. Yes, a friend fixed it.

WAIN. You need the proper tools.

BELLE (*Taking beer to table where she pours glasses*). Oh, he didn't use any tools. (*Realizing.*) I mean, he probably did but I wasn't noticing. Here's your beer. (WAIN *crosses and picks it up.*) Do sit down, won't you? (WAIN *goes to daybed and sits down.* BELLE, *after a slight hesitation, sits down on the daybed too. There is a pause.*) Well, how have you been?

WAIN. Not too bad.

BELLE. Any exciting new work?

WAIN. New York in summer—is it dead!

BELLE. How about your TV Western pilots? Have you heard anything?

WAIN. Not a word. It's pretty tough, I don't mind telling you. Pretty tough.

BELLE. Oh, I am sorry.

WAIN. Know what they paid me for those pilots? Equity minimum. Ost and Raden—a couple of crooks if you ask me.

BELLE. How disgusting when they must be so rich.

WAIN. What you need's a good agent or you're screwed all along the line. Talent, personality. Goes for nothing without an agent.

BELLE. And you haven't got one?

WAIN. Agents. You bum around the offices. Know what you are— just so much flesh.

BELLE. That's New York. Oh, if you know how mad I get all the time. False standards, blindly following trends. A lot of mad sheep. To think they don't have enough sense to appreciate you.

WAIN. I've got a special line all worked out, too. A gimmick, to make it different. Most of those kids, they just imitate Brando or Elvis or someone. But come along with something new? It makes me sick.

BELLE. Poor Wain.

WAIN. Discouraged too.

BELLE (*Her flattery is genuine*). I can't imagine you getting discouraged—with your talent.

WAIN (*Interested*). You think I've got talent?

BELLE. Oh, of course, I'm no expert and I've never actually seen you perform. But I think one can tell those things.

WAIN (*Hopeful*). Like star quality, maybe?

BELLE. Well, yes, a kind of glitter. I always thought you had it, and Jennifer too. Back at Taylor High, just looking at you, you could tell you belonged to a different species from . . . well, Leroy Archer, Buck Sedlitz, and all of those nonentities.

WAIN. Buck Sedlitz. Bet he took over in his father's real estate. Bet he's on the up and up now.

BELLE. But who would want to be like Buck Sedlitz?

WAIN. Those teeth, remember? Snaggly.

BELLE. Of course. I got a letter from Mom last week. I'd told her I'd seen you. She was thrilled. They are all thrilled. Old Mrs. Johnson said, "I guess he's a big movie star by now." They all think you're just wonderful.

WAIN (*Pleased*). Old Groversville. What a dump.

BELLE. And you've got your looks too. Oh, Wain, it's absurd for you to be discouraged. You've only got to wait.

WAIN (*Really looking at her for the first time*). That's a real cute robe.

BELLE. Oh, do you really like it?

WAIN. It's cute as a button.

BELLE. It's nothing really. I got it at Gimbels, no, at Bloomingdale's. Not on a sale or anything. But it wasn't expensive.

WAIN. Know something? You're a nice kid.

BELLE. Oh, I do hope so. It's so difficult to tell oneself, isn't it?

WAIN. Was I down when I called you this morning!

BELLE. And you thought of me. I am glad.

WAIN. Well, not exactly. But was I low! And now . . .

BELLE. Maybe it's the beer.

WAIN. I never remember you too well from Groversville. Guess we weren't in the same age group.

BELLE. Nobody noticed me very much.

WAIN. How old are you?

BELLE. Nineteen. I'm Virgo.

WAIN. A virgin?

BELLE. Well, I . . . That is, what I meant actually was that I'm Virgo. That's my astrological sign. Of course it's all so ridiculous. I don't know why one keeps on referring to it. It's such a terribly outworn convention, isn't it?

WAIN. So, back in Groversville, you thought I was something special.

BELLE. Oh, yes.

WAIN. Little old Sally Dort.

BELLE. Not Sally . . . Belle.

WAIN. That's right. Sally—Belle. Two of them. You're Belle.

BELLE. That's right.

WAIN. Hot in here, isn't it? Even with the air-conditioner.

BELLE. Well, yes, it is rather warm.

WAIN. I guess you don't think I'm so wonderful anymore—bumming around New York, no work, nothing going right.

BELLE. Oh, that doesn't make any difference. How could it?

WAIN. Can't be more than twelve-fifteen-thirty. (*Puts his hand on her knee.*) You're a sweet kid.

BELLE. I . . . I . . . I mean I don't want you to think . . .

WAIN (*Slipping his arm around her waist*). A summer afternoon, a sweet kid . . . You're not strait-laced, are you?

BELLE. Oh, no.

WAIN (*Moving around her, pulling her to him, bringing his mouth down*). How about it, baby? (*He kisses her. She is rigid at first, then passionately responds.*)

BELLE. Oh, Wain . . .

WAIN. Shut up, baby, uh? (*Kissing her again.*)

BELLE. But you don't have to. Please, please, you don't have to.

WAIN. What a kid. (*Kissing her some more and then drawing away, looking at bedroom.*) This daybed—springs just as lousy as ever. Come on, honey. What do they make bedrooms for? (*He gets up, stoops over her.*)

BELLE. But, Wain, I never thought . . .

WAIN. Who's thinking? (*Lifts her up in his arms.*)

BELLE (*As he starts to carry her*). But, Wain . . .

WAIN. Everything's okay.

BELLE. But I mean . . . I've got to say it. I don't know . . . I mean, it's ridiculous, nineteen and everything . . . but I never have . . . I mean, oh, Wain, if it doesn't happen properly.

WAIN (*Carrying her toward bedroom*). Over the threshold we go.

BELLE. Wain, put me down, please. All that—across the threshold. It's different.

WAIN. You're not scared, are you, kid?

BELLE. When I've never done it, when . . .

WAIN. Don't you worry, baby. Some things come naturally.

BELLE. Oh, yes, it must be natural. That's the point. Two people just wanting each other . . . no overtones, nothing mental, nothing mixing it all up. (WAIN *kisses her passionately. Just as they reach the door, he stumbles over the little step.*)

WAIN. That goddam step. Always forgetting it. (*He carries her into the bedroom, the door closes, the curtain falls.*)

SCENE II

The same—one hour later. The bedroom door is closed. From the bathroom off the kitchen we can hear WAIN *singing a loud, lugubrious folk ballad as he takes a shower. For a while the stage is empty, then the bedroom door opens and* BELLE, *in a cotton dress but no shoes, comes in from the bedroom. She moves around the room uncertainly. She goes past the table where the hair spray is, touches it, goes to the mirror, looks at her reflection, goes back to the table, picks up her glasses, returns to the mirror, puts on the glasses, and gazes at herself again.* WAIN, *fully clothed, comes through the kitchen from the bathroom. He is carrying his old guitar with which he fiddles through the scene.* BELLE *hears him, takes off the glasses, and turns to him shyly.*

BELLE. Hello.

WAIN (*Faintly uneasy, hitching up his jeans*). Hi there, kid.

BELLE. Would you like a beer?

WAIN. Sure, sure, that's just what we need.

BELLE (*Looking at coffee table*). We never finished the others. They'll be terrible and warm. (*She picks up the bottles and glasses and starts for the kitchen.* WAIN *stands in her way, puts his arms around her.*)

WAIN. Hey, kid, how you feel? (*With the same faint uneasiness which comes out as swagger,* WAIN *pulls her to him and kisses her on the mouth.*)

BELLE. Oh, Wain, Wain ...

WAIN. You're a sweet kid, know that?

BELLE (*Slipping away, laughing*). Do let me get that beer. (BELLE *goes into the kitchen.* WAIN *glances quickly at his watch, runs his hand over his hair, and sits down on the daybed.* BELLE *comes in with the beer.*) They're the last two, I'm afraid. I never buy enough of anything. (*She puts the beer down on the coffee table and pours them. Then she sits down next to* WAIN *on the daybed.*)

WAIN (*Picking up his beer*). Here's to you.

BELLE (*Raising her glass*). To you. (*There's a pause.* BELLE, *blurting.*) Isn't it funny? I feel the same. I mean, something like that, something so terribly important, and you feel the same.

WAIN (*Nettled*). Gee, thanks for the compliment.

BELLE (*Horrified*). Oh Wain, I didn't mean that. I mean essentially the same. You'd think there'd be a huge gulf. The old you on one side, the new you on the other. But it isn't. Essentially you're the same.

WAIN. Listen, kid, I feel bad. I mean you saying it was the first time and then it being it and ...

BELLE. Oh, all that's so antiquated. What's the body for? And when it's spontaneous, natural, when both people feel the same ... Oh, I can't tell you how strange it was, having thought about you for so long. There were two yous, the old you I made up for myself, and the real you, both there together. So strange.

WAIN (*Dubious*). Then you're not mad or anything?

BELLE. But how could I be when I wanted it too? Oh, I do hope I wasn't too coming on or coquettish and all that—which I despise so much. But it was what I wanted too.

WAIN (*Reassured*). Gosh, kid, you've really got something, know that?

BELLE. Oh, Wain, I can talk, can't I? Please. I know boys hate it when you talk, but it's so important. I've got to make you see.

WAIN. See what?

BELLE. That I make no claims. When something wonderful's happened, when you're happy—especially if you're a woman, I guess—every instinct cries out, "Hold on. Stake your claim." But I won't ever because it twists and tarnishes. That's what corrupts it with the mind. You do see, don't you?

WAIN. I get the general idea, I guess.

BELLE. Then you do feel absolutely free, don't you?

WAIN. Sure. That's something I always feel. I feel free okay.

BELLE. There. You see? If there's no misunderstanding, if you always keep communications open . . . (*Snuggles against him.*) Wain.

WAIN (*Mostly reassured but still with traces of uneasiness, tightens his arms around her*). Hi, sugar.

BELLE (*In his arms*). Think of it. Maybe we'll go for days on end without seeing each other, without even calling each other, but we'll always know when the time comes . . . (*Smiles up at him, pulls his glass down and takes a sip.*) Now that everything's so straight between us, I can tell you something. It doesn't matter. It doesn't change anything in the slightest degree. But I've always been in love with you.

WAIN (*Uneasy again*). That's kind of a big word, isn't it, honey?

BELLE. Of course it is and it's criminal to use words inexactly. But it's true. At first there was always Jennifer which made it hopeless anyway. But even then I didn't realize it properly. I thought it was purely a carnal thing. You see, I always thought you were kind of limited.

WAIN. Me limited? That'd be the day.

BELLE. I mean, I always thought that when I fell in love it would be with someone sensitive to books and painting and everything. But of course that was ridiculous, wasn't it, because love *is* physical. I should have known it from Lawrence.

WAIN. Olivier?

BELLE. No, no, D. H. Lawrence. There's everything there really, but of course you have to grow into it. There's a poem. Oh, Wain, can I read it? Please, can I?

WAIN (*Glances surreptitiously at watch*). It isn't too long, is it?

BELLE. Oh no, he's never too long. (*She jumps up, goes to books and takes out her complete D. H. Lawrence. She opens it, peers, remembers her glasses, goes to the table, puts them on, finds the poem and stands by the table.*) It's from the ones called "Look, We've Come Through." Song of a man who has come through.

Not I, not I, but the wind that blows through me!
A fine wind is blowing the new direction of Time.
If only I am sensitive, subtle, oh, delicate, a winged gift!
If only, most lovely of all, I yield myself and am borrowed
By the fine, fine wind that takes its course through the chaos
      of the world
Like a fine, an exquisite chisel, a wedge-blade inserted;

If only I am keen and hard like the sheer tip of a wedge
Driven by invisible blows
The rock will split, we shall come at the wonder we shall find
    the Hesperides.

WAIN. The what?
BELLE. The Hesperides.
WAIN. Oh.
BELLE (*Going on*).

Oh for the wonder that bubbles into my soul,
I would be a good fountain, a good well-head,
Would blur no whisper; spoil no expression.
What is the knocking?
What is the knocking at the door in the night?
It is somebody wants to do us harm.
No, no, it is the three strange angels.
Admit them, admit them.

(*She puts the book down on its face on the table, still open, turns to* WAIN.) Do you? Do you see a bit?
    WAIN. It's pretty.
    BELLE. If only, most lovely of all, I yield myself. . . . He knew. He understood everything.
    WAIN. You read it pretty too.
    BELLE. Oh no, I didn't. (*She remembers her glasses, takes them off, crosses to the daybed and sits down next to* WAIN. *She moves to lie against him. He, quite deftly, disengages himself.*)
    WAIN. Look, kid, don't you want your beer?
    BELLE (*Laughing, picking up her glass*). Oh yes, after that. (*Turning to him.*) You musn't mind about what I told you. I mean about the love thing. It puts you under absolutely no obligation. It's just something for me. And I only told you because—well, if one isn't completely frank . . . (*Holding up her glass.*) Let's drink to Groversville.
    WAIN (*Indicating glass-raising*). Old Groversville.
    BELLE. Strange. I used to despise it so much—all that smugness, marrying everyone else next door, going into their father's business, so utterly unawakened. But maybe I was smug too. Maybe all of them feel that way at least once—that sensation of coming through. (*Lifts her glass.*) Dear Groversville.

WAIN. Say, honey, you got the correct time?

BELLE (*Glancing at her watch*). It's one-thirty. Why? Do you have to go somewhere? Because if you do—please, please, feel absolutely free.

WAIN. No, it isn't that. I was just wondering. My watch loses, then gains. A real crazy watch.

BELLE. That's the sort of watch I like—refusing to be the slave of time.

WAIN. Look, kid, this thing—you and me. Don't get me wrong. I feel the way you do and all that. But you're not going to tell Jenny, are you?

BELLE. Oh, not in a letter. She never answers my letters anyway.

WAIN. But I mean—when you see her . . .

BELLE. You think I shouldn't? You think it would hurt her?

WAIN. Yeah. What with everything.

BELLE. Perhaps you're right. Of course I admire her immensely but she is vain. That's perfectly natural, of course. All actresses have to be. But, yes, you're right. I think it's cruel to hurt people even in their vanity.

WAIN. Then we're agreed. We never tell Jenny?

BELLE. Not if you want it that way.

WAIN. Promise?

BELLE. Of course.

WAIN (*Gets up, goes to table*). Any cigarettes? . . . Oh, yes, here. (*Picks one up and lights it.*) You fixed the bed and all, didn't you?

BELLE. Oh yes.

WAIN (*Turning*). Look, kid, I don't know how to say this.

BELLE. But, Wain, you can say anything.

WAIN. I mean, when I came here, I didn't have any idea . . . I mean, about you and me.

BELLE. But of course you didn't.

WAIN. I mean, I was real low and you're such a sweet kid—and, well, I guess those things happen.

BELLE. But we've gone into all that.

WAIN. You get an impulse. That's only natural. You said it. Particularly when you're low and you feel everything's against you and there's this sweet kid . . . (*Blurting.*) Jenny's coming. She's due now.

BELLE (*Getting up*). But how do you know?

WAIN. She called me at the Y last night from San Francisco. Seems the designer for the show's sick in New York. She's got to fly East for a new dress. She's due here between one-thirty and two.

BELLE. Now?

WAIN. Yeah.

BELLE. And she asked you to meet her here?

WAIN. That's right. She can't stand the Y.

BELLE. And that's why you came?

WAIN. I told you. When I came I had no idea about . . .

BELLE. . . . and you were low in your mind.

WAIN. That's it.

BELLE. And Jennifer wants you back?

WAIN. Gosh, she didn't say. But with that big show on the Coast, with her going places and everything . . .

BELLE. I see.

WAIN. I mean, after all, she is my wife, and if she called from the Coast . . .

BELLE. Of course.

WAIN. I kind of wish it hadn't happened. (BELLE *stands saying nothing.* WAIN *goes to her.*) No, I don't mean that. It was wonderful, baby. A big thrill. And you being so wonderful about it. No claims, being free and everything. (*Takes her arms.*) You're not mad at me, are you?

BELLE. I've got to get out of here. (*Trying to release herself.*) Please. I've got to get my shoes.

WAIN (*Not letting her go*). Baby, baby, sweetie, don't be that way. Stick around. Jenny'll want to see you. Jenny's crazy about you.

BELLE. Please let me go. (*She struggles out of his arms and starts running away into the bedroom.*)

WAIN (*Going after her*). Belle. (*At bedroom door, looking in after her.*) Belle, you're not going to tell her. You promised. (BELLE *comes out of the bedroom pushing past him, carrying her shoes. She goes to a chair, sits down, starts wildly trying to put the shoes on.*) Look, kid, you don't want to go out like that.

BELLE. Like what? What's the matter with me? There's nothing the matter with me. (*The shoes are on. She gets up while* WAIN *hovers. She starts for the door. The phone rings. She stops, looking at the phone.* WAIN *looks at her. The phone rings again.*)

WAIN. Aren't you going to answer it? (BELLE *neither replies nor moves. The phone rings again.* WAIN *picks it up, watching* BELLE.)

WAIN (*On phone*). Hey, Jenny. Wait a minute. Belle's here trying to grab the phone away from me. (*Holds phone to* BELLE.)

BELLE (*Taking it*). Hello, Jennifer. . . . Yes, I'm all right. I'm fine. I . . .

WAIN (*Grabbing phone back*). Belle just wanted to say hello. . . . Sure, Jenny, just the same, kid. . . . Not too good. To tell the truth, I'm pretty discouraged. . . . No kidding! Gosh, Jenny, not a part in your show! . . . Better than that? But . . . Brother, you mean it? . . . Jenny, you're wonderful. . . . Sure, sure, right away. How'm I ever going to thank you, baby? (*He laughs at her reply.*) Okay, girl, ten minutes flat. (*He drops the receiver and turns to* BELLE, *beside himself with delight.*) Hey, kid, guess what? I've got an agent. (*He pauses a moment to let the great news seep in.*) Jenny fixed it all up with Mr. Mizer. Didn't I always say Jenny would come across? Look, they flew in together; they're waiting for me at Sardi's. I've got to get out of here so fast you can't see me for dust. (*Pats her arm.*) See you, kid. (*He starts away from her.*) Boy, are all my troubles over! (*Remembers, turns back.*) Jenny says to give you her love. (*Comes to her and kisses her.*) You're a sweet kid. (*Exits boisterously.* BELLE, *miserable, humiliated, despising herself, moves forlornly around the room. She sees* WAIN's *guitar and pauses, looking at it. The door buzzer sounds. Can it be* WAIN *back? Hopeful and hating herself for the hope, she runs to the door and opens it.* BOBBY *stands on the threshold. He is keyed-up, with the air of Someone to Whom Something Important Has Happened.*)

BELLE. Bobby!

BOBBY. Hey, Belle, I gotta talk to you. (*He closes the door and comes in.*) I broke with Arthur.

BELLE. You did?

BOBBY. Yeah. Give him back the identification medal. Everything.

BELLE. What happened?

BOBBY. Gosh, I dunno exactly. I ate the shrimp cocktail like always. And suddenly— Can you imagine? With him being so good to me and all? Suddenly I look at him and I think: Bobby, are you crazy or something? And I hear myself saying: "Hey, Arthur, this gotta stop. This ain't right. For chrissakes, man, we're both men." Pretty dopey, wasn't it? I mean, when we know there's all sorts—men, women, in between. But I hadda do it. . . . (*Notices* BELLE.) Hey, Belle, what is it? Something wrong?

BELLE. I'm all right.

BOBBY. Did old Wain notice your hair? (BELLE *doesn't answer.*) Boy, it happened? What you know! Was it okay—like you figured it would be? Mindless rapture and all? (BELLE *doesn't answer.*) Don't want to talk about it? That it?

BELLE. Jennifer came back.

BOBBY. Boy, when?

BELLE. She called him from the Coast. That's why he came here—to meet her.

BOBBY. The bastard, the goddam bastard.

BELLE. No, no. Why wouldn't he want her? Who wouldn't prefer Jennifer? (*She is utterly dejected.* BOBBY *watches her anxiously.*)

BOBBY. Hey, Belle, things ain't so bad, maybe. Look on the bright side. Leastways your body got freed, didn't it? Well, that's something, ain't it? (*There is no reaction from her. Trying again.*) You like a record? Dylan Thomas, maybe?

BELLE. No, thank you.

BOBBY. Not Bach even? Like you say? When you're real low—Bach? Don't worry. You'll figure it out with your great big brain. Gosh, Belle, sometimes I think you know everything there is.

BELLE. (*Outburst*) I don't know a thing.

BOBBY. Hey, Belle.

BELLE. I don't. You know how I talk—jabber, jabber, jabber, pouring my stupid brains out. I told him I loved him. But it didn't matter, I said. It made no bond. He'd got to feel absolutely free, I said. But it isn't true. All that from Lawrence. (*Sobs.*) Two individuals—free with no ties. It wasn't like that. It isn't. I'm just like anyone else from Groversville. I don't care what he is. I want him for me. I want him to love *me*.

BOBBY. Hey, Belle, don't be that way, please. (*She is sobbing hopelessly now.* BOBBY *hovers. He puts out a hand and then withdraws it. He sees the Lawrence poems on the table and picks them up. He opens the book.*) Hey, Belle, it's the one you go for. Song of the Man That Come Through. (*Rather awed but rather proud too, he starts to read.*)

> Not I, not I, but the wind that blows through me,
> A fine wind is blowing the new direction of Time.
> If only I am sensitive, subtle, oh, delicate, a winged gift,
> If only most lovely of all, I yield myself. . . .

(*Looks up, delighted with this unexpected new talent.*) Hey, Belle, listen. Me reciting!

CURTAIN

Act Three

SCENE I

The same day—six-thirty p.m. SKIP, *a big, dark sailor of 24, is lounging with immense self-confidence on the daybed, drinking beer out of a bottle.* BOBBY, *with a beer too, is sitting on the edge of the bed.* BELLE, *in her working Doubleday clothes with her glasses on, is sitting opposite them in the chair.*

BOBBY (*All out to make the party go*). Hey, Skip, no kidding! You really been in a real Geisha house?

SKIP. Have I been in a Geisha house? Brother.

BOBBY. Gosh, Belle, traveling all around the world. Seeing all them different places with their different customs. Ain't that . . . ?

SKIP (*Interrupting as he feels in his blouse pocket. He is being the amiable monarch*). Hey, what you got to do for a butt around here? Yodel?

BOBBY. Sure, Skip, we got cigarettes, ain't we, Belle?

BELLE. There are some on the table.

SKIP. Then shape up, kid. Make tracks.

BOBBY (*Jumping up happily*). Okay, Bro. Okay. (*He goes to the table, comes back with the cigarettes and offers them to* SKIP.) Here ya, Skipper. (SKIP *takes the pack, takes out a cigarette, puts it in his mouth, tosses the pack back onto the table and tilts his chin, indicating* BOBBY *should give him a light.*) Light? (*Fumbles in his pocket.*) Sure, Skip.

SKIP (*Still the amiable monarch*). Boy, have you got sloppy with me away, kid. I'll have to straighten you out. (*To* BELLE.) You should have seen him before I went into the service, miss. I had him trained real good. (BOBBY *produces matches and lights* SKIP'S *cigarette.*) That's my boy. Sit down, kid. Sit down. (BOBBY *sits down again next to him.* SKIP *drags on the cigarette.*) Them Geisha girls? Brother. Me and a couple of the kids and Evans, the yeoman, we all ended up at this dump one night. You should have seen me doing that fancy stomach dance right along with

49

the girls. Was I loaded! It's that stuff they keep pouring into you—saki, they call it. Seems like nothing—but watch out. (*To* BELLE.) You ever drunk saki, miss?

BOBBY. Hey, it's Belle. Call her Belle.

BELLE. As a matter of fact, I haven't. I almost went to a Japanese restaurant once but something went wrong.

SKIP. Boy, I was floating around that room with all them paper walls and everything. And there's this big vase with a flower in it. Over it goes. Bang. I busted her fan too. Boy, was she riled—old Lotus Blossom.

BOBBY. Hey, Skip, was that her name? Old Lotus Blossom?

SKIP. They're all called like that—like flowers. Lotus Blossom, Peach Blossom, God knows who blossom. Real cute, too. But was she riled. Said it was her mother's fan. If you ask me, half them dames don't know who their mother was even.

BOBBY. Old Skip—what a mess!

BELLE. I do hope . . . I mean, you did give her something to get the fan repaired, didn't you?

SKIP. Sure, gave her a couple of bucks, threw in a couple packs of Chesties too. But, boy, do they gyp you in that clip joint. For what we paid out, she could have bought a whole crateload of fans. Don't worry, though. I got my money's worth okay. Old Lotus Blossom . . . bet she had to take a vacation for a couple of days.

BOBBY. Hey, Skip, watch it!

SKIP. Watch what?

BOBBY. That ain't no way to talk in front of Belle.

SKIP. She ain't shocked. Anything goes with Belle. You said so in your letter. Ain't that right, Belle?

BELLE. Oh yes. Of course.

SKIP. What a night! Evans? A couple of us had to drag him out of that place almost—to get him back to the ship on time. Those Geishas—there's nothing like them, I'm telling you.

BELLE (*Rather breathless*). Then I don't think they can have been real Geishas.

SKIP (*Slightly defensive*). Uh?

BELLE. I mean, I don't think it can have been a genuine Geisha house. Of course I have no personal experience, but one reads and I always understood there was nothing like that . . . I mean, nothing between the Geishas and the clients.

BOBBY (*Impressed*). Boy, is that right?

BELLE. Oh yes. It's all—well, aesthetic really. It's part of the Japanese culture. They prepare the meals and talk and dance and play those instruments and recite. They've been trained to it from the cradle. But the whole idea that they're sort of—well, prostitutes—that's a complete fallacy.

SKIP (*Thunderous*). You accusing me of lying or something?

BELLE. Oh, no, no. Of course not. I just meant I don't think it could have been a genuine Geisha house. They probably told you it was, but . . .

SKIP. You think I don't know a Geisha house from just some crummy waterfront dump for gobs?

BELLE. Oh, of course you can, Skip. And I'm certain . . . well, there must have been so many changes since the occupation. But . . .

SKIP. Either I had Lotus Blossom or I didn't. Right?

BELLE. Of course.

SKIP. Okay, okay. (*There is a rather awkward pause with* SKIP *prepared to be surly,* BELLE *ill-at-ease, and* BOBBY *desperately pretending that the party is going well.*)

BOBBY. Hey, Belle, ain't you gonna break down and have another beer?

BELLE. I'd love to, but I just can't go reeling into Doubleday's, can I? (*Tries a little laugh to win* SKIP. *It doesn't work.*) I've got to go any second too. I've simply got to.

BOBBY (*Grabbing* SKIP's *empty bottle*). Okay, Skipper, let's fill 'em up.

SKIP (*Keeping the bottle, taking* BOBBY's). I'll do it.

BOBBY. Hey, Skipper, this is our party for you. You don't have to do nothing. Just sit there.

SKIP (*Getting up with bottles*). I'll get 'em. Got to go to the head anyways. (*Goes into the kitchenette.*)

BOBBY. Gosh, Belle, he shouldn't have talked that way about the Geishas.

BELLE. Oh, that doesn't matter. I was the one who did it all wrong.

BOBBY. You wrong? That'd be the day. But it's interesting, isn't it? Learning all them real live facts.

BELLE. Of course.

BOBBY. Old Skip ain't too educated. But he's tops, honest, when you know him.

BELLE. Oh, I'm sure he is.

BOBBY. You like him? No kidding?

BELLE. No kidding.

BOBBY. Boy, was I scared for a while. I thought: "Old Skip's different somehow. He and Belle ain't gonna go for each other." But it's okay?

BELLE. Of course it is.

BOBBY. See how it's just like I said? "Hey, Bro, get me a cigarette. Hey, Bro, I'm gonna straighten you out"? Thinks the world of me, old Skip. Look, Belle, you wouldn't do something, would you? A real favor?

BELLE. What is it?

BOBBY. When you leave—well, it okay if I kiss you when you leave?

BELLE. But of course. (SKIP *comes out of the kitchen with two open bottles of beer.*)

BOBBY. Hey, hey, here's the barman. (SKIP *gives one bottle to* BOBBY *and stands looking at* BELLE.)

SKIP. It said it. In great big letters—slapped right across the front of the building. "Genuine Geisha House."

BELLE. Then of course it must have been genuine.

SKIP (*Mollified*). Okay, okay. (*Sits down next to* BOBBY.)

BOBBY. Little old Japan. Wow! Them temples. You see all them temples?

SKIP. I've seen them all.

BELLE. Oh, did you go to Kyoto?

SKIP. Don't exactly recall that name.

BELLE. That's where all the wonderful temples are.

SKIP. If you ask me—all that heathen stuff—it's crap.

BELLE (*In spite of herself*). Oh no, you can't say that.

SKIP (*Prepared to be belligerent*). You a Christian?

BELLE. Well, yes, I suppose so. I mean, if you're born into a Christian culture, you're really a Christian whether you want to be or not, aren't you?

SKIP. And you go for that heathen stuff?

BELLE. It's not going for it. It's just that it's terribly important to realize that in all religions, along with all the bad, there's always a germ of truth. The same truth. In all of them. Christianity, Buddhism, probably voodoo, too.

BOBBY (*Admiring*). Gosh, listen to her, Skip. Ain't she something? A real Einstein. Din't I tell you?

BELLE (*Getting up*). It's awful, but I've really got to go this very minute.

BOBBY. Gosh, Belle—already?

BELLE. Gloria'll be having a fit. She's got a big date.

SKIP (*The drink showing a bit*). You crazy about the Japs?

BELLE. As a matter of fact, I don't think I've ever met one.

SKIP. When they killed our kids by the thousands—Guadalcanal, Iwo Jima . . . all them suicide planes?

BELLE. But that was war. That's not just the Japs. That's everyone. That's . . . Oh dear, it's silly, isn't it, getting into topics like this when I've got to leave? (*Going toward* SKIP.) Good-bye. I have enjoyed meeting you.

SKIP (*Getting up, very correct*). Likewise.

BELLE. I know you and Bobby have a million things to say to each other so it's just as well I've got to go.

BOBBY (*Getting up*). But we'll pick you up at Doubleday's at midnight, eh, Belle?

BELLE. If you're really sure . . .

BOBBY. If we're sure! Listen to her, Skip. Boy, will we hit the town. Three musketeers, three little pigs, three blind mice.

BELLE (*Holding out her hand to* SKIP). Well, good-bye for the moment.

SKIP (*Taking her hand*). 'Bye.

BELLE. Well, good-bye, Bobby. (*She turns to him. For a second they stand awkwardly. Then* BOBBY *kisses her with what he hopes is airy sophistication.*)

BOBBY. 'Bye, baby.

BELLE. Good-bye. (*She lets herself out of the door and closes it behind her.*)

BOBBY. Hey, Skip. You like her? You like old Belle?

SKIP. Walking dictionary, ain't she?

BOBBY. Is she a mental genius!

SKIP. Keyoto. Where she dug that one up? Some one-horse town no one ever heard of.

BOBBY. Belle's heard of everything. She reads books all the time. History, geography. Music too. Is she a whiz at music! Makes you see . . .

SKIP. Seems like she should be a schoolteacher or something.

BOBBY. Oh, sure. Belle could teach school.

SKIP (*Rolls up the pants of his left leg, exposing his knee*). I've got work for you. (*He bangs the couch.*) Hey, kid. Come over.

BOBBY (*Looking at the knee*). It still acting up?

SKIP. Been pretty near killing me since morning. It's Manhattan. This goddam humidity. Okay, kid, action.

BOBBY. Maybe I lost the knack.

SKIP. Na, you got the knack okay. Get at it. (*With some reluctance* BOBBY *kneels down and starts massaging the knee.*) Ah, that's more like it. Know something? Once over in Tangier I like to died with it and I thought: "Boy, if only old Bro was here."

BOBBY. Didn't they have no medics or nothing?

SKIP. Them pharmacists' mates. You should see some of 'em. You could pass out almost from the pain and would they care? Dirt. That's what you are to them. Dirt. Boy, is this like old times!

BOBBY. Sure, Skip.

SKIP. Bet you missed me when I was gone.

BOBBY. Sure did, Skip.

SKIP. I took good care of you, didn't I? Like a brother almost. That's a tough neighborhood if you don't have someone real hep to look out for you.

BOBBY. That's right.

SKIP. Millie Brownlow. Remember? Any night after nine-thirty back of Sampson's Garage. Listen, kid, we really stuck with her tonight?

BOBBY. What you mean stuck?

SKIP. A whole bunch of the kids is meeting up at the Crossroads. Rarin' to go. They know all about you. My mascot. How about it, kid?

BOBBY. And stand Belle up?

SKIP. Won't kill her, will it? Okay. She comes back here and reads a good book. (BOBBY *abruptly stops massaging and stands up.*) Hey, don't lay off. It's still killing me.

BOBBY. If it's that bad you should go see a doctor.

SKIP. What's the matter with you?

BOBBY. Nothing.

SKIP. Then fix my knee.

BOBBY. I don't feel like it.

SKIP. You don't feel like it? You got pretty big for your britches, ain't you?

BOBBY. If you wanna meet up with your friends—okay.

SKIP. And you'll go pick up your girl friend at that bookstore?

BOBBY. That's right.

SKIP. Your girl friend! (*Imitating.*) "I don't think it can have been a genuine Geisha house." (*Imitation over.*) Brother! And them eyeglasses. Read about her in your letter you'd think she was Marilyn Monroe.

BOBBY. When'd I say she was like Marilyn Monroe? When'd I write that? Belle ain't like no crummy Marilyn Monroe.

SKIP. You telling me!

BOBBY. You criticizing Belle?

SKIP. For Chrissakes!

BOBBY. *You* criticizing Belle! Just meeting her, you oughta feel proud.

SKIP. Is that right?

BOBBY. Is that right! You been most every place in the world. Paris,

Japan. What'd you learn? Did you study them temples? Did you go visit all them paintings and stuff in the Eiffel Tower? Belle ain't been no place —just where she come from and New York City—but she knows. Not just facts, not just like that. But how to figure things right? How to get everything doped out right? Why, Belle . . .

SKIP. You lay her? You telling me you lay her?

BOBBY. For Chrissakes, you think all girls gotta be like—like Millie Brownlow?

SKIP. What's wrong with Millie? She knows what a guy needs, okay.

BOBBY. Yeah. Like an animal. Like a dog or something. Millie Brownlow—a cheap lay-around anyone can have for the price of a Hershey bar.

SKIP. You mean *you* done it with Millie for the price of a Hershey bar?

BOBBY. Aw—who couldn't?

SKIP. You couldn't.

BOBBY. What you mean?

SKIP. You never had Millie.

BOBBY. Me? You crazy? I had Millie fifty, a hundred times.

SKIP. You think I'm a dope or something? You think she never told me how she made a pass back of Sampson's Garage, how you turned yellow in the face and ran? You think she never told me that?

BOBBY. Millie—she'd lie about her own old dad.

SKIP. Boy, did the kids on the sub laugh when I told them that one! Know what they called you?

BOBBY. I don't care what no one calls me.

SKIP. No, I said. You got the kid wrong, I said. He wrote me. He's got a girl friend. Seems like she's like Marilyn Monroe almost. You and your girl friend! Boy, was I green before I went into the service. All them years. Buddy-buddy. Hey, Bro. Hiyah, Bro. Was I green! (*Pats the couch.*) Hey, kid. Come over here.

BOBBY. Why?

SKIP. You been waiting long enough, ain't you? Well, everything comes to him who waits, as the saying goes.

BOBBY. You crazy or something?

SKIP. What you scared of? It's the ideal setup for you, ain't it? A nice elegant apartment, no one disturbing us, your old boy friend with a couple of beers under his belt. (SKIP *gets up very nonchalantly, walks to the door, throws on the safety catch. He turns to* BOBBY.) Okay, Bro. Okay.

BOBBY. Get outta here.

SKIP (*Hitching up his pants and starting toward* BOBBY). Who d'you think you're kidding? Little faggot. Goddam little son-of-a-bitch faggot. (*He continues ominously toward* BOBBY *as* BOBBY *picks up a beer bottle.*)

BOBBY. Get outta here—or I'll kill you.

CURTAIN

SCENE 2

The same—12:30 a.m. the same evening. The lights are all on. The empty beer bottles from the "party" are still in place and there is a certain amount of wreckage, indicating some sort of violence has taken place—for example, an overturned table and lamp lie beside the daybed. At the rise of the curtain, JENNIFER, *very tense, comes out of the bedroom, carrying a suitcase.*

JENNIFER. Press on. Press on. You are an American woman. Nothing can defeat you. (*She opens the suitcase and inspects contents.*) Panties, bras, underarm deodorant. (MILTIE, *wearing his sunglasses, enters from the kitchen.*)

MILTIE. Just as I suspected. The cupboard is bare. Not even the dregs of her great aunt's blueberry cordial. (JENNIFER, *stepping back, trips over the lamp.*) Damn, damn, goddam lamp.

MILTIE. What on earth are you doing?

JENNIFER. Tables and lamps strewn all over the place. God knows what Belle's been up to. (*Goes into bedroom.*)

MILTIE. With her weakness for juvenile delinquents, she's probably been staging her own private rumble. I can see her right now, leading an attack on O'Malley's candy store, swinging a bicycle chain.

JENNIFER (*Returning with dresses on hangers*). Oh no, she'll still be at Doubleday's. I can't imagine why they stay open so late. Who's going to lurch in at midnight and order the collected works of St. Thomas Aquinas?

MILTIE. Some call-girl who has FOUND GOD perhaps.

JENNIFER (*Throwing dresses into suitcase*). Ha-ha. Terrible green dress, terrible beige dress. Oh well, put them in. You never know.

MILTIE. Rather agitated, aren't you, Mrs. Dumke?

JENNIFER. Who wouldn't be, after that cute little, true-blue little con-game at Sardi's?

MILTIE. Dear Mrs. Dumke, your performance with your husband was a masterpiece. If only I could say the same for that little demonstration of acting singing you offered the world in San Francisco.

JENNIFER. If you ever mention that again.

MILTIE. It's merely to remind you that twenty-four hours ago you were the most emphatically fired actress in history. Now, thanks to Milton M. Mizer and that cute little con-game, you at least stand a sporting chance of making it as a housewife.

JENNIFER. . . . while you get a hernia, I hope, dragging that ten percent to the bank. It *was* ten percent, wasn't it? You and your revolting lawyer didn't squeeze any extra blood out of that pitiful defenseless boy?

MILTIE. Tut, tut, Mrs. Dumke. Is nothing sacred?

JENNIFER. Oh God, why does real life have to be so real with you around? (*Slams suitcase, nips her finger.*) Ouch! Lousy, bitchy, Mark-Cross type suitcase. (*Bangs suitcase.*)

MILTIE (*Bitchy*). Keep calm. Be sophisticated at all times. K.C.

JENNIFER. If this were a Barbara Stanwyck movie, I'd shoot you. (*The door opens.* BELLE, *wearing her glasses, comes in and pauses, blinking momentarily at the lights.* JENNIFER *sweeps toward her.*) Ah, there she is. There's my friend. There's my dear cherished friend.

BELLE. Hello, Jennifer.

JENNIFER. Let me look at you. But, darling, the hair—it's a miracle. You've positively blossomed. You remember Miltie Mizer, don't you?

BELLE. Yes, I remember him.

JENNIFER. Miltie, say something nice to Belle. You were so beastly last time. Remember? That poor little friend of hers?

MILTIE. I hope your poor little friend is as fit as a fiddle. Is that nice enough? (*Dazzling smile.*) Hello, child.

BELLE. Hello.

JENNIFER. Darling Belle, what on earth have you been at? Another of your orgies?

BELLE. I had some friends in for beer before I went to work. I thought they were going to pick me up at Doubleday's. I suppose they forgot. (*To* MILTIE.) I'm sorry, Mr. Mizer. If there's any beer left, would you . . . ?

JENNIFER. There isn't any, but it couldn't matter less. We're bursting with news far headier than the foamiest Lowenbrau, aren't we?

MILTIE. Far headier.

JENNIFER. Darling, the most fantastic coincidence. Guess what?

BELLE. I'm never very good at guessing.

JENNIFER. Aren't you? You poor sweet child. Then, listen. You know

I persuaded Miltie to represent Wain. Well, you're never going to believe this, but just a few hours—literally—after the contracts were signed, Miltie discovered that the Western pilot crashed through. They're insane about Wain. A huge sponsor. A fantastic salary. The dear boy's ecstatic. Just wait till you see him.

BELLE. He's coming here?

JENNIFER. He's picking up his things at the Y—and then the blissfully reunited Dumkes, with their splendid agent, wing their way to L.A. on some wildly eccentric plane which leaves at four a.m.

BELLE. You mean you're going too?

JENNIFER. Of course.

BELLE. But what about your show in San Francisco?

JENNIFER. Oh that!

BELLE. You're giving it up?

JENNIFER. Where could I possibly be now but at my husband's side? Darling, aren't you thrilled to the marrow?

BELLE. I think I'm more muddled than anything.

JENNIFER. Of course, darling, everything happening so quickly.

BELLE (*Pause*). You knew in San Francisco, didn't you?

JENNIFER. Knew what, darling?

BELLE. About Wain. That's why you came back—to get him before anyone else did.

MILTIE. What a sly little mind she has.

BELLE (*Bewildered*). But—but why doesn't he see what you're doing?

JENNIFER. But, my poor sweet Belle, all we're doing is rallying around. A brilliant agent. . . .

MILTIE. A brilliant wife. What more could the dear boy ask for?

JENNIFER. After all, what is success if it isn't shared? Who said that? Schopenhauer? Oh no, it was my mother. (WAIN *enters.* JENNIFER *runs to him.*)

WAIN (*Wildly excited, to* BELLE). Hi, Belle. What you know, baby? I made it. Didn't I always say? (*Pulls keys from his pocket.*) Hey, what'll I do with the keys to this firetrap?

MILTIE. Dear boy, throw them out of the window.

WAIN (*Tossing keys to* MILTIE, *to* BELLE). Boy, isn't it something? Me out on the Coast in a fancy villa with a swimming pool? Just wait till they hear in Groversville. (*Embraces* BELLE.)

BELLE. I think you'd better go now.

WAIN. What's the rush?

BELLE. I think you'd better go.

MILTIE (*Conscious of possible complications*). Dear boy, the child is right. There's not much time. And you never know what may happen on the way to the airport.

JENNIFER (*Equally eager to be gone*). A blow-out, a head-on collision—those divine Con Edison men digging because they must. The suitcase, Miltie.

MILTIE. With pleasure, Mrs. Dumke. Just the one, isn't it?

JENNIFER. Just the one. (*To* BELLE.) Darling, do take care of yourself. And if Doubleday's ever opens a branch on the Coast, get yourself transferred—instantly. Bye bye, dearest friend. (*She hustles* WAIN *out.*)

MILTIE (*At door*). Farewell, little girl. (BELLE, *alone, stands looking around the apartment. They have gone. A few hours ago this would have seemed the end of everything. Now, unexpectedly, what she is feeling is a sense of liberation. They are out of her life. The apartment is hers now. Almost ritualistically, proving the point, she moves a chair from one position to another. As she does so, there is a tap at the door. She goes to open it.* BOBBY *comes in. His face is cut. He is holding himself together by an immense effort of will.*)

BELLE. Bobby.

BOBBY. I seen Wain come. I waited. When they come out, I slipped in. It's okay. They didn't reckernize me.

BELLE. But—your face. What's happened?

BOBBY. Ain't nothing. I'm okay.

BELLE. But what happened with Skip?

BOBBY. Nothing happened. Look, Belle, I'm sorry, Belle, but could you loan me a couple of bucks—four bucks, maybe?

BELLE. But of course I can. (*She goes to her bag on the table and searches.*)

BOBBY. Was it okay? Wain coming back? You got it straightened out better with Wain?

BELLE. I'm never going to see them again.

BOBBY. Gosh, Belle, that's too bad. Three bucks is enough maybe.

BELLE (*Handing him the money*). Here's five.

BOBBY. You sure you can swing it?

BELLE. Of course.

BOBBY. I'll pay you back Friday, honest. I'd of slept in the park or someplace. But them cops—give them half a chance, they pick you up.

BELLE. You mean that's what you want the money for? To get a place to sleep?

BOBBY. It's okay. I know a place. Good clean room and all. (*Starts for the door.*) Well, thanks, Belle. So long, Belle.

BELLE. But you're not going.

BOBBY. It's real late and I been walking.

BELLE. But, Bobby, you know you can stay here.

BOBBY. That wouldn't be right.

BELLE. But that's ridiculous.

BOBBY. Nah. I don't wanna. I don't wanna.

BELLE. But, Bobby, please. Don't leave for a while. At least have a cigarette. (BOBBY *hesitates.* BELLE *picks up the cigarette pack. He comes to her from the door. She lights cigarette for him.*) Aren't you going to tell me what happened?

BOBBY. Nothing happened. I told you.

BELLE. But you and Skip had a fight, didn't you? I know you did.

BOBBY. Nothing got broke, did it? If it did, I'll pay.

BELLE. It was me, wasn't it? Saying all that about the Geishas and everything. I antagonized him. I knew it. I get so worked up and feel I've just got to speak my mind. Oh, it's so stupid. I'm so sorry.

BOBBY. It wasn't you. (BELLE *goes hesitantly to him and puts her hand on his shoulder. He reacts away from her hand violently.*) Don't touch me.

BELLE. But, Bobby . . .

BOBBY. Don't touch me. (*In sudden collapse, he throws himself face downward along the daybed.*) Don't touch me. Don't touch me. (*While* BELLE *hovers unhappily,* BOBBY *lies stretched out, rigid, engulfed in misery. After a long pause, his face pressed against the bed, muffling the words.*) What he said—it ain't true!

BELLE. What Skip said?

BOBBY. All of 'em. Why? What is it? What's in their filthy minds? Why don't they keep their hands off of me? What've I done?

BELLE. Nothing, nothing.

BOBBY. My buddy. From way, way back. He done something—I done something. Always together. And nothing like that. I'd rather die in the street than ever think nothing like that. And he stood there and he called me . . . Bastards, all of 'em. Skip, Arthur, all of 'em. Mom, too.

BELLE. You've been home?

BOBBY. Mom—sitting there in that old leather chair, with her feet up. (*Imitating.*) "Hey, Bobby, you call Arthur this minute. He's been calling and calling. Bobby, you make it up with him quick. He's a good friend to you and to me." (*Stops imitating.*) And I look at her and I think, "You know the score okay. You know what Arthur is and you don't give a damn what he done with me so long as you get asked to the Broadway theater with a martini cocktail at Schrafft's." Boy, I coulda spit. All of 'em on your back, pushing you. Why, Belle, why? Is it me? (*He puts his hands up to cover his face.*)

BELLE (*Urgently*). No, Bobby, no. It's them.

BOBBY (*Dropping the hands from his face*). Skip knew you wasn't my girl friend. He sat there and he says: "She your girl friend? You kidding me? You—you lay her?" And I said: "For Chrissakes, you think every girl gotta be a cheap lay-around like Millie Brownlow that anyone can have for the price of a candy bar?" And he said, "You never had Millie." And I said, "Sure I had Millie, I had her fifty, a hunnerd times." But it wasn't true. I never done it with Millie. She tried one time back of Sampson's Garage. Come on, Bobby, she says. All the other kids been there. What you waiting for? And I tried—and I couldn't. I got sick to my stomach and ran.

BELLE. You've never told that to anyone, have you?

BOBBY. You kidding?

BELLE. And all this time it's been in your mind.

BOBBY. It happened, din't it? I tried—and I couldn't. All that I say about sex—how it's dirt—for the birds . . . it's lies. It's just because I can't do it. I ain't like Arthur, even. Being like old Arthur, at least that's something. But me—I'm nothing. That's what I am. Have I got plenty of nothing! Brother! (*Starts to leave.*)

BELLE. But, Bobby, that's ridiculous, that's . . . Don't leave. Please, Bobby, stay.

BOBBY. And have you tell me things to make me feel good?

BELLE. No, Bobby. It isn't that. I want you to stay because—well, all this—the apartment—it's mine now. It's nobody but me. And I want you to be my first guest.

BOBBY (*Looking around from the door*). Yeah. That's right. You got everything switched around, ain't you?

BELLE. I think the chair looks so much cozier like that, don't you? I've always wanted it that way. And I was going to move the table. (*She picks up the phone table. A leg drops off.*) Oh dear. (BOBBY *closes the door, comes back into the room, squats and examines the table.*)

BOBBY. Maybe it ain't so bad. You got any glue?

BELLE. Why, yes. There's some in my desk. (*She runs to get it.* BOBBY *on the floor turns the table over, in his element, very competent.* BELLE *brings the glue and drops down beside him.*)

BOBBY (*Expertly spreading glue on the broken leg*). Hey, hold the table. (*Indicating.*) Hold it like that.

BELLE (*Holding the table but awkwardly*). Oh dear. You see? I'm so clumsy.

BOBBY. You're okay. You're holding it real good. (*As he works.*) What havoc! Boy, you should of seen Skip when I got through with him. If you think I'm bedraggled, you should see him. (*With a flourish, he brings the broken leg and the table together, pressing to make the glue hold.*) There. Good as new. You can have a real big fat guy sitting down on that. And—Rock of Gibraltar! You just see next time you give a party.

BELLE. I don't imagine I'll be giving many parties.

BOBBY. Just because you tossed out Wain and them? Don't you worry, Belle. You just wait. Someone'll come along. Some guy. Nothing crummy like old Wain. But some real bright guy with a great big brain. Good-looking too.

BELLE. No, no. That isn't for me.

BOBBY. You kidding? When you got everything? When there ain't no one wouldn't be proud just to be walking down the street with you?

BELLE. Dear Bobby, dear sweet Bobby.

BOBBY. Sure, Belle. You got me. You know that, don't you? You always got me. (BELLE *nods.*) We're friends, ain't we? (BELLE *nods.*) Not just because we got no one else, but because we're real friends. A team.

BELLE. Yes.

BOBBY (*Handing her the glue*). Here's old Elmer's glue. (*She takes it.* BOBBY *takes her hand.*) Know something? You got real pretty hands.

BELLE. I never remember my nails.

BOBBY. They're real pretty. (*He looks at the hand. Very shyly, he raises it to his lips and kisses it. They sit together on the floor, looking at each other.*) Belle. Gee, Belle.

BELLE. Bobby.

BOBBY. If . . .

BELLE. Yes?

BOBBY. I mean, if . . . Belle? (*Pause.*) You and me? (*He takes her in his arms. He kisses her.*) Wow! What you know? Live and learn, don't you?

THE CURTAIN FALLS

ON
Look: We've Come Through

Theater people are terribly neurotic about failure. With an almost superstitious dread of the subject, actors quietly omit from their biographies all mention of their parts in past flops, while producers delicately sidestep references to productions that failed, projects that fell apart. Whenever the word "flop" comes up in a conversation among theater people, there is much shuffling of feet, shrugging, coughing, throat-clearing, and a really impressive variety of ingenious attempts to change the subject.

By way of contrast, a casual reference to Hugh Wheeler's *Look: We've Come Through*, which opened at the Hudson Theatre on October 25, 1961, and lasted through the end of the same week, provokes not only a genuinely warm response, but also a strong inclination to relive past history—even on the part of those individuals whose personal involvement with the production would presumably make remembrance an unnecessary pain. Characterizing the play as "a beautiful, beautiful play," its producer, Saint Subber, declares, "I'm prouder of what I've done with this show than *Kiss Me, Kate*. I look back on my career and it has included some real humdingers of successes. But my two favorite plays are *The Grass Harp* and *Look: We've Come Through*." Considering that Saint Subber's "humdingers" include William Inge's *The Dark at the Top of the Stairs* and Paddy Chayefsky's *The Tenth Man*,

63

and practically every Neil Simon play produced on Broadway, that is indeed some testimonial.

The show's director, Jose Quintero, not only affirms that he "absolutely loved" the play, but even today—with such productions as *The Iceman Cometh, Long Day's Journey into Night,* and *Summer and Smoke* to his credit—insists that "it was one of the best jobs that I've ever done." Quintero claims, in fact, that the show brought him "more letters than any other play I've ever done."

Perhaps even more significant than the continued enthusiasm of the play's producer and director is the uncharacteristic championing of *Look: We've Come Through* by a number of professional theater critics who were publicly appalled by the production's short-lived career on Broadway. Resurrecting the subject in a piece called "The Anatomy of a Valiant Failure," which appeared in *The New York Post* after the play had closed, theater critic Richard Watts wrote, "I admit to a feeling of great frustration when a play which I have high regard for, and am virtually alone among the reviewers in applauding, encounters a hasty failure." After reiterating the reasons for his admiration of the play and its production, Watts then went on to admonish gently his fellow critics for their insensitive and narrow readings of the play's content and their spurious evaluation of its author's dramatic talents.

Writing in the *Village Voice,* Jerry Tallmer was more vociferous in his condemnation of his fellow critics for failing to appreciate what he called "one of the few altogether moving love stories I have ever experienced in the theater." Announcing himself "appalled and exhausted" by what he characterized as "an episode of love and death, beauty and murder," he focused his anger at the play's brief life-and-death chronicle on *The New York Times's* critic, Howard Taubman, faulting him specifically for his repetitive use of the word "impotence" within the context of his review. Even *Newsday's* critic, George Oppenheimer—generally too courtly a gentleman to chastise his colleagues—took them to task for damning the play with faint praise.

Ironically, the play which piqued these critics into the rare and uncharacteristic behavior of scrapping in public with their fellow reviewers is itself gentle and totally nonbelligerent. Essentially the tender treatment of two adolescents who might be characterized as "losers," or, less harshly, as "little people," the play explores the fragile core of their characters. With bittersweet humor, playwright Hugh Wheeler uses the device of sexual encounter to reveal his characters in all their vulnerability. In *Big Fish, Little Fish,* which had a Broadway production the previous year, Wheeler also wrote about a group of losers—but these gray, twilight "little people" had so capitulated to their own character weaknesses and to the dehumanizing forces of the society which declares them "losers" that they did not "come through." In both plays, although with far more optimism in *Look: We've Come Through,* Wheeler indulges his self-acknowledged fascination for "people who can't conform and have no hope of success." Of his characters, the playwright observes, "If you're looking for human qualities in an increasingly dehumanized world, where you're apt to find them is in the misfits. Wherever you look for what might be the redemption of the human race, you'd be more likely to find it in the misfits of society than you are in the rest of civilization."

Look: We've Come Through achieves an added degree of warmth and tenderness because Bobby and Belle, its young misfit hero and heroine, eventually do find their way to each other to share a private, "little-people" joy. The play's plot follows the pair through an episodic series of painful and yet often very funny emotional encounters with other, "golden" people whom they idolize and try to emulate. In contrasting his young losers with the winners of the world, Wheeler offers some fascinating observations on contemporary social values. "I compare my misfits with those people doomed to material success with all the coarsening that accompanies it," Wheeler says. "All the other characters in the play—Jennifer, Wain, and the agent—have all been corrupted by the success bit. But it isn't their fault. They're victims, too."

Ultimately, then, Hugh Wheeler's basic dramatic concern is with the society which creates losers by defining them as such; which creates them by imposing on them a bogus sense of values. The people in his play are not merely failures but victims of the phony standards which their society insists they follow. As Wheeler himself makes quite clear, the American success syndrome is at the root of this system of false values. *Look: We've Come Through* is a refinement of this basic theme because it examines a key aspect of the success syndrome—its insistence on the importance, the desirability, the *necessity* of beauty.

Explaining, in the play, why she avoids her idols, Jennifer and Wain, and prefers to worship them from afar, Belle says, "I was ashamed . . . of being skinny and clumsy—but mostly of the braces on my teeth. It was sacrilege, I thought—to confront Beauty with the Beast." Patently a victim of false social values, Belle mirrors her culture's obsession with beauty as a definitive quality of success. Conditioned by our cultural code of the Beautiful to evaluate people on the basis of their physical assets, Belle rejects herself as "unworthy," and in a total misplacement of values, lavishes all her love and admiration on the beautiful but shallow Jennifer and Wain.

Wheeler's young people are all the more intriguing because of a further dimension to their characters. Jennifer, the brittle, materialistic golden girl who scrambles over other people's feelings in her ambitious climb to success as an actress, is no cartoon villainess, but in her fashion as much a victim of perverted cultural values as is Belle, her doormat-roommate. Jennifer's belief in the success syndrome, as defined by the superficial trappings of beauty, glamour, sophistication, and casual morality, is neither more nor less false than Belle's set of standards. Both codes, in fact, are remarkably similar. The difference is that Jennifer is a winner, rather than a loser like Belle—which means that she has the opportunity to actually live her life by these misguided principles. Belle happily is saved by the fact that she is a loser. With Bobby, she comes to examine the insides of people; to see that her beauty values are without substance and her love objects without interior worth. She and Bobby learn to question the values of their society, to judge them worthless, and to formulate new values of their own.

Critical reaction to this gentle but not unsubstantial play was quite curious. Although only a few critics wrote absolute rave notices, the praise lavished by the critics of such publications as the *Post*, the *New Yorker*, *Newsday*, the *Village Voice* and the *World-Telegram and Sun* easily would have furnished enough material for an impressive "quote ad." On the other end of the spectrum, a small number of reviewers passionately despised the play. The New York *Daily Mirror's* man, Robert Coleman, wrote a vicious pan, topped only by the scathing review turned in by the New York *Daily News's* critic, the late John Chapman, who wrote, "I almost loathed it."

From an overview, the notices were curious in two respects, the first being a common tendency to voice their praise in the most laconic, uninspiring, almost grudging fashion. When analyzed for specific critical evaluation, a large majority of the reviews proved to be favorable in substance, but their overall tone was flat and turgid and quite lacking in a sense of vital excitement. Walter Kerr, for example, writing in the New York *Herald Tribune*, distributed accolades with one hand, while simultaneously snatching them away with the other. By liberally sprinkling his notice with such dampish words as "tidy," "tiny," "humble," and "small," he effectively squelched the value of his positive critical judgments.

Similar ambiguous verdicts were delivered by the *Journal-American*,

Women's Wear Daily, and the weekly magazines. But most damaging of all for *Look: We've Come Through* was the fact that the almighty *New York Times* delivered its favorable critical commentary in the same laconic fashion. Howard Taubman's notice is, in fact, a perfect example of the damn-with-faint-praise review to which critics resort when they admire a show's virtues but consider its production flawed, its subject ignoble, or its content of interest only to a limited audience. In the theater's greener years, the so-called "mixed review" would still have assured a show a modestly successful run. In earlier days, when production and operating costs were manageable and theater audiences larger and more enthusiastic, such a notice would still manage to reach that segment of the theatergoing public which would enjoy and support the show. In today's marketplace, and similarly, if to a lesser degree, in 1961, nothing less than all-out critical raves can keep a show alive. The mixed review thus becomes a treachery, a clear verdict of doom.

Aside from the fuzzy-mouthed and stiffly restrained manner in which many of the critics delivered up their accolades, the reviews of *Look: We've Come Through* were quite respectable and not at all deserving of Saint Subber's charge that the critics killed his play. "They destroyed a beautiful play unfairly," the producer declares. "I have produced thirty plays in my career and I've never had an argument with the reviewers. I have never said that any of my failures were unjust—with the single exception of *Look: We've Come Through.* That's the first time in my career that I have felt the critics destroyed a play unfairly."

According to Saint Subber, the critical establishment shaped up quite differently ten years ago. At that time, the television critics wielded little power, which was then concentrated in the critics of the *Post,* the *News,* the *Herald Tribune,* and the *Times.* The *Post* delivered a rave; the *Times* and the *Trib,* qualified and grudgingly stated approval. The *News* notice was a killing pan, and that was the one which incensed Saint Subber.

"Oddly enough, the *News* was a more important paper in 1961," the producer says. "Today the weight has changed and the power is definitely with the *Times.* But in those days, the *News* critic, John Chapman, had much more weight than he has today . . . AND CHAPMAN CAME DRUNK! He arrived drunk after the curtain was up and he left before the play was over. He reviewed a play he did not see, and that he did not see sober! Is that loud and clear?"

In seizing on the *News's* critic (who was still alive and in critical power at the time of the producer's denunciation of him) as the villain of the tale, Saint Subber reduces the issue of the play's failure to a simplistic black-and-white case of Beauty devoured by the Beast. But the situation is hardly this clear-cut. Far more crucial than a single critic's insensitive reaction to the play was another curious tendency on the part of the critics—almost all of them analyzed the drama as a sexual treatise of sorts, and in particular as a study in adolescent homosexuality.

Whatever else it is about, *Look: We've Come Through* manifestly is not centered on the issue of sex—homo-, hetero-, or otherwise. The play is a study of young people caught up in a system of false values, a story about adolescents who, after some struggle and pain, eventually discard these values and assume more viable principles to live by. It is a drama about people who "come through" and find each other. Certainly sex figures in the play, but only as dramatic illustration of how muddled these kids really are. Belle's sexual capitulation to her adored Wain is hardly a scene of searing sexuality, but a dramatic device to show her tragicomic attempt to be included in the sexual-freedom code of her generation. Eventually, the play exposes the libertarian sexual code as just another of society's false standards for the "new freedom." Within this context, Belle's affectations at being sexually liberated are no less bittersweetly touching than her romantic affectations of Art.

Hugh Wheeler puts the play's sexual scenes in their proper context when he says, "I had hoped also to poke a little bit of fun at my misfits, the so-called hero and heroine of the play. They, in their way, are ridiculous too, as all human beings are. Perhaps that style of being half-funny, half-not-funny was bewildering to people then. If you poke fun at your hero and heroine, maybe that confused people. Looking back, my scene of a comic rape of my heroine *might* indeed have seemed rather shocking in 1961."

To Wheeler, adolescent stumblings with sexual liberation make young people humanly appealing and dramatically interesting, today, as much as in 1961. "I suppose today's kids do worry less about sex than the boys and girls in my play," he says. "But I bet the ordinary kids still have terrible hangups about their sex lives. They may feel more 'liberated'—the long hair and the weird clothes and all—but beneath those surface trappings of liberation I'm sure they're just the same underneath as Bobby and Belle."

Wheeler emphatically states that the sexuality in his play is in-

tended to be viewed within the drama's total context, which empha-
sizes how difficult it is for young people to avoid society's pressures to
conform. "My characters are definitely 1950's people," he says. "I
think that today society is putting infinitely more pressures to conform
than it did ten years ago. Thank Gòd, there is a huge resentment
against it today, and the young are standing up against many of the
things which I was attacking in that play. But society's pressures are
also more subtle. Unhappily, the terrible Machine starts exploiting that
very spirit of rebellion—and there you have it. Whether young people
can survive all that or not, I just don't know."

It is Wheeler's judgment, then, that the critics were repelled by
the seriocomic treatment of sex in *Look: We've Come Through* and
unable to see the humor-pathos mixture in his treatment. All they
were able to see, in fact, was the big bogey, Sex. "It was hard for me
to understand why people were shocked," he says. "But one must remember that it was still Tennessee Williams time in the theater. Plays
dealt with sex, of course, but it was all so tremendously serious, so
agonizing, so self-pitying—which all seemed so much more acceptable
in a sexual situation than humor. Of course, you do have the proto-
Neil Simon sort of play, where people sort of giggle around the edges
of sex. But people still do, by and large, treat sex so terribly, terribly
seriously—which I never do. If a playwright has a rather different voice,
it might indeed bewilder and antagonize people."

Wheeler's contention that his humorously off-beat treatment of
sex might have confused, if not actually antagonized, the reviewers
seems valid when one examines some of the notices. Walter Kerr saw
the play's subject as merely the "sexual coming-of-age of two baffled
moppets." *Variety* found the treatment of sex "tasteless," while *Wom-
en's Wear* reported that "sex, both sacred and profane, is the author's
chief concern." In his notes on the abridgment of the play which appeared in *The Best Plays of 1961–62*, Henry Hewes summarized most
succinctly the critics' rather extraordinary fixation on the play's sexual
elements when he stated that Wheeler "made the mistake of presenting
too explicitly and objectively the sordid deflowering of his heroine, and
the detailing of the homosexual past of the young man with whom
she goes on to establish a truer relationship."

As squeamish as the critics were about the play's overall treatment
of adolescent sexuality, they really recoiled at Wheeler's handling of the
theme of homosexuality. "Their reactions were *bizarre*," Saint Subber
stated, with not a little justification. Within the play, Bobby is not a

definitive homosexual anyway, but a boy who has had homosexual experiences. And within the play these homosexual experiences have a distinct dramatic function. On the one hand, they parallel Belle's painful sexual experience. In addition, Bobby's sexual relations with an older man and the rugged treatment he gets from a friend he worships serve the deeper purpose of illustrating a general disillusionment with sex *per se*. Because he himself has been used as a sexual object, he comes to regard sex as an animalistic and inhuman function. With Belle, he learns to reverse his values and see sex as the outgrowth of affection for another human being. It hardly matters whether that human being's sex is male or female; the important factor is Bobby's re-awakened ability to love—anyone.

The treatment of homosexuality is handled so gently and with such tender understanding in the play that one wonders, as Richard Watts of the *Post* wondered at the time, how so many critics could see it as "a tasteless drama of perversion." *Variety* was particularly vigorous in its moralistic condemnation of the play. "Although it's become an accepted theatrical subject," the *Variety* critic wrote, "sex perversion is a questionable ingredient in box-office terms. . . . It obviously has identifiable appeal for only a limited public."

Given the unabridged freedom with which homosexuality is treated in the theater today, it seems ludicrous to be compelled to defend a play which depicts homosexuality on the cautious level which *Look: We've Come Through* does. And yet it certainly needs defense, for its treatment was almost completely misunderstood. To begin with, and on the most ironic level, the question of the boy's homosexuality is not intrinsic to the play. According to his own statement, Ralph Williams, the actor who portrayed Bobby, did not play the character as a homosexual. "I don't believe that Bobby really was a homosexual," he says. "What happened was—*Look: we've come through!*" In Saint Subber's view, "The play is *not* about a queer boy. It's about a boy who *thinks* he might be queer, who asks himself questions, who, when he was a child, had a love for another boy. I'd like to know the case history of a child who is *not* like that."

Even if one allows for a certain disingenuousness in these comments, it is still clear that beyond the question of whether Bobby is a garden-variety homosexual or not lies a more pertinent question: How is the subject treated dramatically? And even the most cursory reading of the play reveals that it is treated with infinite tenderness, good taste, and gentle-humored understanding. From the reviews, it seems apparent that the critics overreacted to the subject itself and were somehow insensitized to the thoughtful way in which the subject was handled.

As anachronistic as it seems to defend the play for dealing with homosexuality as a dramatic sub-theme, it is even more absurd to condemn the critics for their revulsion to it. Although it appears that their antipathy for the mere subject of homosexuality led the reviewers to write hesitant, self-conscious notices which were in large measure responsible for the play's unjustified failure, it should also be apparent that the critics were themselves victims of prejudices and misunderstandings engendered by the social mores of their times—ironically, the *real* subject of *Look: We've Come Through.*

It should be remembered that, prior to 1961, homosexuality had been treated but rarely on the stage, and then, in the most discreet fashion imaginable. Plays such as *A Taste of Honey, Period of Adjustment, Advise and Consent, Five Finger Exercise* (all produced in 1960), and *The Devil's Advocate* and Wheeler's own *Big Fish, Little Fish* (both done in 1961) all illustrate the careful and exceedingly delicate manner in which homosexuality had been drawn on the stage up to this point. To put the theatrical climate of the times in sharper perspective, one need only remember the struggle which the embattled London theater was waging against its censorship laws. Harold Hobson, the drama critic of the London Sunday *Times,* has noted that it wasn't until 1958, in "a trivial farce by Denis Cannan, *Who's Your Father?* that the word 'homosexuality' was pronounced for the first time upon the public stage in Britain." Hobson further observed that although plays like *Five Finger Exercise* and *A Taste of Honey* exhibited "strong undercurrents of homosexuality, they evaded the censorship by not mentioning the thing explicitly."

Given the temper of the times, *Look: We've Come Through* was certainly much more daring a venture than it now seems from our more sophisticated contemporary vantage point. Quintero accurately categorizes the production as a high-risk venture for its producer. "Saint took a play that touched upon something—homosexuality—which, at the time, was taboo," Quintero says. "At that time, he was taking a real risk."

The theatrical climate of the early, transitional 1960's is most vividly chronicled in an apocryphal article written by Howard Taubman which appeared on the front page of the Sunday Arts and Leisure section of *The New York Times* on November 5, 1961. Entitled "Not What It Seems," with the subhead "Homosexual Motif Gets Heterosexual Guise," the piece opens with the statement: "It is time to speak openly and candidly of the increasing incidence and influence of homosexuality on New York's stage."

The gist of Taubman's thesis was the observation that writers were forced to evade the issue of homosexuality entirely, or else forced to disguise it in other forms. "The insidious result of unspoken taboos," Taubman wrote, "is that sincere, searching writers feel they must state a homosexual theme in heterosexual situations. . . . But dissembling is unhealthy. The audience senses rot at the drama's core." After complaining that the "infiltration of homosexual attitudes" had appeared on many theatrical levels—some pathetically obvious and some offensively vulgar—the critic concluded with a plea for an end to all subterfuge and a demand that playwrights speak their piece without the "dissembling" which Taubman considered theatrically "unhealthy."

The irony of the article was that, in calling for an end to an "insidious" practice, Taubman was dealing an equally insidious blow to *Look: We've Come Through* by misinterpreting its theme and its author's dramatic intention in his zeal to make his own point about the current dramatic attitude toward homosexuality. The long, evidently well-thought-through piece shed quite a bit of light on the *Times*'s critic's ambiguous opening notice on the play, illuminating in particular Taubman's reticence to deliver his praise in more forthright terms, and his equivocally stated and unexpounded contention that the play had not been structured into "a dramatic sum." What Taubman avoided stating in his first notice, and what he revealed in his Sunday piece, was his suspicion that Hugh Wheeler had been afraid to be explicit about his hero's homosexuality.

After lauding Wheeler for treating the issue with "humor, warmth, and acute sensibility," Taubman established that he was not convinced by the boy-girl relationship. "It was suggested that he was changing," Taubman wrote, "but everything about him said that he would not." It was the critic's belief that Bobby would remain "a sad, passive homosexual in spite of himself," and so he took Wheeler to task for not being thoroughly honest about his character, for fudging on his theme. "For all its virtues," the article went on, "the play was lamed. For all his courage, had Mr. Wheeler dared enough? Did inhibitions imposed by the theme lead to a sense of troubling incompletion?"

Sadly, and not a little unfairly, the most influential of all the critics had castigated Hugh Wheeler over a play he never wrote. The play which Wheeler actually wrote is not a drama about homosexuality—obfuscated or otherwise—but a play about a couple of young misfits who successfully survive the dehumanizing pressures of their exploitative society. Taubman himself proved Wheeler's dramatic thesis about the power of the forces of conformity by his inability to see the play on any but the most conventional level of meaning, as an evasive, and perhaps even dishonest, drama about a homosexual stereotype.

Irrespective of its function and weight in the play itself, the mere issue of homosexuality was enough to affect adversely the fate of *Look: We've Come Through*—not only for the automatic bias which it aroused in the critics, but also for the impact which that critical bias had upon the play's producer, who gave it a most hasty burial.

According to Jose Quintero, Saint Subber had the courage to take the initial "risk" of putting on the play, but backed down when the critical fires got too hot. "Today, homosexuality has become a thing that people go to the theater and the movies for," Quintero says. "But at that time it was different. I remember that the critics—Chapman especially—made an issue out of the homosexuality. Well, Saint got scared. That's the truth. He got scared and he pulled it. He got scared because it touched upon a subject that at that time had an entirely different color to it. It reflected upon the people who were doing the play. Today it does not, but then it did—it reflected on us. I didn't care, but Saint did. He felt that it pointed a finger at all of us.

"It wasn't *him*, but the *times* that were wrong. It was very sad, because the times have since turned around. But at the time I think Saint felt the finger pointed out at our own personal lives."

Certainly *something* must have shaken up Saint Subber, because the show had an unusually abrupt closing, considering that it had some appreciative notices. For all his current uninhibited evaluations of the critics, his comments at the time of the play's closing were markedly subdued. An ad which ran in all the newspapers on Friday, October 27, 1961, contained the following muted statement: "We, Saint Subber, Hugh Wheeler, and Jose Quintero are withdrawing our play, *Look: We've Come Through*, tomorrow evening. We wish to thank those critics and audiences who feel that this production has value. We believed and still believe in what we are presenting at the Hudson Theatre. It is possible that we are right. . . . P.S. We have nothing but admiration and love for our young cast." At that time, Saint Subber's harshest words for the critics were a mild statement quoted by Louis Calta in a *New York Times* article which accompanied the closing notice. "I'm prouder of what I've done with this show than *Kiss Me Kate*,"

Saint Subber told Calta. "But I'm told by the critics that its milieu is not right for it, and that it's not commercial. I'm bowing to their opinions."

According to Saint Subber, the play had to be closed immediately because the critics "destroyed" it. "From the time of opening night and the notices," the producer recalls, "box office attendance vividly and dramatically decreased. There wasn't a single person at the box office window the morning after the opening. It would have been very foolish of me to run a play that got poor notices and had poor attendance." To the suggestion that the show might have been closed prematurely and out of its producer's personal pique with the critics, he responds, "The answer to that is that I am a very emotional person—a very, very emotional person—and all of my decisions are based on emotion. Consequently, I surround myself with a staff. My general manager is the coolest cat in the world. My accountant has no emotion whatsoever; he just counts—one-two-three-four-five. My accountant, general manager, and press agent—all the people involved in the business end of the show with me—they all said to forget it."

Notwithstanding Saint Subber's protestations that the closing was economically inevitable, other professionals involved in the *Look: We've Come Through* production indicated surprise at the swiftness with which the closing notice was posted, and registered the opinion that, with the help of its more enthusiastic critical notices, the show might have caught on. "It wouldn't have cost that much money to keep going," Ralph Williams feels, noting that he and his fellow actors "were only making peanuts." His opinion is confirmed by Quintero. "I felt we should have kept the play running because the cost of the cast was so little."

They are all quick to point out, however, that their own opinions would hardly have carried any weight with Saint Subber, because the producer never consulted them. According to Quintero's recollection of the opening night, "Hugh and I went to a party and afterwards we took a long walk. We should have stayed with Saint, I suppose, but neither one of us thought the show would be closed like that. The next morning, we were simply told the play was closing."

In Quintero's judgment, the producer's decision to withdraw the play without conferring with either its director or its author was a rather unusual procedure and contrary to the standard practice. "With other plays, you all get together the next day and decide whether or not you have a chance to run," Quintero says. "But no. Saint just went ahead and made his decision and that was it. I think he *should* have consulted Hugh and myself, but he didn't. He didn't consult anybody. He just went ahead and did it."

"I know I got screwed," is Hugh Wheeler's succinct appraisal of the manner in which Saint Subber closed his play. "It is absolutely true that I was not consulted. If I was indeed 'consulted,' it was when I was in an exhausted state. Saint is very extravagant in his talk. He came to see me and said, 'Darling, we've been slaughtered. This is absolutely hopeless.' It was all like the gesture of the great artist who was not prepared to cast his pearls before swine—that was how it was presented to me. I was told all these terrible things and was exhausted, so I went to bed."

The next day, Saint Subber composed the closing notice and his announcement to the newspapers. "This was all done without my or the director's knowledge," Wheeler says. "If I'd gotten in touch with Quintero, we could all have talked it out, but before anyone could say anything, it had all been done. The director copped out, and I copped out, too."

Wheeler's naïveté becomes even more affecting when one considers that it is shared by all but the most experienced writers in the business. The large majority of Broadway playwrights are quite alarmingly innocent about their function—and, even more important, about their *rights*—in regard to the production of their works. When one hears Hugh Wheeler's rather wistful recounting of his experience with *Look: We've Come Through* ("It was the artistic love affair of all time. I was wooed as if I were Shakespeare. Of course, I didn't know so much about Broadway then, because I was new at it. Now, I've come to look with a fairly cold eye at the realities of Broadway."), one cannot help but deplore the extent of the power wielded by playwrights' agents, and the totally inadequate guidance which all but a few offer their lamblike clients.

Had Saint Subber, Wheeler, and Quintero conferred together and decided to stand by the play for a few more weeks, instead of closing it in four days, the decision would have been based on the belief that the play had a potential audience. Both Quintero and Wheeler insist that such an audience did, indeed, exist for *Look: We've Come Through*. "I think that people would have come," Quintero said. "But it would have needed a kind of campaign to reach them. Maybe that movement of young people that we have today—so open, so apparent— maybe that would have been our audience. It could have been tapped, but nobody knew it was lying there."

Although several people involved in the production, from the pro-

ducer and director to individual cast members, all mentioned the unusually enthusiastic reception given the play by its preview audiences,
it was Hugh Wheeler who best defined the nature of the potential
audience for *Look: We've Come Through*. According to Wheeler, his
play had appeal for a limited and quite special audience—a segment of
theatergoers set apart from what he calls the "foreign land" of the
mass Broadway audience. Speaking of the peculiar pressures which the
Broadway system imposes on the writer of nonformula plays, the playwright notes, "The sort of thing that a Broadway audience obviously
wants is not really what I want to write. Standards are so confused at
the moment."

In Wheeler's view, civilization is effecting "the total dehumaniza-
tion, the depersonalization of people," which is having an incalculably
adverse effect on the theater and its audiences. "People seem to like
substitute emotions rather than real emotions," he says, using the film
Love Story as a concrete example of his point. "They only *think* they're
feeling, but when they are faced with real emotions, they get very un-
comfortable, they become bewildered. Under the circumstances, I can
understand why people write plays of tremendous shock value. In a
way, it seems to be the only way to jolt and get through to people who
are in the process of being dehumanized. But I don't write that sort
of play, because I love human beings. My plays depend on the humanness of people, on the human emotions which, by and large, people
don't seem to be feeling anymore. I seem to be terribly arcane."

If Wheeler is a bit hasty in pronouncing himself obsolete, he is
astute, nonetheless, in recognizing that his gentle brand of humani-
tarianism does indeed place his plays well outside the mainstream of
current dramatic fashion and of appeal only to a select audience.

Any play manifestly of interest to a limited and special audience,
demands delicate treatment from its producer if it hopes to have a
chance of success on Broadway's commercial market. It was the ill-fated
luck of *Look: We've Come Through* to have been produced with few
discernible concessions to its unconventional theatrical realities. In particular, no special steps were taken to tap the real but subsurface audience which existed for the show.

Look: We've Come Through was quite low-budgeted, even for
1961; having been capitalized at $100,000, it actually cost around
$90,000 to produce. Its notably low break-even point was a mere (to-
day's producers would say "negligible") $25,000 per week. The pro-
duction's modest mounting hardly seems realistic for a show which

needed all the support it could get to stay afloat until the word-of-mouth got out to its limited audience of potential enthusiasts.

Saint Subber did initiate one experimental production practice which proved effective in helping the play find its own audience. Instead of taking the show out of town for traditional previews, the producer offered six half-price preview performances right at the Hudson Theatre.

One wishes that Saint Subber had been as keen in his selection of the theater itself. Despite the producer's vociferous denials, the Hudson's dimensions were hardly on the intimate scale demanded by the play. A few critics noted that the theater was too large a house for the play and tended to dwarf it—an opinion shared by the author, who called it "a horrible theater," and by its director, who refuted Saint Subber's contention that "the theater couldn't have been smaller." According to Quintero, "The Hudson is *not* a small theater. It's a *big* theater. *Too* big. I am sure that Saint went to the Shuberts to get another theater. But I'm also sure that, because the show had no protection in terms of big stars, the Shuberts said no. I think Saint took the only theater that he could get."

Quintero's reference to the show's young cast brings up an especially crucial aspect of the production, and one which contributed in large measure to the unusual brevity of its career. Unlike most Broadway productions of plays by relatively unknown writers, this show was cast with four young performers whose names meant even less to the theatergoing public than the name of Hugh Wheeler. Normally, a director tries to secure the services of popular star figures as a form of "insurance," to offset the built-in commercial risks of a straight play. In the case of Hugh Wheeler's play, however, the very nature of the script made such a move impossible.

"It would have been wrong of me to cast the show with a star," Quintero says. "Then, it would have become a play about one person. If an actor has a name, he acts it, and an audience knows that he has already 'come through.' But Hugh wrote a play about four little lost people, still trying to find their way. Therefore, I had to find four marvelous actors who themselves were still stumbling, still trying to 'come through' as actors. The play demanded it. It could never have been a vehicle for a star."

To Saint Subber's immense credit as a producer, he supported these casting choices. "It wasn't a matter of saving money at all," Saint

Subber says. "I don't cast plays that way. I cast the best people. And this play was cast exactly as I wanted it to be cast."

"The show was very hard to cast," Quintero affirms. "And Saint had his qualms. But it must have been very difficult for Saint to raise money for that play, with no names to raise it on. Maybe it was a mistake, after all, not to use stars. I think that was one of the reasons the show closed so quickly. What did Saint have to fight with, to gamble on? He had nothing—four unknown actors and a marvelous but unknown writer. Nothing."

Critical judgment eventually supported Quintero's casting decisions, and indeed, most of his artistic choices about the play's production. There were occasional carpings about Quintero's pacing of the show, and Hugh Wheeler was never quite satisfied that Collin Wilcox was sufficiently naïve in the role of young Belle. But according to professional critical pronouncements, and in the opinion of the creators of the show, *Look: We've Come Through* had avoided major production blunders. "The only *crucial* problem which arose during production was the color of Collin's shoes," is Saint Subber's final evaluation.

In retrospect, it does seem as if the show's single serious production flaw was the initial decision to produce it on Broadway. Commercially risky because it was a straight play by a little-known writer; lacking the insurance of star performers; of limited audience appeal by virtue of its modestly scaled dramatic concerns; and potentially vulnerable to public misinterpretation of its homosexual thematic elements, the production was blatantly unsuitable for Broadway. It wasn't killed; it committed suicide. Today, it seems perfectly obvious that *Look: We've Come Through* should have been done off Broadway, for which it was perfectly scaled.

Quintero now thinks that the play would have worked off Broadway, although he admits that he never raised the question with Saint Subber back in 1961. Interestingly, the producer claims that initially he had conceived of an off-Broadway production. "I did ask for this production to be done off Broadway originally," Saint Subber said, "but I was turned down by the author. So I quickly said, 'All right—if I can't do it off Broadway, I'll do it *on* Broadway.' But my original conception was that it should have been done off Broadway." But according to Hugh Wheeler, the possibility of an off-Broadway production simply never arose. "In those days, Saint didn't think of himself as an off-Broadway producer," the author said.

Regardless of who actually squelched the idea of doing the show off Broadway, if, indeed, the subject was ever raised at all, the significant point here is that the theatrical climate was quite different eleven years ago. Off Broadway had neither the respectability nor the cachet which it has today, when it is almost a miniaturized version of mainstem theater.

In 1961, a producer was still taking a risk if he chose to produce off Broadway. Broadway audiences were still hesitant about venturing downtown, and consequently, profits were still quite modest, making an off-Broadway project decidedly limited in its appeal to a producer of Saint Subber's rank. It all seemed rather much of a risk and a good deal of energy to expend on something which was not likely to return a worthwhile profit.

So, in a sense, it was the economic structure of the theater industry which dealt the crucial blow to *Look: We've Come Through*. A textbook example of a nonformula show—in subject, in professional production, in its basic audience appeal—the play needed special treatment if it was to survive under a Broadway system which is intrinsically inhospitable, if not indeed hostile, to anything the least commercially unconventional. And although its producer was willing to take some chances in backing his maverick project, he couldn't override the inhibited social climate which conditioned the critics to instinctively resist and misinterpret Hugh Wheeler's fragile and lovely play. As the author himself notes, "I still think it was the right play at the wrong time."

THE BEAUTY
PART

by S.J. Perelman

CAST OF CHARACTERS

OCTAVIA WEATHERWAX

MIKE MULROY

MILO LEOTARD ALLARDYCE
DU PLESSIS WEATHERWAX

LANCE WEATHERWAX

SAM FUSSFELD

APRIL MONKHOOD

BUNCE

VAN LENNEP

HAGEDORN

VISHNU

HYACINTH BEDDOES LAFFOON

GODDARD QUAGMEYER

GLORIA KRUMGOLD

SEYMOUR KRUMGOLD

HARRY HUBRIS

ROB ROY FRUITWELL

MAURICE BLOUNT

BORIS PICKWICK

CHENILLE SCHREIBER

KITTY ENTRAIL

VERNON EQUINOX

MRS. YOUNGHUSBAND

GRACE FINGERHEAD

CURTIS FINGERHEAD

FISH-MARKET BOY

EMMETT STAGG

WORMSER

NELSON SMEDLEY

ROWENA INCHCAPE

RUKEYSER

WAGNERIAN

SHERRY QUICKLIME

SECRETARY

HENNEPIN

POTEAT

CAMERA MAN

HANRATTY

COURT STENOGRAPHER

POLICEMAN

JUDGE

HERMAN J. RINDERBRUST

BAILIFF

ROXANA DE VILBISS

JOE GOURIELLI

MRS. LAFCADIO MIFFLIN

Act One

SCENE I

Scene: *The library of the luxurious Park Avenue triplex of Mr. and Mrs. Milo Weatherwax. The decor is posh Madison Avenue Oriental crossed with Ginsberg and Levy early American. Constance Spry flower arrangements, a Buddha head, a vase, and two abstract paintings on walls.*

Time: *Late afternoon.*

At Rise: *As the stage lights up,* OCTAVIA WEATHERWAX, *a chic, poised woman in her late thirties, paces nervously D.S.L. and R., a crumpled handkerchief pressed against her lips.* MIKE MULROY, *a private eye in the classic Raymond Chandler tradition, stands nearby consulting a pocket notebook.*

MULROY (*As* OCTAVIA *crosses D.L.*). No use being huffy, Mrs. Weatherwax. A private eye like I—like me, that is—I've got to know which skeleton's in what closet.

OCTAVIA (*Crosses D.S. by L. end of couch*). Your line of work makes a man pretty nosy, I daresay.

MULROY (*Crosses U.S., puts hat on C. table*). Look, Mrs. Weatherwax. I've got a dusty office in the Arbogast Building. My clients pay me a hundred dollars down as a retainer and ten cents a mile, but that doesn't entitle them to poke into my psyche.

OCTAVIA. Then we understand each other. Suppose you give me your report. (*Sits couch, R. end.*)

MULROY (*Sits armchair. Nods*). Mr. Weatherwax left the house at 11:14, took a hack to a dairy restaurant on Second Avenue, and had a plate of soup containing kreplach. I checked that out with the manager. He lives in the Bath Beach section of Brooklyn. Mr. Weatherwax then made a seven-minute call from a pay phone to a party on the Regent exchange.

OCTAVIA. A woman?

MULROY (*Evasively*). Well, I really don't like to say—

OCTAVIA (*Rises and crosses L. of* MULROY). See here, Mulroy—I hired you to investigate my husband's extramarital didoes. Let's not be coy. (*Crosses L., sits on couch.*)

MULROY. Yes, ma'am.

OCTAVIA. Now, who was she? Who is this person?

MULROY. A television actress, Mrs. Weatherwax.

OCTAVIA. A what?

MULROY (*Rises, crosses L.*). Well, not really an actress. She poses for commercials.

OCTAVIA. What kind?

MULROY (*Crosses L. of chair*). Er—ladies' underthings, I believe.

OCTAVIA. What kind?

MULROY (*Crosses R. of chair*). Gee, Mrs. Weatherwax, does that make any difference?

OCTAVIA. *What kind?*

MULROY. All right. Brassieres.

OCTAVIA. I deserve it for asking. How old is she?

MULROY. She's no chicken—at least twenty-three. A very ordinary girl—long legs—tiny waist. Her lips are too lush—kind of ripples when she walks—(*Crosses R. to front of chair.*)

OCTAVIA. What does?

MULROY (*Pantomimes*). Her hair. It's chestnut and she wears it loose— (*Sits chair C.S.*) cascading down her shoulders—and when she laughs—

OCTAVIA (*Rises, crosses R.* MULROY *rises. Sharply*). That'll do, Mulroy. You needn't launch into a rhapsody.

MULROY. Yes, ma'am.

OCTAVIA. This apartment you spoke of is where?

MULROY. East 73rd, between Park and Lex. Modified French Provincial furniture with mirror accents and white wall-to-wall carpeting. Foam chairs in fake zebra and a coffee table made out of an old set of bellows. (*Refers to notes.*) The bedroom is done in pink, with ruffles—

OCTAVIA (*Crosses L., front of* MULROY *to front of couch*). Never mind. I can visualize it.

MULROY (*Steps L.*). I'm sorry, I realize what a shock it always is. I haven't been a private snoop nine years for nothing—

OCTAVIA. Thank you. Nice of you to empathize.

MULROY (*Steps L.*). Mrs. Weatherwax, I'm not very good at putting my thoughts into words.

OCTAVIA. Say it in your own way.

MULROY. May I kiss you?

OCTAVIA (*Crosses L. of* MULROY). If you like. (*They embrace. She turns D.S., his arms around her.*) Oh, Mulroy, what's to become of us?

MULROY. I don't know. I don't care. All I know is that you've spoiled me for other girls.

OCTAVIA. I felt that in my heart's deep core.

MULROY. Octavia—

OCTAVIA (*Back L.*). How dare you call me by my first name!

MULROY (*Sheepishly*). Maybe I overstepped.

OCTAVIA (*Sits R. end of couch*). You have. I'm one of the richest women in America, Mulroy. A mere nod from me creates a convulsion in Wall Street. My son, Lance, is Skull and Bones at Yale. It's time for you to leave the room.

MULROY. Yes, ma'am. (*Crosses U.C. table, picks up vase. Taking it from stand.*) My, that's lovely. Genuine Sèvres, isn't it?

OCTAVIA. Yes. How did you know?

MULROY. Oh, I dabble in porcelain a bit.

OCTAVIA. Isn't that strange? I rather sensed you had a flair.

MULROY (*Puts vase back; picks up hat*). I haven't been a private snoop twelve years for nothing.

OCTAVIA. It was nine last time.

MULROY. It seemed like twelve till you came along. (*Kneels R. of* OCTAVIA.)

OCTAVIA. That will be sufficient, Mr. Mulroy.

MULROY (*Rises, crosses front of couch to L. of couch. Chagrined*). Yes, I'd better get back and relieve my partner, Costello. He's on the fire escape outside her flat.

OCTAVIA. Yes, you'd better.

MULROY (*Sits, L. end of couch*). You ought to meet that Costello. He's the talented one. He's been exhibited at the Guggenheim.

OCTAVIA. Oh?

MULROY. He does these collages out of seawood and graham crackers.

(*Offstage squeal and "Oh, Mr. Weatherwax!"*)

OCTAVIA. It's Milo. He's home.

MULROY. Hasta luego. (*Exits L.*)

(*screams from off* R.)

OCTAVIA. Milo!

(MILO *enters.*)

MILO (*Crosses back of chair*). Now, look here, Octavia, I just had to give our French maid a severe dressing down.

OCTAVIA. So I heard.

MILO (*Crossing U.R.*). There's loose rubies all over the foyer. A person could break their ankle! What are we living in, a pig pen? (*Opens painting to reveal bar.*)

OCTAVIA. How was your board meeting, dear?

MILO (*At bar, pouring drink*). Meeting? Why—er— (*Busies himself with glasses, then crosses D.S.*) I didn't attend. I had other fish to fry.

OCTAVIA. Yes, and they crackled, didn't they? (*Crosses U.S. of chair.*) Milo, this is the handwriting on the wall. Our marriage is washed up—napoo—*ausgespielt.*

MILO (*Turns to her*). You're trying to tell me something.

OCTAVIA. I mean that I'm restless, unhappy, bored, and you are, too. (*Sits in chair.*)

MILO. Maybe you're right. I'll admit I've been chafing at the bit a bit. (*Crosses L. of* OCTAVIA.)

OCTAVIA. Ah, well, the fat's in the fire. How are we to break the news to Lance?

MILO (*Crosses D.S.*). What Lance is that?

OCTAVIA. Why, our twenty-year-old son, which he's home from Yale on his midyears and don't suspicion his folks are rifting.

MILO. Of course, of course. (*Crosses L.*) Reached man's estate already, has he? (*Front of couch, he sits. Shakes his head.*) Where is our cub at the present writing?

OCTAVIA. In the tack room, furbishing up the accouterments of his polo ponies.

MILO (*Acidly*). Far better to be furbishing up on his Euclid, lest he drag the name of Weatherwax through the scholastic mire.

LANCE (*Off R.*). Dads! Mums!

OCTAVIA. Shush! Here he comes now. (*Crosses L.*) You had best handle this. I'm laying down on my chaise lounge with a vinegar compress. (*Exits.*)

(LANCE *enters.*)

LANCE (*Crosses R. of C. chair*). Hi, Dads! Where's Mums?

MILO (*Rises, crosses L. of C. chair*). Son, we are facing a family crisis. The Weatherwax union has blown a gasket.

LANCE. I don't dig you, Guv.

MILO. To employ the vulgate, your mother and I .have split out!

LANCE (*Sobered, a hand on MILO's shoulder*). Rum go, Dads.

MILO (*Crosses front of couch*). Yes, it's hard on us oldsters, but it isn't going to be easy for you, either.

LANCE (*Frightened*). You mean I've got to go to work?

MILO. Don't be asinine! Not as long as there's a penny of your mother's money left. (*Sits couch.*)

LANCE (*Crosses R. end of couch*). Look, Pater, I—that is, me—aw, jeepers, can I ask you something man to man?

MILO. Lance, a chap with a sympathetic sire don't have to beat about the bush.

LANCE (*Crosses back of couch*). Thanks, Pop. Well, I've been running with a pretty serious crowd up at New Haven—lots of bull sessions about *Lolita* and Oscar Wilde.

MILO. That's the stuff to cut your eye-teeth on, son. A fellow has to learn to crawl before he can walk.

LANCE. Reet. (*Crosses L. to L. end of front of couch.*) And I've been wondering more and more of late. Where does our money come from?

MILO (*Evasively; rises*). Why—er—uh—the doctor brings it. In a little black bag. (*Crosses C.*)

LANCE (*Sits L. end of couch*). Aw, gee, Dad, I'm old enough to know. *Please.*

MILO (*Pacing L. and R.*). My, you children grow up quick nowadays. (*Crosses R.*) Very well, have you ever heard of the Weatherwax All-Weather Garbage Disposal Plan?

LANCE. You—you mean whereby garbage is disposed of in all weathers by having neatly uniformed attendants call for and remove it?

MILO. Yes. That is the genesis of our scratch.

LANCE (*Clenches his fists to control himself*). Oh, sir, I want to die!

MILO (*Crosses, puts hand on LANCE's shoulder*). Steady on, lad. After all, think of the millions which, were it not for our kindly ministrations, their homes would be a welter of chicken bones, fruit peels, and rancid yogurt.

LANCE (*Voice breaks*). I'll never be able to hold up my head in Bulldog circles again.

MILO (*Crosses R. and L.*). Nonsense, lad. Why, you wear the keenest threads on the campus and you're persona grata to myriad Eli frats.

LANCE (*A pause. Rises*). No, Father. (*Crosses R.*) This is the end of halcyon days in the groves of Academe. I'm going away. (*Crosses front of chair.*)

MILO. Going away? Where? Why?

LANCE. No, Dad—it isn't only your revelation that turned my world topsy-turvy. There's another reason I've got to prove myself. I've fallen in love with a wonderful person.

MILO (*Steps L.*). Hm-m-m, I thought there was a colored gentleman in the woodpile.

LANCE. No, Dad, this is a girl—I met her last Christmas in Greenwich Village.

MILO (*Crosses to bar, puts down glass*). Well, you mustn't fling your cap over the moon. (*Turns L.*) Remember, an apple knocker like you could easily fall into the hands of an adventuress.

LANCE (*Hotly; Upstage side of chair*). Adventuress? April Monkhood's the most sincere human being who ever lived!

MILO (*Crosses R. of chair*). April Monkhood! (*Turns to* LANCE.) I didn't quite catch that name.

LANCE. She's a designer.

MILO. It figures.

LANCE (*Sits chair*). You'd love her, sir, honest you would. She's spiritual—vibrant—artistic to the nth degree. April awoke something in me I never knew existed. A thirst for beauty, and I've got to express it somehow—in words or paint or music.

MILO (*Crosses L.*). I know, my boy, I know. I had the same creative urge when I was your age.

LANCE. What became of it?

MILO (*Front of couch*). I sublimated it. Nowadays I sponsor a few gifted individuals on the side—sopranos—drum majorettes . . .

LANCE. Each of us has to work out their own salvation, Dad. What was yours?

MILO. Sex, and plenty of it.

LANCE (*Rises, puts chair on C. platform. Crosses D.C.*). Mine's in the arts somewhere, in what branch I can't say until I try them all. But I'm not going to compromise. April's never compromised, and if I'm going to be worthy of her, I've got to hew to my resolve.

MILO (*Rises, crosses L. of* LANCE. *Shrugs, extracts envelope*). Very well, then. Before you start, I want you to have this keepsake.

LANCE. Gee, Dads.

MILO. It won't buy much except dreams, but it's been in the family for generations.

LANCE. What is it?

MILO. A letter of credit.

LANCE (*Crosses L., squaring his chin*). I can't take it, sir. To me it's like—tainted.

MILO (*Crosses R. of* LANCE). Great Scott, lad, you can't leave here empty-handed. You'll need money, introductions, shelter—

LANCE. No, Dad.

MILO. But I won't let you sleep in the street! There's our old railroad car underneath the Waldorf Astoria. Take it—it's only using up steam.

LANCE (*Simply*). I'm sorry, Dad. From now on, I walk alone. (*He exits.*)

(OCTAVIA *enters, looking nonplussed after the exiting* LANCE.)

OCTAVIA. Why, goodness, whatever ails the child? Milo, my woman's intuition tells me you've just had a stormy colloquy with Lance.

MILO. What Lance is that?

OCTAVIA. Why, our twenty-two-year-old son, which he's home from Yale on his midyears and don't suspicion his folks are rifting.

MILO. Of course. If you need me I'm laying down on my chaise lounge with a vinegar compress. (*Exits R.*)

OCTAVIA (*Throws up hands despairingly*). Incorrigible boy! I wonder where it will all end.

(*She exits L. Music starts. And we revolve to:*)

SCENE II

Scene: *April Monkhood's apartment. A standard village locale such as is occupied by any young career woman, but re-*

cently redecorated to express the personality of the occupant.
Fishnet looped around walls, interspersed with glass spheres.
Two or three score notary seals, both gold and red, pasted in-
discriminately on window-shades, drapes, and in box on sofa.
A profusion of fake leopard-skin upholstery, fake Negro sculp-
ture and any of the claptrap extant along East 8th St. judged
suitable.

Time: *Two days after Scene 1.*

At Rise: April, *sitting C. platform. As unit stops, crosses*
up, mounts a small aluminum stepladder hanging a small fern.
Downstage, at end-table, FUSSFELD, *a telephone repairman, has*
been working on the instrument, his tin kit on the settee.

FUSSFELD (*Upstage of couch, on phone*). Checking ALgonquin
4-1014 . . . (*Phone rings.*) Loud and clear. (*Hangs up, addresses* APRIL
as he reassembles kit.) Well, you're O.K. now, Miss Monkhood.
(*Crosses D.S., R. of phone.*)

APRIL (*On ladder putting fern in holder*). Thank heavens—I was
on the brink of suicide. Absolutely bereft! I get so many calls in my
business I couldn't exist without a second phone.

FUSSFELD (*At tools, R. end of couch*). Oh? What line you in, may
I ask?

APRIL. Well, several, but chiefly jewelry design. Abstract things—
you know, conversation pieces.

FUSSFELD. You don't say.

APRIL (*Crosses, pulls pouf D.S., crosses L. of couch, picks up box*).
I handle just a few connoisseurs. If someone comes to me—say, a cynic
with an appetite for subtle blasphemies—or a woman in a black gown
with a sense of what's stark and dramatic—or a man whose id cries out
for a massive and tortured ring—I distill their personality. (*Crosses U.S.,*
back of couch.)

FUSSFELD (*Crosses C.*). I pegged you for some artistic field when
I walked in your place.

APRIL. Yes, I've been redecorating. Of course, it's incomplete as
yet. (*Looks about worriedly.*)

FUSSFELD. I'd sprinkle a couple of magazines around, or maybe a
dish of cashews. They're tasty and they help soak up the humidity.

APRIL. No, no, what it really yearns for is a great splendid tree right
over there—I've ordered a Bechtel's flowering crab.

FUSSFELD. A tree? Wouldn't the landlord raise the roof?

APRIL (*Sunnily*). Oh, yes, he promised he would. (*Sound of door buzzer off.*) Would you just let in whoever that is on your way? (*Rises, puts box on window sill.*)

FUSSFELD. Sure. G'bye. (*To himself, as he exits S.L.*) Raise the roof!

LANCE (*Off*). April! April!

APRIL (*Crosses R. of* LANCE *as he enters*). Lance Weatherwax! Whatever in the world are you doing here?

LANCE (*Crosses C., tensely*). April—I've got to talk to you. Right away.

APRIL (*Crosses L. of* LANCE). Of course, dear. Come in— (*With concern.*) You look so distrait. Has something happened? (*Takes off his coat.*)

LANCE. Well, yes—kind of. I bet I've walked fifty miles the past couple of days, trying to think things through.

APRIL. You must have been in real travail.

LANCE. I was.

APRIL (*Crosses U.L., hangs up his coat*). You poor boy.

LANCE (*Crosses front of couch. Reacts to decor for the first time*). What—what's going on here?

APRIL. I've had it done over. Isn't it delectable?

LANCE. Oh, it's great. I mean, it like hits you right in the eye.

APRIL (*Crosses L. of* LANCE). Does it say anything to you? You don't feel it's overdone?

LANCE. Overdone? It's underdone! You couldn't omit a single detail without damaging the—the entire concept.

APRIL (*Hugs him*). You old sorcerer. You know just the words to thaw a woman's heart. (*She kisses him and crosses back of couch.*) Let's have a drink to celebrate. Set ye doon— (*Pushes him gently onto couch.*) and I'll open a bottle of Old Rabbinical. (*Crosses U.S. of couch, and whisks bottle from window sill. The phone rings; she answers hurriedly.*) Yes? . . . Who? . . . Oh, hi! . . . No, I can't. I have people here. . . . What? No, I have to wash my hair. . . . Yes, silly. . . . Why don't you do that? I'm always here. . . . 'Bye. (*Hangs up.*) Honestly, some men are just impossible. They think all they have to do is whistle. (*She picks up glasses, crosses D.S., L. of couch.*)

LANCE. Who was that?

APRIL. My ex-fiancé, of all people.

LANCE. Hanh? You never told me you'd been engaged.

APRIL (*Gives* LANCE *glass*). Oh, Sensualdo and I haven't seen each other in ages. He's a monster—an absolute fiend. (*Pours* LANCE *drink.*)

LANCE. Sensualdo? His name sounds Mexican.

APRIL. Uh-uh—Peruvian. (*Pours own drink.*) One of those insanely jealous types. Tried to stab a man I was having a Coke with. That's what broke up our engagement. (*Crosses U.S., puts down bottle.*)

LANCE. Is he—er—back there now?

APRIL. In Peruvia? Well, he shuttles between there and Staten Island. Something to do with vicunas or emeralds, I believe—I really don't know. . . . I haven't been in touch with him in ages! (*Crosses to pouf.*)

LANCE (*Urgently*). April, there is something very important I—

APRIL. As a matter of fact, he was a prince compared to my first fiancé. Did you ever hear of Benno Vontz, the sculptor?

LANCE. No, I can't say that I have, but—

APRIL. Benno designed that abstract saddle on top of Neiman-Marcus's in Dallas. A brilliant boy, but terribly neurotic. (*Sits pouf.*) He used to wake me up in the middle of the day, claiming I'd had affairs with all kinds of people—osteopaths, car-hops, bakers. It was a nightmare, my dear—an absolute *cauchemar.* I was practically on the verge of a neurasthenia when I met Ricky. (*Rises.*)

LANCE. Ricky?

APRIL (*Crosses L. of couch*). He was an auctioneer that I met in Atlantic City. Naturally, one thing led to another. (*Crosses L. of* LANCE.)

LANCE. And you got engaged.

APRIL (*Crosses back of couch, takes glasses to bar*). No! Benno found out! One night Ricky and I were driving home in a downpour and his brakes overheated near Asbury Park and we had to take refuge in a motel. (*Sits back of couch.*) Next thing we knew, Benno was all over us with flash bulbs. (*A tragic Mrs. Malaprop.*) My *dear*, it was too sorbid.

LANCE (*Takes her hand*). You poor kid. It's a wonder to me you could live through so much and still remain gay and joie de vivre.

APRIL (*Crosses R., sits end of couch*). That's because I sublimate myself in my work, Lance. Whenever life gets frantic, why I rush to my bench and fashion a brooch or earrings that crystallize a dewdrop of ecstasy. Your great craftsmen have always done that, right back to Cellini.

LANCE. April, if you only knew how your eyes light up when you talk about art.

APRIL (*Leaning nearer*). Do they?

LANCE. There's a kind of a glow in them. They're like mysterious violet pools, full of wisdom and understanding . . . and—oh, terrific tolerance. Not like those empty-headed little debs I used to date before I met you.

APRIL. Why, Lance, I've never heard you so articulate before. It's as if you'd been freed, somehow.

LANCE (*Vehemently*). I have. I've come to a very important decision about my future, April. I have to know right away how you feel.

APRIL (*Placing finger on his lips*). Please, Lance, for both our sakes—don't say anything you might regret.

LANCE (*Rises*). No, no—I've got to. You see, this door suddenly opened in my mind and I realized what truly matters to me.

APRIL (*Tempest-tossed*). Oh, Lance, do you know what you're saying?

LANCE (*Kneels L. of* APRIL). Yes, yes, I do. April, I've decided to become a writer.

APRIL. You *what?*

LANCE. Or maybe a painter.

APRIL (*Barely suppressed irritation*). Oh, Lance, don't be an Airedale.

LANCE (*Rises, wounded*). What's the matter? Don't you think I have the ability?

APRIL (*Rises, crosses L. of pouf*). Er—of course, but—well, I was just a little overwhelmed. I mean, it's such a tremendous challenge.

LANCE (*Crosses R. of pouf*). I want to accept that challenge—I want to unleash whatever creative powers there are inside me. But my problem is—how do I become a writer?

APRIL. Buy a magazine—or maybe a chain of them. I understand the *Saturday Evening Post* is up for grabs—

LANCE (*Rises, crosses R.*). No, siree, I won't be a lousy dilettante. I'm going to start humbly, get the smell of printer's ink . . .

APRIL (*Rises, R. of pouf. Lighting up*). Wait—wait! Eureka!

LANCE. I beg your pardon?

APRIL. What a blind little fool I've been! The perfect way to express yourself—it's right in front of you!

LANCE. I don't follow.

APRIL (*Sits* LANCE R. *of her on couch*). Let's plunge into the depths together. Scale the heights together.

LANCE. How?

APRIL. Well, you know what a disorganized scatterbrain I am away from my workbench—I haven't a clue to facts or figures. I need someone with divine good taste to counsel me—someone whose judgment I respect.

LANCE. But where would I contribute my creative talent?

APRIL. Why, in a hundred ways. . . . Right here, for example— (*Extracts crumpled paper from under phone.*) this came in the morning mail. What does it mean?

LANCE. It's from the bank. It says they're returning your check for $471 due to insufficient funds.

APRIL (*Rises, crosses D.S.*). It must be that consignment of turquoise nut-picks I ordered from Santa Fe. Those Navajos are so grasping. What should I do about it? (*Crosses L. of couch.*)

LANCE. You must put the money in the bank to cover the overdraft.

APRIL (*Triumphantly*). There—you see how much more practical you are than I? Very well—you handle it, love.

LANCE. How do you mean?

APRIL. Why, when you leave here, just drop by the Centerboard National and deposit that amount—until I get straightened out.

LANCE. But I haven't any money.

APRIL. Of course—how dense of me. Nobody carries that much around. Well, here's a thought—ring up your father's accountant and tell him to deposit it.

LANCE. I don't think you understand, April—I've cut myself off. I've broken with my family.

APRIL. But you haven't broken with your accountant, surely.

LANCE. With everybody.

APRIL. You're teasing.

LANCE (*Exhibiting a few coins*). This is all the money I have.

APRIL (*Instantly*). Lance, I don't think we're quite ready to work together. Obey your original impulse—go and get the smell of printer's ink. Go see Hyacinth Beddoes Laffoon, right away.

LANCE. Who is she?

APRIL. The woman who publishes all those magazines—*Gory Story* —*Sanguinary Love*—*Spicy Mortician*.

LANCE. But they're just pulp fiction, full of blood and thunder. . . .

APRIL. My dear Lance, wake *up*. Some of our most enduring American authors come out of that milieu.

LANCE (*Fired*). Maybe you're right, April. Maybe I ought to contact her.

APRIL. Without further ado! Now you buzz right over to Laffoon House and storm the redoubts. I'd help you storm except I have to rush out to an appointment.

LANCE (*As she turns away*). When am I going to see you again?

APRIL. *Quien sabe corazon?* (*A sudden inspiration.*) I'll tell you what—why don't you drop in at my house-warming next Tuesday? And dig up an itty-bitty case of Scotch on the way, will you? There's a dear. (*Pushes him out, turns back into room. Phone rings; she answers brusquely.*) Yes? . . . Who? . . . Oh, it's you again. Now listen, Sensualdo, I told you, no monkey business—what? What new emeralds? (*Second phone rings.*) Look—hold on just one minute— (*Snatches up other receiver.*) Hello?—Who? . . . Well, stranger! . . . Of course I have, Benno darling—absolutely heartsick. . . . No—no, I couldn't. . . . Anselmo who? . . . Olivetti? Not the *typewriter* Olivettis? . . . Honey, wait one second, my other phone . . . (*Clasps phone to her, jabbers into the other.*) Look, Sensualdo, I just stepped out of my shower and I'm holding a big bag of groceries. Why don't we meet at the Drake about midnight and you bring along the adding machine . . . I mean the emeralds. . . .

(*The scenery has been moving during end of speech, and now segues into:*)

SCENE III

Scene: *Office of Hyacinth Beddoes Laffoon. A chamber devoid of furniture and of uncompromising severity with only enough indications to stamp it as a publisher's sanctum. The walls may display a couple of lurid pulp magazine covers with violent themes and broad mammary exposure.*

Time: *A week later.*

At Rise: BUNCE, VAN LENNEP, HAGEDORN, *and* VISHNU—*four typical crew-haired and brain-washed editorial assistants, Christmas tigers all—are grouped R. They wear identical blazers with breast patches exhibiting the letter "L" (cf. employees of Prentice-Hall), and buzz between themselves as they look over at* LANCE *isolated at L.*

VAN LENNEP (*From R.*). When did you hear about it?

HAGEDORN (*From R.*). I didn't—when I arrived this morning, there was a strange polo coat in my locker.

BUNCE (*Worriedly*). I was told not one word by Mrs. Hyacinth Beddoes Laffoon about a new editorial assistant.

VAN LENNEP. Nor me. She usually gives me an intimation—if only a wink—

HAGEDORN (*Crosses L. of* VAN LENNEP). She kind of winked at me at yesterday's meeting.

VAN LENNEP (*Superior*). No, I saw that. It was a belch.

VISHNU (*Crosses L. of* VAN LENNEP). That's right. She took a spoon of bicarb right after.

BUNCE (*Crosses L. of* VAN LENNEP). Besides, which magazine's got a vacancy? We're full up.

VAN LENNEP. He might be taking over that gland column—"You and Your Gonads."

VISHNU (*Crosses L. of* VAN LENNEP. *Aghast*). Say—you don't suppose it's the doctor she spoke of?

HAGEDORN. What one?

VISHNU. She said we all needed a good proctologist.

VAN LENNEP. Cheese it! Here she comes now!

(*With the silken smoothness of a Cadillac, an executive desk glides in, behind it* HYACINTH BEDDOES LAFFOON. *She is the epitome of female editors* (*cf. Mesdames Luce and Cowles*)— *chic, sleek, and murderous. Desktop holds a neat stack of magazines, dictagraph.*)

HYACINTH. Good morning, good morning, good morning! (*Cordially.*) How are you, Weatherwax?

LANCE. Fine, Mrs. Laffoon.

HYACINTH. Men, I want you to welcome a new member to our editorial family—Mr. Lance Weatherwax.

(*Ad lib greetings; the staff bestow saccharine smiles as they scan* LANCE.)

BUNCE (*Delicately*). Er—how would you describe Mr. Weatherwax, Chief? Is he a writer?

HYACINTH (*Coldly*). I don't believe in labels, Bunce. When I smell a fresh, original talent in the marketplace, I buy it. This young man is going to be a dynamic addition to our team. All right, now, drain the sludge out of your think-tanks. (*Sits.*) We're going to brainstorm. (*Men step D.S. Chattering sound.*) What's that chattering sound?

BUNCE (*Leans in to* HYACINTH. *Eagerly*). It's Hagedorn's teeth, Mrs. Laffoon. I've been meaning to squeal on him. Gosh, you ought to hear the noise he makes over the partition! A man can hardly concentrate.

HYACINTH. Oh, you have trouble concentrating, do you?

BUNCE (*Back up*). No, no—it'd take a lot more than that to upset *me!* I could work in a boiler factory!

HYACINTH. You may yet. Meanwhile, Hagedorn, let's have those choppers out before our next conference.

HAGEDORN. I'll see my extractionist in the lunch hour, Chief.

HYACINTH. Well, see that you do. Now, then, I've had my ear to the ground lately and I get a very—strange—impression. Some of you disagree with the policy of my new magazine—*Shroud.*

VAN LENNEP. Hell's bells, Hyacinth! Where'd you ever pick up a crazy idea like that?

HYACINTH. From the dictaphone I had installed in the water cooler. Does this sound familiar, Van Lennep? (*Reads from flimsy.*) "Just give the old windbag enough rope. You'll see, the public'll pin her ears back."

VAN LENNEP (*Squirming*). I—I was referring to Miss Lovibond, who solicits those ads for lost manhood. You said yourself the magazine needed more chic.

HYACINTH. Well, you squirmed out of that one all right, but watch your step. I'm sentimental enough to think this organization can't function without one-hundred-percent loyalty.

VISHNU. And you've got it, Mrs. Laffoon.

BUNCE. Why, we venerate the ground you walk on!

VAN LENNEP. Right down the line.

HAGEDORN. I'll say, Chief.

HYACINTH. At the same time—no ass-kissing! I want honest, sturdy, independent reactions—is that clear?

BUNCE. Like crystal!

HAGEDORN. Boy, I wish I could express myself so forcefully!

VAN LENNEP. She really cuts it, doesn't she?

VISHNU. What an editor!

HYACINTH. O.K. Well, I've just had a couple of skull-busters that I'd like to try out on you. (*Rises, crosses to L. of* BUNCE, *crosses D.S., front of desk.*) First, those covers we've been running. Look at this one— who's responsible for this? (*Taps pile of them on desk.*) A naked girl tied to a bed-post and a chimpanzee brandishing a whip. No more punch than a seed catalogue. (*Throws magazine on desk.*)

VAN LENNEP. I see the structural weakness.

BUNCE. Demands too much of the reader.

HYACINTH. Correct. We've got to drill him right between the eyes. Now, I visualize a cover with a real revolver barrel pointing at you.

OMNES (*Men close in—kneel—eyes lighting up*). Hey . . .

HYACINTH. And a wisp of smoke curling out. The smoke would be engendered in a mechanism hinged to the back cover.

OMNES. Hey!

LANCE. But, Mrs. Laffoon, wouldn't it be kind of bulky?

HYACINTH. Yes, and we could run afoul of the Sullivan Law.

VAN LENNEP (*Rises*). Nah, that can all be worked out.

HAGEDORN (*Rises, crosses R.*). Baby, what an inspiration.

VISHNU (*Rises, crosses L. of* HAGEDORN). It'll knock Publishers' Row right back on their heels!

BUNCE (*Rises, crosses L. of* VISHNU). Hyacinth, I don't say these things lightly. This idea's got undertow.

VAN LENNEP. I can hear those dimes and nickels showering down!

HYACINTH. You bet you can. It's the cashier counting your severance pay. So long, Van Lennep! (VAN LENNEP *crosses.*) Sayonara! (*As he exits chopfallen.*) There's no room at the top for a yes-man. Good thinking, Weatherwax. (*Crosses R. of* VISHNU.) As of today, you take over Van Lennep's duties. (*Crosses, sits L. of desk.*) You can wear his blazer till yours comes through.

LANCE. Gee, thanks, Mrs. Laffoon.

HYACINTH (*Sits, L. end of desk*). Now, let's see how my next idea appeals. What about a country-wide golem contest?

VISHNU (*Crosses to R. of desk*). Could you clarify that a bit for us, Chief?

HYACINTH (*Crosses to* VISHNU). A competition among our teen-age readers for the best Frankenstein monster built in a home workshop. (*Crosses R. to L. of* BUNCE.) How does that lay on the stomach, Bunce?

BUNCE. It stirs me and yet it leaves me cold.

HAGEDORN. I want to throw my arms around it, but something holds me back.

VISHNU. It's as broad as it is long.

BUNCE. How do you—

VISHNU. —feel about it—

HAGEDORN. —yourself?

HYACINTH (*Crosses L. of* VISHNU; *simpers*). Well, of course it's my idea.

VISHNU. And you can afford to crow. . . . I know I'd be proud of it.

HYACINTH. Well, I'm not—it's a *bomb*. (*Crosses R., significantly.*) Vishnu, I wish you'd reconsider leaving us. We need you here.

VISHNU. And I feel there's a place for me.

HYACINTH (*Crosses L., front of desk*). Not right here, but in the stockroom. Scout around, find an opening (VISHNU *exits.*), and clean it. Arrivaducci! (*As* VISHNU *exits R.,* HYACINTH *crosses R. of* LANCE.) By the by, Weatherwax, I didn't catch your reaction to my idea just now.

LANCE. What idea?

HYACINTH. Ho-ho, that's foxy of you—very good! Pretended you didn't hear it! You've got real executive stature, lad. (*Crosses behind desk.*)

LANCE. Gee, thanks, ma'am!

HYACINTH. Nothing at all. Now, leave me, all of you—run along. You stay, Weatherwax.

BUNCE (*Back R. with* HAGEDORN). But you might need us, boss.

HYACINTH. Go—go—go!

HAGEDORN. Oh, he's the palace favorite now, is he?

(BUNCE *and* HAGEDORN *withdraw, exit R., casting black glances at him.* HYACINTH *has withdrawn lacy handkerchief which she presses to her lips with anguished expression.*)

HYACINTH. Oh, the jealousies, the intrigues— (*Sits, shoulders heaving.*) Oh, it's too much. It's insupportable.

LANCE (*L. of desk*). What is?

HYACINTH. I feel so alone—so inadequate. I'm only a woman in a man's world, trying to cope.

LANCE. But you're on top—I mean, you're in charge. What you say goes.

HYACINTH (*Emotionally*). Do you think that way lies true happiness, Weatherwax? Under this artificial exterior there's a helpless creature that wants to be dominated—to be adored. . . .

LANCE (*L. of* HYACINTH). Everybody loves you, Mrs. Laffoon. Honest they do.

HYACINTH (*Rises, crosses R.*). No, no—you're all toadies, parasites. There's not a single living thing I can rely on. Not even a dog.

LANCE (*Fervently*). You could depend on me. Just try.

HYACINTH (*Blinking at him through unshed tears*). You mean it?

LANCE. Oh, I do! Really I do!

HYACINTH. Oh, how wonderful to hear those words! (*Sits desk.*) Weatherwax, as I sit here, I suddenly have a vision. I see a vast publishing enterprise, with two of us at the helm. Not one of those cockamamy affairs that Henry Luce runs, but a far-flung empire embracing every printed word. (*Buzzer sounds. She flips switch: a raucous, unidentifiable bark.*) Hello! The who? . . . The Weatherwax Trust & Loan Co. Good—put them on. . . . (*Grabs phone, sugar and spice.*) Well, are we getting that little half-a-million loan for *Shroud* magazine? (*Her face clouds over.*) Oh, we're not! (*Cradles phone, outraged.*)

LANCE. You were saying . . .

HYACINTH. That you're clean and straight and fine, and I say to you —get out before it's too late.

LANCE. But I only started this morn—

HYACINTH (*Rising*). Are you getting out, or do I have to have you thrown out?

LANCE (*Crosses L., stops, turns R.*). Er—yes, ma'am—I only thought—

HYACINTH (*With a snort*). Hit the road! (*He exits confused.* HYACINTH *resumes seat, picks up documents and glares after him.*) He only thought. That's the trouble with the world nowadays . . . too much thinking. (*She flips dictagraph switch.*) Lorna? Get me Barry Goldwater. (*The desk begins moving as she utters the foregoing, and segue into:*)

SCENE IV

Scene: *Goddard Quagmeyer's studio, Greenwich Village. The studio of a professional painter, devoid of any hint of dilettantism. Skylight at rear facing into street. At C. an easel with a partially-complete abstract painting, beside it a taboret laden with pigment, fixative bomb, etc. At rear also, an antique Greek plaster cast of a head, tableful of sketch pads, jars of brushes, pencils, dividers, maul-stick. A disordered cot dimly in evidence in background. A small radio on a table near easel; phone.*

Time: *A spring morning, several days later.*

At Rise: *The studio is empty of human life. Then a key is heard in the lock and* GODDARD QUAGMEYER *enters carrying a paper bag. Switching on radio, he picks up ashtray heaped with butts, crosses to door, and empties them into hallway. He now snaps door-bolt shut and proceeds to sip coffee from a container he extracts from bag, nibbling on a Danish butterhorn and intently considering the painting on easel. He has picked up palette and begun to work on canvas when a knock sounds at door.* QUAGMEYER *reacts with irritation, attempts to continue. Another couple of knocks, more insistent.*

QUAGMEYER (*Calls Off, attention glued to canvas*). Go 'way—nobody's home! (*Another knock; he half-turns.*) Quiet—we're recording! (*Repeated knock; he shouts.*) Stop that, will you? Someone's dead here!

(*Still another knock.* QUAGMEYER *starts convulsively, crosses to door, unbolts it.* LANCE *enters tentatively.*)

LANCE. Mr. Quagmeyer.

QUAGMEYER. Yes—what is it?

LANCE (*Steps R.*). You probably don't recall me.

QUAGMEYER. Your intuition is faultless.

LANCE (*Steps R.*). I'd like to talk to you if I could.

QUAGMEYER. Well, you can't. I've got a gouache to finish and it's drying on me.

LANCE. My name is Weatherwax. I'm not trying to sell anything.

QUAGMEYER. But *I* am.

LANCE (*Steps R.*). Lance Weatherwax. My mother owns two of your paintings.

QUAGMEYER (*Reacting*). Oh? . . . Yes, that's right—she does. (*Takes container of coffee.*) And as I remember, she paid a tidy little sum for them.

LANCE (*L. of chair C.*). Mr. Quagmeyer, how can a person like me tell whether they really have the creative spark?

QUAGMEYER. If it sets fire to your pants.

LANCE. Oh, I know how naive it sounds—me, Lance Weatherwax, aspiring to the arts.

QUAGMEYER. You've got plenty of company. Every housewife in the country's got a novel under her apron.

LANCE (*Turns chair around, sits*). No, I'm more interested in the visual—

QUAGMEYER (*Crosses L. to R. of* LANCE). And the dentists are even worse. Do you realize there are twice as many dentists painting in their spare time as there are painters practicing dentistry? (*Crosses to easel.*)

LANCE. I have to fulfill myself, Mr. Quagmeyer—

QUAGMEYER. All over this tremendous country, millions of poor worn-out bastards are schlepping home to frozen casseroles because their wives are out studying psychoceramics.

LANCE. If I could like write the perfect sonnet or paint one masterpiece, I'd die happy.

QUAGMEYER (*Sits chair on No. 3 unit*). Well, you'll never die of starvation, that's one comfort. Your folks have more bread than the Sheikh of Kuwait.

LANCE (*Rises, with spirit*). They can keep it. The whole six hundred million.

QUAGMEYER (*Rises*). Look, headstrong boy . . . (*Crosses L. of* LANCE.) Even Lorenzo de' Medici and Huntington Hartford didn't go that far. . . . But, tell me, what do you want from me?

LANCE. Mr. Quagmeyer. From the little you've seen of me, do I have the raw material to be a painter?

QUAGMEYER. Sonny—I'm pressed for time, so you'll excuse me for being blunt. Lay off the Muses—it's a very tough dollar.

LANCE. It's not the financial rewards I'm striving for, sir—it's self-realization! Like Gauguin was searching for when he went to the South Seas.

QUAGMEYER (*Crosses easel*). Oh. Well, in that case, you might have to do the same thing.

LANCE (*Crosses R. of easel*). Do you mean it? Do you think maybe I ought to lose myself in some place like Tahiti—live like the natives do?

QUAGMEYER. Yes, but easy on the poontang.

MRS. KRUMGOLD (*Offstage*). Do me one favor, Seymour, and shut up!

(MR. *and* MRS. KRUMGOLD *enter.*)

MR. KRUMGOLD. Last stop! Last stop! You said that an hour ago at the place we bought the Siamese fighting fish.

MRS. KRUMGOLD (*D.S. of No. 3*). Oblige me once in your life and button your lip!

MR. KRUMGOLD (*Crosses R.*). Now you drag me down to Greenwich Village and make me climb five flights of stairs. Me with my duodenal. (*Sits chair.* MRS. KRUMGOLD *sneers.*) You can laugh. Laugh! I was so tensed up last night, I could hardly hold my pinochle hand.

MRS. KRUMGOLD. That'd be a tragedy, all right!

QUAGMEYER (*Crosses L. to L. of* MRS. KRUMGOLD). Excuse me.

MRS. KRUMGOLD. Don't interrupt, please! (*Crosses L. of* MR. KRUMGOLD.)

MR. KRUMGOLD. You'd like to see me keel over, wouldn't you? (*Crosses R. of C. chair.*) Any woman that sits around the house studying her husband's insurance policy.

MRS. KRUMGOLD. I resent that deeply!

QUAGMEYER. I beg your pardon.

MRS. KRUMGOLD (*Crosses L. of* MR. KRUMGOLD). You keep out of this!

MR. KRUMGOLD (*Rises*). I wouldn't put it past you to hire assassins.

MRS. KRUMGOLD. You're paranoid!

MR. KRUMGOLD. What about those two truck drivers that stopped me for a light just now? The one wearing mascara looked like a pretty tough customer.

MRS. KRUMGOLD. Those were Bennington girls.

MR. KRUMGOLD. I'm glad I don't have your dirty mind. (*Crosses U.S.*)

MRS. KRUMGOLD. Oh, shut up! (*Crosses R. of* QUAGMEYER.) I'm terribly sorry we're late. Seymour was trapped with his tax consultant.

MR. KRUMGOLD. That lousy crook!

QUAGMEYER. I think you've made a mistake, lady.

MRS. KRUMGOLD. Aren't you Goddard Quagmeyer? I'm Zimmy Vetlugin's cousin. He's your art dealer, isn't he?

QUAGMEYER. Yes.

MRS. KRUMGOLD. Well, I'm Gloria Krumgold. We're here about the painting.

QUAGMEYER. Oh—oh—of course. Now—which canvas was it? It's slipped my mind.

MRS. KRUMGOLD. That Zimmy—I can see he didn't tell you anything.

MR. KRUMGOLD. Gloria, for God's sake— (*Crosses R. of* MRS. KRUMGOLD.)

MRS. KRUMGOLD. Seymour!

(MR. KRUMGOLD *crosses U.S.L. on No. 3.*)

QUAGMEYER. Perfectly all right, Mrs. Krumgold. What sort of thing are you looking for?

(MR. KRUMGOLD *holds chair,* MRS. KRUMGOLD *sits C. chair.*)

MRS. KRUMGOLD. We have a special problem—I better describe it. You see, Seymour and I have just built this very lovely home in Passaic Hills. The last word in modrun, except for the stables.

QUAGMEYER (*Steps R.*). Sounds very attractive.

MRS. KRUMGOLD. We need something for the living room. The idea is, in the center there's a sunken conversation pit.

QUAGMEYER. Sounds dangerous.

MRS. KRUMGOLD. But that's not our problem. It's the free-standing fireplace in the middle. We need a picture that would be suitable.

QUAGMEYER (*L. of* MRS. KRUMGOLD). To do what?

MRS. KRUMGOLD (*Gestures*). To go around it.

QUAGMEYER (*Crosses slightly away*). I don't paint round pictures.

MRS. KRUMGOLD (*Patiently*). Canvas wouldn't work naturally on a fireplace, so we thought maybe you would do it on formica. Not only would it be heat-resistant, but it would be easy to wash.

QUAGMEYER. Well—I've never done anything quite like it before, but I suppose we all have to move with the times.

MRS. KRUMGOLD. Marvelous. Seymour, I told you.

MR. KRUMGOLD (*Crosses R. of* QUAGMEYER). Let's not start celebrating. We haven't talked price.

QUAGMEYER. I'm sure we can come to some agreement. But look here —there's one thing we've overlooked—the subject matter.

MRS. KRUMGOLD. Oh, who cares? So long as it doesn't clash with the drapes. They're silver blue.

MR. KRUMGOLD (*Crossing to* QUAGMEYER). And my mother comes to dinner every Friday night. It shouldn't be smutty.

MRS. KRUMGOLD (*Brightly*). Well, now that it's all settled, when can we expect it?

QUAGMEYER. Never.

MRS. KRUMGOLD. I beg your pardon.

MR. KRUMGOLD. What kind of a way is this to do business?

QUAGMEYER. My way.

MRS. KRUMGOLD (*Lightly*). Well—if that's how you feel about it. Could you recommend a good restaurant around here?

QUAGMEYER (*Crosses R.—inhales deeply*). Lady, I'm a quiet, middle-aged man with a receding hairline and most of my own teeth—by profession a painter.

MRS. KRUMGOLD. So?

QUAGMEYER. So every morning, while nine million people are rushing to Wall Street and the Garment Center and Radio City, I come here to my little nook and ply my craft. By no stretch of the imagination would you confuse me with Giotto or El Greco or Picasso, but I don't bother anyone.

MRS. KRUMGOLD. Look, there are plenty of other painters—

QUAGMEYER (*Holds up his hand as she starts to speak*). Please—I'm not finished. Now, don't think I'm complaining. I make a mediocre living, but my career suits me. I'm adjusted to it, the way a maple tree manages to grow in a cement sidewalk. The only drawback to my existence, though, is the hyenas.

MRS. KRUMGOLD. The what?

QUAGMEYER. Every so often, the door opens and a couple of hyenas walk in. You can't tell they're hyenas because they walk like people, dress like people, and they have bank accounts (MRS. KRUMGOLD *rises.*), but you know 'em the minute they open their mouths. Well, I'll tell you how I protect myself. Over here behind the curtain, I keep a heavy club. First I warn them, and if they don't heed my warning, I count to ten and go for the *club. (Crosses L.)* One . . . two . . . three . . . four . . . (*Crosses R. of* MRS. KRUMGOLD. *The* KRUMGOLDS *exit precipitately.*) five . . . six . . . seven, eight (*Crosses R.*), nine, ten!

LANCE (*Crosses L.*). That was an experience, Mr. Quagmeyer.

QUAGMEYER. Nothing unusual.

LANCE (*U.S. to R. of* QUAGMEYER). Integrity in action. It was a privilege to see it.

QUAGMEYER (*Grimly*). Yes, no doubt. (*Crosses easel.*)

LANCE (*By C. chair*). I'm just beginning to realize what discipline an artist has to have.

QUAGMEYER. Well, then, your time hasn't been wasted.

LANCE. If you had a secretary or an assistant, like, to protect you, you'd be free to concentrate.

QUAGMEYER. Are you proposing yourself for the post?

LANCE. I could be real helpful, Mr. Quagmeyer. I'll run errands, take messages, and in between, you could give me various pointers on your craft.

QUAGMEYER (*Crosses L., nodding*). Like those apprentices the Old Masters used to have. (*Sits chair.*)

LANCE (*Crosses L. of* QUAGMEYER). That's it, sir—exactly!

QUAGMEYER. I see. Well, forget it. The last thing I need here is a nudnick asking a lot of damn fool questions.

LANCE. I wouldn't get in your way.

QUAGMEYER. I refuse to consider it, I tell you.

LANCE (*L. of* QUAGMEYER). Couldn't we give it a trial—please? If it didn't work out . . . (QUAGMEYER, *indomitable, shakes head.*) Mr. Quagmeyer, when you were just beginning, didn't anyone ever lend you a hand?

QUAGMEYER (*Pause*). Well—O.K. (*Rises. As* LANCE *brightens.*) But remember, you're on probation. If I bounce you into the street, no spaniel eyes or bawling—do you hear?

LANCE. Don't you worry.

QUAGMEYER. Right. (*Glances at wrist watch.*) Now, look—the morning's shot. I've got to get some stretchers. While I'm gone, you can begin your first lesson. (*Gets coat.*)

LANCE. Yes, sir.

QUAGMEYER. In oil painting, the brushwork is everything. (*Produces long-handled floor brush from behind stove L.*) Get into those corners. And if you shape up, I may let you wash the skylight.

(*He exits.* LANCE *stands holding brush, exhales slow sigh of delirious happiness. He moves about for a moment, inspecting studio. Then puts broom on No. 3, crosses to easel; he timidly picks up palette and brush, poses himself in his conception of painter at work. A pause, then, heralded by a perfunctory knock at door,* HARRY HUBRIS *enters L.*)

HUBRIS (*Stops short, fastidiously dust sleeves*). Hi, there, Maestro. Harry Hubris—Hubbub Productions.

LANCE. Harry Hubris?—the movie producer?

HUBRIS (*L. of C. chair. Surveys studio with distaste*). Roger! Say, are you kidding? Those terrific abstractions of yours—you don't actually *paint* them here?

LANCE (*Puts palette down*). No, I'm only the apprentice—Mr. Quagmeyer's not here—

HUBRIS (*Crosses easel; amused scorn*). Listen, I know that dodge. Your dealer told me about your publicity phobia. (*Crosses L. to below No. 3, gazes around studio, shakes head.*) Go figure it. It always kills me an artist should hole up in a flea-bag to conceive a masterpiece. Still, everybody to their own ulcer. (*Crosses U.L., sets attaché case down.*)

LANCE (*Urgently*). Mr. Hubris, I'm trying to tell you. I'm not Goddard Quagmeyer.

HUBRIS (*Turns L. of* LANCE; *overtaxed*). Pops, will you drop dead on that Salinger kick? I recognized you the minute I walked in. And I want you to know that I consider you one of the nine foremost painters of our time. (*Crosses L.*)

LANCE. Who are the other eight?

HUBRIS (*Turns, crosses L.*). Don't get me started, pal. I've got maybe the most important collection in the L.A. area. Four Jackson Pollocks, three Ben Shahns, five Lipschitzes, one of yours— (*Crosses L.*)

LANCE. Which one?

HUBRIS (*Impatiently*). Ask my wife, that's her department. (*Crosses U.S.*) All I know is she bought it in 1956, right after I had my thyroid out. . . . (*Sits L. armchair.*) But look here—let's get down to basics. Did you perchance read *The Tortured Bostonian?*

LANCE. What is it?

HUBRIS. The biography of John Singer Sargent—by Irving Stone-henge.

LANCE (*Crosses R. of* HUBRIS). Oh—oh, yes—I think I read the plot in *Time* magazine. It was very intriguing.

HUBRIS. I paid two hundred and seventy big ones for the picture rights—that's how intriguing. (*Extends index finger at* LANCE.) Just imagine Rob Roy Fruitwell in the lead!

LANCE. Who is he?

HUBRIS (*Rises*). Rob Roy? Only the biggest potential draw in pictures today. Properly handled, Fruitwell could be another Kirk Douglas, *and*— (*Crosses D.S., taking* LANCE *with him, lowers voice.*) I'll exhale you something in the strictest confidence. Next season you won't be able to tell them apart—after Fruitwell has his dimple deepened! (*Starts L., knits brow purposefully.*) But my immediate headache is this. Rob Roy's a born actor, and he'll play the hell out of Sargent, but what he requires is— (*Crosses L.*) a little coaching from a professional artist like you.

LANCE. How could anybody teach a man to paint in one lesson?

HUBRIS (*Crosses R. of* LANCE). For God's sake, smarten up, will you? This lug don't know from the muse. All you got to do is show him how to hold a brush . . . (*Indicates palette.*) what that board is for . . . which end of the tube the paint comes out. Two years ago he was a bus-boy in Fort Wayne. (*Crosses L.*)

LANCE. I've never dealt with actors. I haven't any clue to their mentality.

HUBRIS. Mentality's one problem you won't have with Rob Roy Fruitwell. Strictly a matzo ball.

LANCE. But John Singer Sargent was a genius.

HUBRIS (*Triumphantly*). That's the beauty part. (*Sits* LANCE *in C. chair, paces L. of him.*) This cluck is a sensitized sponge that he'll soak up the info you give him and project it. So, in view of the fact that we start shooting Friday, I had Rob Roy sky in from the Coast last night solely on purpose to huddle with you.

LANCE (*Rises, crosses easel*). Well, you're wasting your time, Mr. Hubris. There's one thing you'd better understand. Money won't buy everything.

HUBRIS (*Crosses L. of* LANCE). I consider that a highly un-American attitude. What are you, a Red or something?

LANCE. This is the studio of a dedicated painter—a person with ideals. You're asking a man to betray his birthright.

HUBRIS. You know, fellow, I'm deeply disenchanted with you. You talk like a mouth-breather.

ROB ROY FRUITWELL (*From doorway*). Hey, Harry!

(ROB ROY FRUITWELL *slouches in from L. He is a standard prize bullock with Brando tonsure and capped teeth, in Sy Devore silks and gooseneck sweater exposing thorax.* HUBRIS's *irritation instantly turns to saccharine.* ROB ROY *crosses D.S. of No. 3 chair.*)

HUBRIS. Hiya, Rob Roy, sweetheart? (*Crosses L.*)

ROB ROY (*L. of* HUBRIS; *looks around with distaste*). Man, where's the Board of Health? It's like Roachville here.

HUBRIS (*Crosses L. of* ROB ROY). Don't mind this rat trap, baby. In the picture, you're going to have a studio the size of Carnegie Hall.

ROB ROY. Big deal. O.K., come on—what's the action? I left a broad in the kip.

HUBRIS (*To* LANCE). It's a technical term. Rob Roy, this is the artist I told you about.

(ROB ROY *crosses L. of easel.*)

LANCE (*Crosses L.*). But, Mr. Hubris—I'm trying to tell you—

ROB ROY (*Facing easel*). Hey, Jack, this doodle here. What's it supposed to be—a woman?

LANCE. Of course. Don't you see the various female elements?

ROB ROY. Man, you need therapy.

HUBRIS (*Crosses L. to* ROB ROY). Well, I wouldn't go *that* far, Rob Roy. You know, a artist reacts to the world around him cranium-wise— through the old noggin.

ROB ROY. Don't give me that bushwa. I've dated Mamie Van Doren, Jayne Mansfield, and Diana Dors, and take it from me, Clyde, they don't have any corners. This moke's in trouble.

HUBRIS (*Crosses bag at No. 3, with wild gaiety*). Ha-ha—who isn't? . . . Now, Rob Roy, doll, I just want to check on a couple of scenes to insure we don't make a booboo. (*Whips open attaché case, produces smock and beret, crosses L. of* ROB ROY.) Here, slip these on so you'll get used to the feel of 'em.

ROB ROY. What the hell are we making, a costume picture? You said I wear a sweatshirt and jeans.

HUBRIS (*Dripping with sucrose*). In the love scenes, pussy-cat. But when you're sketching and dreaming up your different masterpieces, we got to blueprint you're an artist. It establishes your identity.

ROB ROY. The way a sheriff puts on a tin star?

HUBRIS. Or a bus-boy his white coat. (*Crosses L.*)

ROB ROY (*Reacts, wheels towards* HUBRIS). What did you say?

HUBRIS (*Gets script from No. 3, turns to* ROB ROY). Me? Not a thing, honey—nothing. (*Muttering,* ROB ROY *dons smock in reverse.* HUBRIS *gropes a script from attaché case. Crosses R. of* LANCE, *behind* LANCE.) Now, first of all, Rob Roy, run through the situation where Vincent Youmans tries to win you back to your wife.

LANCE. Vincent Youmans, the composer? How does he come into this?

HUBRIS (*Crosses, pushes* LANCE L.). A dramatic license we took to justify the score. You see, Youmans is a young music student at Harvard that Sargent befriends. (*Crosses L. of* ROB ROY.) Can you remember the lines, Rob Roy?

ROB ROY (*Contorting forehead*). I don't know. There's a coupla hard words.

HUBRIS. Never mind. Spitball some dialogue to give the sense. Go ahead, I'll cue you. I'll be Youmans. (*Crosses C.*) "Good morrow, Sargent!"

ROB ROY (*Crosses L. to* HUBRIS. *Tonelessly*). Hello, Youmans. Where you been, man?

HUBRIS. And he don't even know Lee Strasberg. (*Reads dialogue from script.*) "Oh, just studying my counterpoint over in Cambridge. But you certainly are a storm center these days, John Singer. All Beacon Hill is agog the way you threw up your job as stockbroker and abandoned your family. Can a pair of saucy blue eyes underlie this move, as waggling tongues imply?"

ROB ROY (*Crosses R., with a purportedly cynical hoot*). Women! I'm tired of those silly little creatures casting their spell on me. I want to paint—to paint, do you hear? (*Crosses L.*) I've got to express what I feel deep down inside me! The agony, the heartbreak!

HUBRIS. Beautiful—beautiful! Sweetheart, don't change a word, a syllable! Do that on camera, and I'll guarantee you an Oscar! (*Wheeling toward* LANCE.) How did it sound? Does it ring true from the artist's point of view?

LANCE. Well, yes, on the whole, but I noticed one thing wrong. Mr. Fruitwell's got his smock on backwards.

HUBRIS. You're dead right—the audience might mistake him for a barber. Watch that, Rob Roy.

ROB ROY (*Crosses L., as one crucified*). Damn it, Harry, you gonna hang around this mother-grabbin' place all night? I got an eight-man team of writers from the New York *Post* waiting to interview me!

HUBRIS (*Crosses L. of* LANCE). Be patient another ten seconds, baby —I got to corroborate one more detail. The key scene where you get your big break from the hotel manager. (ROB ROY *crosses U.S., sits chair on No. 3.* HUBRIS *takes* LANCE R. HUBRIS L. *of* LANCE.) The plot point here, Maestro, is that Sargent's down and out in New York. It's Christmas Day, the landlord's shut off the gas, and he's starving.

LANCE. The landlord?

HUBRIS. No, no—*Sargent.* (*Sorely impatient.*) Anyway, just at his darkest hour, in comes Tuesday Weld, the hat check girl at the St. Regis Hotel, which she's been secretly in love with him. She's persuaded the Hotel Manager to let Sargent paint a mural of Old King Cole . . . in the men's room. (LANCE *nods.*) How would a painter react in those circumstances? What exact phraseology would he employ?

LANCE (*Ponders*). Well, let me see. (*Crosses R. of C.*) Sometimes they smite their forehead— (*Demonstrates.*) and use a simple Greek word, like "Eureka!"

ROB ROY (*Rises, crosses D.S., taking off beret, L. of* HUBRIS). And for this you fly me from the Coast, you *schlep!*

HUBRIS (*Crossing to him*). I only did it for your good, baby—

ROB ROY (*Raging*). Don't try to con me, you muzzler! I'm walking off your stinking picture!

HUBRIS. Now calm down, you're tired—

ROB ROY. You bet I am! Tired of being pushed around by you and that turpentine peddler. (*Taking off smock.*) I'm calling my agent, Monroe Sweetmeat, right now to break my contract! (*Crosses to chair No. 3.*)

HUBRIS (*Crosses R. of* ROB ROY, *takes him D.C.,* HUBRIS R. *of* ROB ROY. *Panicky*). Rob Roy, I sensed you were unhappy in this role—I had a premonition. I've decided to buy you the property you begged me for— *Laughing Stevedore.* Tomorrow I ink a new pact with Monroe doubling your salary to five-fifty a week!

ROB ROY (*Crosses L.*). Ink your head off! You're a loser, Hubris. I'm planing to Rome tonight to see Carlo Ponti! (*Crosses L.*)

HUBRIS (*Crosses L. to R. of* ROB ROY). Ponti?

ROB ROY. You heard me!

HUBRIS. That pizza peddler! What can he give you?

ROB ROY. Top billing and some of the greatest zook in Europe!

HUBRIS. Yeah? (*Scrabbles in pockets, extracts a fragment of paper and leads* ROB ROY *D.S. out of earshot of* LANCE. *Then the ensuing four speeches are read* sotto voce.) Can Carlo Ponti give you that? . . . Answer me!

ROB ROY. "April Monkhood, 33 Perry Street." (*His eyes narrow lustfully.*) Is she built? Is she stacked?

HUBRIS. Who cares? She's alive and she's there!

ROB ROY (*Starting toward door*). Come on!

HUBRIS. Go ahead—I'll folly you. . . . (*Turning back to* LANCE, *with intense conviction—crosses to chair* L.) A household word in two years! That's what I predict for that young man!

LANCE (*Dubiously*). Yes, he seems to be very gifted. . . .

HUBRIS. He's a lot more than that, Buster—he's going to be an annuity for my old age. Well, thanks for the dope you gave me. (*His voice sweetens.*) Say, Rembrandt—in view of all the publicity you're getting, you ought to present me with a little token of your esteem. This sketch here, for instance . . .

(*As he crosses to easel and removes painting,* QUAGMEYER *enters carrying a couple of stretchers.*)

QUAGMEYER. What are you doing there? Leave that alone!

HUBRIS (*Crosses R. of chair. Belligerently*). Yeah? Why should I?

QUAGMEYER. Because it's mine—that's why. Drop it, I said! (*Takes painting from* HUBRIS, *sets it on easel.*)

HUBRIS (*Puzzled, to* LANCE). Who is this bird?

LANCE. He's Mr. Quagmeyer—the one you came here to see! (*To* QUAGMEYER.) I tried to tell him I wasn't you, but he was too bullheaded to listen!

HUBRIS (*Crosses L. of* QUAGMEYER; *sunnily*). Oh, well, what's the diff, so long as we finally connected? Quagmeyer, I'm Harry Hubris of Hubbub Productions, in Hollywood—and I badly need a technical advisor for my new picture—based on the life of John Singer Sargent.

QUAGMEYER (*Turning away*). Save your breath, Mr. Hubris—you just want to use my name to merchandise your junk—

HUBRIS. Yeah? Well, you listen to me, pal: What if I gave you complete control over the whole artistic end?

QUAGMEYER. You mean absolute authority?

HUBRIS (*Crosses L. with* QUAGMEYER *on his R. Transported*). I'll tell you how absolute. You need a certain statue from the Louvre? I'll glom it for you. You want a particular type beret for Sargent's head? I'll steam it for you. You'll be the chief shamus of the whole God-damned production!

QUAGMEYER. Well . . . that's different.

HUBRIS. You bet your rosy pratt it is. (*Crosses R.,* QUAGMEYER R. *of* HUBRIS.) Now, as to the fee, we don't expect anything free gratis. I'm buying a reputation, and I'm prepared to lay it on the line.

QUAGMEYER. What did you have in mind?

HUBRIS. One-fifty a week, a four-week guarantee, and half your bus fare.

QUAGMEYER. That doesn't seem like very much. . . .

HUBRIS. Fifteen hundred a week!

QUAGMEYER. We're in business.

LANCE (*Outraged*). Mr. Quagmeyer—how can you lend yourself to such practices? I thought you had some integrity—that you stood for something clean and straight and fine. But there's nothing people won't do for the almighty dollar, is there? . . . O.K., go ahead and sell your soul to the Devil. I for one won't watch it! (*He exits violently.*)

HUBRIS (*Blandly*). Typical. A rebel without a cause. (*He dismisses it with a wave.*) But getting back to our deal, Quag. Instead of fifteen hundred in a lump sum, what about thirty-five dollars down, fifty at the preview, and the balance the minute the negative cost is paid off? (*Energetically.*) Or maybe you'd prefer ten bucks now and a percentage deal, like a half share of the Antarctica rights? As a matter of fact, you stand to make twice as much dough that way. . . .

(*As he closes in on* QUAGMEYER, *fraternally clasping his shoulders, we segue into:*)

SCENE V

Scene: *April Monkhood's apartment.*

Time: *Half an hour later.*

At Rise: APRIL's *housewarming, a cocktail party, is in progress.* MAURICE BLOUNT, *a fly-by-night publisher,* BORIS PICKWICK, *a flautist, the* KRUMGOLDS, *and* CHENILLE SCHREIBER, *a beatnik, grouped downstage chattering ad lib.* APRIL *hurries in from kitchen bearing tray of drinks. Subdued Muzak if needed.*

APRIL (*Crosses C., distractedly*). Now who hasn't met who? Oh, Gloria! Maurice, do you know the Krumgolds? They're earth people. Gloria! Seymour! (*To latter.*) Maurice Blount's one of our most distinguished publishers of erotica. . . .

(BLOUNT *rises, puts drink on table.*)

MR. KRUMGOLD. I'm in the textile shrinking game.

MRS. KRUMGOLD. A publisher . . . how fascinating. (*Crosses L. of* BLOUNT.)

APRIL. And, Seymour, this is Boris Pickwick, first flautist of the Utica Symphony . . . (*Crosses U.R.*)

PICKWICK. Where's Vernon? (*Crosses U.R.*)

APRIL. Oh, he'll be along in a wink. (*To* MR. KRUMGOLD.) Vernon Equinox, that is. He writes non-prose for magazines like *Angst*, and he also paints under the influence of mescaline. (*Crosses U.S., gets two drinks from table.*)

MR. KRUMGOLD. I once smoked a reefer with a couple of girls from Bayonne, and boy, was I sick.

MRS. KRUMGOLD. Nobody wants to hear about your orgies.

(*They exchange glances of hatred, separate.* MR. KRUMGOLD *sits pouf.* APRIL *crosses R. and gives* MRS. KRUMGOLD *drink and moves U.S.* MRS. KRUMGOLD *and* BLOUNT *sit couch.* KITTY ENTRAIL, *an intense minor poetess in paisley and hoop earrings enters with* VERNON EQUINOX *from L.*)

APRIL (*Crosses L. of C.*). Kitty, how divine to see you. But where's Rolf?

KITTY (*Crosses L. of* APRIL). He couldn't come, he's laid up with an impacted hip.

APRIL. I'll send him two pounds of caviar tomorrow. Vernon!

VERNON. Who are all these people? My dear, it's the copulation explosion!

APRIL (*Crosses L. of* KITTY). Vernon, when did you get back from Haiti? (*Takes his hand, leads him R.*)

VERNON (*L. of* KITTY). Oaxaca. Nobody goes to Haiti any more.

APRIL. Of course—I forgot.

VERNON (*Crosses L.* APRIL *follows*). Not Oaxaca proper, mind you.

A tiny village sixty miles south—San Juan Doloroso. Sabu and I lived there for three pesos a day.

APRIL. Incredible. But I suppose it's already spoiled.

VERNON. Not inside the volcano. Only on the rim.

KITTY. Darling, I adore your new ambiente. It's too Aubrey Beardsley, isn't it, Vernon?

VERNON (*Critically*). Hm-m-m, I'm not sure about that area over there. I'd like to see a Renaissance credenza— (*Crosses L.*)

KITTY. Or rather, the memory of a credenza.

(*Talk from company.*)

APRIL (*Takes* KITTY L.; VERNON *crosses* U.S., APRIL R. *to* MR. KRUMGOLD). Seymour, this is Kitty Entrail.

KITTY. *Enchantée.*

MR. KRUMGOLD. I'm in the textile shrinking game.

APRIL. Kitty is a minor poetess.

MR. KRUMGOLD. A poetess, eh! I always wanted to know—what do you get for a poem?

KITTY. Heartbreak, Mr. Krumgold, heartbreak.

MR. KRUMGOLD. Same in the textile game.

(KITTY *crosses* U.L., *then* D.S. *of* APRIL. APRIL *crosses* L. KRUMGOLD *sits pouf. Loud talk.*)

BLOUNT (*Crosses* D.C. *to front of couch.* MRS. KRUMGOLD L. *of him*). I can't believe it! (*To* MRS. KRUMGOLD.) Did I understand you never read the memoirs of Polly Adler? You missed one of the great experiences!

MRS. KRUMGOLD. What is it—some kind of a historical work?

BLOUNT (*Crosses L.*). No, more of a true-confessions type thing. I'll mail you a copy tomorrow in a plain wrapper.

MRS. KRUMGOLD (*Archly*). Do I have to read it in a plain wrapper?

BLOUNT (*Crosses R.*). I got a closetful of fancy ones. Come up to my place and we'll read it together.

MRS. KRUMGOLD (*Slaps his hand away*). Don't get fresh with me, you measle.

BLOUNT (*With dignity, crosses L.*). Excuse me, I got to correct some proofs. (*Crosses* U.L.)

(*Loud talk.*)

MRS. KRUMGOLD. Oh, my goodness. (*Laughs. Sits couch.*)

CHENILLE (*Crosses D.S.*). But, Boris, MacDougal Alley's the very reason I left Bridgeport. (*Crosses front to R. end of couch.*)

(VERNON *crosses R. of* APRIL. BLOUNT *crosses L. of* VERNON.)

PICKWICK (*Crosses L. above couch*). The trouble with MacDougal Alley is, it has only two dimensions. The people over there is strictly a lot of cheap crumbs. Now in my winter home, in Cortina d'Ampezzo—

KITTY (*Crosses L.*). Cortina d'Ampezzo! The echolalia of that name! It's so—so steeped in the bright black creosote of authenticity.

PICKWICK. You see what I mean?

KITTY (*Ecstatically*). Oh, I do, I do!

PICKWICK. Then explain it to me.

KITTY. Get that woman away from me!

APRIL (*Crosses D.S. with* VERNON). Vernon, I'm furious with you. Everyone's avid to see those puppets you twist out of pipe-cleaners.

VERNON (*Crosses table R., gets tray*). I'm through with that dilettante stuff. I've been designing some nonobjective marionettes—a combination of dance and mime. Aaron Copland's wild to do the music.

APRIL. Oh, do let him.

(VERNON *crosses L. of* APRIL.)

MR. KRUMGOLD (*Rises, crossing D.R. of* MRS. KRUMGOLD). Gloria, for God's sake! . . . I . . .

GLORIA (*Shouts*). Seymour! (*Turns back smiling.*)

APRIL. By the way, how do you like the Krumgolds?

VERNON (*Sincerely—eating canapé*). They're the most delicious things I've ever eaten. (*Crosses D.S. of couch.*)

(LANCE *enters R.*)

LANCE (*Crosses L. of C.*). April! April!

APRIL. Lance Weatherwax! Whatever in the world are you doing here?

LANCE. You invited me!

APRIL (*Crosses R. of* LANCE). Then where have you been, for God's sake? I've had to do everything myself.

LANCE. I'm sorry, April. I had a terrible experience. I went over to see Goddard Quagmeyer about my problem.

APRIL. You can tell me all about it tomorrow. (*Pushes him across to her R.*) Run and get a muscatel for Kitty.

LANCE. I will, but when you hear what that man did—

APRIL (*Impatiently*). Now, really, Lance—is this the time or place to air your petty personal concerns? (*Turning toward guests; raises voice.*) Out in the hall, everybody! Dinner's ready on the stairs!

(GUESTS *drift off, but* LANCE *delays* APRIL.)

LANCE. You told me to go see him—

APRIL. Who?

LANCE. Quagmeyer. You were wrong—he's as corrupt as anybody else. (*Crosses L.*)

APRIL (*Crosses telephone table*). Are you still harping on him?

LANCE (*Crosses R.*). Anybody that sells out his principles for fifteen hundred dollars. It was disgusting! (*Crosses L.*) You wouldn't believe it. There was this movie actor there—Rob Roy Fruitwell— (*Crosses C.*)

APRIL (*D.S. of couch*). Rob Roy Fruitwell! That hoodlum! I've seen those movies of his—he's an animal. (*Crosses R. of* LANCE.)

LANCE. I'll admit he's very masculine, but Mr. Quagmeyer—

APRIL. Masculine? He's like something out of the primordial ooze. Is that what you admire in people?

LANCE (*Crosses L. of* APRIL). No—no—no—

APRIL. Lance, I'm surprised at you, I detest everything he stands for.

(ROB ROY *enters from D.L., crosses R.*)

LANCE. Yes, yes—but Mr. Quagmeyer—

APRIL. I know his type, believe me. He thinks all he has to do is look at a girl, nod in her direction— (ROB ROY *looks at* APRIL *as he passes her and exits R.*) and she'll go lusting after him. (APRIL *follows* ROB ROY *out R.*)

LANCE. April! (*D.S. of couch.*)

(HARRY HUBRIS *enters jovially from L.*)

HUBRIS (*Crosses L. of* LANCE). Say, have you seen Rob Roy Fruit-well?

LANCE. She's gone!

HUBRIS (*Recognizing* LANCE). It's the mouth-breather. (*Chuckles.*) I got to hand it to you, Clyde, I really mistook you for an artist before.

LANCE (*Brokenly*). I knew it couldn't last. I was only deceiving myself.

HUBRIS. Well, you fooled me, and I'm a pretty tough customer.

LANCE. She's left me—abandoned me. Oh, what am I going to do?

HUBRIS. For openers you could clean up these olive pits. (*Crosses L.*)

LANCE. She was my guiding star—my beacon (*Crosses L. of C.*), but there's no point in life any more.

HUBRIS. Hey, Willie, you need some fresh air. (*Looks at initial on* LANCE's *sweater.*) Back to the "Y" and take a cold shower.

LANCE (*Bitterly*). I've been on the wrong track all along. What good is art if it only leads to heartbreak? (*Crosses, sits pouf.*)

HUBRIS (*Crosses U.S., L. of* LANCE). Say, this is a soul in torment.

LANCE. I'm through with the ivory tower. I'm going to work in the mass media. I'll show her what beauty I can create—

HUBRIS (*Patronizingly*). Listen, bub, what are you—a chicken-flicker? An elevator operator in a one-story building? (*Crosses R.*)

LANCE. One day when I'm immortal, she'll know the sacrifices I made.

HUBRIS. Sacrifices? A rabbi—is that what you are?

LANCE (*Rises*). She'll remember me to her dying day, you wait. She'll remember the name of Lance Weatherwax.

HUBRIS (*Crosses R. of* LANCE. *Electrified*). Lance Weatherwax? Not the Weatherwax All-Weather Garbage Disposal Plan?

LANCE. Yes.

HUBRIS (*Crossing*). Then I'll tell you what you are—you're a movie director! (*Takes* LANCE *D.S.*) You're going to direct my new picture, *The Guns of Appomattox*, the biggest grosser in the next ten years! The Music Hall's got it pencilled in for Easter Week, and it's not even written yet! (*Hitting* LANCE *hard on shoulder to emphasize remarks.*) And you're the bozo that's going to direct it!

LANCE. I never directed before—

HUBRIS. A fresh mind, a primitive! Willie Wyler wants to do it but he's too shallow. John Huston wants it—he's too deep. You're the logical man! (*Arm business again.*)

LANCE. Golly, sir—are you really serious?

HUBRIS (*Encircling* LANCE's *shoulders*). I'll tell you how serious. To show my faith in you, I'm going to let your folks put up the money for an independent production! (*As he steers* LANCE *out.*) Hollywood— here you come! (*Crosses L.*)

CURTAIN

Act Two

SCENE I

Scene: *Mrs. Younghusband's Agency, an employment office for select domestics in Santa Barbara, California. A fairly shallow set, approximately one-and-a-half. The furnishings are simple: a desk at R.C., matching chair and filing cabinet, wall calendar, a large photo of Del Monte coastline with twisted cypresses. Facing desk, two wicker chairs for clients. Door to exterior at L.*

Time: *Morning, two weeks later.*

At Rise: MRS. YOUNGHUSBAND, *a desiccated gentlewoman in her forties, professionally* hochgeboren *and attired in a cardigan sweater set and pearls, sits at desk, speaks animatedly into phone.*

MRS. YOUNGHUSBAND (*Into phone*). Now, Chang Fat, I have a simply marvelous situation for you—a yachtsman down at Balboa. He's got a 63-foot yawl with a balloon jib, and he needs a wideawake Chinese boy to do for him. . . . What? . . . No—only the summer. In the winter, he lives at Pancreas Hall, that sanitarium in Glendale. . . . No, poor man, he thinks a weevil is eating his liver. . . . All right then, three o'clock— Good-bye.

HUBRIS (*Entering from L. Crosses L. of desk*). Dolores, Dolores, Dolores.

MRS. YOUNGHUSBAND (*Rises. Gummy*). So generous of you to come up to Santa Barbara, Mr. Hubris. I know how valuable your time is.

HUBRIS (*Sits L. of desk*). Dolores, Tom Younghusband—your husband—may he rest in peace—was the greatest stunt man that ever worked for me. The day that Egyptian temple fell on him, I made a resolve his widow would never want for a thing.

MRS. YOUNGHUSBAND (*Sits R. of desk*). There should be more people like you, Mr. Hubris. This world would be a better place.

HUBRIS (*Rises, crosses L.*). Of course! Now you said you got a problem. You said you got a client needs a first-rate houseboy.

MRS. YOUNGHUSBAND. The Rising Sun Domestic Employment Agency handles only top quality Oriental personnel.

HUBRIS (*Crosses L. of desk*). I got him. I got him . . . a Cambodian.

MRS. YOUNGHUSBAND. These people, Mr. and Mrs. Fingerhead, are terribly particular. One thing they won't tolerate is a jazz baby. You know the type gook I mean.

HUBRIS. They can rest easy, dear lady. Wing Loo studied three years at UCLA. He was on the dean's list morning, noon, and night. (*Sits L. of desk.*)

MRS. YOUNGHUSBAND (*Makes note*). And you can vouch for his cooking, can you?

HUBRIS. Don't ask me—ask a gourmet like Darryl Zanuck—Hedda Hopper—Duke Wayne—people which they make a shrine of their stomach. Every time I throw a luau, they're in the kitchen trying to hire Wing Loo away from me.

MRS. YOUNGHUSBAND. An authentic Cambodian, you said?

HUBRIS (*Rising*). Right off the boat—a greenhorn. Look, you'll see for yourself. (*Rises. Calls through door.*) Oh, Wing Loo, Wing Loo! (*Crosses L.* DOLORES *crosses R. of C.* LANCE *enters L., his appearance perceptibly altered. He wears Chinese garb, pigtail. His eyes have a strikingly Oriental slant and his skin is a distinct yellow. Carries a cheap cardboard suitcase.*) Did I exaggerate?

MRS. YOUNGHUSBAND (LANCE *bows.* MRS. YOUNGHUSBAND *nods approvingly*). Yes, he's the real thing, all right. (MRS. YOUNGHUSBAND *crosses R. of* HUBRIS.)

HUBRIS. Like night and day from a false Cambodian.

MRS. YOUNGHUSBAND. You've just had the most glowing reference, Wing Loo. I hope you create a good impression on the Fingerheads, now.

LANCE. It sounds like a golden opportunity.

MRS. YOUNGHUSBAND. It is!

HUBRIS (*Moves R. Elaborate nonchalance*). Now—correct me if I'm wrong but did I hear you say the lady of the house was a writer, no?

MRS. YOUNGHUSBAND. Her husband, too. They're both experts on the Civil War. Written scads of books about it. Well, it's all set. (*Crosses R.*) If you'll excuse me, I have to run next door to the vegetarian bar. (*Crosses to door.*) I have a very serious iron deficiency. The doctors gave me only nine hours to live. I have to go get my parsnip juice.

HUBRIS (*As she exits*). A parsnip condition, she should wear a metal tag. (*Energetically.*) Now, look—we can't waste any time. You remember my instructions?

LANCE. To find out the plot of Mrs. Fingerhead's new Civil War novel. The one I'm going to direct.

HUBRIS. Right.

LANCE. Golly, Mr. Hubris, it was a great day when I met you. And now I'm going to express myself in film. Directing movies— (*Gratefully.*) You sure have been swell, Mr. Hubris.

HUBRIS (*Crosses R.*). Nothing at all—nothing at all!

LANCE. The only thing . . . (*Indicates makeup.*) What does all this have to do with making movies?

HUBRIS (*Crosses R. of* LANCE). It's the most important part—stealing the property! Everybody in the trade'll be shooting a Civil War spectacular on account of it's the Centennial. We got to be there fustest with the mostest—*vershsteh?*

LANCE (*Dubiously*). I guess so . . .

HUBRIS. You're the undercover man, the camera eye recording every little detail. And if you can heist the manuscript, so much the better.

LANCE. The whole thing?

HUBRIS. As much as you can carry. How's the makeup?

LANCE. The adhesive tape hurts my eyes.

HUBRIS. Take it off at night. But don't forget—keep that Jap-a-lac on your face, and lots of Scuff-Koat on the hair. (*Crosses L. of* LANCE.)

LANCE. What about the meals?

HUBRIS. Don't worry! They're Southerners. Just look mysterious and give 'em grits.

LANCE. Suppose they order something fancy.

HUBRIS (*Crosses L. to L. of C.*). I'll send you a couple of books. *The Joy of Cooking* and *Love and Knishes*, by Sara Kasdan.

LANCE. Mr. Hubris—what I'm doing—are you sure it's legal? . . . Couldn't I get arrested?

HUBRIS. For what? Impersonating a Cambodian?

LANCE. It just doesn't seem right.

HUBRIS (*Crosses L. of* LANCE). Of course it ain't! It's sneaky—lowdown—beneath contempt! But you listen to me. Suppose Harry Lime refused to water down that black-market penicillin in the *The Third Man?* (*Crosses R.*) Suppose Janet Leigh didn't take that shower in

Psycho? (*Crosses* LANCE.) Suppose Simone Signoret didn't shack up with that guy in *Room at the Top?* Where would this great industry be today?

LANCE. Gosh, I never thought of it that way.

HUBRIS. Of course!

(*Steps D.S. of* LANCE. *They start to exit L.* HUBRIS *looks out front, registering satisfaction at the logic that has convinced* LANCE. *As they exit, we segue to:*)

SCENE II

Scene: *Kitchen of the Fingerhead residence. Window rear over a sink unit flanked by work counters and cupboards. Wall phone. At C., a table bearing a silver pitcher, creamer, spoons and forks, candlesticks, silver polish, rags. Door to living room L., door to garden R.*

Time: *Noon, five days later.*

At Rise: LANCE, *in houseman's striped apron, is polishing silver. After a moment,* GRACE FINGERHEAD *enters from living room wearing a floppy garden hat, carries flower basket containing shears over arm.* LANCE *on chair R. He rises.*

GRACE (*Crosses to counter*). Good morning, Wing Loo.

LANCE. Good morning, Mrs. Fingerhead.

GRACE. The lobelias look so lovely this morning I can't resist them. I'm going down to the lower garden and snip off their little pods.

LANCE (*Sits*). Yes, ma'am.

GRACE (*At counter, turns R.*). Whose motorcycle was that I heard in the driveway just now?

LANCE. The fish-market with our order.

GRACE (*Crosses back of L. chair*). Oh, your halibut squares . . . Wing Loo, I know you're making every effort, but I wish you'd stick to the menu I give you. Now that noodle ring you made for dinner last night!

LANCE. I'm sorry, Mrs. Fingerhead. I guess I put in too many raisins.

GRACE (*Crosses L. of L. chair*). And just because your last employer loved frozen blintzes, I see no reason to get them three nights running.

LANCE. Yes, ma'am.

GRACE (*Crosses to behind counter*). Is Mr. Fingerhead up yet?

LANCE. No, ma'am. He worked all night again. I heard him dictating into his machine.

GRACE. A lot of good it'll do him. My book'll be out long before his. Congratulate me. Wing Loo, I've just completed the final chapter —the burning of Natchez. (*Crosses R.*)

LANCE (*Reacting*). Oh? You're all finished?

GRACE. Four years' work! Why, I've *discarded* more than a million and a half words. (*Crosses behind table.*) Even so, the manuscript runs to eleven hundred pages. (*Crosses R.*)

LANCE. I hope Madam has a great success.

GRACE (*R. of* LANCE). Well, thank you, dear. I feel I deserve it. Nobody before ever looked at the Confederacy through the eyes of a Creole call girl. (*Picks up clipping from desk. Crosses desk.*) Call me visionary, Wing Loo, but some day the character of Stephanie Lavabeau will stand with Madame Bovary and Becky Sharpe. (*Crosses desk.*) What's this?

LANCE. Mr. Fingerhead left it here for you. He cut it out of *The New York Times Book Review.*

GRACE (*Crosses R. of* LANCE. *Hands it to him*). What does it say?

LANCE. "Curtis Fingerhead, one of our most constant observers of the Southern literary scene—"

GRACE (*Angrily*). What are they talking about, the idiots? I've observed it twice as much as he has! (*Crosses behind table.*)

LANCE. "—is promising a new novel for the fall season based on the loves of Stonewall Jackson."

GRACE (*Grabs clipping, tears it up; spitefully*). Promising is right! He wrote two chapters of the wretched thing and bogged down. And even if he got it done, I doubt whether he'd sell more than twelve copies. (*Throws scraps on C. table, crosses L., sits stool.*)

(CURTIS FINGERHEAD *enters, attired in bathrobe.*)

CURTIS (*Coldly; steps to D.S. end of counter*). I heard that. And may I observe that anyone whose conception of the Union breastworks at Vicksburg is so Freudian—

GRACE. Thank you, my dear. I didn't realize you'd ever read my best seller *Spoon Bread and Powderhorns.*

CURTIS. I haven't, but I occasionally do run across your reviews.

(*Producing clipping from bathrobe pocket.*) This one, for instance, from the Nashville *Scimitar:* "Author Grace Fingerhead betrays her usual ineptitude—"

GRACE (*Crumples it and puts it in pocket*). Mr. Fingerhead! Must you vent your spleen in front of the help? Not that I think Wing Loo is indiscreet.

CURTIS (*Crosses L. of L. chair*). Oh, I've met a couple of gabby Chinks in my time. Boy, did they run off at the mouth! (*Chuckles.*) Or maybe it was two other Chinamen, they all look alike to me.

GRACE. I doubt whether Wing Loo is very interested in your past.

CURTIS (*Crosses behind table*). Well, I'm interested in his. Bet you saw plenty of orgies down there in Hollywood, eh? (LANCE *lowers eyes modestly.*) Lots of naked little starlets chasing around in—what do they call 'em—teddies?

GRACE. Curtis, what a thing to say.

CURTIS (*Back of table*). Ah, everybody knows what goes on. Swimming pools full of champagne, mixed bathing— (*Crosses R.*)

GRACE. Well, Wing Loo won't encounter that sort of thing at our house.

CURTIS. No, he sure won't. (*Exits swinging door.*)

GRACE (*Crosses swinging door, crosses back to chair L., sits*). Do you want to know how downright evil some people can be? (*Looks around quickly.*) I've a notion he's trying to steal the manuscript of my book!

LANCE (*Petrified*). Ma'am?

GRACE. Well, you've noticed that old-fashioned safe upstairs in my closet?—behind my dresses?

LANCE. Uh—I'm not sure. . . .

GRACE. Oh, naturally, you'd have no reason to go poking about up there, but anyway, that's where I keep it, the manuscript, that is, and someone's been fooling with the combination recently. I put some axle grease on the knob a day or two ago, and sure enough, it's all smudged!

LANCE. Why—why would Mr. Fingerhead do a thing like that?

GRACE. Because he's consumed with jealousy, don't you see? It's killing him that Emmett Stagg, the head of Charnel House, wants to publish my novel. (*Sharp bark of laughter. Crosses to counter, gets basket.*) Well, Curtis won't get away with it. (*Crosses U.S. of table.*) I bought a fingerprint kit! (*Crosses R. of* LANCE *behind him.*)

LANCE. Holy Moses.

GRACE (*Shrugs*). Oh, well, I suppose one should be more compassionate. His last urinalysis came out 94 percent cognac. (*Exits swinging doors.*)

(*She exits.* LANCE *crosses swiftly to phone, dials.*)

LANCE (*Crosses desk, sits and dials. On phone. Rises*). Hello? Hubbub Productions? Give me extension 354— Yes, yes, it's urgent! . . . (*Sits.*) Listen, Miriam, this is Lance again—I have to speak to Mr. Hubris right away. . . . (*Rises.*) What do you mean, you can't find him? You *have* to find him—get a message to him. . . . He *knows* that. I told him all about Stephanie Lavabeau—I told him it was in the safe but I couldn't—what? Look—tell him I'm in danger, they suspect something—

GRACE (*Offstage*). Wing Loo!

LANCE. I got to hang up, someone's coming— (*Crosses L. of table.*)

GRACE (*Crosses above R. chair. Excitedly reenters*). Wing Loo— Wing Loo! I have the most thrilling surprise for you! Guess who just walked into the laundry area! (*Crosses L. of swinging door. He gapes.*) Your father! From Cambodia!

(*As* LANCE *emits a startled exclamation,* HARRY HUBRIS *enters past her. He is also garbed as a Chinese.*)

HUBRIS (*Crosses front of R. chair, drops bag. Emotionally, as he beholds* LANCE). My little tiger-cub. Come to me, pride of your ancestors.

LANCE (*Frozen with fright, advances to him, bobs jerkily*). Honored sire.

(*Bowing to each other.* LANCE *keeps bowing.* HUBRIS *stops him.*)

HUBRIS. Enough already!

GRACE (*Crosses D.S., R. of* HUBRIS. *Eyes protrude in awe*). Filial respect . . . it's a tradition . . .

HUBRIS (*Turns to her, speaks in stilted English*). Five thousand years ago, the great sage, Matzo Tongue, he say, "If pepper seed take wing, it will turn into a dragonfly. But if dragonfly lose wing, it will not turn into pepper seed." That is what the sage he say, five thousand year ago.

GRACE. The inscrutable wisdom of the East. (*Sighs.*) But I mustn't intrude—you two have so much to say to each other. (*Exits swinging door.*)

HUBRIS (*Crosses L. to D.S. of stool*). O.K., enough with the laundryman bit. Where's the safe?

LANCE (*Follows R. of* HUBRIS). Mr. Hubris, I just called you— we're in trouble!

HUBRIS (*Reassuringly, indicates portmanteau*). Relax. The tools I got there can open anything.

(LANCE *starts to pick up bag.*)

GRACE (*Offstage*). Wing Loo-oo!

(LANCE *drops bag—bows to* HUBRIS—*speaks Chinese.* LANCE *lapses into Chinese.*)

HUBRIS. V*uss?*

GRACE (*Enters*). Wing Loo, do offer your father a cup of oolong. He looks exhausted. (*Exits.*)

LANCE. The safe's upstairs.

HUBRIS (*Crosses L. of* LANCE). Well, go and get it!

LANCE (*Horrified*). You mean, carry the whole safe out?

HUBRIS. Certainly. You're a big strong boy, you could lift a house. I can't lift on account of my thyroid, but I'll supervise. (*Energetically.*) Here's the dope. First—you're positive the whole script is inside, no loose fragments laying around?

LANCE. No, it's all there— She told me the plot—it's mostly sex.

HUBRIS. That's the two most important drives. Sex and what I got— hunger. . . . Okay. You beat it upstairs and carry down the box while I stand guard. Capisco?

LANCE. But we're going to need a truck, or a car—

HUBRIS. I made a deal with a motorcycle kid from a fish market. The safe goes into the side-car. And the two of us can hang onto the kid. Go on, now, upstairs and work fast.

(LANCE *gets bag and exits L.* HUBRIS *runs to swinging door R., hears someone coming and runs L. and hides behind the counter L.* CURTIS *enters swinging door and goes stealthily across stage and out L.* FISH MARKET BOY *enters immediately U.R., looks around, and goes out swinging door.* GRACE *enters U.R., looks around, sees* HUBRIS, *screams, and exits through swinging door.* EMMETT STAGG—*owl-faced, bouncy—bespectacled, a pipe stuck jauntily in teeth—enters. Surveys kitchen cursorily, exits U.R.* HUBRIS *reappears from behind counter, crosses to swinging door, listens, and then runs to table. He picks up silverware and starts to stuff it into his coat.* GRACE *enters swinging door humming to herself.* HUBRIS *drops silver and crosses D.L.* GRACE *picks up microfilm package from desk and walks D.R. and addresses audience.*)

GRACE. Well, well. So—my envious husband reckons to steal my manuscript. Well, I'll fix his wagon. Here it is, transferred to microfilm and all that remains is to smuggle it out of the house. Hello—this guileless Oriental is meet for my purpose. He should yield readily to my blandishments. (*Crosses R. of* HUBRIS. *To* HUBRIS.) Well, Mr. Loo, how did you find your son?

HUBRIS. I rook around—I see him.

GRACE. Ha ha—very nicely phrased. Mr. Loo, would you do me a favor?

HUBRIS. Me do anysing fo' plitty lady.

GRACE. Would you just drop this in the nearest mailbox? It's a wedding present for my niece.

HUBRIS (*Takes package, puts in pocket*). Me keepum light here, next to ticker.

GRACE. Why, how gallant of you, Mr. Loo. I'm much obriged.

HUBRIS. Obliged.

GRACE. Of course. Thank you so much. (*Starts R.*)

HUBRIS (*Bowing her off R.*). My preasure. My preasure.

GRACE. Charming. You're too kind.

(*She exits.* HUBRIS *assures himself she is safely out of the way, recrosses to living room door and looks off anxiously. He then returns to the table at C., picks up silverware again.* CURTIS *enters furtively, steals downstage.* HUBRIS *sits R. chair—starts to polish silver.*)

CURTIS (*Aside*). Well, my devious stratagems are coming to fruition at last. (*Exhibits duplicate of Grace's brown package.*) Thanks to technological advance, I now possess a duplicate microfilm copy of Grace's novel. To fob it off as my own, I shall need a cat's-paw. (*Descries* HUBRIS *upstage.*) Oh, by jove, the very man. This wily Oriental, skilled in intrigue, is meet for my purpose. . . . I say there, Wing Loo! (*Crosses U.S. back of L. chair.*)

HUBRIS. Yassuh— Yassuh, Bwana?

CURTIS (*Stares at him*). Humph. I don't know what it is about Santa Barbara, but it sure ages people. Look, boy, can you run an errand for me chop-chop? (*Sits L. chair.*)

HUBRIS. Solly, no can do. Missy tell me stay here, shine silber.

CURTIS. Oh, banana oil! I'm the one that pays your salary, do you hear? (HUBRIS *bobs assent.* CURTIS *addresses package.*) Now run out and mail this manuscript for me.

HUBRIS (*Pricking up ears*). Manusclipt?

CURTIS. Yes, you wouldn't understand, but it's my novel of the Confederacy as seen through the eyes of a Creole call girl.

HUBRIS (*Reaches eagerly for it*). Yes siree. Me complihend! (*Takes package.*)

CURTIS (*Takes package, rises, breaks L.*). On second thought, maybe I shouldn't entrust it to the mails—

HUBRIS (*Rises, crosses R. of* CURTIS). Me velly careful—me insure it! (*Takes package.*)

CURTIS. No, wait a minute. (*Takes package.*) Film's got to be packed in a fire-proof container— (*Crosses L.*)

HUBRIS. Me packee! Me packee! Me *packee!!* (*Crosses L., grabs package.*)

CURTIS (*Holds on to the package. They wrestle for it. Suspiciously, thrusting it behind him*). Oh, no, you won't, you cunning heathen. Nobody's handling this but yours truly— (*Gets package.*) not after the pains it's cost me. (*Exits L. door.* HUBRIS *crosses L. door and crosses behind counter.*)

(EMMETT STAGG *reenters from U.R.*)

STAGG (*Crosses front of counter. Entering U.R.*). Grace!! Grace!! Anybody home? (*Breezily.*) Hi there, John. I'm Emmett Stagg, Mrs. Fingerhead's publisher. I'm on my semiannual lecture tour of the West Coast, playing to packed houses everywhere, and thought I'd stop in.

HUBRIS. I bereave I see you on terevision.

STAGG. Every Sunday night, unless you're blind. (*Crosses front of table to R. Crosses U.S.*) Well, I can't wait. Lenny Bruce and eighteen of America's foremost sick comics are throwing me a—ha-ha—Stagg dinner at Hillcrest. (*Fumbles out calling card and pencil. Crosses counter.*) Here's my number—I'm staying with Tony Curtis in Bel Air. . . .

HUBRIS. Tony Curis in Berair.

STAGG. You're dead right—Tony wouldn't want his phone bruited about. Tell you what, I'll leave Burt Lancaster's—

(*As he bends down to write,* CURTIS *reenters.*)

CURTIS (*Crosses L. of L. chair, looks about vaguely*). Where's that almond-eyed son-of-a-bitch was in here a minute ago?

STAGG. Hello—ha-ha—Fingerhead—

CURTIS. Emmett! What are you doing in this neck of the woods?

STAGG. Well, I'm on my semiannual lecture tour of the West Coast—playing to packed houses everywhere—thought I'd drop in.

CURTIS (*Crosses R.*). Fine. But what am I being so cordial to you for? You're only here to see Grace.

STAGG. Curtis, that was unfair. Bring me a piece of work you've got faith in, and by tarnation, I'll paint your name across the sky!

CURTIS (*Sneering*). Do you think that pipsqueak firm of yours is big enough to handle a runaway best-seller? (*Sits R. chair.*)

STAGG (*Crosses L. around table, sits L. chair*). Who copped the National Book Award last year? Charnel House—with our number one smash hit, A *Child's Life of Liberace.*

(HUBRIS *crosses R. of* CURTIS, *tries to pick package out of his pocket.*)

CURTIS (*Querulously*). I've got a taste in my mouth like a motorman's shoe. Where's that slippery Mongolian? (*He catches sight of* HUBRIS.) Hey, you! Fix me a highball—and heavy on the brandy.

HUBRIS. Me bling whole bottle. (*Crosses R. through swinging door. He moves off slowly, straining to catch the drift of the others' conversation.*)

STAGG. Curtis, I see a sly little look in your eye. (*Wheedling.*) Have you got a book in the oven?

CURTIS. A book, for God's sake? A cataclysm—a Vesuvius!

STAGG. You think there's a movie in it?

CURTIS. Ho ho—and how! Why, there are scenes in it that'll make

Grace Metalious look like Mother Goose! (HUBRIS *enters, crosses above table, pours drink.*) Wait till you read about the orgies at Rebel head-quarters, the mixed bathing! No one before has ever looked at the Confederacy through the eyes of a Creole call girl.

STAGG. Man, we'll have to print that on asbestos—

CURTIS. All honeysuckle and spitfire—that's Stephanie Lavabeau!

(HUBRIS *reacts.*)

STAGG. Who?

HUBRIS. Stephanie Lavabeau. . . .

CURTIS (*Gleefully*). See that, Emmett? That heathen ignites at the name and he doesn't even speak the language.

(HUBRIS *crosses front of counter.*)

STAGG (*Excitedly*). Now listen to me, pal, because I mean business. You let me have that book and I'll print a hundred and fifty thousand copies before publication.

CURTIS. Peanuts. Simon & Schuster offered me that for the outline. All I have to do is pick up a phone.

STAGG. *I'll* pick up a phone. (*Rises, crosses to phone R., dials.*)

CURTIS. Who are you calling?

STAGG. What does the phrase "movie sale" mean to you?

CURTIS. Now you're cooking!

STAGG (*Sits phone chair; into phone*). Goldie? Mr. Stagg— I'm up in Santa Barbara. Give me a tie line. Hollywood— Hubbub Productions. . . . That's right. I want to speak to Harry Hubris personally.

CURTIS. Harry Hubris, the movie mogul? You know *him*?

STAGG (*Sits chair*). We've never met vis-a-vis, Curtis, but in the aristocracy of success, there are no strangers.

(HUBRIS, *his astonishment at* STAGG's *effrontery mingled with admiration, moves Downstage and addresses audience.*)

HUBRIS (*With relish*). Why, the four-eyed weasel—there goes my plan to steal the manuscript. Oh, well, I'll just have to buy it.

STAGG (*Into phone.* CURTIS *rises, crosses L. of* STAGG). Yes, I'm on . . . Hubbub Productions? This is Emmett Stagg. Put me through to Harry Hubris. . . . Harry? Emmett Stagg. How are you, Harry?

HUBRIS. I'm fine—how are you?

STAGG (*Into phone, unctuously*). Harry, I've got a book. 'No, I'm not going to let you read it. I'm just going to tell you one thing. (*Chuckles.*) It'll be a tidal wave, and I'm letting you on my surfboard. You've got first crack at the movie rights for three hundred G's!

HUBRIS (*Crosses back of table*). Three hundred?

STAGG (*Into phone*). Correct, dear heart, but you better talk fast— I've got Otto Preminger on the other phone!

HUBRIS. Two-fifty.

STAGG (*Into phone*). Why, you cheap scavenger, you presume to haggle over a symphony?

HUBRIS (*Steps R.*). Two-seventy-five.

STAGG (*Into phone*). Make it two-eighty and we call it *schluss*.

HUBRIS. You got a deal.

STAGG. O.K., Harry—the rest is bookkeeping. (*Slams up phone, revolves around.*)

LANCE (*Enters L. door. The three turn.* STAGG *rises.* LANCE *is doubled over, the safe in a sling on his back*). I've got it! Mr. Hubris, I've got the manuscript, Mr. Hubris!

HUBRIS. Shhh!—Shut up—shut up!!

STAGG. Who the hell is that?

HUBRIS. Could be Atlas. (*Virtuously.*) I never saw him before in my life!

STAGG (*Crosses R. of* HUBRIS). Hubris—? (*He stares at him dumbfounded.*) Why, you low-down crook! Beating me down while all the time you were stealing it!

CURTIS (*Wheeling on* STAGG). Emmett Stagg, you phony bastard!

HUBRIS (*Crosses L. of* CURTIS. *To* CURTIS, *indignantly*). You should talk, you pickpocket! You copped the whole thing from your wife! (*Turning on* STAGG.) And you sold it to me! That makes you a receiver of stolen goods—a fence!

STAGG. I acted in all good faith! He told me he had a novel—

CURTIS (*Producing his brown paper package*). And so I have, right here!

HUBRIS. Then what are we all foompheting about? That's the property I bought—we've got a deal!

STAGG (*Turning to* CURTIS). By God, we have, haven't we?

LANCE (*Puffing, eyes on floor*). Is everything all right, Mr. Hubris?

HUBRIS (*Crosses R. of* LANCE. *Outraged*). What do you mean, all right? We caught you stealing a safe, young man! (*Righteous.*) Now, take that box upstairs and clear out while I still have pity on you. Go on. (*He gives* LANCE *a push toward door L. and latter totters out.* HUBRIS *turns, crosses R.*) Where's the story?

CURTIS (*Hands him brown package*). Here.

HUBRIS. We're going to make a bundle with this, boys.

GRACE (*Emerging from behind portal*). Oh, no, you won't, gentlemen. All you've got there is a hodge-podge of recipes from *Love and Knishes*.

HUBRIS (*Crosses L. of* GRACE). Then where *is* the novel?

GRACE. Right next to your ticker, where it's been reposing all along. Do you want to hand it over, or would you prefer the police to search you?

HUBRIS. Dear lady, we're all friends here. Why should we wash our dirty linen in public? (*Crosses R. of* STAGG. *Points to* STAGG.) He's got a contract to publish your book, Mrs. Fingerhead. I got a deal to make a blockbuster out of it. All we need is a top-flight screen writer. (*Points to* CURTIS.)

CURTIS. Gee, thanks, Harry.

GRACE (*Crosses L.*). Well, this has been a most profitable encounter. Shall we adjourn to the rumpus room for a libation on the altar of friendship. (*She exits L.*)

CURTIS (*Crosses L.*). I'll mix you my special long-life gimlet—Somerset Maugham's recipe. (*Exits L.*)

STAGG. Nothing like a drink when the day's work is done. Join me, Harry?

HUBRIS (*Crosses L.*). Emmett, it's a pleasure to do business with a momzer like you. (*As he takes the latter's arm to go.*) You know, regarding the picture—instead of two-eighty big ones, how about an escalator deal?

STAGG. How do you mean?

HUBRIS. A hundred bucks down and fifty percent of the Transylvania rights . . .

(*They start to exit U.L. as:*)

CURTAIN CLOSES

SCENE III

Scene: *Conservatory of the Pasadena estate of* NELSON SMEDLEY, *millionaire founder of the Smedley Snacketerias, a coast-to-coast restaurant chain. The set, a two-dimensional tracery of metal in the Art Nouveau style, is so constructed as to suggest glass behind it. Several exotic plants (philodendron and century plants intertwined with liana) ranged at front. At stage L., an ornamental high-backed Hong Kong rattan chair; at stage R., a stone bench.*

Time: *Three days later.*

At Rise: *Stage deserted. After a moment,* WORMSER, SMEDLEY's *private secretary, enters, beckoning to* LANCE, *who bears manila envelope under his arm.*

WORMSER (*Crosses C. with oily deference*). Right this way, Mr. Weatherwax, and welcome to Pasadena. Mr. Smedley was so delighted to get your telegram. (*Indicating bench.*) Do sit down, won't you?

LANCE (*Sits R.*). Thank you.

WORMSER (*Winningly*). I don't know *how* our restaurants could function without the Weatherwax All-Weather Garbage Disposal Plan.

LANCE. I'm not here representing the company, Mr. Wormser. It's about a television program I'm planning—

WORMSER. Oh, doesn't matter in the least—just having you drop in will be such a treat for the Commander. He'll be down as soon as he has his paraffin injection.

LANCE. Golly, is it ever hot in this conservatory here. It must be close to 95.

WORMSER. 112, actually, but one gets used to it in time. (*Extracting paper.*) Ah—just one trifle—this questionnaire you completed at the lower gate. Now, among your various clubs, you've listed something called the Y.C.L. (*Sudden harsh note.*) Now, what does that signify—the Young Communist League?

LANCE. Oh, no, sir—the Yale Camera Lovers. It was my extracurricular activity.

WORMSER. Of course, of course. But you do understand, we can't be too careful with all this subversion around. I'll fetch Mr. Smedley.

(*He exits L. As* LANCE *proceeds to examine plants,* APRIL *enters garbed in nurse's World War I uniform à la Edith Cavell, pushing wheeled medicine tray.*)

LANCE (*Rises*). April!

APRIL (*Crosses L. of* LANCE). Lance Weatherwax! Whatever in the world are you doing here? (*Before he can recover.*) The last time I saw you, you were standing in the middle of my living room creating a scene. I've a good mind not even to speak to you. (*Puts tray down.*)

LANCE. I wasn't to blame for that, April. I tried to explain, but you got me all rattled.

APRIL. And I can see you're still just as confused, dear boy. Why are you staring at me in that extraordinary fashion?

LANCE. Well—uh—you look different somehow—

APRIL (*On the seventh astral plane*). I *am* different, Lance—as utterly and totally different as can be from the person you used to know.

LANCE. I don't understand—

APRIL (*Infinitely patient, infinitely sweet*). Ah, there's so much you'll never understand, my dear. If I could only bring you to comprehend the change I've undergone. (*Sits L. chair.*) Lance, do you know what it's like to come under the influence of a truly dynamic individual?

LANCE (*Still smarting*). You mean that Rob Roy Fruitwell? (*Sits bench.*)

APRIL (*With contempt*). That hoodlum—of course not. I mean Nelson Smedley—the founder of Smedley Snacketerias.

LANCE. Well, I know he's a genius in the restaurant game—but what else does he do?

APRIL. He lives life to the fullest. He's vital—uncompromising. He rises above the drab, petty things of life. He inspires every single person around him to serve, to give unstintingly. But of course, you haven't any conception of what I'm talking about, poor boy. You're still the same sweet naïve creature.

LANCE (*Rises, crosses R. of* APRIL. *With warmth*). Oh, no, I'm not. I had some very rough experiences after I struck out for myself, April. I was pushed around and abused by all kinds of sharpers, like that Harry Hubris . . . but I've learned my lesson.

APRIL (*Patronizingly*). Which is what?

LANCE. To create my own opportunities (*Kneels R. of* APRIL.), to make myself worthy of you, April. I want to earn your respect—to prove myself, so that one day I can claim you.

APRIL. Oh, Lance, you have so far to go.

LANCE. No, no. (*Taps envelope.*) Wait till Mr. Smedley hears the idea I've got in this folder . . . about the Chocolate Soda Rhapsody! He'll flip, I guarantee you!

APRIL. Now I hope you're not going to upset him. (*Rises.*) Mr. Smedley is a very delicately balanced man.

(NELSON SMEDLEY, *supported by* WORMSER, *totters on. He wears a smoking jacket and skull-cap, is swathed in muffler, shawl and afghan.*)

WORMSER (*Enters L., U.S. of* SMEDLEY, *helping him*). Be careful, Mr. Smedley.

SMEDLEY (*Pulling his arm away*). Keep your paws off me! I can walk as good as the next man— (WORMSER *removes his arm, and* SMEDLEY *falls to the floor.* APRIL *crosses U.S. of* SMEDLEY. *They help him up.*) Pushed me again, didn't you? Always pushing—push, push, push, push— (*They cross to big chair,* WORMSER *L. and* APRIL *R.* WORMSER *helps him into his chair.*) Who turned off the heat? It's an icebox in here!

WORMSER. It's 118, Mr. Smedley. The putty's melting in the windows.

SMEDLEY. The hell with it. Tell the janitor to put on another coal.

WORMSER. But the boilers are red-hot.

SMEDLEY (*Agitated*). What? What's that about red? Who's red? There's reds in the house! Reds in the house!

WORMSER. No—no—it's all right. Don't get alarmed. . . . April, help me—

SMEDLEY and WORMSER. No—no! No—no! (APRIL *and* WORMSER *soothe* SMEDLEY, *lower him back into rattan chair.* SMEDLEY *meanwhile utters peevish whines and grunts like a baby teething. He suddenly catches sight of* LANCE.) Who's he? What's he after?

WORMSER. It's the young man who wired you, sir.

SMEDLEY. Did you screen him? (WORMSER *nods.*) There's a bulge in his pocket? It's round—it's a hand grenade—it's a hand grenade!

LANCE (*Producing orange*). No, sir, it's an orange. I found it on the lawn.

SMEDLEY (*Shrilly*). He tried to steal my orange! Stop, thief! Stop, thief!

WORMSER (*To* LANCE, *affrightedly*). Look, give it back—quick—

(*Ad libs*—APRIL, LANCE, WORMSER. LANCE *extends it to* SMEDLEY, *who burrows it into his coverings like a chipmunk, chattering his teeth.*)

APRIL (*Resentfully, to* LANCE). Now you got him all worked up. Aren't you ashamed?

LANCE. I'm sorry . . .

APRIL (*She removes pill from bottle, pours water from carafe, extends both to* SMEDLEY). All right, Commander dear. Down goes the liver spansule.

SMEDLEY (*Gritting his teeth*). No, no! Won't take it! Won't take it!

APRIL. There's a brave little boy.

SMEDLEY. Can't make me. Can't make me!

APRIL. All right, Mr. Stubborn—we won't have our five-o'clock romp.

SMEDLEY. I'll take it.

WORMSER (SMEDLEY *spits out pill*). Now, Commander! (*Maneuvering* LANCE *up to* SMEDLEY.) This is Lance Weatherwax, Commander—you know, the party you consented to see.

SMEDLEY (*Suspiciously*). He looks like the other one—the one that stole my orange. Stop, thief! Stop, thief!

WORMSER. No, that one went away. This is Milo Weatherwax's son.

SMEDLEY. Milo Weatherwax! Knew him well. We were the same class at Groton. Dirtiest feeder in the school—always covered with farina!

WORMSER. This is Milo Weatherwax's son.

LANCE (*Seeking to ingratiate*). My dad often mentions you, Mr. Smedley.

SMEDLEY. Yeah? Well, tell him to give me back that elastic supporter he borrowed. What do you want?

LANCE (*Withdraws place-mat from envelope*). Well, I tell you, sir. I've got a sensational idea. I happened to drop into one of your Snacketerias between here and Santa Barbara, and this place-mat caught my eye—

SMEDLEY. Hold on there! Stole that from one of my restaurants? Stop, thief!

WORMSER. No—no! That thief went away.

SMEDLEY. Oh? He went away?

LANCE. I bought it at the souvenir counter.

SMEDLEY. Check on that, Wormser.

LANCE. The thing is, sir—are you familiar with what it says? The text about the chocolate soda? Let me read it to you—

SMEDLEY (*Snatching it*). I can read, you young squirt. I went to Groton. (*As he starts to read his hands shake.* APRIL *and* WORMSER *steady him. Clears his throat volcanically.*) "Hymn to a Chocolate Soda." (*Hands shake again.* APRIL *and* WORMSER *steady him.*) Stop shaking! (*Returns to place-mat.*) "Arise, ye troubadours, and sing a song of nectar. See the great satin ball of mouth-watering mocha, the luscious bubbles whose every secret cell is pledged to arouse—" (*Breaks off abruptly.*) Secret cell? Wormser! Wormser, where are you?

WORMSER. Right here, Commander.

SMEDLEY. Who wrote this Commie propaganda? What's all this about cells?

WORMSER. I'll have that deleted pronto, sir. Don't you worry.

SMEDLEY (*Growling*). Musta been written by one of those wetbacks. Goddam aliens come in and use up all our paper towels. . . . Goddam foreigners—hang 'em all—hang 'em! Kill 'em—kill 'em all—goddam foreigners!

APRIL (*Indignantly, to* LANCE). Really, Lance, you deserve to be locked up, raising Mr. Smedley's blood pressure with such nonsense! } (*Ad libs.*)

LANCE. I wasn't trying to excite him—

SMEDLEY. Shut up—a man can hardly hear himself read. Where's all the printing? It went away! Now, where was I? You made me lose my place! Oh, here we are! (*Hands shake again.* WORMSER *and* APRIL *steady him. Returning to place-mat.*) "Now gird yourself for the climax supreme. Discard the straw, tilt back your head, and treat your tonsils to the celestial ambrosia of flavor, action and chill." (*He looks up.*) Who the hell wrote this?

WORMSER. You did, sir.

SMEDLEY. Fire 'em! Fire 'em!

WORMSER. No, you don't understand. You wrote it yourself.

SMEDLEY. Pretty good!

LANCE (*Eagerly*). Do you see it, sir? Do you get it?

SMEDLEY. What?

LANCE. It's a natural—the germ for a sensational TV documentary—a spectacular! "Rhapsody in Bubbles"—an hour TV program showing the importance of the ice-cream soda in our culture!

SMEDLEY. M-m-m, I don't know.

LANCE. Now, wait till you hear my production plans, sir! Step one—I send a crew to the high Andes to film the life cycle of the cocoa bean. (*Kneels R. of him.*) Step two—we move a unit into Hershey, Pennsylvania, and live with the syrup as it evolves. (SMEDLEY *falls asleep.*) Step three—the marriage of the siphon and the scoop. And mind you—that's only the background for the titles!

WORMSER (*Shakes* SMEDLEY). Commander!

SMEDLEY. Get away from me! I want to hear this. Might have possibilities. . . .

LANCE (*R. of* SMEDLEY. *Encouraged*). I haven't even touched the story, sir! We plant candid cameras in a drugstore—reproduce an actual *soda fountain* and for the music I see a really great score—Virgil Thomson—

SMEDLEY. No—no—no—no! That wouldn't sell a lemon phosphate! You haven't thought it through. (*Gives* LANCE *place-mat.*)

LANCE. In what way, Mr. Smedley?

SMEDLEY (*Pontifically*). Now let me tell you something, young man —the story of the ice-cream soda—is the story of Nelson Smedley. You gotta combine the two!

LANCE. By Jiminy, sir, that's a genuinely creative idea! You're dead right!

SMEDLEY. I'm always right! I'll tell you how it should be done. You open the program with me sitting on a big banana split, with a large chocolate float on each side. (*To* WORMSER.) What d'ye think of that, Wormser?

WORMSER. Commander, you want my honest opinion? The night they televise that, Khrushchev better barricade himself in the Kremlin!

(ALL *laugh*. SMEDLEY *goes suddenly to sleep.*)

LANCE (*Exultantly*). Boy oh boy, we'll knock 'em cold with that opening—won't we, April?

APRIL (*Crosses R., sits bench*). I really wouldn't know, Mr. Weatherwax.

LANCE (*Wakes up* SMEDLEY). Well, Mr. Smedley, what do you think? Would you sponsor a program like that?

SMEDLEY. I don't know. I'd have to see a budget first! The scenery alone could cost a fortune.

LANCE. That's right, Mr. Smedley. We've got to be practical about this. (SMEDLEY *back to sleep.*) What we want is an estimate for the entire production. I better get going. (*Turns to* APRIL.) April, I may have something pretty definite to say to you the next time we meet. . . . (*Turns back to* SMEDLEY, *taps his shoulder.*) I'll be reporting back to you shortly, Commander. (*He exits quickly.*)

SMEDLEY (*He wakes*). Who's that? What'd he steal?

WORMSER (*Calms him*). No, no, sir—that was the young man about the television show, Lance Weatherwax.

SMEDLEY (*Awakening*). Oh, yes—yes. Milo's boy. Seems a pretty bright fella. . . .

APRIL. Yes, you always bring out the best in people, Commander. It's fabulous the way you handle them. You instinctively sense what they want.

SMEDLEY. Damn tootin'. That's why I drew up that document this morning.

APRIL. What document?

SMEDLEY. Tell her, Wormser.

WORMSER (*Crosses R. of* SMEDLEY). Well, Mr. Smedley felt that inasmuch as you've behaved with such devotion and selflessness, he ought to take cognizance of it.

APRIL. Oh, Nelson, you shouldn't have. Your gratitude is enough reward.

WORMSER. So he's left you his old watch-fob—and the rest of his money goes to the fight against Social Security.

APRIL. He WHAT?

SMEDLEY. That's right, honeybun.

APRIL. You're . . . you're joking.

SMEDLEY. Never joke about money, dumpling.

APRIL (*Rises*). Why, you—you— That's the last straw! I gave up everything for you. My emotional life, my career, my friends. And for what? (*Crosses L.*) I won't remain in this house a moment longer! (*Turns R.*) I wouldn't demean myself! (*She exits outraged.*)

SMEDLEY. He he he! A clever little minx, but they have to get up early in the morning to pull the wool over Nelson Smedley.

WORMSER. They sure do. (*Glancing at watch.*) Well, Commander, it's almost three.

SMEDLEY. Yup—time to watch television. Help me up, Wormser (*He helps him up, R. of him.*), and we'll go see who we can blacklist. (SMEDLEY *pulls his arm away.*) Get your paws off me! I can walk as good as the next man!

(WORMSER *removes his arm and* SMEDLEY *crashes to the floor once again.*)

BLACKOUT

(*And* CURTAIN *opens into:*)

SCENE IV

Scene: A corner workshop, the Whirlaway Scenic Studios in Los Angeles. The deeper end of the set, L., contains a little of flats, lumber, and scenery paint pots. At R., a sculptor's workstand displaying the head of a collie carved from soap; beside it a taboret with chisel, mallet, etc. Exit to shop far R.
  Time: *Noon, two days later.*
  At Rise: ROWENA INCHCAPE, *a matron in her advanced thirties, is engaged in work on the collie's head. She is garbed in a green smock, has an uncompromising henna-colored Dutch bob, wears heavy horn-rimmed spectacles. A short pause, and* LANCE *enters uncertainly.*

  LANCE (*In door*). Pardon me, would this be the Whirlaway Scenic Studios?
  ROWENA (*Without looking up*). It would.
  LANCE. They said you build displays for parades and department stores—all kinds of floats—
  ROWENA. They hit the bull's-eye.
  LANCE. Then this is the place. I'm Lance Weatherwax.
  ROWENA. Hallelujah. I'm Rowena Inchcape. (*She resumes work with her spatula.* LANCE *draws nearer, his interest in her sculpture plainly aroused.*)
  LANCE. Excuse me. Is that an actual portrait, or more of an idealized conception, like?
  ROWENA. Half and half. I based it on our Timmy. He passed over several weeks ago.
  LANCE. Oh—I'm sorry.
  ROWENA. It was about time, if you ask me. He was twenty-three.
  LANCE. You don't say. (*Crosses L. Sympathetically.*) Did he die of natural causes?
  ROWENA (*On step*). No, he fell down a well. Nobody's been able to drink out of it since. (*She regards* LANCE *steadily for a moment, nods toward sculpture.*) Do you like it?
  LANCE. Well, you certainly got a good likeness. Of course, I never knew Timmy. . . .

ROWENA. You bet you didn't. If he were alive, you'd never be standing there. He'd have torn you limb from limb.

LANCE. They're great pets, collies. I guess his death was a real loss.

ROWENA. I can't imagine to whom. He bit everybody, right up to the man who chloroformed him.

LANCE. I . . . I understood you to say he fell down a well.

ROWENA. After they chloroformed him. That's how ornery he was. (*Appraising him coolly over her shoulder.*) But I suppose you're one of those sentimentalists who get mushy about animals.

LANCE. Yes, ma'am—I mean, no, ma'am. . . . May I ask what medium you're using there?

ROWENA. Soap—castile soap. I'm doing it on a Procter & Gamble Fellowship. (*Crosses U.S. behind dogs.*)

LANCE. A head like that must take quite a few bars.

ROWENA. There's enough here to wash a family of fifteen.

LANCE. I always wonder how creative people get started. Were you interested in sculpture from a child?

ROWENA. No, it was an afterthought. I had a joint on Hollywood Boulevard where I eternalized baby shoes.

LANCE. I beg pardon?

ROWENA. Dipped 'em in bronze for ashtrays and souvenirs.

LANCE. But that didn't fulfill you, I guess. The artist is a special case.

ROWENA. The artist is a leech. (*Starts down to second step.*) Scratch any one of 'em and you'll find there's money from home.

LANCE. Ah, that's most interesting. Tell me, which way from here is the float department?

ROWENA. I don't read you, stranger. (*Crosses down steps to front of platform.*)

LANCE. I'm interested in placing a quite sizable order. I have in mind a banana split approximately eighteen feet long and twelve feet high.

ROWENA. How deep?

LANCE (*Crosses D.S.*). Oh, only about six or eight inches. . . .

ROWENA. I see. Do you want nuts on it . . . or just the usual whipped cream?

LANCE. I don't think I've made myself clear. That's only part of it. I also need a chocolate float on each side, maybe—oh, thirty feet high.

ROWENA. Listen, Tom, you're a nice upstanding kid. Why don't you kick that nose candy? There's no future in it.

LANCE. Oh, no—you don't understand. You see, I'm doing this TV spectacular—"Rhapsody in Bubbles"—for Mr. Smedley—you know—of Smedley's Snacketerias.

ROWENA (*Crosses L.*). Look, you're telling me more than I want to know.

LANCE. We have this great opening shot of Mr. Smedley posed against this banana split.

ROWENA. Yeah, yeah. What did you say your name was? Weather what?

LANCE. Wax.

ROWENA. Look, Wax. I only rent studio space here for my work. The party you want is Rukeyser, the foreman of this drop. Hey, Virgil! Well, Tom, nice to talk to you. Good luck with the spec.

(RUKEYSER *enters.*)

RUKEYSER. What's up, Rowena?

ROWENA (*Crosses L. of* RUKEYSER). This civilian's got problems. Get out your slide rule. Abbadabba. (*She exits L.*)

RUKEYSER. O.K., sonny. What's bugging you?

LANCE (*D.S. of steps*). Well, I've got a two-float order, Mr. Rukeyser, and I need an estimate for it—I had some rough drawings made to show you. Here— (*He spreads them on the floor.*)

(As RUKEYSER, *with a long-suffering sigh, bends to examine the drawings,* WAGNERIAN *bursts on from L.*)

WAGNERIAN (*Crosses D.S.*). Now look here, Mr. Rukeyser, I am calling my union.

RUKEYSER (*Rises, crosses R. of* WAGNERIAN). Just a minute, sonny. What's the matter now, Wagnerian? Isn't the pie finished?

WAGNERIAN. How can I spray on the white of egg until I know if the mechanism works?

RUKEYSER. We're waiting for the broad they ordered for the stag banquet. The clients are coming over for a demo.

WAGNERIAN. She's here! (*Crosses L.*) She's been cooling her heels for thirty minutes. . . .

RUKEYSER. Then tell her to get undressed.

WAGNERIAN (*Turns R.*). I can't do that! I'm engaged!

RUKEYSER. Do I have to do everything around here? Handle the clients—run after strippers—?

WAGNERIAN. Very well! . . . But I'm calling my union! (*Exits L.*)

(*As* RUKEYSER, *with a long-suffering sigh, bends to examine the drawings,* GODDARD QUAGMEYER, *followed by a* GIRL, *enters R. He is a changed man; his manner is brash and assertive, and sartorially he has become a Hollywood peacock. The* GIRL *is a standard film-colony bimbo.*)

QUAGMEYER (*Crosses R. of C.* GIRL *stays R.*). Listen, Rukeyser, what's with those blueprints I sent over for the waterfall set?
RUKEYSER (*To* QUAGMEYER). Hiya, Quagmeyer! Didn't you get my message?

(QUAGMEYER *crosses L.*)

LANCE (*Rises. Reacting*). Mr. Quagmeyer!
QUAGMEYER (*Waving him aside*). Please, no autographs! . . . We've lost two days' shooting already!
RUKEYSER. I told you—we ran into complications—
QUAGMEYER. For God's sake! An ordinary fifty-foot waterfall with some iridescent rocks!
RUKEYSER. Where the hell do I get the mother-of-pearl for the rainbow?
QUAGMEYER. Call up a button factory—a jewelry-supply house—how do I know? I've got enough aggravation.
RUKEYSER (*Aggrievedly*). And my life is a peach Melba, I suppose!
LANCE. Mr. Quagmeyer—
QUAGMEYER. I told you I was busy, didn't I?
LANCE. Don't you remember me, sir? Lance Weatherwax?
QUAGMEYER (*Turns. Crosses L. of* LANCE, *pats his shoulders*). Bubby! What are you doing out here?
LANCE. I'm a producer.
QUAGMEYER. It figures. Anything can happen in Tomorrowland. Look at me. (*Crosses L. of* GIRL. *To* GIRL.) The last time this joker saw me, I was schmeering my heart out in a New York tenement—I was so hung up on art and all that fakery, I'd have been there yet if it wasn't for him.
LANCE. For me?
QUAGMEYER. That's right! Remember the day you bawled me out—said I had integrity poisoning?

LANCE. Did I say that?

QUAGMEYER. Yeah. That sank home, Weatherwax. I brooded over it all night and finally realized what a fool I was. Yes, siree, you gave me a whole fresh set of values.

LANCE. But I didn't mean—

QUAGMEYER (*Boisterously*). Who cares what you meant? (*Crosses R. to L. of* GIRL.) All I know is I've got a five-year contract at Fox, a white Jag, and the sweetest little head since Helen Twelvetrees.

GIRL (*Slaps his hand away*). Is this your idea of a fun time, shooting the breeze in a junk shop?

QUAGMEYER. All right, gorgeous, we go toot sweet. (*Smirks at* LANCE. QUAGMEYER *crosses* R.) You see? I'm her slave. . . . Well, thanks again, fella, be seeing you. If you ever feel like a hot meal, just contact me through my flesh peddler, Monroe Sweetmeat, which he handles Rob Roy Fruitwell and all the biggies.

(*He waves, exits with* GIRL. RUKEYSER *turns back to* LANCE.)

RUKEYSER (*L. of* LANCE). All right, bud, what's your pleasure? I haven't got all day.

LANCE (*Kneeling by the drawings again*). We need an exact replica of a chocolate float in duplicate, Mr. Rukeyser.

(WAGNERIAN *and* ELMO *appear, wheeling a large papier-mâché pie, roughly five feet in diameter by twenty inches deep, on a dolly.* ELMO R. *of pie.*)

WAGNERIAN (*L. of pie*). Sure, it's heavy. You put a zoftick dame in a deep dish pie and you've got engineering problems.

RUKEYSER (*Crosses R. of pie. Pushing* ELMO *aside*). O.K., Elmo, I'll handle this. (*To* WAGNERIAN, *as* ELMO *exits.*) I hope she can breathe in there.

WAGNERIAN. She's in clover. I put in plenty of air holes.

RUKEYSER. Well, as long as the mechanism works. If it don't we got a nice little lawsuit on our hands.

(HENNEPIN *and* POTEAT, *two gentlemen of distinct executive bearing, in homburgs, enter.*)

HENNEPIN. Mr. Rukeyser?

RUKEYSER (*Turns, steps R.*). Speaking.

HENNEPIN. I'm Hennepin of the banquet committee.

POTEAT (*Crosses R. of* RUKEYSER). And I'm Poteat. You know—the send-off we're giving Floyd Geduldig, our associate in the utilities field?

(WAGNERIAN *crosses D.L. of pie.*)

RUKEYSER. Yep. Well, there's your prop, but let me tell you, brother, it's the last pie I build without specifications.

WAGNERIAN. The whole thing was guesswork.

HENNEPIN. No doubt, no doubt. (*Crosses L. Major Hoople cough.*) However, in such a delicate matter, you can't very well expect us to put anything on paper.

POTEAT. The slightest breath of a scandal . . .

RUKEYSER. What's scandalous? You're throwing a feed where a bimbo comes out of a pie and dances with a gorilla. Whose business is that?

HENNEPIN. Ha ha—quite—of course. (*Inspects pie critically.*) Frankly, Mr. Rukeyser, I envisioned something a good deal smaller, with a real biscuit crust.

POTEAT. We were planning to distribute a wedge to everybody after the lady pops out.

RUKEYSER. Biscuit crust? Are you nuts? How would she pop out if she's laying under ninety pounds of dough reinforced with chicken wire?

HENNEPIN. He's got a point, Poteat—it does sound a bit unwieldy. Will this cover of yours lift off readily?

RUKEYSER. Watch. (*Calling offstage.*) Start the music!

(*He presses a button on exterior of pie; the crust jackknifes skyward, and* APRIL MONKHOOD, *clad in the world's scantiest bikini, springs forth.* RUKEYSER, WAGNERIAN *help* APRIL *out of pie.*)

APRIL. Whee! (*She dances a few sinuous steps, climaxing in a bump as* LANCE *gapes at her open-mouthed. Then she turns upstage as a figure clad in super-realistic* GORILLA *costume emerges from behind flat. The latter seizes her in his arms and they execute short tango routine Downstage, at climax of which* GORILLA *bends* APRIL *backward.* APRIL, *carried away, moans in ecstasy.*) Bombo—you're crushing me in your mighty arms! Release me, Bombo!

RUKEYSER. She's a mental case! Stop the music, stop the music!

LANCE. April!

APRIL (*Blinking as she regains perspective*). Lance Weatherwax? Whatever in the world are you doing here?

HENNEPIN (*Crosses L. of* APRIL; POTEAT R. *of* LANCE). O.K.—That's jim-dandy. (*Producing card-case briskly.*) Los Angeles Vice Squad. Young lady, you're under arrest for conspiracy to come out of a pie and dance with a gorilla.

(RUKEYSER, WAGNERIAN *and* GORILLA *push pie off* L.)

APRIL. Why, you rotten, contemptible slobs—

(APRIL *crosses* R. POTEAT *stops her* R. *of* LANCE. *She turns to flee;* POTEAT *grabs her wrist,* LANCE *springs forward to unhand* APRIL.)

LANCE (*L. of April*). Let go of her, you!

HENNEPIN (*Crosses R. of* APRIL. *Thrusts him aside*). Lay off, punk, or we'll take you along, too!

LANCE. You're going to regret this, you wait! That lady's innocent.

POTEAT. Yeah, it's another Dreyfus case. (*Yanks* APRIL's *wrist.*) Come on. You can explain it all to Judge Rinderbrust. (*Starts off* R.)

LANCE. Oh, April, how could you ever get involved in such a sordid awful mess?

APRIL (*Crosses R. of* LANCE. HENNEPIN, POTEAT *follow*). Don't you criticize me, you mealy-mouth! I'd never have been here if it wasn't for you!

LANCE. For me?

APRIL. That's right! You rejected me at my darkest hour—I offered you love and understanding—

HENNEPIN (*They pull her* R. *Impatiently*). Get going—you're breaking my heart.

APRIL (*Crosses R. of* LANCE. HENNEPIN *and* POTEAT *follow her. Hysterically, to* LANCE). Go back to your polo ponies, you rotten little poseur! You're nothing but a dilettante—a playboy! And you can marry the whole Social Register for all I care—I hate you!

(HENNEPIN *and* POTEAT *drag her off.* LANCE *stands overwhelmed a moment.*)

LANCE (*Crosses L. With a groan*). Oh, my God—what kind of a selfish, spoiled brat have I been? Nelson Smedley and his chocolate soda be damned! I've got to save the woman I love!

(*Squaring his jaw, he rushes off, and we segue to:*)

SCENE V

Scene: *A courtroom in the Los Angeles Hall of Justice.*
Time: *Three days later.*
At Rise: A TELEVISION MAN *pushes on a camera.* SECRETARY *and* HANRATTY *enter L.*

CAMERA MAN (*Crosses R. of* HANRATTY). Bring it in—push the dimmer up, Voltage. Where the hell's Judge Rinderbrust? We go on the air at one o'clock sharp.

HANRATTY (*Crosses R. of* CAMERA MAN). He's officiating at a baby derby in Cucamonga. Probably got caught in traffic. Don't worry about Herman J. Rinderbrust. In addition to being the foremost jurist in Southern California, he's all show biz. Kefauver and McClellan pointed the way, but Rinderbrust put the cherry on the parfait. (*Crosses up to desk.*) Real-life court cases—living offenders tried before your very eyes. (*Crosses R. of* CAMERA MAN.)

CAMERA MAN (*Crosses to camera*). We go on network at ten a.m., East Coast time. If we got to throw in *The Mark of* Zorro once more, the agency'll have our heads.

HANRATTY. Rinderbrust'll be here. He's a real trouper.

(JUDGE RINDERBRUST *hurries on clad in his judicial robes.*)

JUDGE (*Crosses R. Angrily*). See here, Hanratty, I get a new makeup man by air-time tomorrow, or I don't go on!

HANRATTY (*Crosses R.*). I'll call the account exec right after the session, your Honor.

JUDGE. That flunkey! Don't deal with ribbon clerks. Call the sponsor direct!

HANRATTY. Yes, sir.

JUDGE (*Crosses R. of* HANRATTY). And burn his keyster about that feature story in *TV Guide*. It's cheapening. (*Patting toupee girlishly.*) By the way, Hanratty, how do you like the new rug? Mrs. Rinderbrust says it makes me look like David Susskind.

HANRATTY. The women viewers'll eat it up.

JUDGE (*Thoughtfully*). We won't know till the mail starts coming in . . . O.K., what's on the docket?

HANRATTY (*Reads from pad*). Just routine stuff, except for a murder charge and a conspiracy to come out of a pie and dance with a gorilla.

JUDGE. Um—gorilla dancer—not bad. I'll throw the book at her. Should goose the rating. (*Crosses R.*) What's the commercial for today!

HANRATTY (*Producing cue-cards*). The usual for Respighi's Bubble Gum—and a new splot for Glo-in-the-Dark Falsies.

JUDGE. Glo-in-the-Dark Falsies? Out, out—I don't plug any product I don't believe in.

(BAILIFF *enters, sits in his chair.*)

CAMERA MAN. Thirty seconds to air and we've got a new advertiser, the Elysian Fields Cemetery Guild in the 1100 block on Lankershim Boulevard.

JUDGE (*Crosses R. to L. of* CAMERA MAN). Cemetery? What are you talking about? I own a row of stores on that block.

HANRATTY. It's the property out back.

JUDGE. Out back is a bog, ten feet under water. A stiff wouldn't last a day in there.

HANRATTY. They're piping the water into fountains, with colored lights. It's a great effect—like Mardi Gras.

JUDGE. Well, that's different. I'll buy that, so long as it's dignified.

CAMERA MAN. Judge Rinderbrust! Ten seconds to air! (JUDGE *crosses to bench—looking at mirror held by* HANRATTY.) Five, four . . . three . . . two . . . whoof!

JUDGE (*Into camera*). Good morning, fellow-citizens, and welcome to *The Scales of Justice*—the only program that brings you real law-breakers, malefactors and hoodlums—people like yourselves in a peck of trouble. Yours, truly, Judge Herman J. Rinderbrust starring! (*Raps gavel.*) All right—bring on the first culprit.

(POLICEMAN *enters from L., crosses L. of bench.* ROXANA, *in skimpy nurse's uniform, follows to front of witness chair.*)

BAILIFF. The people of the State of California, the County of Los Angeles, versus Miss Roxana DeVilbiss.

JUDGE (*Licking his lips*). And what's the charge against this little transgressor?

BAILIFF (*Sitting*). Operating an unlicensed massage parlor.

JUDGE (*Regards* ROXANA's *garb intently*). So you're a masoose, are you? My, what a lovely turtle-neck sweater.

ROXANA (*Indignant hauteur*). Your Honor (*Sits.*), this is a miscarriage of justice! I'm a respectable college grad—the Slenderola Body Institute in San Berdoo. (*Leans forward.*)

JUDGE. This court has a very warm feeling towards San Berdoo. They raise the largest casabas in the West.

ROXANA. Thank you, Judge. Now, me and my colleagues at the Idle Hour Massage Parlour— (*Skirt over knee.*) —perform a very important role in the community.

JUDGE. You restore men's souls as well as their bodies—right?

ROXANA. Exactly! By what we call psycho-massage.

JUDGE (*Emotionally*). You nurse your fellow man back to health, you bring roses to his cheeks.

ROXANA. Oh, definitely, Judge!

JUDGE. In short, you rediscovered the Fountain of Youth.

ROXANA. Yes!

JUDGE (*Angrily*). And for this those lousy Puritans—those keyhole peepers—seek to penalize you! (*Turns majestically into camera.*) Ladies and gentlemen of the TV audience, I want you to look upon this tiny defendant, and I want you to remember another frail little person without a license—Florence Nightingale. (*Rising.*) As long as I wear these judicial robes, the sovereign state of California will remain a haven and a refuge for all healers of the feminine gender, with or without certificates! Case dismissed.

ROXANA. Gee, Herman, you've been a peach.

JUDGE. I'll drop in at your store to see that my orders are carried out.

ROXANA. I'll tell the girls!

BAILIFF (*As* ROXANA *exits*). The People of the State of California, the County of Los Angeles, versus Joe Gourielli, alias the Truth Swami, Haroun Azeez.

(GOURIELLI *enters, clad in tuban and business suit.*)

JUDGE (*With papers*). Swami, you're charged with creating a public disturbance. On the night of the 24th, at the intersection of La Paloma and Alta Yenta, you did willfully stage a human sacrifice. Think fast, Gourielli.

SWAMI. The sacrifice, yes—the disturbance, no. The Apostles got over-heated and started to grab souvenirs from the funeral pyre.

JUDGE (*Outraged*). Who do you think you are, knocking off citizens like they are clay pigeons!

SWAMI. They're followers!

JUDGE. Makes no difference! This is America, Gourielli, and everybody's entitled to four square meals, a second car, and the right to croak when he sees fit—not when some wog sets fire to him. This is an extremely grave offense.

HANRATTY (*Anxiously, with papers*). Judge, just a minute. (*Faces camera.*) Ladies and gentlemen, while the Judge is pondering the facts of the case, we pause briefly for station identification. (*To* JUDGE.) Don't be too tough on him, Judge. Remember, our new sponsor, the Elysian Fields Cemetery Guild.

JUDGE. By Jove, you're right! We mustn't discourage business. This zombie is good for forty plots a week. Give me a close-up. (BAILIFF *holds up mirror.* JUDGE *looks, slaps his hand away.* HANRATTY *gets cue card from R. Holds it high over camera from rear.* JUDGE *climbs on stool to read it.* HANRATTY *then stoops down in front of camera.* JUDGE *tries to read.*) Ladies and gentlemen—on due— (*To* HANRATTY.) I'm reading your thumb. (HANRATTY *crosses to U.S. of camera.* JUDGE *reads; into camera.*) Ladies and gentlemen—on due consideration, everybody's entitled to religious freedom and to a fine, decent funeral at reasonable prices. If you have a loved one who has recently given up the ghost, insure their future through the Elysian Fields Cemetery Guild. Make their journey to the Happy Hunting Grounds a memorable experience for relatives and cadaver alike. (*Carried away, he starts to sing "Dear Old Girl," stops himself. To* SWAMI.) All right, Gourielli, back to your devotions but keep your nose clean.

(GOURIELLI *exits L.*)

BAILIFF. Miss April Monkhood. Charged with conspiracy to come out of a pie and dance with a gorilla. (APRIL *has entered, clad in virginal coat.*)

JUDGE. Ah, the Gorilla Dancer! (*Into camera.*) Television viewers . . . once in every jurist's career, he is confronted by a case so shocking that the mind reels. The one you are about to witness surpasses anything in my vast experience. The culprit did knowingly plot and agree with accomplices unknown, to emerge from a pastry and engage in a lascivious dance with an anthropoid. Behavior like this would have the most dubious effect on your American womanhood, and I, as its legal guardian, intend to squelch it root, branch, lock, stock, and barrel. (*Turns to* APRIL.) Now, then, young woman, what do you have to say for yourself?

APRIL (*Crosses, sits witness chair*). I was tricked, your Honor. They claimed it was an experiment.

JUDGE. None of your shilly-shally. How do you plead—guilty or not?

(A *hubbub at* L. *from which emerge voices of* BAILIFF *and* LANCE *as latter struggles to enter.*)

BAILIFF. Stand back there, you!

LANCE. I'm involved in this case, I tell you! Let me } (*Ad libs.*) in!

JUDGE. Who's that? What does he want?

LANCE (*Struggling*). Judge Rinderbrust—please! I've got to talk to you!

JUDGE (*Beckoning*). Come up here. (*Severely.* LANCE *crosses* L. *of* C.) Look here, you, you're in a court of law. What do you mean, creating this uproar?

LANCE. I want to testify for the defendant, Your Honor—

JUDGE. Have you got any new evidence?

LANCE (*Emotionally*). Your Honor, you're making a terrible mistake! This lady's innocent—I've known her for years. She's a distinguished artist . . . a cultivated, refined person. . . .

JUDGE. Don't waste my time with character references! Produce your evidence!

LANCE. I saw the performance, Judge—there was nothing offensive in it! She did a little dance—

JUDGE (*Raps his gavel—rises majestically*). Now you listen to me, young fellow. The law explicitly states, *ex parte* and *nolens-volens*, that he who comes into court with clean hands is *sub judice* prejudiced *a priori*. In other words, "*Exceptio probat regulam de rebus non exceptis.*" Once and for all, before I pronounce sentence on the accused—have you any evidence relevant and germane in this matter?

LANCE (*Produces an envelope*). I have, your Honor.

JUDGE. Well, give. Hand it to the clerk of the court. (LANCE *gives envelope to* BAILIFF.) But I warn you, there are no extenuating circumstances in this case. Okay, what does it say?

BAILIFF (*Takes envelope, extracts checks, reads*). "Pay to the order of Herman J. Rinderbrust—five hundred thousand dollars. Signed, Octavia Weatherwax."

JUDGE (*Thwacking gavel*). Case dismissed!

(APRIL *and* LANCE *react joyfully, dissolve into embrace. As* JUDGE RINDERBRUST *raises his hands in benediction over them, a couple of* PRESS PHOTOGRAPHERS *run on, blaze away at the couple with flash bulbs, as we segue into:*)

SCENE VI

Scene: *The Weatherwax Library.*
Time: *One month later.*
At Rise: APRIL, *a bride's headdress and veil surmounting her head, stands arm-in-arm with* LANCE, *both their faces set in the strained grimace of the conventional society wedding photograph. The two* PRESS PHOTOGRAPHERS *crouch at opposite angles, aiming their cameras.* OCTAVIA *fidgets impatiently nearby. In background,* MRS. LAFCADIO MIFFLIN, *a majestic dowager well-boned over the diaphragm, with avian headgear and a froth of ruching at her throat, alertly observes the tableau.*

FIRST PHOTOGRAPHER. Hold it!
SECOND PHOTOGRAPHER. O.K., now—personality! Just one more!

(*Their flash bulbs explode.* OCTAVIA *steps between them.*)

OCTAVIA (*From R., moves chair D.S. Imperiously*). All right, gentlemen, that's quite sufficient. You've held up the wedding rehearsal long enough. (*Crosses D.S. of couch, moves with* APRIL, LANCE *as they go off.*) Run along, children, it's almost time—I'll be along directly.

(PHOTOGRAPHERS *mumble ad-lib thanks, exit. As* LANCE *and* APRIL *hurry off in opposite directions,* MRS. MIFFLIN *joins* OCTAVIA.)

MRS. MIFFLIN (*Crosses back of C. chair, rubs finger along top of chair for dust*). Octavia, love. Your daughter-in-law couldn't be more captivating.

OCTAVIA. Oh, Milo and I are enraptured with her.

MRS. MIFFLIN (*Sits R. end of couch*). And so well-bred for a theatrical person.

OCTAVIA (*Crosses L. end of couch. Tinkly little laugh. Crosses behind couch*). My dear, that phase of April's was just puppy fat. Started way back when she was a senior in Miss Hewitt's classes.

MRS. MIFFLIN. I thought you said she was at Foxcroft.

OCTAVIA (*Crosses R. back of couch to R. end. Adroitly*). Both, darling—you know how volatile these girls are nowadays. Well, her mother was determined to send her to Bryn Mawr, of course—family tradition—

MRS. MIFFLIN. Was that Alicia Monkhood who captained the field hockey there in Tucky's year?

OCTAVIA (*Crosses behind chair, sits chair*). Oh, no, this was the Scottish branch. They derive from Llewellyn Fitzpoultice, ninth Viscount Zeugma.

MRS. MIFFLIN (*Nodding*). Of course. That's where she gets that fair English skin.

OCTAVIA (*Crosses L.*). And her willfulness, dear child. Nothing would do— (*Rises.*) but she must run off and join Martha Graham's troupe— (*Pulls MIFFLIN up.*) and when Lance saw her at Jacob's Pillow, he naturally fell head.

MRS. MIFFLIN (*Crosses R. with OCTAVIA. Pouting*). Wretch. I still think you might have shared the secret with your eldest friend.

OCTAVIA (*Hurried kiss, maneuvering her off*). You'd have spread it all over Prout's Neck—you know you would.

MRS. MIFFLIN. Shall we see you at the Dingbats' Thursday?

OCTAVIA. No, I believe Milo's tied up that night at the Luxor Baths.

MRS. MIFFLIN. Well, tell him how happy we are for the both of you. (*Fluting as she exits R.*) Good-bye—ee-ee. . . .

(LANCE *and* APRIL *reappear, his demeanor clearly rebellious.*)

LANCE (*Crosses R. of chair;* APRIL *crosses L. of couch*). Gosh, Mater, do we have to go through all this mumbo-jumbo?

OCTAVIA. Indeed you must, and you may as well put a good face on it.

LANCE. But the things that really matter are spiritual—aren't they, April dearest?

APRIL (*Guardedly*). Well . . .

OCTAVIA (*Crosses front of couch*). Lance, darling, you talk like a sausage. The things that matter are objects one can touch—viz. and to wit, diamonds and furs and blue chip securities. Only we on the distaff side understand that. (*Sits R. end of couch.*)

APRIL (*Crosses front of couch to L. of chair and back of couch*). You sure are cooking on the front burner. I may be horribly naïve, but blindfolded in a London fog, I can tell mink from stone marten, and it's all thanks to you, Mother Weatherwax! (*Sits couch.*)

OCTAVIA (*Graciously*). I like your spirit, April. My first reaction when our son brought you home to our stylish Park Avenue triplex was that you were a cheap little tramp. Nothing you've done since has caused me to alter that opinion.

APRIL. Thank you, Mother Weatherwax.

OCTAVIA. But what can be keeping Milo?

LANCE. What Milo is that?

OCTAVIA. Why, your father, which he is probably handling the management reins of our far-flung interests.

MILO (*Entering briskly from R., kisses* OCTAVIA's *hand*). Wrong as per usual, my pet. A young protegée of mine—a geology student— was showing me some rare stones over at Cartier's.

OCTAVIA (*Acidly*). And you totally forgot the surprise we are giving Lance.

MILO. Applesauce. The relevant documents repose inside this very envelope. (*Extracts same.*) Lance, I hope your creative Odyssey has taught you something.

LANCE (*R. of chair*). It did, sir. I found there's an awful lot of prejudice against money. Especially from people that don't have any.

MILO. They should be machine-gunned.

OCTAVIA. Hear, hear!

APRIL. You can say that again!

MILO. I will! They should be machine-gunned. (*Crosses L. of* LANCE.) But paradoxically, Lance, you also have a responsibility to them.

LANCE. I don't dig you, Guv.

MILO. It's up to you to stamp out that prejudice tooth and nail. (*Handing him envelope.*) My boy, I've set up a mighty foundation in your name—tax free—to bring culture into every American home.

LANCE (*Glowing*). Gee, Dads, me—the final arbiter of truth and beauty!

MILO. You may meet resistance to your concept of what's clean and straight and fine, but if you do, just cram it down their throats.

LANCE (*Crosses R. of* MILO). Will do, Dad!

MILO (*Crosses D.C.*). But remember that in this weary old world, there's one value that transcends all others.

(ROXANA DEVILBISS, *in nurse's uniform, enters* R. *bearing fancy baby basket trailing swaddling clothes. She passes it to* LANCE, *who transfers it to* MILO.)

OCTAVIA. Why, Milo, there's a suspicious moisture in your eye.

MILO. Yes, I'll 'fess up to same, hardened cynic though I am. (*Clears throat.*) Friends, this little bundle of happiness is everybody's joy. We must cherish it—share it with us, won't you?

(*As he tilts basket forward, revealing it crammed with green-backs, dips into it and starts broadcasting it over* LANCE *and* APRIL *like confetti:*)

CURTAIN

ON
The Beauty
Part

Within the New York theater community, there is an unofficial but loyal confraternity of people who saw *The Beauty Part*, loved *The Beauty Part*, and to this day derive enormous pleasure from swapping fond remembrances of *The Beauty Part*. "I'm always running into people who saw that show," someone who was connected with the production told me. "Their faces light up and they want to talk about how great it was. And we always wind up playing: do-you-remember-the-bit-where . . . It's crazy—it's like having been together at Krakatoa, or something."

Although each play in this collection is a nonpareil, nevertheless, there is something additionally remarkable about *The Beauty Part*, which was written by S. J. Perelman, starred Bert Lahr, opened at the Music Box on December 26, 1962, and closed some two months later. Even by standards of the blasé Broadway community, the production remains a unique event in theater annals. It was that ironic phenomenon, that rare bird—the hit that failed.

The circumstances of that failure are interesting enough when examined individually, but when one considers that each separate element dovetailed into the next, the saga of the production life and death of *The Beauty Part* really takes on the aspect of a complex and not unmoving drama—a miniature comi-tragedy that reveals much that is inept, rigid, and simply unfair about the Broadway system.

Because it opened during the debilitating New York newspaper strike of 1962–63, *The Beauty Part* illustrates first of all the truly crucial importance of the daily press to the health of the theater industry. Secondly, because it was critically caught between two interim book- ings, the show also illustrates the complexities of producing and man- aging a Broadway show—a single judgmental error on the part of a pro- ducer, and even a popular show can lose its momentum and suddenly fold. Finally, because the comedy is a satire, and one whose pungent wit is aimed directly at the class of people who comprise the bulk of the general Broadway audience, *The Beauty Part* is eloquent proof of the extraordinary difficulties faced by nonformula shows trying to suc- ceed within Broadway's conventionally structured producing system.

No analysis of Perelman's play will succeed in conveying the sheer hilarity of the 1962 production. It was a mad show, a happy marriage of the most refined wit with the most insane low-comedy traditions. It was eighteenth-century rococo literary humor laced with pit humor. It was the world of baroque in tandem with the world of burlesque. It was a howl.

Structurally, the plot is sublime chaos. In a series of loosely con- nected scenes, the play follows the picaresque adventures of a modern- day Candide named Lance Weatherwax. Lance is the son of a mil- lionaire garbage-disposal manufacturer who rejects his father's tradi- tional values and goes off in search of the *real* meaning of life. His quest for ultimate truth and beauty leads him to Art—actually, to *all* the arts, which he assaults one by one in his pursuit of the eternal verities. To his utter disillusionment, the innocent lamb discovers that Art and Artists have all been corrupted by society and have become commodities just like everything and everyone else within the contem- porary cultural system. Finally, chastened by his experimental educa- tion, Lance returns to embrace his father's values—religious worship of the omnipotence, beauty, truth, and goodness of the American dollar— which, as the boy has discovered, is the same system of values embraced by today's artists.

According to various interviews which Perelman gave prior to the opening of *The Beauty Part*, the play's thematic structure is "the frightening notion that everybody has to be creative; the barber has to paint pictures, the housewife has to take ballet lessons. Nobody's happy unless he's creating something. . . .

"It's got to the point where—as I say in the play—every housewife in America has got a novel under her apron. The culture bit, the need for self-expression and all is fine, as long as you don't get carried away with it, as long as you remain an amateur. . . .

"I haven't anything against culture. My play is a spoof of the amateurs. It's designed to be amusing. I'm not really attacking anything. I'm all for the Sunday painters, the housewives who model in plasticene, the girls who hammer out jewelry, the dentists who compose music. I'm all for them as long as they remain amateurs. But the amateurs everywhere are taking themselves seriously. They're trying to sell their stuff. They actually consider themselves serious artists. That, in the language of our time, bugs me."

S. J. Perelman's ingenuous insistence that he is "not really attacking anything" notwithstanding, *The Beauty Part* is actually a very tough play. Although totally succeeding in its intention to be "amusing," the comedy is also a devastating satire on American values, with especial acidic scorn for society's debasement of art and culture into bogus fabrications of their pure selves. In Perelman's vision of culture-consuming America, the acclaimed artist is he who prostitutes his principles to become a pseudo-artist. Success descends not on the creator of pure art, but on the dilettante practitioner of pseudo-arts, like interior decorators and designers, and on the cultural scavengers like agents, editors, and producers, who batten off the talents of true creators.

At the core of Perelman's satiric thrust is the observation that for Americans the basic unit of value is the dollar, and everything is measured in terms of it. According to this measurement unit, art and artists also become commodities to be bought and sold.

In his quite marvelous biography of his father, John Lahr makes an insightful correlation between this specific aspect of *The Beauty Part* and the personal life experience of Bert Lahr, the star of the play. "His favorite part was Harry Hubris," John Lahr writes, in *Notes on a Cowardly Lion*. "Like Hubris, a conniving theatrical agent, he saw himself as a product, and the world as a marketplace where the gaudiest object earned the highest bid."

Although *The Beauty Part* drips with scorn for the artist who calculatedly sells out to the system, and for the various no-talents who pursue art in the debased forms of their own contrivance, there is even more satiric disdain in the play for the materialistic principles which have created the national climate to begin with. Artistically insecure, culturally a swaddling country, America is still nonplussed by the phenomenon of art and the nature of its creation. Intrigued by it and possessed of a vague respect for its parts, Americans—essentially, the educated middle class—express this fascination by an urge to acquire culture and somehow "hold" it. But they can only "have" culture on the terms taught by their society—to possess culture, they must *purchase* it. Operating under the dollar-value system they've been taught, the middle class thus becomes a horde of culture-mongers who, in the process of pursuing the superficial trappings which they interpret as real art, manage to debase the genuine article in the process. And the nature of this corruption, Perelman seems to imply, is nonetheless destructive because of its innocence.

At the crux of Perelman's satirical toughness is the fact that he doesn't compromise. His characters are monsters—brilliantly funny cartoons, but travesties of human beings, nonetheless. Television comedians such as Red Skelton and Jackie Gleason also rely for their humor on the creation of galleries of grotesques, but the principle is quite a different one. Whereas these comedians inject affectionate compassion into their character portraits to make them sympathetic, Perelman's satire allows his gargoyles no redeeming virtues other than the obvious one of being human—not even the virtue of innocence through stupidity. Character warps which in the work of other comic writers are foibles and quirks, in Perelman's writing emerge as unmistakable follies. John Lahr makes it clear that his father, for one, was fully aware of this uncompromising quality in Perelman's gargoyle characterizations. "The predicaments of the characters were as familiar as the general cultural boom," the younger Lahr writes. "He understood the forces of greed and ego that whittled at their hearts."

The greatness of Perelman's humor, then, is partially due to the man's courage to make moral judgments about people, about society, about an entire country's cultural climate and the principles on which it is founded. This commitment to his own strict code of ethics gives Perelman's satire a dimension which far supersedes the mere brilliance of his flawless prose, the extraordinary richness of his inventive vocabulary, and the genius of his comic cadences. *The Beauty Part* thus becomes comedy of the highest rank—a real classic of the satiric genre, and one that should have run for years and years.

The critics agreed that *The Beauty Part* was a wonderful show and bestowed upon it such lavish praise in their reviews that it appeared as if the show would indeed run for years and years. Several critics noted the episodic nature of the madly incoherent story line which Perelman blandly referred to as his "plot." "It is more like a collection of *New Yorker* sketches played out on the stage than a comedy," observed *Theatre Arts*, shrewdly recognizing that Perelman had delved into his *New Yorker* file for many of his characters; indeed, for some of the situations and lines of dialogue, as well. Adapting the material into a cohesive comedy for the stage was a devil of a job, and it was the general critical consensus that the rampant inventiveness of Perelman's literary humor was frequently stymied by the restricting needs of plot development. Some reviewers suggested that the show would have been enhanced by song and dance, and *Newsweek* characterized it as "a revue without music."

But the critical community, once having observed the show's structural flaws, airily dismissed them to revel in the sheer fun of it all. Everybody loved *The Beauty Part*, and as far as the reviewers were concerned, there was a brand new hit on Broadway. According to Harvey Orkin, then S. J. Perelman's agent, "The reviews were raves, and we thought the show was a smash. All the talk between us and the producers was about what we should do with the show in its third year, and who should be cast in the road company when the show went on tour, and whether to take the profits in spread. Sid was really flying high, and he took a trip to Africa. When we closed the show two months later, I finally had to cable Sid in Africa. He wrote a *New Yorker* piece about that cable, and in it I think he referred to his agent as 'Toby Swindler.'"

Its glorious notices notwithstanding, *The Beauty Part* folded after its eighty-fourth performance. Although it is generally assumed within the theater community that the show was killed off by the paralyzing newspaper strike, a more careful look into the play and its production history reveals that a number of other factors contributed to its premature demise, although admittedly not in as dramatic a fashion as the strike.

To begin with, there is the fact that S. J. Perelman is a comic writer of genius, but a writer whose style is subtle, refined, and distinctly literary—a style not normally irresistible to the majority of Broadway theatergoers. Although Michael Ellis, the show's producer, acknowledges that "Sid is basically a verbal writer, and *The Beauty Part* is a special play for special people," it is the show's publicist, Bob Ullman, who states the case of Perelman's uniqueness with the most candor. "This was the kind of show that would have had a struggle anyway, even though it got the most brilliant notices," he insists. "Perelman's wit is really caviar for the masses. Unless you had seen the show 20,000 times, like I had, and could pick up the nuances that he just dropped along the way like pearls from a broken necklace, you could never begin to appreciate fully his use of words, his command of vocabulary, his phraseology. The show just went over the heads of the great mass of the public. They were laughing at Bert Lahr clowning."

That Perelman's wit *is* special, that his is not the mass appeal of a Neil Simon, seems clear from the fact that his theatrical excursions are rare events, although, as Harvey Orkin states emphatically, "Sid loves the theater, and he loves show business." Perelman himself is aware that the eccentric brilliance of his style is not easily adapted into the currency of the commercial structure of Broadway. *Time* magazine noted, when *The Beauty Part* was announced for Broadway production, that the venture was Perelman's first flirtation with the theater since "he swore off theatrical writing after a minor disaster called *Sweet Bye and Bye* closed on the road in 1947." In May of 1971, Perelman was still wary of writing for the theater, although it was obvious that the stage holds a distinct fascination for him. "It's awfully hard to look into the crystal ball and tell whether I would be tempted to work again in the theater," he said then. "But the theater is a very attractive medium. It's so much better than pictures, because it allows you absolute autonomy. You have so much more power. You can't have some piece of electronics change everything around on you, because you are the playwright and you're protected by the Dramatists' Guild. Nevertheless, in the theater, you are subject to tremendous accidents of fortune."

The Beauty Part adds another level to the inherent singularity of Perelman's style, because the play is a satire, and a particularly potent one at that. Dealing as it does with the contemporary middle class's almost hysterical infatuation with "Kulchur," the play is a comic attack—but an attack nonetheless—on the very audience which it had to woo and win to become a Broadway success. As John Lahr has observed of the play's satirical thrust, "The serious target of the laughter, the well-aimed barbs at America's cultural pretenders, was surprisingly new to Broadway entertainment. It confused some observers, who, while enjoying themselves, were quick to dismiss the play as a cartoon. . . . Broadway was, perhaps, the wrong location to launch a debate about democracy and culture. But Perelman as a satirist wanted to bring his vision into the enemy camp. With Lahr as a vehicle of exchange, he had a fine chance to infiltrate middle-class imaginations. Perelman was bold enough to place the show in front of the audience it was about. This was a moralist's tactic, as well as the instinct of a commercial writer."

While the pungency of the satire may not actually have kept audiences away, it must have contributed some measure of uneasiness in the play's appreciative, but not fanatically supportive audiences. Certainly there was something awry in the cool reception which the show's pre-Broadway tryout received in Philadelphia, despite ecstatic critical notices. Producer Mike Ellis recalls, "We got very, very good notices in Philadelphia, but we did *no business*. We were there for the three weeks before Christmas, which is not a terribly good time for business, usually. But still, in those three weeks we grossed just about $25,000 *total*—which must be the all-time low for a show that got good notices."

Ellis decided that Bert Lahr simply didn't draw in Philadelphia, but this seems a simplistic conclusion, and hardly consistent with the fact that the critical reviews were so enthusiastic that the show should have drawn full houses even if its star were Frankenstein's bride. And since Philadelphia had no newspaper strike, that excuse is instantly ruled out. It seems more likely that something about the play itself—the eliteness of Perelman's rococo wit, the acidic sting of his satiric barbs—turned off the Philadelphia audiences.

Ellis disagrees that the satiric element was the audience cooler, and falls back on Broadway's traditional response to failure—fatalism. "What sells tickets and what keeps people away is at best an intangible thing," he says. "Where are they tonight? Well, you know the old answer: There's a dance in Newark. It's as good an excuse as any."

It's a great joke, a typically Broadway joke. It makes one picture some poor slob whose trousers have just fallen down around his ankles, while he stands in the middle of Times Square, trying to laugh at the joke on himself. But as philosophy, the crack is indubitably inadequate. The fact is that *The Beauty Part* is a biting piece of satire aimed squarely at the follies of the very segment of the middle class which comprised the bulk of the traditional Broadway audience. Some degree of audience alienation was inevitable. This satiric basis of the show, plus the baroque nature of Perelman's literary wit, combined to put *The Beauty Part* into the category of a "special," a show of appeal to a limited segment of the Broadway theatergoing population. And anything at all "elite" must scramble for its life within the Broadway system.

If there is anything else intrinsic to the play which might have put off audiences, it is probably its structural formlessness. In the second act, especially, Perelman gets so ensnared by the need to advance his cockamamy plot that the mechanics frequently become intrusive. A scene like the one in Whirlaway Scenic Studios, which exists primarily to set up the hilarious courtroom scene with Judge Herman J.

Rinderbrust, is necessary to shift the action of the plot. But it lacks a satiric point of its own and thus slows down the frenzied pace of the act as a unit.

The play's episodic nature and its zany attempts to cling to a plot couldn't have mattered less to the dedicated Perelmaniacs who were familiar with the humorist's singular brand of wit. But they might have disconcerted the traditional Broadway audience primed by past experience to expect the predictable formula perfection of the standard Broadway comedy. And they might have unsettled theatergoers who found it difficult to follow Perelman's verbal humor as it was "translated" from the pages of the *New Yorker* into stage terms.

David Doyle, a Broadway actor who appeared in the show, offers this impression of the show's audiences: "The audiences were either with it from the very beginning—realizing that they were in for something saucy and sassy—or it just sailed right past them. The majority of audiences knew exactly what they were coming to see, and they just roared. It was just like the old Marx Brothers comedies. But there were some audiences who just sat on their hands." The show's director, Noel Willman—who, the previous year, had directed the *very* literary *A Man for All Seasons* on Broadway—acknowledges the difficulty of "adapting Perelman's style to a dramatic idiom of comedy." Willman saw Perelman's own comic idiom as "eighteenth-century literary—almost purely literary. His use of words is marvelous, of course, but it is not entirely dramatic. Perelman himself found that as he went on he had to alter, shape, and change—partly for Lahr, of course, because he was the central figure, but in more general terms, for the *theater*."

Given the strongly individualistic nature of Perelman's writing and the equally strong collectivism of the theater's own collaborative nature, one might well inquire whether the clash between these two apposite forces in any way impaired the show's production. Specifically, one might also wonder if there was any conflict between the strong personalities of Perelman and Lahr. "I had worked with Bert Lahr before," Perelman says. "I had done a thing with him on television called *The Wonderful World of Burlesque*, and we got along very well. I had great admiration for him. For some happy reason, I could write almost anything for him. He had a way of taking my material, and because of his personality, it attained a kind of secondary value. I felt that he was able to take whatever I wrote and perfectly interpret it. From my point of view it was an ideal collaboration."

As unlikely as it seems, there did indeed seem to be a unique rapport between this great literary stylist and this great burlesque clown. This rapport seems to have gone deeper than mere personal harmony—to an unusual rapprochement between the apparently diverse artistic styles of two comedy giants. Perelman himself attributes it to the fact that burlesque humor, Lahr's personal style, always made a social comment. Although physical, rather than verbal, in its comic approach, burlesque humor was based on making fun of rich people and their pretensions, and therefore was as deflationary in its own peculiar style as Perelman's more literary brand of satire.

Not that the collaboration was without its tensions. According to the people who worked with him, Bert Lahr as an artist and a human being was a complex individual beset by needs which were often plainly neurotic. In his biographical study of his father, John Lahr mentions the comic's deep artistic insecurities, his almost fanatical drive for perfection, his tendency to reshape his material, his need to feel a personal command over the direction a production was taking. Director Noel Willman notes that, in the specific case of *The Beauty Part*, "Lahr, like so many actors of talent, if indeed not genius, was always trying to rewrite things. Often, to Perelman's rage, he would suddenly take lines and change them. Perelman hated Lahr to change a line, or to substitute one of his own, or slightly change it, or anything like that. He *hated* that. But then, most playwrights do, of course." As *Time* magazine noted, about the show's 1961 tryout at the Bucks County Playhouse, "On opening night Perelman was horrified to hear star Bert Lahr forgetting half his lines, filling in the gaps with Chinese proverbs of his own invention."

For his part, Perelman hardly had the temperament of St. Francis of Assisi. The author could be obdurately cantankerous in moments of crisis, and the production history of *The Beauty Part* was rife with crisis. Although theater people are notoriously loath to "bad mouth" their co-workers, the reminiscences of people who worked on the production contain oblique acknowledgments of the Perelman temper. Anger, in fact, is every satirist's stock in trade, and like satirists from Aristophanes on, Perelman is not always as just as he is funny. For the June 3, 1967, issue of *The New Yorker*, he wrote a deliciously witty, but really quite unkind profile of a character named Smiley Grimes—clearly based on Bert Lahr. In the sketch, Lahr comes off as an inflated egotist and much of a dunce—hardly Perelman's personal view of his colleague and friend, but a portrait irresistible to the "other," professional Perelman, the writer of satire.

The beauty part of the collaboration on *The Beauty Part* was the fact that, despite their two quite different personalities and different approaches to comedy—Perelman's genius being literary precision and Lahr's being spontaneous invention—there was ultimate harmony. It might even be said that the very tension between the two artistic approaches served to create a new style of comedy that was separate and unique on its own special terms. Perelman certainly recognizes the happy phenomenon when he comments on the difficulty Lahr had in pronouncing some of the words he had written for him. "It didn't really matter," Perelman acknowledges. "Once in a while he strayed into an accidental thing which was much funnier than what I had written originally." Speaking about the same harmony-through-tension principle, John Lahr observes, "Lahr had difficulty with some of Perelman's convoluted literary cadences. Perelman's combination of hifalutin English and Yiddish jargon could keep Lahr's exuberance from taking control. . . . Perelman struggled to adapt his most baroque rhythms to Lahr's vocal range. The tension was healthy but frustrating. Perelman's language took on an economy and dramatic impact it sometimes lacked on the printed page."

The single purest example of how the separate comic styles of Perelman and Lahr combined to create a distinct but quite marvelous new idiom of comedy is evident in "the Smedley scene" of *The Beauty Part*. Nelson Smedley is the sublimely funny co-creation of S. J. Perelman and Bert Lahr. He appears in Scene 3 of Act II of *The Beauty Part*—the magnate of Smedley Snacketerias; a crabby, senile old John Bircher who sees the Communist menace lurking in every shadow; the inspired comic embodiment of the right-wing political fanatic.

The evolution of the character of Nelson Smedley is a miniature drama in itself. According to Perelman, the scene was conceived in New Haven and written in Philadelphia. "We were having big trouble in the second act," Perelman recalls. "There was a real mushy thing right in the middle of the second act and we didn't know how to get out of it. Noel Willman and I drove up to New York to see Sid Caesar in *Little Me*, just hoping to refresh ourselves, because we were awfully close to the show. En route, we kept talking about different ways of filling up this hole. Now, I'm a great admirer of Raymond Chandler. On two occasions in his detective novels he had scenes laid in a hothouse, once with a rich old character in Pasadena. There was something about the steamy quality of a hothouse that attracted him and that I hadn't forgotten. So I said to Willman, 'What about a scene in a hothouse with Bert? He can be a real reactionary—not a red-baiter exactly, but a man who is fixated on the whole thing.' Well, back we came, and I wrote the scene, and as it turned out, that was the most popular scene in the whole show."

Perelman remembers that Lahr was very wary of the character. "I think that Bert was a little frightened at first, because I think he thought that it was a little too political. He said to me, 'Wouldn't somebody think that this was a defense of communism?' And I said, 'Oh, what are you talking about, Bert, for God's sake? Everybody is so fed up with red-baiting that we might have an unexpected success with it. Try it, anyway.' He was still very wary about it, but he finally got it out on the stage in Philadelphia. And the minute that those laughs began to roll back, I saw that Bert wouldn't part with this thing—ever."

Because Perelman had written the scene under duress, and had not had the opportunity to refine it with the same meticulous care he usually afforded his writing, the Smedley segment remained more of a sketch than any of the other scenes, thus giving Bert Lahr more freedom to invest it with his own comic inventiveness. "The basic scene was Perelman's invention, of course," Noel Willman says. "But it was then kind of realized by Lahr in rehearsal. If you examine that sketch, you'll find that it's less Perelman wit, less Perelman rococo-type writing than the other scenes. It's much simpler, much more like a burlesque sketch. Basically, that's because Perelman hadn't had the time to polish it—it was panic-time, in a way. Then, what Bert did was to give it this *frenzied* subjective quality which made it wildly funny and ultimately the best thing in the show."

Perelman himself came to a similar analysis of why the Smedley scene was a rare example of perfect theatrical collaboration. "Bert took this stuff which was pretty wild to begin with, and he gave it an extra dimension. He blew it up. Even though he wasn't partial to the scene and was frightened of it and didn't want to get mixed up with the political angle, by his own personality he was able to take this thing and really give it tremendous dimension."

If an analysis of the play's production reveals no further rationale for its commercial failure—reveals no blundering misinterpretation of the script's intentions, and no destructive antagonism between the production principals of author, star, and director; reveals nothing, in fact, but evidence of a rather rare case of artistic collaboration—where, indeed, are the additional causes for that failure? Where, then, are the villains?

"I guess Bertram Powers was the real heavy," is S. J. Perelman's terse comment about the single most disastrous piece of bad luck that hit *The Beauty Part*—the New York newspaper strike. On December 8, 1962, the International Typographical Union, the printers' union, struck New York's nine metropolitan dailies. The papers, which had a combined circulation of 5,500,000 copies a day, did not resume publication until 114 days later. It was the single longest news blackout experienced by New York City, and its effect on the legitimate theater is to this day incalculable. In a *New Yorker* "Profile," Bert Lahr offered a concise summary of the strike's effect on *The Beauty Part.* "It's been murder with this newspaper strike," he was quoted as saying. "Normally, with the kind of reviews we got, we'd be sold out for two months in advance, but as it is, we're selling out performance by performance, with a steady line of maybe six customers at the box office all day long."

In the minds of all the people connected with the show, there is not the slightest doubt that the newspaper strike was the responsible agent for the closing of *The Beauty Part* after only eighty-four performances. "I'm the producer, and I'm biased," Mike Ellis says. "But I'm trying to be objective about it, and I say now—ten years later—that had it not been for the newspaper strike, that show would have run."

Over in Africa, Perelman raged, and eventually channeled the rage into a typically brilliant *New Yorker* piece. In later years he chose to review the incident less passionately and more philosophically. "It was a distressing experience to have worked that long and then have had this thing come out of left field," he says. "But it was just one of those things—who could have predicted a newspaper strike that would last 114 days?"

His then-agent, Harvey Orkin, has a rather more offbeat view of the strike. "You've gotta know something about Sid," he says. "He's like that character out of Al Capp, Joe Bltsfks. Whenever he's around you know *something's* gonna happen. It's like having a picnic: you have this right and that right and everything's all set; you got the sandwiches, you got the martinis—but you forget the gas. With *The Beauty Part*, it was opening in the middle of the newspaper strike—that was the thing that really licked Perelman. There's no doubt in my mind that if we had had the newspapers, we would have run."

Writing in the *Manchester Guardian*, Alistair Cooke made a significant observation that most American journalists, in evaluating the effects of the strike, failed to recognize. Analyzing the theater's fatal dependence on the New York newspapers, Cooke realized that it was but a reflection of the theater's larger dependence, as an art form, on the nonartistic economic system of the commercial marketplace. "The curse of the theater's financial vice," Cooke wrote, "is that one tends to look back more in sorrow than in anger on the many stirring or bad plays that might be memorable if they had been permitted to plant themselves and flourish in a healthy system."

To appreciate the full calamitous effect which the 1962–63 strike had upon the Broadway theater, one must first grasp the degree of dependence in which the press holds the theater. On the simplest level, the theater relies on the newspapers to publish critical judgment of its offerings. Through a variety of causes—mounting ticket costs; the complexities of the sheer physical mechanics of theater attendance; the marked decrease in shows opening each season; the easier accessibility of movies and television as popular art—all of which have intensified the theater's tendency to be a "special event," the public has become less inclined to frequent and casual theatergoing. An excursion to the theater has become a special event—more a social affair than an artistic experience—and one representing an appreciable investment in terms of time, money, and personal commitment. Today's theatergoer, wary of his investment return, has grown increasingly more reliant for guidance on the opinions of the critics.

In an attempt to surmount the first hurdle imposed by the newspaper strike—the blackout of this important critical opinion—the producers of *The Beauty Part* concocted a number of ingenious gimmicks to alert the public to the enthusiastic notices of the play which the critics wrote, but never saw printed in their publications.

"We did all kinds of things," producer Michael Ellis recalls. "We had a million bookmarks made up with reviews of the show, and laid out in every cigar store in town. We had fliers about the size of the *Daily News* printed up with all the reviews in them and then had them distributed by people in Revolutionary War costumes going all over the midtown area, preceded by a town crier ringing a bell. We made a deal with Consolidated Laundries to put these review-flyers into 100,000 packages of laundry, and we made another deal with Arrow Photos to do the same thing with 100,000 packages of developed film. We even used skywriting." And yet, with all his myriad "deals," Ellis is forced to admit that, "There is something inherent in the idea of the immediate impact of total reviews, within the first week of the opening of a show, that seems to have a major effect."

Aside from the most tangible and most immediate blow inflicted by the printers' strike—the loss of the "immediate impact" of its positive reviews—*The Beauty Part* suffered a deeper damage; namely, it lost the means of hawking its wares on a day-to-day basis on the public market-place. Operating as it does within Broadway's commercial structure, the theater is a commodity like any other piece of package goods, and as such must constantly sell itself as a product to its potential consumers through our traditional economic procedures of advertising and publicity. That *The Beauty Part* failed to market itself successfully illustrates not only the power of newspapers as a merchandising aid, but also the basic in-justice of a production system which reduces theater art to the status of a laundry detergent.

Although apparently unexercised by this more insidious implication of the theater's bondage to daily newspaper exposure, producer Ellis nevertheless is quite cognizant of the immediate effect of losing the day-by-day merchandising assistance of the newspapers. "What you miss from the newspaper is not only the reviews, but the daily ad," he says. "You have to put the ticket prices and information right in front of people, so they can order by mail—mail order is fifty percent of business in the theater—and we must have the newspaper ads to do that." According to Ellis, $40,000 was spent in advertising devices during the first few weeks of the play's run, in an attempt to offset the absence of the daily news-papers; $10,000 was spent for the first 250,000 brochures of critical re-views. More thousands were spent in subsequent weeks, as the manage-ment struggled to make the public aware even of the existence of *The Beauty Part*. Hamburger stands on Long Island held *Beauty Part* con-tests; gorgeous showgirls wandered around town handing out literature on the show; delicatessen chains plastered Bert Lahr's picture in the windows; people found fliers in their laundry, in their supermarket pack-ages, in Pepsi-Cola cartons, in candy boxes, in beer containers, in pack-ages of blintzes. "Every possible kind of deal that could be made to spread the word about that show was made," Ellis says. "But it just isn't the same thing as having that newspaper in your hands."

Even before the show actually had opened, Ellis had tried to buck the newspaper blackout by more drastic measures. "I immediately went to Equity to try to get a reprieve on the show's opening," he says. "But Equity said I couldn't do anything about it. If I wanted to lay off, I'd have to lay off for eight weeks, paying the actors continuously." Then he tried to initiate ticket-cutting, but found the theater owners intransigent. "That was nothing new," he says. "I've tried many times to introduce half-price twofers for the first few weeks of a show that had no advance sale. But the Shuberts would not permit it; they said I would 'immediately cheapen the show.' A lot of people, understandably, don't want to be the one to go out on a limb and experiment. But if you do want to try experiments, like student discounts, charge cards, or cut-price tickets, I don't know how you can *make* the theater owners go along with you. Maybe David Merrick and Hal Prince have control of their theaters when they go into them, but all the rest of us go into the theaters with what they call 'mutual control' with the theater owners."

Summarizing his disastrous personal experience in attempting to buck the newspaper strike, Ellis offers this wry conclusion: "I'm a firm believer that the newspapers are the main pillar of the Broadway theater."

In Broadway's typically ironic fashion, *The Beauty Part* has assumed a special position of interest within the theater community precisely because of the "victim-of-fate" role it played in the newspaper blackout. As such, it has become almost a symbolic example of the "luck," "chance," "fate," or "odds" which the theater industry believes rules the destiny of the theater. Broadway's superstitious belief in "the breaks" is a colorful aspect of its collective personality, but it is also a convenient camouflage for human error and ineptitude. "We didn't get the *Times*" or "We opened too late [or too early] in the season" or "There were too many comedies [or dramas or satires or one-man shows or spoon acts] already this season" or "The theater was on the wrong side of Broadway" or, simply, "We didn't get the breaks"—these are the solemnly advanced alibis one hears whenever a show flops. Better "There was a dance in Newark," Broadway theater philosophy contends, than an admission of human culpability.

Without minimizing the enormously detrimental effect which the newspaper strike had upon the theater season of 1962–63, and upon *The Beauty Part* in particular; nevertheless, within the Broadway mythology, it did become a kind of apotheosis of the "bad luck" alibi, a really awesome manifestation of "the breaks" which made all the time-worn excuses pale by comparison.

In the case of *The Beauty Part* it served to distract attention from a disastrous production error which actually contributed far more effectively to the show's premature closing than did the newspaper strike.

To evaluate the extent of this lapse in managerial judgment, one first needs a bit of background on the production economics of *The Beauty Part*. "It was an expensive show," producer Michael Ellis says. "It was done in 1962 for $150,000, plus an overcall, and that was *very* expensive then for a straight play. There were seventeen people in the show and they played forty to fifty parts, so there was an enormous number of costumes, which meant there was a large costume staff backstage. It broke even at about twenty-eight, twenty-nine thousand dollars a week, and for a straight play in those days, that was a very high break. And remember that over the break point only about fifty percent of everything that comes in is profit. Thirty percent goes to the theater; ten percent to the author; ten percent to the star—so that only fifty cents of every dollar is really profit."

Thus, *The Beauty Part* was a very costly show to mount and an even costlier show to operate. As only one example of the play's high operating costs, Ellis mentions a minor scene change which, because it necessitated extra musicians and an additional stagehand, somehow mushroomed operating costs into an additional $1,500 a week. The show, it should be remembered, had already lost $40,000 during its inauspicious Philadelphia tryout, and Ellis himself had had to float a personal loan to bring the show into New York. "I ended up in terrible, terrible debt with that show," Ellis says. "Eighty-four thousand dollars of debt is *real*. And I'm not out from under it yet."

Hamstrung by its high operating costs, *The Beauty Part* couldn't afford the luxury of hanging on until the good word on it penetrated the newspaper blackout and stirred audience interest; it had to "find its audience" or fold. Under the circumstances, any additional production crisis could prove cataclysmic. The cataclysm came in the shape of Broadway's shortsighted and frantically managed policy of interim booking. Interim booking is a cross between musical chairs and Russian roulette. Essentially, it is a chaotic system of chance whereby a play will open in a theater which is temporarily empty but awaiting a previously booked show. Although rarely practiced in these days, when theaters so far outnumber productions that a large percentage of them remain "dark," or untenanted, for a good portion of the season, interim booking was a common policy in 1962, when shows often went begging for theaters. It's a chancy system, to say the least. The producers of the temporary-tenant show are taking the chance that, if their property proves to be a solid hit, the theater's future tenant will fold out of town or conveniently find another theater.

According to Michael Ellis, the theory goes like this: "You say to yourself, if you don't have a hit, it doesn't matter, because you'll close. And if you do have a hit, you can always get another house. No hit has ever been kept out of New York." Ellis claims that the policy is common

Broadway procedure and hardly qualifies as an extraordinary production measure. "I would guess that half the shows that open on Broadway open on interim bookings." But the raw fact of the matter is that the procedure is considered by producers to be a last-resort measure and is therefore scrupulously avoided unless absolutely necessary. According to David Doyle, a cast member of *The Beauty Part* who has appeared many times on Broadway, "That was the only play that I have ever appeared in which opened in a theater on a temporary basis, with the producers fully aware that we would have to get out."

In a kind of *tour de force* of mismanagement, Ellis finagled *The Beauty Part* into not merely one, but *two* interim bookings. Ellis today pleads confusion on the details, which he now recalls as "hazy," but in outline the facts are these: Ellis booked the play into the Music Box, a prime theater in the desirable location of Forty-fifth Street, knowing he had to vacate the house sometime before the end of February because the theater was previously committed to the Gertrude Berg comedy, *Dear Me, the Sky Is Falling*, which was already set for a March 2 opening. According to Perelman's agent, the fact was known to Ellis but not to any of the other principals in *The Beauty Part* enterprise until after the commitment was made. "A week before the show opened," Harvey Orkin recalls, "Mike told us we only had the theater for six weeks. So there we were on Forty-fifth Street with a good show in a good house, a show the audience liked, and the show had to be moved."

A tricky maneuver under the most favorable circumstances, an interim booking arranged amidst gathering rumors of a newspaper strike seemed to be courting disaster. Without newspapers to publicize the subsequent move to higher ground, a show might as well be moving to Tasmania. As David Doyle notes, "We knew that we had to get out of the Music Box, but we didn't know where we were going to go. This was a detriment to the chance of the show's going on to a successful run, because in not knowing what theater we were going to go to, we couldn't sell any advance tickets at the window."

There was consideration given to moving the production into a theater on Forty-eighth Street, but Ellis was hesitant to lose his choice Forty-fifth Street location. Accordingly, he decided to sit out the opening of Jack Richardson's *Lorenzo*, which was booked into the Plymouth, across the street from the Music Box, on Forty-fifth Street. When *Lorenzo* folded, Ellis promptly secured the Plymouth, and *The Beauty Part* moved in and reopened on February 25, 1963.

But the damage had been done. The move across the street cost five thousand dollars, to begin with. The management had been unable to advertise the move or, even more important, to accommodate advance sales, until the fate of *Lorenzo* was definitely determined. According to a story in *The New York Times* written by Howard Taubman, "While *The Beauty Part* waited for the Plymouth, it was unable to sell tickets for performances beyond its term at the Music Box. The advance sale languished and all but evaporated . . . the public was slow in discovering the show's new location."

The real kicker in this tense game of musical theaters is the fact that the Plymouth engagement was also an interim booking, and, again, one that nobody seemed to know about until after the commitment had been confirmed. S. J. Perelman, for once, was too stunned even to write a witty *New Yorker* sketch about the matter. "In addition to the newspaper strike, which was ghastly, I think that there was much mismanagement and inefficiency," is his quite somber reaction. "I think that Mike Ellis and everybody concerned with the show really mishandled it." His agent, Harvey Orkin, stiffly shoulders some of the responsibility. "We all made the mistake," he says. "As far as business was concerned, the production wasn't extremely well handled by any of us. We didn't look at the contracts to see how long we had the Plymouth. I think the day before we moved in we realized that [producer] Kermit Bloomgarden had the house in two weeks' time for Lillian Hellman's play *My Mother, My Father, and Me*, which closed a week after it opened."

There was thought given to moving the play once again, into a theater which would be available March 18, when *Lord Pengo* was due to close, but it was decided instead to close *The Beauty Part*. And close it did, on Saturday, March 9, 1963. In a passage in his biography of Bert Lahr, John Lahr recalls his father's reaction when he was told that the show was closing. Summing up the whole sorry mess, he said, "It's economics . . . simple economics. It's just one of those things. . . . Don't ask me to explain it. I don't understand it either. This is probably the best material I've had since the forties. . . . It confuses me, though. It's a lot of things, but the main thing is—well, it's such good material."

It would be easy to lay the blame for the mismanagement of the production totally on producer Michael Ellis' already debt-laden shoulders. Certainly many people did just that. The show's publicist, Bob Ullman, speculates out loud that, "If you had a producer who had some kind of leverage, like David Merrick," the play would not have closed in two months. "If David Merrick had been the producer," Ullman hypothesizes, "he would never have accepted an interim booking on a major production like that." Someone else connected with the show entertains a rather more elaborate fantasy. "Whether you like him or not," he says, "David Merrick would have gone into the Music Box and he just wouldn't have left. He'd have told Irving Berlin [the owner of the theater] to piss off. He just would have stayed there. He *never* would have left that theater—he would have blown up somebody or something. And he would have gotten publicity out of it. You've got to be ruthless. If you believe in the show, you'd *kill* somebody. What could they have done to Mike, really, if he refused to move from the theater—put a sheriff there? It would have been good publicity for the show."

It's always easier to be brave, or ruthless, or brilliantly cunning ten years after the deed. If any of Michael Ellis' gambles had paid off—*if Lorenzo* and/or *My Mother, My Father, and Me* had closed out of town; *if* the newspaper strike had been settled a few weeks earlier (it ended two weeks after *The Beauty Part* closed); *if* all those wild-and-woolly publicity gimmicks had suddenly paid off—the producer would probably be hailed today as a bold wildcat businessman. But the fact is, he lost every gamble. Besides forcing the obvious conclusion that Ellis was a hapless gambler, the extraordinary case of *The Beauty Part* also illustrates the intrinsic idiocy of Broadway's commercial theater system. Because the theater is an art form forced to function as an industry, it ends up being one of the most mismanaged industries in the entire free-enterprise system. But the difference, of course, between the chaotically run theater industry and any other inept business enterprise is the fact that the theater's commodities are not widgets or two-way light bulbs, but the infinitely less durable substance of art and artists. And that makes it virtually impossible to evaluate the full extent of the artistic and human damage suffered whenever a play closes in a state of disaster. What makes the confraternity of *Beauty Part* boosters such a remarkable little band is its sense of irony—the abrasive bit of knowledge that the waste would have been unnecessary if only the Broadway theater could, in Alistair Cooke's words, "be permitted to plant itself and flourish in a healthy system."

THE LAST ANALYSIS

by *Saul Bellow*

CAST OF CHARACTERS

PHILIP BUMMIDGE

BERTRAM

LOUIS MOTT

IMOGEN

WINKLEMAN

MADGE

MAX

PAMELA

AUFSCHNITT

BELLA

GALLUPPO

MESSENGER

TANTE FRUMKAH

FIDDLEMAN

KALBFUSS

Act One

At curtain, we discover BUMMIDGE lying in a barber chair, completely covered by a sheet. IMOGEN sits by her desk on a swivel chair, legs crossed, eagerly transcribing notes from a stenographic pad to large file cards. Enter WINKLEMAN.

WINKLEMAN. Imogen, where's my cousin? Oh, there. Now, Bummy—

IMOGEN. Please, Lawyer Winkleman. I just got him to rest. The strain of today's broadcast is twisting his nerves.

WINKLEMAN (Looking about). Ah, television equipment. But not the real thing. Only closed-circuit. There was a time when my cousin Bummidge was king of the networks—the greatest comedian of his time. Now look at him, almost destroyed by his ideas, mental experiments—home-brewed psychoanalysis. Poor has-been. (BUMMIDGE quivers under the sheet.) He spends his day in an old loft with his colleagues (A gesture at IMOGEN.) acting out his neuroses. His traumas. The psychological crises of his life. It's very painful.

IMOGEN. It's almost deliberate, Mr. Winkleman, the way you refuse to understand.

WINKLEMAN. What's to understand?

BUMMIDGE (Tears off sheet). Don't waste your time, Imogen. He pretends to be a genuine lowbrow, a plebeian. You know, Winkie, why I act out my past life.

WINKLEMAN (With heavy irony). Yeah, self-knowledge.

BUMMIDGE. If a man like me needs insight, why should he go to some punk? I have my own method—Existenz-Action-Self-analysis.

WINKLEMAN. Once you were in a class with Bert Lahr, Groucho Marx, Jerry Lewis. Big money. Now I foresee you waiting in an alley for a handout of dried eggs.

IMOGEN (To BUMMIDGE). Finish your rest. You have to have it.

WINKLEMAN. Lowbrow! For you no brow could ever be high enough, that's your trouble. At this time of your life, to plunge into theories—Science, Originality, the Pleasure Principle, Nirvana, and now the final brainstorm, spending your last dough on a closed circuit television broadcast to the American Psychiatric Association. Wasted. Sheer waste!

BUMMIDGE (*Nettled*). Waste? They jumped at the chance to see my work.

IMOGEN. Rest . . . I don't know how his organism stands the strain. (*She draws the sheet over him.*)

WINKLEMAN. And whose equipment is this? (*Reads label.*) Diamond Electronics. I thought so. Louis Mott, your old Hungarian sidekick and errand boy. That swindler. Bummy, listen to me. We have ties. Why, my mother brought you into the world.

BUMMIDGE (*Sits up*). Oh, Tante Frumkah! That ancient thing, she still exists. She delivered me. She could clue me into the Unconscious in a dozen places. Where is she?

WINKLEMAN. Very busy, in her old age. She said you telephoned her.

IMOGEN. You haven't rested, haven't eaten in two weeks. You must relax a while before you face the cameras.

BUMMIDGE. Today my powers must be at their peak. I must convince everyone.

(*Enter* MOTT.)

MOTT. Well, my assistant is here. We can hook up the equipment. But first there's one matter to be took up—money, the balance.

(BUMMIDGE *pulls the sheet over his head.*)

WINKLEMAN. I knew you'd be mixed up in this, you devious Hungarian. Whenever he's on the brink of disaster, you're always right behind him.

MOTT. Go blow it out, Winkleman. I stood by him for years.

WINKLEMAN. Only because there were broads around. And now this TV racket. I bet you can't transmit to the Waldorf.

MOTT. I could transmit all the way to China, if I wanted. Maybe you fool your pals at the Harvard Club, but not me. I know about your old-people's-home racket.

(WINKLEMAN *flinches.*)

IMOGEN. Nursing home?

MOTT. You bet. Cousin Winkie bought an old luxury hotel and filled it with ancient, senile old-folks.

WINKLEMAN. Perfectly legitimate. The old Ravenna Towers. Gorgeous! A work of art. The space, the gilt cornices. The doorknobs themselves are priceless.

MOTT. Three bunks to a single room. And your old lady is like the camp commandant.

(WINKLEMAN *is glaring.*)

BUMMIDGE. Imogen—tell them to wrangle outside.

MOTT. Bummy, the office insists on the final payment. Five grand.

IMOGEN. What about the thirty-five thousand he already paid you?

MOTT. I can't help it. And no funny stuff, Bummy.

BUMMIDGE (*Sits up, the sheet clutched to his throat*). I thought you were pulling with me, Louie. I've invited all those distinguished people. They want to see the results of my research.

MOTT. Okay, fine. But the office . . .

BUMMIDGE (*Earnest*). Don't sell out to the bookkeepers. This is of universal significance.

IMOGEN. I'll look for the checkbook.

BUMMIDGE. Wink. (*Beckons him near, speaks sotto voce.*) Let me have the dough for a few days.

WINKLEMAN. Cousin, you're joking.

BUMMIDGE. Why joking? I need it. You made millions on me.

WINKLEMAN. Ancient history! That was when you let me do the thinking. I'd like to help. But I have my principles, too, just like you.

BUMMIDGE. O money! O Plutus! O Mammon!

WINKLEMAN. Is anything more horrible than a solemn buffoon. Where are your savings?

BUMMIDGE. In the separation Bella cleaned me out. Two millions.

WINKLEMAN. You made her furious. Your mistresses used her charge accounts.

BUMMIDGE. Don't you know what Freud says about gold? What does the color remind you of?

WINKLEMAN. Try giving Louis here (*Gestures.*) the other substance. See if he'll take it.

BUMMIDGE. For thirty years you sold me to the lousy public like dry cereal.

WINKLEMAN. Lousy? You lost your touch. They stopped laughing.

BUMMIDGE. I can make those apes laugh any time. At will. (*Pause.*) It's just that I can't stand the sound they make. Laughter without meaning is music of the madhouse.

WINKLEMAN. And you're going to cure the ravaged psyche of the mass. Poor cousin!

BUMMIDGE. You exploited me. Dragged me down into affluence.

MOTT. Let's not forget that check.

IMOGEN (*Crossing to desk*). You see me looking for it, don't you?

BUMMIDGE. You made me change my name. Lead a false life. Maybe an actor must— I'll give you that much— But— (*With fervor.*) Now I want insight. Value. I'll die without value. And finally I've succeeded in getting off the mere surface of life. Wink, back me today.

WINKLEMAN (*Sits on couch*). You're not the only one in trouble.

IMOGEN. I came to Mr. Bummidge's door with a questionnaire. Instead of answering my questions, he took me by the hand and said, "My dear, what do you consider funny?"

MOTT. What did you say?

IMOGEN. I just said, "Me, coming to your door to ask if you eat soup." And he laughed, and hired me. I believe in him. (*Her hand is on her breast.*) Mr. Winkleman, leading scientists have agreed to watch. Dr. Gumplovitch, Dr. Ratzenhofer, the giants of American psychiatry. And people from Princeton and Johns Hopkins, the Ford Foundation. They know they're dealing with a great artist.

MOTT. I'm waiting.

BUMMIDGE. Calm! (*Throws himself back in the chair.*)

MOTT. Here's a check. Israeli Discount? What kind of bank is that? Fill it in. Five zero zero zero and no one hundred cents.

(IMOGEN *writes.*)

WINKLEMAN. Between Bella, and his son Max, and his broads, especially the present one, Pamela, the ex-chorus girl, I figure he's been taken for ten million. Your sister Madge and I are worried. Your real friends. Sometimes I think he is ruining himself to get revenge on the whole bunch of us.

BUMMIDGE. Why don't you conduct services elsewhere, in the name of the Golden Calf, Winkie. The Calf? Calves' Foot. . . . Oh my God, *Kalbfuss!*

MOTT. Let's have the signature, now.

BUMMIDGE (*As he signs*). Imogen, we must check out a few things.

Where's Bertram? And Kalbfuss! Make sure Kalbfuss will be watching me. Phone his shop.

WINKLEMAN. Kalbfuss? Shop?

(*Enter a* TECHNICIAN.)

TECHNICIAN (*To* MOTT). Louis, is this the joint? The floor doesn't look solid enough. These boards waggle like loose teeth. (*Seeing* IMOGEN.) Well—hello, Miss.

IMOGEN. Bertram went to the Waldorf to see about the canapés and champagne.

WINKLEMAN. Champagne? And who is this Kalbfuss—the lord high egghead? (*Speaking to the* TECHNICIAN *and then to* IMOGEN.) The suckers had their mouths open for yucks—he fed them Aristotle, Kierkegaard, Freud. Who needs another homemade intellectual to tell them West Cincinnati is in a bad way?

TECHNICIAN (*Pushing a television camera*). Look out, friend.

WINKLEMAN. Reading! Booksellers were like dope-pushers to him.

IMOGEN. All I can say is that he's done great things for my mental development. He saw more than these externals. No other man has ever been willing to look past them.

(*The* TECHNICIAN *whistles at her.*)

MOTT (*Sniffing her*). She's like a mound of nectarines— Business first. I'll run down to the bank. (*Exits.*)

BUMMIDGE. Oh! (*Sits up.*) The time is short. I've got so much mental preparation to make, and I'm hampered, hindered, held back, obstructed, impeded, impaired. (*To* WINKLEMAN.) Where is your mother? I need those sagging bones. I want her here today. (*Crossing stage.*) And Bertram—Kalbfuss. He's crucial. Come, Imogen. (*Exit stage Right.*) (*As* IMOGEN *follows, the* TECHNICIAN *pinches her.*)

IMOGEN. Yes, Mr. Bummidge. (*To* TECHNICIAN.) Please. (*Exits.*)

WINKLEMAN. No matter what Bummy masterminded, no matter what he brewed, I could make use of it. It brought me a buck, and a tax-clean buck, too. With phantasmagoria like his there's only one thing to do: sell them! When he wanted to weave rugs, I put him into a Fifth Avenue window. If he wanted to paint action pictures, play the organ like Albert Schweitzer, I'd make a deal. But now he's lost his image with the public, he's confused the Plain Man, and that's the sonofabitch that pays for the whole show. (*He starts to leave.*) Wipe your glasses, Winkleman. Lurk in the bushes. Hide, wait, listen—watch from the fringes, and you'll get benefits. (*Exit.*)

(*Enter* BUMMIDGE *with a timer.*)

BUMMIDGE. Hours and minutes! No time. Curse that interfering Winkleman. I know he wants to exploit me. There's some intrigue. (*He wipes it away with a gesture.*) Now I am alone. Ultimate reality— that's what we want. Okay, Bummy. (*Sits.*) What's on your mind? Come, boy, let's have it. Begin with the dreams you dreamt last night. Each dream is a tiny psychosis. The sleeper is a tranquil criminal. All right —the dreams. . . . What I dreamt! A huge white animal climbed into my bed. I thought, "A polar bear." I looked again and saw pig's feet. A white sow. But wait—I didn't do anything to her. A nursing pig. What's the symbolism of it? (*Ponders, then shrugs.*) I thought, "Live and let live. Let her lie there." I moved over on the diagonal. Part of my basic sub-missiveness. At least I didn't have to make love to her. But the dream, the dream! The pig squirmed and writhed like a phantom knockwurst, and turned into a fat, enormous man in a baggy sweater with little candy milk bottles sewn in rows. Like Hermann Goering with his medals. But was this fat man a man? In the unconscious, to be obese is female. Oh, that unconscious! Is it ever cunning! Repression! The power of the Id! This was a male with breasts. (*Rises.*) I want notes on this, for the rec-ord. (*Calls.*) Imogen! Is that girl slipping, libido-wise? Wait, there's more. (*Crosses over and sits on his analytic sofa.*) Then he/she lay in bed with me, shaking, and all the little bottles clinked and jingled. He/she was laughing (*Laughs in several keys, assuming various characters.*) He-he-he! Ha! Hoo-hoo-hoo! That laughter! (*Now he is grave.*) A nightmare. The creature mocked me. I'm afraid I may not be taken seriously in the field of science. In the dream I threw a fit. I puffed up with rage like a squid. My psyche let out angry ink. I almost levitated from the bed. And I cried out in many tongues—"Nefesh, Ish. Ecce homo. Ho thanatos," in Hebrew, Latin, Greek, and bared my chest in the dead eye of the floating moon. And . . .

(*He staggers a bit. Enter* IMOGEN, *with the* TECHNICIAN *close behind her.*)

IMOGEN. Please! You must let me alone!

BUMMIDGE. Imogen, is this one of your sexual lapses?

IMOGEN. Of course not, Mr. Bummidge.

BUMMIDGE (*To the* TECHNICIAN). I'm going to request that you leave this broad alone.

TECHNICIAN. *I*, let *her* alone? (*Laughs.*) Do I wear lipstick, use perfume, waggle my behind? *She* does it.

BUMMIDGE. Is your home life so inadequate that you become inflamed before dinner? (*The* TECHNICIAN *laughs.* BUMMIDGE *is enraged.*) Listen to that laugh. Is that neurotic, or is that neurotic?

TECHNICIAN (*To* IMOGEN). Is he serious? (*Laughs.*) Is that Bummidge the comedian? He's lost his marbles. (*Exits.*)

BUMMIDGE. You'd better adjust yourself a bit.

IMOGEN. It makes me so unhappy. I try to communicate with people, but they only pay attention to my body.

BUMMIDGE (*Sympathetic*). Ah, yes.

IMOGEN (*Sits on his knee, filially*). That's why I understand when you try to speak seriously. They don't know how profound you are.

BUMMIDGE (*He has picked up a hand mirror and is grimacing into it*). I look frightful. Can people accept my message of sanity and health if I look like death or madness?

IMOGEN. But you're making faces before you look.

BUMMIDGE (*To the mirror*). Come on, you! I know your lousy tricks! Humankind must tear itself away from its nonsense.

IMOGEN. I just know you'll win today. It's bound to be a triumph. I feel it.

BUMMIDGE (*Eager*). You think so? Thank you, Imogen. You help me bear my burden. What time is it?

IMOGEN. Two-oh-nine.

(*Both rise quickly.*)

BUMMIDGE (*Crosses stage*). I haven't decided on an opening for my TV appearance. What music shall we begin with?

IMOGEN (*Looking through records*). Well, we have Wagner, Grieg, and here's *Les Sylphides*.

BUMMIDGE (*Stands beside a bust of Freud*). Where shall I stand? Here? Maybe with this bust of Freud. Just the two of us. I'll wear a special coat I designed. Aufschnitt is bringing it. He'll want money, too.

IMOGEN. Here's classical guitar music.

BUMMIDGE. No, something wilder. Remember who'll be watching at the Waldorf. I've invited not only psychologists and analysts, but artists, too, and comedians. I want the comedians to see how the analysts laugh. I want the analysts to see how seriously the comedians take me. I must reach everyone. Everything. Music to denote that I've roused the sleeping Titans of the instincts. Wham! Crash! Thunder! . . . Oh, Imogen, I'm frightened. My fingers are freezing.

IMOGEN (*Chafing his hands*). You'll do it.

BUMMIDGE. The enterprise is bigger than me, but there's nobody else to do it. What are these fabrics?

IMOGEN. For a papal-throne effect.

BUMMIDGE. I've also invited the clergy. Where is Bertram? Louie— at the bank with my bad check. I must raise the money. Meantime, my schedule. My inner self. Oh-oh—my sordid sister.

(*Exit* IMOGEN *and* TECHNICIANS, *as* MADGE *enters.* MADGE *is conservatively dressed; the matron from New Rochelle is what she tries to be.*)

MADGE. Well, Bummy, what's all the excitement?

BUMMIDGE (*At first, trying to charm her*). Madge, dear, what a surprise! But I knew you'd come.

MADGE. Naturally. You were weeping on the phone. I thought you were dying. How nice to see TV equipment again. A reminder of your former greatness.

BUMMIDGE (*More charm*). Madge, I've missed you. You have Mama's sense of humor.

MADGE. The good old days! The big time, the celebrities, the beautiful trips. I'm often sorry for you, Philip.

BUMMIDGE. You think I goofed.

MADGE. Are you as prosperous in psychoanalysis as you were in show business?

BUMMIDGE. How's Harold?

MADGE (*Indifferently*). The same.

(*They kiss.*)

BUMMIDGE. Madge, I need five thousand dollars.

MADGE (*Laughs*). Oh, Bummy!

BUMMIDGE (*Behaves oddly when she laughs; puts his ear to her chest like a physician*). That makes you laugh? Laugh again.

MADGE (*Pushing him off*). First you read these books, then you turn

FRIEDMAN-ABELES

into a mad scientist. You have to broadcast your message on a closed-circuit . . .

BUMMIDGE. Any minute, Louis Mott will be back from the bank with a bad check.

MADGE. You're putting me on. It's just your idiosyncrasy to live in this warehouse and play psychologist with a dumb doll and a ratcatcher. You didn't let Max and Bella and Pamela take *every*thing!

BUMMIDGE. Why leave yourself off the list? Madge, we're siblings. Sib-lings! From the same womb. It's not like being registered in the same hotel, different nights.

MADGE. I'm grateful to you for what little I have. But don't forget *my* problems. Why, Harold alone—first his eyes, then his coronary, then his prostate!

BUMMIDGE. I wish I were a modest failure like Harold—no broad perspectives, no ideas, adrift with bifocals. All I'm asking is five—

MADGE (*Laughs*). Peanuts, to a former millionaire.

BUMMIDGE. Your laughter fascinates me. Mama had a throaty laugh. Yours has little groans and moans in it. (*Imitates.*) But don't make a poor mouth. You took your diamonds off in the street. I can see the marks.

MADGE. Your sister will show you how broke she is. My very slip is torn. (*She shows the lace of her slip; it hangs loose.*)

BUMMIDGE (*Voice rising*). Oh, my Lord! Your underwear. Your underwear!

MADGE. Now even you can understand how it is.

BUMMIDGE. Wait! What's happening? My unconscious is trying to tell me something. What, you primitive devil—guilt? Lust? Crime? Tell me! (*Prods his head.*)

MADGE. I hope you're satisfied.

BUMMIDGE. I hear the groaning past. (*He makes a deep sound in his throat.*) Madge, you've mobilized ancient emotions.

MADGE. I can't stay.

BUMMIDGE (*Clinging to the lace*). Wait!

(*They both tug.*)

MADGE. Let go my slip.

BUMMIDGE. Answer some questions about Williamsburg, where we lived behind the store.

MADGE. Hideous place. I was ashamed to bring a boy to the house.

BUMMIDGE. The scene of my infancy.

MADGE. So, put up a plaque—you're tearing my clothing, Bummy.

BUMMIDGE (*Now on his knees*). The stages of the psyche—polymorphous, oral, anal, narcissistic. Madge, look deep! Infinite and deep!

MADGE. You want me to be as confused as yourself? Freud is passé. Even I know it.

BUMMIDGE (*Tearing the lace from her slip*). I need this. (*Puts it to his nose.*)

MADGE. You're stripping me!

BUMMIDGE (*Rises*). It's coming back to me. Ah! A sealed door has burst open. Dusty light is pouring out. Madge—Madge!

MADGE. I'm leaving.

BUMMIDGE (*Stops her*). No. You have to share this with me—this trauma you gave me at eleven. You caught me fooling with the things in your dresser. We'll re-enact it. Eleven and thirteen. You catch me. Scream for Mama.

MADGE. No, I won't.

BUMMIDGE (*Stamps his foot*). You will. You owe it to me. You damaged me. (*Changing tone.*) It'll do you good, too.

MADGE. Twenty-four hours a day, I have to defend myself from insanity.

BUMMIDGE. This is the dresser. You surprise me as I fondle your step-ins. Clutch my arm and shout, *Mama, Mama!* (BUMMIDGE *in pantomime opens a drawer and feels silks with adolescent lasciviousness.*)

MADGE. Mama! Mama!

BUMMIDGE. That's not right. Give it more. Again, and use your nails, too.

(*Enter* MAX *from upper door and* WINKLEMAN *from lower door.*)

MADGE. Mama!

BUMMIDGE. You're beginning to have that bitchy tone I remember. But more.

MADGE (*Piercing*). Ma!

(*Enter* BERTRAM *from elevator.*)

BUMMIDGE. More yet. (*Pinches her.*)

MADGE (*Fiercely*). You nasty, sneaking little bastard.

BUMMIDGE (*Triumphant*). The old Madge. You can hear it yourself.

MADGE (*Inspired*). Look what I caught him doing, Mama. I'm the daughter, the only daughter, and I have no privacy in this filthy, foul, horrible hole. Look what I caught him doing. He'll end up with the whores yet. Dirty, snotty, cockeyed little poolroom bum!

BUMMIDGE (*Squatting*). Right—right! And I crouch there, trapped, quivering, delight turning to horror. I'm the human Thing—the peculiar beast that feels shame. And now Mama's swinging at me. (*He ducks.* MADGE *swipes at him with her purse.*) Don't hit me.

WINKLEMAN. If this isn't spooky. Playing with dead relatives.

MADGE (*Shaken*). Who *am* I, anyway?

MAX (*Angry*). Hey, what about a minute for a living relative? It's me, your son, your only child. Remember? You damn well will. I'll see to that.

BUMMIDGE. One generation at a time. Bertram, did you see this?

BERTRAM. I sure did. You're all shook up.

BUMMIDGE. A petticoat. Lace. Hem. I was hemmed in. A boy's awakening sex cruelly suppressed. A drawer. Drawer—coffin—death. Poor things that we are. Binding with briars the joys and desires. Madge, you see how I work?

MADGE (*Matronly composure beginning to return*). Ridiculous!

MAX. That's what I say. A crude joke.

BUMMIDGE (*Turns to him*). Can you tell me what a joke is? (*Starts to leave.*)

MAX. Stay here. Once and for all, we're going to have it out.

BUMMIDGE. Come, Bert—Imogen. Help . . . upstairs. Consultation . . .

MAX. Pop, I warn you . . .

IMOGEN. An artist like your father is entitled to respect.

MAX. Artist? Feet of clay, all the way up to the ears.

BUMMIDGE. Wink. Your mother. Tante Frumkah. Bring her. I need three minutes of steam.

IMOGEN (*To* MAX). Your father needs three minutes of steam.

(BUMMIDGE *exits with* IMOGEN *and* BERTRAM, *smelling* MADGE's *lace.*)

WINKLEMAN. Would anyone pay to see him carry on like this?

MAX. An obsolete comedian? His generation is dead. Good riddance to that square old stuff. . . . What are you doing here, Winkie—you want to con something out of him?

WINKLEMAN. How delightful to hear a youthful point of view.

MAX (*To* MADGE). And what's your angle? You didn't come to give him a glass of Yiddisher tea.

MADGE. I'm his agent still. And Wink's his lawyer.

MAX. Parasites, germs, and viruses. You two, and Pamela, the famous Southern choreographer. . . .

MADGE. You went through quite a chunk of money yourself. What do you want with him?

MAX. Yesterday my old man raised thirty-five thousand on the property in Staten Island. It's mine in trust. He's spending it on this TV production. . . . Pathetic show-off slob. But I'm going to stop him, I'll tell Louis. (*Exits, angry and determined.*)

WINKLEMAN. What's he up to? He probably owes his bookie. He's forever in a booth having long phone conversations with crooks. Dimes are like goof pills to him. I'm glad I never had a son, never married.

MADGE. Why didn't you?

WINKLEMAN. I know my married friends lead *lovely* lives. But me? (*An elaborate sigh mocking himself and* MADGE.) There's an old poem—

To hold a horse, you need a rein,

To hold an elephant, a chain,

To hold a woman, you need a heart . . .

MADGE. Everyone has a heart.

WINKLEMAN. Every restaurant serves potatoes. (*Pause.*) We served too many potatoes to the old people. Now we're in trouble.

MADGE. Does Bummy suspect anything?

WINKLEMAN. So far I've kept it out of the news. Eight cases of malnutrition. If the inspector breaks it to the papers, we're ruined. I socked a quarter of a million into this. I told you we couldn't feed 'em on a buck a day.

MADGE. We could, but your mother took kickbacks on meat, eggs, bread, milk. Face it, she starved them.

WINKLEMAN. You gave her a hopeless budget. Look at these prices. Pot roast thirty-eight cents. Ground meat twenty-three cents. And what about special diets? Some of these people have diabetes, anemia.

MADGE. Why waste time here? I know, we need a lump of money to bribe our way out of a scandal. (*Pause.*) Only think, we used to get half a million a year out of Bummy. But that was before he shot his bolt.

WINKLEMAN. Still, he's never lost his audience sense.

MADGE. He did, he turned solemn, boring, a scold.

WINKLEMAN. Some of our biggest idealists made a career scolding.

MADGE. He should have stuck to his nonsense.

WINKLEMAN. But that's just it. The great public is tired of the old nonsense-type nonsense. It's ready for serious-type nonsense. This psychological setup is just the thing for a comeback. I would have given him the five thousand.

MADGE. Are you out of your head? Today? When we need every penny?

WINKLEMAN. I still say cooperate. I don't know what those highbrows at the Waldorf will think of his shenanigans, but what would Madison Avenue think?

MADGE (*Pondering*). You always were a thoughtful, imaginative angler.

WINKLEMAN. I've been in touch with Fiddleman.

MADGE (*Thunderstruck*). Leslie Fiddleman! But he wrote Bummy off years ago.

WINKLEMAN. At this moment Fiddleman, kingpin impresario, bigger than Hurok, is in his limousine en route to the Waldorf to watch the telecast at my invitation. Don't forget, those people are up against it for novelty. A billion-dollar industry, desperate for innovation. It fears death. It has to come up with something big, original, every month.

MADGE. But would Bummy go commercial again? He's half nuts over Freud. Just as Freud becomes passé.

WINKLEMAN. But on the lower levels the social order is just catching up with psychoanalysis. The masses want their share of insight. Anyway, put a five-million-dollar contract under Bummy's nose, and see what happens.

MADGE. Five! My commission is ten per cent. . . . Winkie, I'm sure he still has money stashed away. In this joint, too.

WINKLEMAN. Crafty he's always been.

MADGE. He'd never hide it. He'd put his dough in an obvious place. For instance, what's this old valise? Locks, chains. . . . It's like the nest-egg ad in *The New Yorker*.

WINKLEMAN. Open it.

MADGE. It's locked. Chained to this barber chair.

WINKLEMAN. He's his own bag man. This is his loot.

MADGE. I'll tip the chair, and you slip the chain out.

WINKLEMAN. Theft? Me? I'm a lawyer. I may be disbarred as it is.

MADGE. Calling me poor-mouth.

WINKLEMAN. Reading me sermons on anality. Ha-ha! That nut. He has charm. You must admit it. (*Shouting is heard above.*) My ridiculous cousin. What's he yelling about?

MADGE. Let's have a talk.

(*They go. Enter* BERTRAM *and* IMOGEN, *supporting* BUMMIDGE *wearing a sheet.*)

BERTRAM. Lucky I heard you. You almost fell out of the window.

IMOGEN. Why did you lean out so far?

BUMMIDGE. I saw Louie coming from the bank. Bertram, stall him. Keep the equipment coming.

BERTRAM. I'll do what I can. (*Exits.*)

BUMMIDGE (*Calling after* BERTRAM). Bring me a sandwich. Imogen, where's the schedule? (*Reads schedule.*) Dreams. Madge. Tante Frumkah. Couch work. I haven't done the couch work. Before the broadcast, I must. There's still a big block.

IMOGEN. You haven't eaten, haven't shaved.

BUMMIDGE. I can't stop. Must barrel through. I'm the instrument of a purpose beyond ordinary purpose. I may be the only man on the Eastern Seaboard with a definitely higher purpose. What a thing to get stuck with.

IMOGEN. Ready for the session. (*Sits with stenographic pad.*) Number eight-one-oh-eight.

BUMMIDGE (*Lying down*). Eight-one-oh-eight. (*Mutters.*) One-oh-eight. (*Rises.*) Imogen, I can't do this alone. I must call in the analyst.

IMOGEN. I understand. The tension must be frightful.

BUMMIDGE. Well, Mr. Bummidge, how is the psyche today? Lie down, stretch out. How do you intend to proceed? I leave you complete freedom of choice, as an analyst should.

(*Throughout this scene, he wears glasses as the analyst. Removing them, he is the patient.*)

BUMMIDGE (PATIENT). Doctor, things are not good. Last night I dreamed of a male with breasts. After this I found myself in a swimming pool, not swimming, not wet. An old gentleman with a long beard floats by. Such a long white beard, and rosy cheeks.

BUMMIDGE (ANALYST). The material is quite mixed. Water stands for the amniotic bag-of-waters. A beard refers to the father-figure.

BUMMIDGE (PATIENT). I have to tell you, Doctor, I'm fed up with these boring individuals in my unconscious. It's always Father, Mother. Or breast, castration, anxiety, fixation to the past. I am sick of them!

BUMMIDGE (ANALYST). You're sick *from* them. Man is the sick animal. Repression is the root of his madness, and also of his achievements.

BUMMIDGE (PATIENT). Oh, Doctor, why can't I live without hope, like everybody else?

BUMMIDGE (ANALYST). Mr. Bummidge, you are timid but obstinate. Exceptional but commonplace. Amusing but sad. A coward but brave. You are stuck. The Id will not release you to the Ego, and the Ego cannot let you go to the Id.

BUMMIDGE (PATIENT). No resolution?

BUMMIDGE (ANALYST). Perhaps. If you can laugh. But face the void of death. Why do you dream of your father?

BUMMIDGE (PATIENT). But was it Papa? Papa had no beard. In his last illness, he shaved his mustache. (*Sits.*) I was shocked by this. Pa . . . oh, Pa, your lip is so white. Age and weakness have suddenly come over you. Too feeble to count out the *Daily Mirrors*. Mustache gone, face changed, your eyes are so flat, they show death. Death, what are you doing to Papa? You can't . . . Is this the mighty hero I feared? Him with the white lip? Papa, don't go from us.

BUMMIDGE (ANALYST). Don't be deceived by surface feelings, Mr. Bummidge. Remember—ambivalence. You may not really feel compassion. An old enemy and rival is going down. In your heart you also exulted. Maybe you wanted him to live only to see your success.

BUMMIDGE (PATIENT). I don't believe it.

IMOGEN (*Applauding*). Good!

BUMMIDGE (PATIENT). You're a hard-nosed man. Why do you prefer the ugliest interpretations? (*Enter* BERTRAM *with a sandwich.*) I loved my old father . . . I want to weep.

IMOGEN. He's giving it to himself today.

BUMMIDGE (ANALYST). Did I invent the human species? It can't be helped. I want to cry, too.

BUMMIDGE (PATIENT). My father couldn't bear the sight of me. I had adenoids, my mouth hung open—was that a thing to beat me for? I liked to hum to myself while eating—was that a thing to beat me for? I loved to read the funnies—is that any reason to whip a child? (*Looks into sandwich and mutters to* BERTRAM.) More mustard. (*His voice rises.*) Killjoy! You attacked all my pleasure sources. But I fought. I hid in the cellar. I ate pork. I was a headliner at the good old Trilby. The good-for-nothing became a star and earned millions, making people laugh—all but Papa. He never laughed. What a peevish face. Laugh, you old Turk. Never! Well, you grim old bastard, I made it. You're dead, and I'm still jumping. What do I care for your grave? Let Madge look after it. Down goes the coffin. Down. The hole fills with clay. But Bummidge is still spilling gravy at life's banquet, and out front they're laughing fit to bust. (*He laughs, close to tears.*) Yes, I am that crass man, Bummidge. Oh, how foul my soul is! I have the Pagliacci gangrene. Ha, ha, ha—weep, weep, weep!

BUMMIDGE (ANALYST). Do you see the Oedipal strain in this situation? What of your mother?

BUMMIDGE (PATIENT). I saw I'd have Mama to myself. *She* laughed. Oh, what a fat throaty laugh she had. Her apron shook.

BUMMIDGE (ANALYST). But what did you want with your mother?

BUMMIDGE (PATIENT). You mean the mother who bathed me in the little tin tub by the kitchen stove? Oh, Doctor, what are you suggesting?

BUMMIDGE (ANALYST). Don't repress the poisonous truth. Go deeper.

BUMMIDGE (PATIENT). How deep?

BUMMIDGE (ANALYST). As deep as you can.

BUMMIDGE (PATIENT). Will there ever be a bottom?

BUMMIDGE (ANALYST). Does the universe have a bottom?

BUMMIDGE (PATIENT). How can I bear it? I, too, am blind. Like Oedipus, grown in corrupt habits. Oh, hubris! I put a rose bush on Mama's grave. But Papa's grave is sinking, sinking. Weeds cover the tombstone. Oh, shame, Jocasta! (*Collapses on floor.*)

IMOGEN. Oh, Mr. Bummidge, marvelous! Those Greek terms! You're so well read!

BERTRAM. Quite extraordinary. If you perform like this on television, the analysts will give you an ovation.

IMOGEN. He ought to have the Nobel Prize. I think psychology is worth every sacrifice. I love it more and more.

BUMMIDGE. My whole brain is like a sea of light. (*He unlocks the valise. Now* BUMMIDGE THE PATIENT *puts twenty dollars on the couch.*) This is one point on which I can't break with orthodox Freudianism. You must pay the analyst.

(*Enter* MADGE *and* WINKLEMAN.)

BUMMIDGE (ANALYST) (*Picks up the money*). Thank you.
BERTRAM. Better lock up the doctor's money.
IMOGEN. Bank it for him.
BUMMIDGE. He prefers cash. He doesn't have to pay taxes.

(*Exit* BUMMIDGE *with* BERTRAM *and* IMOGEN. *Enter* MAX *upstairs, goes into bedroom.*)

MADGE (*Going rapidly to the valise*). Money. He usually puts it in the bag. (*Revelation.*) Loaded.

(*Enter* MOTT.)

MOTT (*Offstage—angry, shaken*). Boy, is he dishonest! Bummy! (WINKLEMAN *runs into the bathroom.*) (*Offstage.*) Where is he, your brother? He wrote a bad check. I wouldn't believe the teller. No funds? "What?" I said.

MADGE (*Soothing*). You won't pull out because of a few dollars. This broadcast is too important, Louie.

MOTT. No sweet talk, please. It's too late. Thirty years ago you turned me down flat.

MADGE (*Shades of youthful allure*). I was a foolish girl. I thought you were attacking me. I'd be smarter now, maybe. You're still so youthful.

MOTT. Excuse me . . . I didn't mean . . . I think you're lovely. Don't get me wrong . . . I used to get such a flash when I saw you—in the old days.

MADGE (*With, alas, antiquated wiles*). You're a dear, Louie. Louie, we mustn't let my brother down. He's been a true friend. He saved you from those Boston hoodlums during Prohibition.

MOTT. True. I was in the dehydrated-wine business. Dry, purple bricks. Add water, make wine. Boston Blackie tried to muscle me out.

MADGE. Bummy saved you.

MOTT. Yes, true. I don't deny it. I tell everybody.

MADGE. He's always helped you. Staked you six different times. Covered for you with women. Even got you this little electronics racket.

MOTT. I admit that. He paid for the course. Enrolled me personally.

MADGE. Don't cry. I know how emotion tears your Hungarian heart.

MOTT (*Moved*). Bummy says I suffer from moral dizziness. No roots. Only loose wires. But when he gives bad checks . . .

MADGE. Louie, I myself will make it good.

MOTT. You? (*All business again.*) Sorry . . . but not in trade. I have to have cash.

MADGE. I'll let you in on a good thing. We have people watching at the Waldorf. Fiddleman . . .

MOTT (*Impressed*). Leslie—the impresario?

MADGE. You know my brother still has greatness in him. Money!

He's due for a revival. He'll be bigger than ever. Money! I want you to pipe the broadcast not only to the scientists but also to an adjoining suite. NBC, CBS, ABC will be watching. With sponsors. The biggest.

MOTT. Is that so? That's clever. Can do. But my balance . . .

MADGE. You'll be cut in. There's enough dough for all. I guarantee it. (*She lightly kicks Bummidge's valise. Enter* TECHNICIAN.)

TECHNICIAN. Well, what gives?

MOTT (*Wavers, then decides*). We work. Start hooking up. (MADGE *and* MOTT *shake hands. Exit* MADGE. *Enter* BUMMIDGE, *now wearing trousers and a T-shirt.* MAX *follows him.*)

BUMMIDGE. Max, don't be destructive.

MAX. Take this crap out.

BUMMIDGE. Oh, Louie. Don't let me down over a few bucks. I know the check was rubber, but—

MOTT. It was a lousy thing to do. But I've thought it over and decided to be big about it. You have another hour to raise the dough.

BUMMIDGE (*Sincerely grateful*). Oh, you generous heart.

MAX (*Seizing a cable*). I'm going to sabotage this whole thing. (*He and* BUMMIDGE *tug at cable.*)

TECHNICIAN. That line is hot. Watch it!

(*The fuses blow. The stage is plunged into darkness. Green and red sparks fly.* BUMMIDGE *screams.*)

BUMMIDGE. My son wants to electrocute me!

MOTT. He blew everything.

BUMMIDGE. Ruined! Lights, lights! Imogen, Bertram!

MOTT. My flashlight! We have to find the fusebox.

(BUMMIDGE *lights a candle,* MOTT *holding a flashlight.* MOTT *and* TECHNICIAN *run out.*)

BUMMIDGE. What the Christ do you think you're doing?

MAX. You're not throwing my dough out the window. I need it today.

BUMMIDGE. Every minute is precious. Guests are waiting at the Waldorf—eminent people.

MAX. Sure, you're the center of everything. Everybody has to wait. You breathe all the air, eat all the food, and lay all the women.

BUMMIDGE (*Alters his tone*). Poor child, master this Oedipal hate and love. You mustn't waste fifty years distorting simple facts. Your father is only flesh and blood. Think, Max, think for dear life.

MAX. You think. Why wouldn't you be Bella's husband, the public's favorite?

BUMMIDGE. You mean a nice, square, chuckling Santa Claus to entertain the expense-account aristocracy with gags?

MAX. What else are you good for?

BUMMIDGE. I'm all for the emancipation of youth. Even at your age. My boy, this war of fathers and sons is a racket. Humankind has an instinct for complaint.

MAX. If we're going to have one of these high-level theoretical talks, you might start by zipping your fly.

BUMMIDGE. Is it open? It isn't worth a glance.

MAX. Let it hang out!

BUMMIDGE. You're just a child fanatic.

MAX. When I drove you and that choreographer to Boston, she was giving me the high sign, open zipper.

BUMMIDGE. Pamela? Why, you crumb— You— You ex-sperm, you.

MAX. Old egomaniac!

BUMMIDGE. Quick, before you provoke me to terrible violence, what do you want?

MAX. You grabbed my property on Staten Island. That's theft. You owe me a good start in life.

BUMMIDGE. I've given you twenty starts. The starting line is worn out.

MAX (*In earnest*). What's the reason for all this analysis? You latch on to everybody who knocks at the door—delivery boys, ratcatchers, bill collectors. You make them act out psychological situations. Are you kidding your way to God? What makes a comic think he can cure human perversity? It'll only take different forms. If you change your vices, is that progress?

BUMMIDGE. Mankind's in trouble. I watched the public laugh at my tired, dull jokes. Ah . . . those stale hearts. Laughing. And how do they laugh in this desperate age? Ha, ha, ha I'm lying. Ha, ha, ha, I'm dying. Ha, ha, I'm nothing. Dust, dust! No hope, no truth, no energy. And funniest of all, life has no meaning. That breaks me up, ha, ha.

MAX. Why take it on yourself? Do your work, draw your dough, and to hell with it.

BUMMIDGE. My work? It's being stolen from me. Everybody is kidding, smiling. Every lie is a pleasantry. Destruction is horseplay. Chaos is amusement. Murder! Sadism! Extermination! This is what drives clowns to thought. (*Gravely.*) To thought.

MAX. Dad.

BUMMIDGE. Max! You called me Dad. Max!

MAX. Pa! (*They are about to embrace. He turns.*) It's just an expression. Don't confuse everything. I'm here to talk business. Listen, Bummy, there's a shipment of toasters from Czechoslovakia refused by the importer because the cords are faulty. I know where to put my hands on the right Japanese-made cords, and there's an importer from Honduras, waiting.

BUMMIDGE. What have I begotten?

MAX. Another father would be proud. I beat those Czechs down to nothing. Ten grand today gets me thirty tomorrow. For twenty I can buy into a frozen-lasagne operation. All I want from you is three grand. Deduct it from the thirty-five you stole from me.

BUMMIDGE. In other words, you have seven and need three. Max, why don't you lend me five and take my note for thirty?

MAX (*Recoiling*). What, invest in your fantasies?

BUMMIDGE. Me you accuse of fantasy? You with the toasters and the guys from Honduras and Japan who'll make you a fortune in lasagne? In the sandbox I watched over you. In the incubator I read to you about the Oedipus complex.

MAX. Lucky I couldn't understand. You would have addled my brains, too.

(*Lights go on.*)

BUMMIDGE. I wanted to lead you out of the realm of projections into the light of sanity. But you prefer the institutionalized psychosis of business.

MAX. Old lunatic!

BUMMIDGE. You may not be my child. Men have been tricked before.

MAX. Profound old fart!

BUMMIDGE. Spirochete! Filterable virus! Your mother took my money. Bug her.

MAX. You hocked my building. (*Jumps up and down in a tantrum.*) You could go to jail.

BUMMIDGE. From a winged boy into a tailored vulture.

MAX. I may have you committed. . . . You wait, I'll be back with a warrant. An injunction. There'll be no telecast. (*In running out, he bumps into the valise,* MOTT, TECHNICIAN, *and* BERTRAM.) Get out of my way! What's this? What are all these chains? (*Exits.*)

TECHNICIAN. What's eating him?

BUMMIDGE. My son has wounded me. Wounded me.

TECHNICIAN. It's the generation business. Well, he's not a junkie and you can still tell his sex, I think?

BUMMIDGE. While I bleed may be the moment to capture the meaning of the pains, which come out from a man's interior like lepers. (*Exits.*)

MOTT. Tough!

(*He and* TECHNICIAN *go about their work.* BERTRAM *is curious, watching.*)

BERTRAM. It all connects, eh? This wire plugs into this wire and it all comes out at the Waldorf?

MOTT. I could transmit to Iceland, if I wanted. . . . I wonder how Bummy'll be.

BERTRAM. Brilliant.

MOTT. Didn't you first come here as the exterminator?

BERTRAM. As soon as I saw the place I realized there were rats. You ask me how? I feel the molding, the baseboards. Rats have greasy fur, and they always run along the wall. Also, a rat drops many pellets.

MOTT. Ugh!

BERTRAM. The expert can date these pellets accurately. By a gentle squeeze of thumb and forefinger. Infallible. He also puts an ear to the wall. Rats must gnaw to survive. Otherwise the fangs'd get too long to chew with, their mouths would lock, and they'd starve. Bummy and I have scientific interests in common. What now?

TECHNICIAN. We hook the A line to this camera.

BERTRAM. Bummy and I hit it off right away. I got involved in psychotherapy. He showed me that to go around killing rats meant I must be compulsive, obsessional. The rat often symbolizes the child, as in the "Pied Piper." The rat also stands for a primordial mystery. Earth mystery. Chthonic. But most of all, my sense of humor fascinated Bummy. I don't laugh at jokes.

MOTT (*Curious*). Never?

BERTRAM. I can't. I'm too neurotic. (*He stands between* MOTT *and the* TECHNICIAN.) I have no sense of humor. I only have occasion to laugh.

TECHNICIAN. When does that happen?
BERTRAM. Mainly when I'm tickled.

(*They tickle him. He laughs horribly. They are aghast.*)

MOTT. Stop! Stop it!
BERTRAM. I know. It's pathological. Tickling shouldn't make a normal person laugh.
TECHNICIAN. Let's see.

(*He and* MOTT *solemnly tickle each other. Enter* IMOGEN.)

IMOGEN. Mr. Bummidge doesn't realize how fast time is passing.

(*Enter* BUMMIDGE.)

BUMMIDGE. To understand Max, I must revisit *my* father.
MOTT (*A bit shocked*). But he's dead. . . .
BUMMIDGE (*Holy, pedantic*). In the unconscious, Louie, there is no time, no logic, and no death.
MOTT. Let's set up these lights.
TECHNICIAN. We need a sound level.
BUMMIDGE. Bertram, you'll play Father. We live behind the candy store in Williamsburg. . . . It was so dark there. Dark. And poverty.
MOTT. Here goes the poor-childhood routine again. How he fetched wood and coal. Was beaten. Peddled papers. Froze his ears. How there was never real toilet paper in the house, only orange wrappers.
BUMMIDGE. Papa wouldn't allow me to have candy. I stole. I'd wolf down the stale chocolates, choking. Now Bert, as Papa, you discover a Mary Jane wrapper floating in the toilet. You clutch my ear and cry out, "Thief! Goniff!"
BERTRAM (*Taking* BUMMIDGE *by the ear*). Thief—goniff.
IMOGEN. I wouldn't want Bertram to pinch my ear.
BUMMIDGE. Harder, Bert. Don't just squeeze—twist. It's essential to feel the pain.
BERTRAM (*Warningly*). It's not a good idea to encourage my cruelty.
MOTT. Go on, Bert, turn it on.

(BERTRAM, *face transformed, twists.* BUMMIDGE *screams.*)

BUMMIDGE. That's it! Unbearable! (*Sinks to his knees.*) I haven't felt such agony in forty years. (*Supplicating.*) Papa, Papa! Don't! I'm only a child. I have an innocent craving for sweets. It's human nature. I inherit it from you, Papa, it's the pleasure principle. *Lust Prinzip.*

IMOGEN. He's read simply everything.

BERTRAM. Mine son stealing?

BUMMIDGE (*Rises*). No, Bert, Papa had a ballsy voice. (*Imitates his father.*) "By thirteen I was already in the sweat shop, brought home pay. God helped, I got this lousy business. All day buried behind a dark counter with broken feet; with gall bladder; blood pressure. I sell egg-cream, mushmellows, cheap cigars, gumballs—all kinds of dreck. But you, your head lays in idleness? Play? Fun? Candy? You'll be a mensch or I'll kill you." (*Himself again. Reflecting.*) A humorless savage, he was. But I loved him. Why won't my son love me? My father whipped me. (*Bending, he canes himself.*)

MOTT. Now he's a flagellant?

BUMMIDGE (*Kneeling, head to the floor*). Flogged.

IMOGEN. Oh, dear, he'll have an attack of Humanitis.

TECHNICIAN. What's Humanitis?

BERTRAM. It's when the human condition is suddenly too much for you.

BUMMIDGE (*Sitting on the floor*). When he punished me, I took myself away and left an empty substitute in his hands. (*Crawls toward exit, sits again.*) That was the beginning of my comic method. (*Explaining the matter to himself, he goes.* BERTRAM *helps him off.*)

IMOGEN. We'll never be ready, at this rate. (*Works on throne.*)

MOTT (*To* TECHNICIAN). Hey, John, go down to the truck and get the rest of those cables. (*Exit* TECHNICIAN.) I talked the office into giving Bummy a little more time.

IMOGEN. That's kind of you.

MOTT. That's the kind of friend I am. . . . Imogen. (*Grabs her waist.*) As soon as I saw you, I had like a tremendous flash!

IMOGEN (*Trying to free herself*). Mr. Mott!

MOTT. You're my erotic type.

IMOGEN. Don't, Mr. Mott. I can't bear to be a sexy joke. I really am a serious person.

MOTT. This *is* serious. I'm a mature man, single, youthful. Sex today is crazy in New York. Plus the danger of V.D. I'm reliable.

IMOGEN. No, no. Someone's coming. (*Flees.*)

MOTT. Drat! And Double Drat! Wish I . . . wait. I could've brought a hacksaw from the truck. There may be a bad link. Is it bonds, something valuable, or just food? (*Shakes the valise and then takes cover as* WINKLEMAN *enters.*)

WINKLEMAN. My nose is like radar. It's not much to look at, but ... it has extrasensory, metaphysical powers. Oh! I've been seen! (*Hides. Enter* MADGE.)

MADGE. Winkie? Are ya still in the bathroom? Money! (*Tries to open valise.*) Quizzing me about diamonds! Or, if Bummy is crazy, I have to have money for a private institution. I'll never put my· brother in a state hospital. It's loosening. I think I can get one end open. Can I squeeze my hand in? (*She does.*) Is it money? It is—it is money! (*She hears* PAMELA *offstage; hand caught in valise, she hides with* WINKLEMAN. *Enter* PAMELA. *She has a slight Southern accent.*)

PAMELA. Bummy? Where are you, dear? I've come to be with you on this important day. (*Thinking she is alone.*) It's sure to be a bomb. Then we can stop pretending. Love, science. "Oh, value, value. I'll die without value." What a drag. Bummy! (*Tickling* MADGE *and* WINKLEMAN *in barber chair.*)

WINKLEMAN. Why, it's Pamela.

PAMELA. Shall we play peek-a-boo? I love to catch people red-handed. Such a luxurious feeling.

MADGE. Help me. (*With* PAMELA *and* WINKLEMAN *helping,* MADGE *frees her hand and falls backward.*)

PAMELA. You'll have to cut me in. Let's not waste time lying. I understand what you're up to. If Bummy gets offers, you'll need my help, my persuasive powers.

MADGE (*As she and* WINKLEMAN *exchange glances, shrug, and accept the inevitable*). Okay.

PAMELA. Life isn't easy for a person like me. If we can put Bummy back in the big time I can lead the respectable life. I'll find out what he's got in this bag. He must carry the keys. Come, let's work out the details. (*She goes off.*)

WINKLEMAN. Why didn't I retire two years ago, when I was ahead? Lead a quiet life? Write the Comedy Humane of New York? (*Exits with* MADGE.)

(BUMMIDGE *and* BERTRAM *enter.* BUMMIDGE *is holding a child's potty.*)

BUMMIDGE. Bert, this was a real piece of luck. This is just like the one Mama sat me on. It will help me to re-enter my infancy.

BERTRAM. You won't sit on that during the broadcast, will you?

BUMMIDGE. I'm not sure. But the Ego has hung a veil, the veil of infantile amnesia, over the earliest facts of life. I have to tear it down. See the bare truth. . . .

BERTRAM. Can it be done?

BUMMIDGE. Shush! (*Finger to lips.*) A quiet corner. A bit of reverie. We were all *body* once. Then we split.

BERTRAM. The trauma . . .

(PAMELA *comes in.*)

BUMMIDGE. O Trauma. O Regression—Sublimation! I think this is a good spot. (*He squats behind the sofa, so that only his head is visible.*)

BERTRAM (*Catching sight of* PAMELA). Don't get settled yet.

BUMMIDGE. History itself has put us in this position.

PAMELA. Lover?

BUMMIDGE (*Leaps up*). Just as I was beginning to feel something. Bert, go clear everything with Mott.

(*Exit* BERTRAM.)

PAMELA. What are you doing?

BUMMIDGE. Therapy, dear. Therapy. I didn't expect to see you.

PAMELA. On a day like this? I came to help.

BUMMIDGE. Where have you been?

PAMELA. Thinking of you. Of your ideas. Our future. (*Sits on sofa.*)

BUMMIDGE. Where were you last night?

PAMELA. Why, darling, I was visiting Mother. We went out to U.S. One for a pizza pie. I told her how happy we'd be if you became a professor of dramatic psychology.

BUMMIDGE (*Lies on couch with her*). I've figured out the main forms of love. A man can love a woman on the tenderness system. That's very good. Or on the lust system. That's better than nothing. Or on the pride system. That's worse than nothing.

PAMELA. You're brain all over. Sheer brain. (*They rise and move toward valise.*)

BUMMIDGE. Sweetheart—that diamond anklet— (*Points.*) Bought when I was flush. I paid Tiffany twelve grand.

PAMELA. Kiss me, Bummy, hold me close. (*Goes through his pockets; gets the key to the valise.*)

BUMMIDGE. I could pawn it for five. Louie Mott would take it.

(*They are now back to back.* BUMMIDGE *holds* PAMELA *by the ankle and removes her shoe. She, meanwhile, is opening the valise.*)

PAMELA. All my life I've looked for nothing but peace, security, quiet, but I always wind up in some absurd mixup.

BUMMIDGE. What large shoes.

PAMELA. You're just a force of nature.

BUMMIDGE (*Removing the anklet*). I've got it.

PAMELA. It's opening. Thousands! (*They fall apart.*) You've got thousands here.

BUMMIDGE. Earmarked for a higher purpose.

PAMELA. My anklet! Give it back!

BUMMIDGE. Where did you get the keys?

PAMELA. You thief!

BUMMIDGE. You picked my pocket. (*He shuts and locks the valise while* PAMELA *tries to recover the anklet.* LOUIS MOTT *runs in.*)

MOTT. Your wife is below—Bella.

BUMMIDGE. Keep her away.

(*Enter* BERTRAM.)

BERTRAM. Bummy, your estranged Missis!

BUMMIDGE (*To* PAMELA). You'd better go.

PAMELA. Without my jewels? Like hell I will. (*In a temper.*) I came to help you.

BUMMIDGE. My scientific demonstration—the biggest thing in my life.

PAMELA. I won't go.

BERTRAM. Where can we put her? The broom closet?

MOTT. What about the toilet?

BERTRAM. The bedroom.

PAMELA. I'll wait a few minutes. I won't go without those diamonds.

(BERTRAM *and* MOTT *hurry* PAMELA *to the bedroom.*)

BUMMIDGE. Certainly, dear, later. Lock that door. Oh, my character has created another typical crisis. My repetition compulsion. (*To statue of Freud.*) O Master, how deep you were! . . . Imogen! Where is she? Astray again? That poor sexual waif. I must stop Bella in the hall. (*Exits with* BERTRAM.)

(*Enter* IMOGEN.)

IMOGEN. Did Mr. Bummidge call me?

MOTT. Imogen, as soon as I see you my pulses jump.

IMOGEN (*Fights him off*). Mr. Mott, don't. It's almost broadcast time.

MOTT. A flash! A red haze. And from below I get this gentle, gentle heat. Here. Feel. . . . Where's your hand?

(*Pounding at the door.*)

IMOGEN (*Struggling*). Someone's coming.

MOTT (*All over her*). I'm oblivious!

IMOGEN. You look so . . . icky.

MOTT. It's virility. You'll be astonished. Ecstatic. Wait till you see. Hungarians are famous that way.

(*Someone is battering the door.* MOTT, *blowing a kiss, takes off.*)

IMOGEN. I'm coming. . . . (*She opens the door. Enter* AUFSCHNITT, *carrying a coat.*)

AUFSCHNITT (*Crossing*). Is Mr. Bummidge here? I am his tailor.

IMOGEN. I thought you were his wife.

AUFSCHNITT. I came with the coat for his broadcast.

(*Enter* BELLA, *large and aggressive, pushing past them into the room, outlandishly dressed. One can see that* PAMELA *has made a study of* BUMMIDGE'*s wife in order to give him—or pretend to give him—all that* BELLA *could never conceivably offer.*)

BELLA. Where is he, that miserable man? And where is that cheap lay of his?

AUFSCHNITT. Mrs. Bummidge, I have your husband's coat. But this time he must pay.

BELLA. Good luck. Imogen, tell him I've come. (*Sits.*)

IMOGEN. I'll try and find him. (*Exits.*)

BELLA. He's somewhere near, listening.

(*She looks for him. We hear the rumble of thunder. Enter* BERTRAM, *instructed to get rid of* BELLA.)

BERTRAM. Mrs. Bummidge, are you looking for your husband?

BELLA. So, where is the great mental wizard? Ah, it's the rat-catcher. You must get your suits in the morgue. Where is he? (*Looking around.*) This place has changed, things have been added—for instance, what is that?

BERTRAM. Well, you know I am a trapper by nature and I have to have devices like snares, cages, and nets. You see a gorilla in a zoo, he has to have a tree trunk to feel at home.

(*Enter* BUMMIDGE *as a little boy, playing hopscotch.*)

BELLA. So. Here's our kiddy. How old are you, little man?

BUMMIDGE. Six and a half.

BELLA. And are you a good little boy?

BUMMIDGE. Yes, otherwise my parents hit me with rulers. They slash me with straps. So I am.

BELLA. And what are you going to be when you grow up?

BUMMIDGE. A little Pagliacci.

AUFSCHNITT. Mr. Bummidge, are you ready for the coat? (BUM-MIDGE *stands as* AUFSCHNITT *fits the coat.*)

BELLA (*Laughing at* BUMMIDGE *in his coat*). Look at that! What a freak he is! Now you'll pay what—sixty G's?—to play psychiatrist to that howling gang at the Waldorf.

BUMMIDGE. Who's howling? Have you been there?

BELLA. Certainly, and a rummier bunch I never saw. Gobbling hors d'oeuvres. Eating and drinking. (*She puts her purse on couch near him and strides about.*)

BUMMIDGE (*When her back is turned, examines her purse*). You saw the gatecrashers. Now Bella, you dear woman . . .

BELLA (*Snatches away her purse, shouting*). I'll never let you snow me again.

BUMMIDGE (*Angrily, pursuing her about stage as* AUFSCHNITT *tries to fit the coat*). Then what do you want?

BELLA. I have my reasons, never mind. Legally I'm still your wife.

BUMMIDGE. You took everything. One, two, three, O'Leary . . . I'm clinging to my theory, four, five, six, O'Leary . . .

BELLA. I had to stop you from squandering every cent on broads. And this choreographer. A whore.

BUMMIDGE. She loves me.

AUFSCHNITT. Don't move your arms too much. It's a rush job. The seams are weak.

(*The* TECHNICIAN *enters with a make-up kit.*)

TECHNICIAN. Let's see you under the lights. Your skin is peculiar.

BELLA. You took her to Europe to see old opera houses. Me you left behind. You think Pamela loves you for your personality? For your brilliant mind? For your bad bridgework? And your belching, and getting up ten times a night to pee? (*Her eye is caught by an open newspaper.*) Oh, Xerox, down three-eighths.

BUMMIDGE (*Smoothing the front of his coat*). Bella, stop bothering me.

TECHNICIAN. Let me see what I can do with this complexion of yours. (*He drags a complaining* BUMMIDGE *to the barber chair.*)

BELLA. You kept me a prisoner for six months on that milk farm in Wisconsin.

BUMMIDGE. You weighed 220 pounds.

BELLA. You put a pistol on my night table to suggest suicide.

BUMMIDGE (*To* TECHNICIAN). I want to emphasize the serenity of my brow.

BELLA. I'm just an old-fashioned, goodhearted broad, an ordinary, practical, loyal woman.

BUMMIDGE. What corn. Aren't you ashamed of yourself? You're turning into a soap opera.

(*We hear another rumble of thunder and* PAMELA *pounding on the bedroom door.*)

BELLA. Why don't you explain to me? . . . I think we're going to have a thundershower.

BUMMIDGE. Listen, Bella, in eighteen fifty-nine Darwin published *The Origin of Species;* nineteen hundred, Freud came out with *The Interpretation of Dreams.* Now me!

BELLA. Now you what? For God's sake, Bummy. Don't go tell those intellectuals what they already know. They'll laugh at you.

BUMMIDGE. They know *nothing* about laughing. . . . Bella, there's something I can't forgive you. Never. (*Leaves the chair.*)

BELLA. What, now? What?

BUMMIDGE. You took the old Trilby Theater, and rented it for a meat market. Where names like "Bummidge," like "Bert Lahr," used to be on the marquee, we now have "The Kalbfuss Palace of Meats. Pork Butts Today."

BELLA (*Giving no ground*). So what?

BUMMIDGE. I'm going to restore it, rededicate it to comedy.

BELLA. Bring back vaudeville?

BUMMIDGE. No. I want to give it to the people. I want to make it a theater of the soul. For my *Existenz*-Action-Self-analysis.

BELLA. You want to bring psychoanalysis to the vaudeville stage? You want to reopen the Trilby. Utopia! Crazy. . . . Oh, one man's jokes are another man's theories. I don't get it.

BUMMIDGE. In this valise I have almost enough to buy the lease from Kalbfuss. I still need money for Louie. (*Runs to desk.*) Somewhere in this mess is the receipt from Tiffany's. (*Pulls out drawer.*) Ah, here. More than I thought. Fourteen thousand.

AUFSCHNITT. I won't leave this coat without you pay me.

BUMMIDGE. Bella, maybe you've got a few bucks.

BELLA. A headache from your theories, that's what I've got. (*Enter* BERTRAM.) Do you have aspirins in the bathroom? I'm sure you have rats in there. (*Exits.*)

BERTRAM. Rats? I slew them all. What does she mean rats?

AUFSCHNITT. Mr. Bummidge, ordinary people understand your cure. I have a daughter who won't even get out of bed.

BUMMIDGE. Single?

AUFSCHNITT. The bed or the daughter?

(*Enter* IMOGEN.)

BUMMIDGE. You and I could work together. In return, you don't bug me for the money?

AUFSCHNITT. For nothing?

IMOGEN. Mr. Bummidge, you have very little time. He's never too busy to hold out a hand to misery.

BUMMIDGE. Now, Aufschnitt, listen to me.

IMOGEN. It's started to rain.

BUMMIDGE. Aufschnitt, I am six years old. My parents have bought my first pair of galoshes for school. Gleaming black. A delicious smell of rubber. But my mother warns me, "Don't come home without those galoshes. Papa will kill you stone dead."

BERTRAM. It's raining out there. A regular monsoon.

BUMMIDGE. Listen, Aufschnitt, my first-grade teacher, Miss Farnum, was a blonde. You be Miss Farnum, and I'll be six.

AUFSCHNITT. What? Farnum is not our name. This is not about my daughter. She's not blonde.

BUMMIDGE. My teacher was.

(*Enter* MAX *and a private detective,* MR. GALLUPPO.)

MAX. Pop, Mr. Galluppo, here, is a private investigator.

BUMMIDGE. I have no time for him.

MAX. Listen to his report.

GALLUPPO (*Gazing about*). So this is what happens to old stars.

AUFSCHNITT. Why should I imitate a young teacher?

BUMMIDGE. Do it for your daughter. This can help her. Like this. (*Enacts Miss Farnum.*)

AUFSCHNITT. Like this? (*He tries.*)

BUMMIDGE. Quite good for a first effort.

AUFSCHNITT. How could it help my poor daughter Sandra?

BUMMIDGE. The other kids have gone home. But I don't dare. My galoshes? (*He and Aufschnitt hunt under chairs for the galoshes.*)

MAX (*To* GALLUPPO). Give your report on his friend Pamela. Where was she last night?

GALLUPPO. In premises at Six-Y Jones Street. She had relations with a gentleman of the other sex. Every night a different person.

BUMMIDGE (*With some hauteur*). You must have the wrong party. (*To* AUFSCHNITT.) Now, Miss Farnum. First you scold me. Then you stick out your tongue. I start to bawl. . . . You call me cry-baby.

AUFSCHNITT. Cry-baby.

(*Enter* MOTT. *The* TECHNICIAN *appears above.*)

MOTT. We've got to try the lights. John—get a sound level.

GALLUPPO. Is this a photo of the party in question?

MAX. You bet. Show it to my father.

IMOGEN (*Trying to interpose herself*). Oh, don't do that. You'll up-set everything.

BUMMIDGE. That's what he wants to do.

(GALLUPPO *shows photo to* AUFSCHNITT, *who can't bear to look.*)

AUFSCHNITT. Why me? I don't recognize these people. They have no clothes on.

GALLUPPO. Monday with a Wall Street broker. Tuesday with a bartender. Wednesday the super of her building. Thursday a blind man.

BUMMIDGE. I'm crying over my galoshes.

AUFSCHNITT. What a cry-baby! (*Puts out his tongue.*)

BUMMIDGE. She tried to make me laugh at my dread.

AUFSCHNITT. Cry-baby!

TECHNICIAN. What's he doing? What goes on?

IMOGEN. It's a cloudburst. They always affect him.

MOTT. Let's try those lights. Bert, give John a hand here. Bummy, you've got only twenty minutes.

BUMMIDGE. What? Louie, take these rocks. Tiffany's. Worth eight grand at least.

AUFSCHNITT. Cry-baby! Cry-baby!

BUMMIDGE. I should have laughed too. (*Tries laughter.*)

MAX. There'll be no broadcast. (*Enter* BELLA.) Mother, what are you doing here?

BELLA (*Pointing to* GALLUPPO). Does he do work for you too? I bet he's investigating the same person.

GALLUPPO. I didn't know you was related.

AUFSCHNITT. Cry-baby!

BELLA. Shut up! My head is splitting. (*Enter* WINKLEMAN *and* MADGE.) I knew they'd show up.

TECHNICIAN. Let's hear you speak a word or two.

BUMMIDGE. Foul! Low blow! (MAX *forces him to look at the photo. Enter a* MESSENGER.) What do you want?

MESSENGER. Western Union.

IMOGEN. I'll take the wire.

(*Exit* MESSENGER.)

(*Enter* TANTE FRUMKAH *in a wheelchair. She carries a cane.*)

WINKLEMAN. Here's Mother.

BUMMIDGE. Tante Frumkah! She's come!

FRUMKAH. Why is it so crowded and noisy?

(*Telephone rings.*)

BUMMIDGE. You were midwife at my birth. From the sightless universe into your hands! Bertram, answer.

(PAMELA *screams offstage.*)

BELLA. Is that a woman screaming somewhere?

BUMMIDGE. The wind! Wind and rain!

MADGE (*Persuasive, cooperative*). Now listen to me, Bummy.

BUMMIDGE (*Mistaking her tone*). You're all in my way.

AUFSCHNITT. You must pay me. Psychology is no pay. (*Tries to remove coat.*)

BERTRAM. It's Dr. Ratzenhofer on the phone. He says how long will the broadcast be? He has appointments.

BUMMIDGE. Oh, Dr. Ratzenhofer? He's sacrificing $50 an hour.

WINKLEMAN. How can you start in all this chaos?

MOTT. How do I know these diamonds aren't fake, or hot?

IMOGEN. The wire is from Kalbfuss. He's standing by.

BUMMIDGE. Kalbfuss! (*Throws his arms upward.*) Thank heaven for his loyalty.

AUFSCHNITT. The seams! The seams are opening!

BELLA. These are the fruits of my husband's originality. Confusion!

FRUMKAH (*Rapping with her cane*). I think this floor is sagging.

WINKLEMAN. Now, look here, Cousin, you've got Madge and me all wrong.

BELLA. Starving old people. Conditions worse than Andersonville.

BUMMIDGE. You've all come to prevent my broadcast.

MAX. That's right.

GALLUPPO (*Pulling out a paper*). I have a restraining order.

BELLA (*To* MAX). Oh, you shouldn't do this to your father.

(MOTT *is about to hit the diamonds with a hammer to see if they are real.*)

BUMMIDGE. Hold it! (*He restrains* MOTT. *There is silence. Then* BUMMIDGE *laughs strangely.*) Ladies and gentlemen. This fits in with today's performance. I invite you to witness a typical moment of human existence, showing mankind as it makes the most of its universal opportunities . . .

(*The next group of speeches is spoken together, jumbled.*)

MAX. Look how he turns the tables.

MADGE. I never know what he's talking about.

FRUMKAH. Why did I ever come?

GALLUPPO. Fifty bucks an hour I charge also. Same as a shrink.

WINKLEMAN. We can't let this go on!

(*They fall silent.*)

BUMMIDGE (*Violently*). Stop! Why are you here? You, a Roman crowd? I, an Asiatic slave?

MAX. Here comes the martyr bit.

BUMMIDGE (*Holds up both hands, fingers widely spread*). Shall I submit?

WINKLEMAN (*Trying vainly to soothe him*). Bummy, don't be carried away.

FRUMKAH. This is New York. 1971 a.d.

BUMMIDGE. All right, where is that staple gun? Imogen. (*He stands on the laundry basket.* IMOGEN *approaches with the stapler.*) Staple Bummidge to the cross. (IMOGEN *hands staple gun to* BERTRAM. *He staples* BUMMIDGE's *cuffs. His arms are outstretched.*)

WINKLEMAN. Wasted! He's using it all up before the broadcast.

MADGE. Save it for the cameras.

TECHNICIAN. I'm kind of impressed. He's like the old Claude Rains, Soulful.

GALLUPPO. This is blasphemy!

IMOGEN. Can't you see he's in pain? He's having an attack of Humanitis. Catch him.

BELLA. No, Bummy, no! I take it all back.

(PAMELA, *drenched, has forced her way in. She is gasping.*)

MOTT. We got just a little time before the broadcast. Let's take a five-minute break. (*He kneels and shoots dice with* FRUMKAH.)

BELLA (*As* PAMELA *collapses at* BUMMIDGE's *feet*). There's the whore in the picture. Now we got the full cast.

MOTT. Okay, roll 'em.

BUMMIDGE. Forgive them, Father, for, for ... What comes next?

CURTAIN

Act Two

(*Minutes later,* BUMMIDGE *has been extricated from his coat, which hangs empty on the wall. Onstage are* PAMELA, *who has wrapped herself, shivering, in the tapestry on the barber chair;* AUFSCHNITT, *who is taking down the coat in order to mend it;* MADGE, MAX, GALLUPPO, *and* BELLA. TANTE FRUMKAH *sits in her wheelchair smoking a cigar and studying business documents.* MOTT *is looking at his wristwatch.*)

MOTT. We may have to call it off.

MADGE. Nonsense! Too much is riding on Bummy for us all. Max understands now.

MAX. I see what you mean. I get it. He's going to do this anyway. We can't like him, so we exploit him instead.

BELLA. You *think* you can outsmart him. Wait. You'll see.

PAMELA. So far, I've lost my jewels. (MOTT *covertly lifts the anklet from his pocket and looks at it.*)

MADGE. Winkie is up in the bedroom with him, explaining that we offer full cooperation. All of us.

FRUMKAH (*To* AUFSCHNITT). And what's he doing?

AUFSCHNITT. Mending the raiment.

MADGE (*Suspicious*). Louis . . .

(*Enter* IMOGEN *and* BERTRAM. BERTRAM *carries an infant in his arms.*)

BERTRAM. Bummy wanted to see a little child. Where is he?

MADGE. The bedroom. . . .

BELLA. This child could use a clean diaper.

BUMMIDGE (*Entering excitedly with* WINKLEMAN). Undress it. I must see the original human material.

BERTRAM. Her mother is an alcoholic. I had to give her a twenty-dollar deposit.

FRIEDMAN-ABELES

IMOGEN. In the bar, across the street.

BUMMIDGE (*Enraptured*). Look at this freedom! How the little belly rises and falls. Everything loathsome about the human species is forgiven time after time, and with every child we begin again.

FRUMKAH. This I don't dig.

IMOGEN (*Explaining*). Heaven lies about us in our infancy. Then comes repression. Then we lost Eternity. Then we get shut up in Time and that's how it goes.

FRUMKAH (*Gestures with her cigar, looks upward*). Big deal. I delivered thousands.

MOTT. Bummy, it's practically zero hours.

BUMMIDGE (*Sentimental*). Take the baby, Bertram. Wait, I must have one last look. (*He looks tenderly at infant, as if to memorize it.*)

(BERTRAM *exits with baby.*)

PAMELA (*Comes forward*). Bummy, I have to have dry clothes. And where is my anklet?

BUMMIDGE (*Hurries to large wicker clothes hamper, opens it*). Here's something for you. (*Struck by an idea.*) There's something here for each of you. . . . Ah, yes. For each and every one. Marvelous! You'll all participate with me in the broadcast. Louie, throw away the old format.

WINKLEMAN. Ad lib? Now? But Bummy—think!

BUMMIDGE. That little infant shows me the way. All impulse. Impulse, the soul of freedom. (*Clutches his head, but smilingly.*)

PAMELA (*Unfolding the garment*). Why, this is nothing but a burlesque stripper's outfit!

BUMMIDGE (*To* WINKLEMAN). You said everyone would stand behind me.

MADGE. To a man! I remember Dr. Ehrlich and the magic bullet.

WINKLEMAN. And Semmelweiss, and Pasteur!

MOTT. Don't forget Richard Nixon. How against him they all were until he went on television with that little dog.

BUMMIDGE. And Pamela? You, too?

PAMELA (*Somewhat reluctant*). Yes, Bummy. You'll give back my diamonds, won't you? (*Exits.*)

BUMMIDGE (*As he watches her go*). The compulsion to suffer is attached to diamonds. Now listen, all of you. I'm going back to my sources and you'll all wear costumes. Imogen, hand them out. Louie, the hoodlum you were during Prohibition. (MOTT *goes to change.*) Madge, these rompers. (MADGE *goes.*) Max, my father. You resemble him. (MAX *puts on a shopkeeper's apron and a broad-brimmed hat.*) Bella, a bridal gown. (BELLA *goes.*) Winkie, wear this.

WINKLEMAN. Must I?

BUMMIDGE. Your cooperation is essential. (WINKLEMAN *goes.*) There's a reason why they're all so obliging. Woe unto you when all men shall speak well of you. (*Enter* BERTRAM.) But it's woe anyway, wherever you look. Imogen, dear, will you assist?

IMOGEN. Of course, Mr. Bummidge.

FRUMKAH. Where do I come in?

BUMMIDGE. This apron. Bertram, in my unconscious it turns out you have female characteristics. Wear this dress.

BERTRAM (*Accepting*). Female? Curious!

AUFSCHNITT. Can I be in the broadcast too? I've never been on television.

BUMMIDGE. Of course! Man! That's who you'll be. Repressed, civilized Man. Thread in your fingers and chains on your feet.

AUFSCHNITT. Fine! Give me chains!

GALLUPPO. And me?

BUMMIDGE. Sly, smiling, menacing . . . I have it! Bella's father. Yes! (*Enter* TECHNICIAN.)

TECHNICIAN. Where's the opening setup?

(*Enter* MOTT *dressed as a neighborhood tough.*)

MOTT. Places! Let's have lights.

BUMMIDGE. Louie, iris in on me here, by this statue of Freud.

IMOGEN. I'm dying of excitement!

MOTT. Time! Five, four, three, two, one—you're on.

BUMMIDGE (*Begins an attempt at smiling refinement*). Ladies and gentlemen of the psychiatric world. Honored guests. You know me as a comedian. But today I invite you to put away that old image. Look at this person, a human being. This hair, these eyes, this chin, stubby hands, a heart that beats: Philip Bummidge, sixty years old. Sixty-one years ago I was literally nothing. I was merely possible. Then I was conceived, and became inevitable. When I die, I shall be impossible. Meanwhile, between two voids, past and future, I exist. Medically, I seem quite sound. Strong as a horse. (*Feels his muscles.*) Twenty-twenty vision. (*Pulls down his underlids.*) Powerful lungs. (*Shouts: Hoy!*) (*Pauses.*) Nothing wrong with the organism, hey? But up here. (*Suddenly gloomy.*)

My mind! Inside my skull. My feelings, my emotions. (*Quite tragically.*)
Is this what we are meant to be? Oh, my character! How did I ever get
stuck with these monstrous peculiarities? Why so vivid within, so dead
outside? I feel like a museum of all the perversity, sickness, and ugliness
of mankind. O Death, take me or leave me, but don't haunt me anymore.
But it's because of death that we are individuals; organisms without death
have no true identity. We are what we are owing to our morbidity. (*In
earnest.*) I bless the day when I discovered how abnormal I was. I read
all the books, and, never forgetting that I was an actor, a comedian, I
formed my own method. I learned to obtain self-knowledge by doing
what I best knew how to do, acting out the main events of my life, dragging repressed material into the open by sheer force of drama. I'm not
solely a man but also a man who is an artist, and an artist whose sphere
is comedy. Though the conditions may be impossible, laughter in decay,
there is nothing else for me to do but face those real conditions. But
rather than lecture, I prefer to illustrate. Let me introduce, briefly, certain
friends and relatives. (*In the following scene, people come forward as
called, in their costumes.*) This is Tante Frumkah, who delivered me.
This, my young bride. This is my son representing my father. This lady,
my sister. And my colleague, Bertram, a mother figure. (*Enter* WINKLE-
MAN *in a Lord Fauntleroy costume.*) Oh, yes, this is my cousin Winkleman, Doctor of Jurisprudence.

WINKLEMAN. One must humor a client, a man of genius with brilliant ideas, a cousin.

BUMMIDGE. Good scout. . . .

(*Enter* PAMELA, *wearing her strip-tease costume.*)

BUMMIDGE. This lady represents the grandeur and misery of the
erotic life. These unfortunates are part of me, and I of them. Now, my
method, on the most elementary level, opens a channel to the past. Like
that old song (*Sings.*) —"I'm just a kid again, doin' what I did again."
(*All sing in chorus.* "When the Red, Red Robin . . ." *He leads them
forward. The group stands about him.*) Look at these miserable creatures.
I shall start with my old aunt. (*Wheels her forward.*) Tante, you bridge
many generations, and you have a long memory.

FRUMKAH. Like a old filing case, I am.

BUMMIDGE. Was mine a difficult birth?

FRUMKAH. On your father's scales you weighed fourteen pounds. It
was tough, but I pulled you through.

BUMMIDGE (*To camera*). She thinks she's being funny. (*To her.*) Now, when was I weaned?

FRUMKAH. Late. On the way to Prospect Park, on your mama's lap, your feet was dragging on the floor of the streetcar. You didn't want the breast, and your mama said, "All right, I'll give it to the conductor."

BUMMIDGE (*To camera*). An old gag. She's full of them. They're really sadistic threats. Now, when was I toilet-trained?

FRUMKAH. As soon as you could sit up.

BUMMIDGE. That's very bad!

FRUMKAH. But nobody could keep you clean. You made in your pants. You were a wild, disobedient boy, like your Uncle Mitchell.

BUMMIDGE (*To television audience*). She thinks she's irresistible.

FRUMKAH. He played baseball. Shortstop. The bus with his team fell in the Passaic River. It damaged his brains. On the Sea Beach Express he exposed himself to some girls from the shirtwaist factory.

BUMMIDGE (*To camera*). Old lobster shells of wit. The meat is gone. Tell the people more. . . .

FRUMKAH. Then there was Uncle Harold. He was a saxophone performer. On the Weehawken Ferry. During the War, he opened a brothel.

BUMMIDGE. From her jokes, you'd never guess what viciousness there was in her. (FRUMKAH *spreads her mouth with her fingers and makes a horrid face at him.*)

WINKLEMAN (*Sternly*). Mother! On the air!

FRUMKAH. Should I say more? Should I tell about Aunt Rose? (*Parodying her own family sentiments.*) All Perth Amboy listened in the street when she sang. Such a woice!

BUMMIDGE. No, enough. Take her away, Winkie. Infinite sadness salted with jokes. But . . . (*Lecturing.*) My method—as follows: I have trained myself to re-enter any phase of my life, at will. By bouncing a ball, rolling a hoop, sucking my thumb, I become like a child. When I want to visit the remote parts of my mind, I take to the couch. (*Lies down.*) Doctor, I had a dream. (*As analyst.*) Tell me all about it. (*As patient.*) I dreamt I was at sea in an old shoebox. (*Rising.*) Thus, ladies and gentlemen, I was able to isolate a hard core of problems, by adapting the methods of Freud—that Genius! (*Turns emotionally to bust.*) The disease I discovered in myself, I call Humanitis. An emotional disorder of our relation to the human condition. Suddenly, being human is too much for me. I faint, and stagger. (*He enacts the sick man. Holds dialogue with himself.*) "What's the matter, Bummidge? Don't you like other human beings?" "Like them! I adore them! Only I can't bear them." "I love 'em like a dog. So ardent, so smoochy. Wagging my tail. This sick, corrupt emotion leaks out of me." I don't have the strength to bear my feelings. (*Lecturing.*) This is the weakness of my comedy. When the laughing stops, there remains a surplus of pain.

BERTRAM. He's going to explain about the Pagliacci gangrene.

BUMMIDGE. The Pagliacci gangrene! Caused as all gangrene is by a failure of circulation. Cut off by self-pity. Passivity. Fear. Masochistic rage. Now (*Smiling and bowing.*) I shall ask you to follow me into the library, where I have prepared an exhibit of charts and diagrams. (*Exits, followed by the* TECHNICIAN *with camera, and by* MOTT.)

FRUMKAH. You think you sell this? I'd walk out. Worst show I ever saw.

MAX. It's like a lecture at the New School, but crazier.

IMOGEN. Every word of it is clear to me.

BERTRAM. Plain as day.

WINKLEMAN. There's millions in it. (*Desperate.*) It's got to work.

MAX. If it doesn't, I've lost out on one of the biggest deals that ever came my way.

PAMELA. I want my jewels back.

BELLA. It's a miracle you can keep them on those skinny ankles.

PAMELA. Better petite (*Illustrates.*) than a ball breaker.

BELLA. Petite! Dry bones. You could do a fan dance with fly swatters. (*They begin to fight.*)

GALLUPPO. Here, break it up. (*Takes a police grip on* PAMELA *as* WINKLEMAN *restrains* BELLA.)

MADGE. No scrapping.

BERTRAM. Bummy won't fail.

WINKLEMAN (*Sweating, he tries to persuade them*). Freud has filtered down to the broad masses. The mental level has to rise—must!

FRUMKAH. Listen to my son! I had only one, but with the brains of five.

WINKLEMAN. Out there are millions of Americans. Faith. I ask you to have a little faith in American capitalism.

FRUMKAH. Wheel me back. Here he comes.

(MOTT *comes in with camera.*)

MOTT. One side. Clear it. Get Bummidge as he enters the doorway. Go, camera.

BUMMIDGE (*Entering*). Such, my friends, is the Pagliacci gangrene, crying as you laugh, and making a fortune from ambiguity. Now let us have a brief look at my career. At twenty I sing and dance at the Old Trilby.

BERTRAM (*Sings*).

> Oh I went to school with Maggie Moiphy
> And Maggie Moiphy went to school with me-e-e.
> I tried to get the best of Maggie Moiphy,
> But the sonofagun, she got the best of me.

(*Another routine.*)

> Lady, lady, put out your can
> I think I hear the garbage man.

BUMMIDGE (*As lady, answering*).

> But Mister, I don't want any garbage.

(*Lecturing again.*) By 1927 we're at the top of our fields. Coolidge and me. I tap-dance in the White House portico. (*Hoofing.*)

BELLA. I almost burst with pride.

BUMMIDGE (*Strutting*). Agents, bodyguards, a Dusenberg; paternity suits. My own cigar vault at Dunhill's next to the Prince of Wales. I charter the Twentieth Century to take me to Saratoga for the races. People laugh at everything I say. "Nice day." (*To group.*) Laugh! (*They laugh uproariously.*) Now the circumstances of my marriage. Bella— Bella . . .

BELLA. Yes.

BUMMIDGE. You be Bella. Now, Bella, what were the first words that kicked us off into matrimony?

BELLA. The first words? It was on the telephone. I need a telephone.

(IMOGEN, *stooping, out of the way of the camera, brings two phones. They ring.* BUMMIDGE *and* BELLA, *back to back, converse.*)

BUMMIDGE. Yes? Hello?

BELLA (*Breathless*). Philip?

BUMMIDGE. Yes?

BELLA. I have bad news. I'm six weeks late.

BUMMIDGE. What? What was that?

BELLA. Late! You know what I'm talking about. Do I have to draw a picture?

BUMMIDGE (*To telephone*). We were just fooling. We didn't even undress.

BELLA. I admit there wasn't much to it.

MAX. They won't spare me a single detail!

BUMMIDGE. I'll come right over. (*Hangs up and speaks to camera.*) Passion on a grand scale is always safe. It's that miserable, neurotic poking around that causes trouble.

PAMELA. She did it on purpose?

BELLA. I was pure and innocent.

BUMMIDGE. Your figleaf turned out to be a price tag. The time is now a beautiful afternoon in May. The Trifflers are having a little party in the garden.

GALLUPPO. We Trifflers are rising in the world.

MADGE. Rising into the upper lower middle class of Brooklyn.

FRUMKAH. Lovely house. Mission-style apricot stucco.

BUMMIDGE. I am sniffing lilacs, unaware that Bella has told her parents she's knocked up. Suddenly old Triffler swoops down and says,

GALLUPPO (*As old Triffler*). What did you do to my child? This you do to a father?

BELLA. I stood under the willow, when my mother ran up. (*Tapping* BERTRAM.)

BERTRAM. Arnold, a houseful of guests. Not now.

MADGE. My opinion was that they were framing him. Bella was an aggressive girl.

BELLA (*Hotly*). A lot you know! But I recall the moment. My mother shouted—

BERTRAM. He's so coarse! Couldn't it be a nice boy, you tramp? His habits are filthy. Look how bad his skin is. He must have syphilis.

BELLA. I told Mama, "He's everything you say."

MADGE. But you weren't getting any younger.

BELLA (*Fiercely*). I was just a kid. My heart told me to marry him.

MADGE. Her heart! She was out to here, already. (*Indicates a swollen belly.*)

BELLA. This proves my suffering never touched your heart, wherever that may be.

BUMMIDGE. I said to Mama Triffler, "Don't you think I'm too immature to marry? I'm not ready yet."

BELLA. You started to blubber.

BUMMIDGE. Then you hit me.

BELLA. Coward! I'll give you something to cry about! (*She strikes him.*)

BUMMIDGE (*Reels*). Ow! (*Angry.*) This was harder than the first time. (*Holding his cheek.*) This is very rich material.

BELLA. You tried to escape out the gate.

BUMMIDGE. You people are railroading me.

BELLA. We were a respectable family.

BUMMIDGE. Your father tried to throttle me, is that respectable? (*To* GALLUPPO.) Choke me.

(*Enter* MESSENGER.)

GALLUPPO. Wait a minute. What's my responsibility if there's an injury? There's a legal point, here.

BUMMIDGE (*Commanding*). My method requires reliving. Choke me.

GALLUPPO. No.

BUMMIDGE. I must have closure. We're on the air. Do it.

GALLUPPO. No!

BUMMIDGE. Somebody— (*Grabs* MESSENGER.) You—choke me.

MADGE. Choke him, and get it over with.

BELLA. Bummy, with all those people watching!

BUMMIDGE (*On his toes, rigid*). Choke me!

MESSENGER (*To* IMOGEN). Hold this! (*He chokes* BUMMIDGE, *who falls to his knees.* BERTRAM *tries to drag* MESSENGER *away from his victim.*)

WINKLEMAN. His face is getting purple.

IMOGEN. Enough! Stop!

MOTT (BERTRAM, *with difficulty, pries the* MESSENGER'S *fingers loose*). This fellow's a killer.

BERTRAM. Who taught you to take life like that?

MESSENGER. He asked for it.

MAX. Pop, are you all right?

BUMMIDGE (*Feebly*). Tip the boy. . . .

IMOGEN. It's a telegram from Mr. Fiddleman.

MADGE (*Grabbing wire*). For Winkleman.

MESSENGER. What's this, a TV show? Is that Bummy? The comic?

WINKLEMAN (*Reading*). Great interest, so far.

MADGE. Oh, Winkie!

(BERTRAM *throws the* MESSENGER *out.*)

BUMMIDGE (*To cameras*). This choking was an orgastic experience. . . . But now, my father has learned of my transgression and engagement, and waits for me on the stoop and strikes me.

MAX (*As Father*). Outcast!

BUMMIDGE. My mother and sister weep in the background, and I am struck. (MAX *flicks him under the nose.*) My nose! Oh, I'm bleeding! Give me something! Someone! A rag! Ice! Vinegar! Bella . . . I'm bleeding. (*He collapses in barber chair.*)

MADGE. Just as things were going good. Take the camera off him.

MOTT. Somebody—do something.

ALL. A cold knife blade! . . . Ice cubes! . . . Take off his shoes! . . . Push his head between his knees! . . . Hold him upside down! . . . Adrenalin!

AUFSCHNITT (*In the center of the stage, stunned, frightened as the camera turns on him*). Ladies and gentlemen, my name is Gerald Aufschnitt. I was born in Vienna, also the home of Mr. Freud. I am now Mr. Bummidge's tailor for thirty years. What a wonderful person. He helps me with my troubles. My daughter's troubles, too. I make his costumes in my little shop on Columbus Avenue. He asked me to play in his show. I was just Man, in the grip of relentless suppressions. I was never in a show before. How do I look?

MADGE. It's a fiasco. Wink, get on camera.

WINKLEMAN. Good evening. Yes, we are relatives. Were playmates. My cousin is a man of genius. Without him, my life would have been very empty. It is becoming rare for any person to need any other specific person. I mean, usually, if death removes the one before you, you can always get another. And if you die, it might be much the same to the rest. Most are interchangeable. But Bummidge is *needed.* . . .

MADGE. Get off with that stuff.

MAX. Pamela! Dance—bumps, grinds—anything!

(BERTRAM *is now before the camera.*)

BERTRAM. For every one of us, there is a rat. One to one. Rats came from Europe. They couldn't cross the continent until there was enough garbage from the covered wagons. They were pioneers too.

MADGE. Pamela, take over.

(PAMELA *performs, something between modern dance and burlesque.*)

BELLA. She's a disaster!

BUMMIDGE (*Rising from chair*). The bleeding has stopped. Where's the camera? Ladies and gentlemen, as you see, I am going backward. But now I am ten. The perils of reality surround the boy. He flirts with death on the fire escape, on the back of the trolley. I run and hide, steal, lie, cheat, hate, lust, crave, and adore.

MADGE. Winkie, if he rambles on like this, we're sunk.

BUMMIDGE. And now I ask you to witness a pair of solemn events. At this moment I am yet unborn. We are behind the candy store in Williamsburg. A January night. (*Counts on his fingers.*) It must have been January. I don't exist. (*Covers his eyes.*) Oh, blackness, blackness and frost. The stove is burning. A brass bedstead. And here they are. (*Points.*) My parents, male and female. Two apparitions. Oh! (*He turns away.*)

MADGE. You're going too far!

FRUMKAH. Of such things the law should prohibit viewing.

BUMMIDGE. My little sister is sleeping. Unaware. And then (*Pointing a trembling hand.*) my father takes . . . And my mother . . . Oh, no, Mama, no! Pa! Ma! Wait! Hold it! Consider! Oh, don't do this to me. (*To the audience.*) It's the Primal Scene. Nobody can come between them. The action of Fate. I am being conceived. No, no, no, no, no! Pray, little Phillip Bommovitch. Oh, pray! (*On his knees.*) But it's too late. My number is up! Bang! (*Claps hands to head.*) I'm doomed now to be born. May God have mercy on my soul—on all our souls.

WINKLEMAN. Even the old name, Bomovitch.

BUMMIDGE (*Rising before camera*). And now, ladies and gentlemen all . . . I will ask you to observe the projection of another most significant event. I shall try to penetrate the mystery of birth. I do this in the hope of renewal, or rebirth. This is the climax of my method. I invite you to watch a playlet which attempts to bring together the ancient and the avant-garde. (*To group.*) I have parts for all of you.

IMOGEN. Here are the parts, Mr. Bummidge.

BUMMIDGE. Hand them out.

WINKLEMAN. Oh, God, now he's a playwright.

MADGE. I've staked everything on this family-type pornography!

GALLUPPO (*To MAX*). You'll get a bill from me, buddy-boy.

PAMELA. I thought it was all impulse.

MAX. What is this?

BELLA. A Greek chorus?

FRUMKAH. I'm no Greek.

GALLUPPO. Why am I the Second Voice?

MADGE. Ridiculous!

WINKLEMAN. Cooperate!

BUMMIDGE. The title of this presentation is "The Upper Depths" or "The Birth of Phillip Bommovitch." Ready . . . get set . . . Go. (*Lies on the sofa.*)

BELLA (*Reading*). The babe is in the womb now.

WOMEN. What far-off force presides over this curious particle of matter?

FRUMKAH. O Kronos!

MOTT (*To* TECHNICIAN). Who the hell is this Kronos?

FRUMKAH. Speak, Tiresias. Speak, holy hermaphrodite. Blind, you know the darkness best. (*Continues to smoke her cigar.*)

MEN. The cells of the babe divide.

WINKLEMAN. Seeming chaos. A terrible order.

GALLUPPO. Iron. Proteins.

MAX. The swift enzymes. Transistors of flesh.

PAMELA. Matter torn away from other forms of being.

ALL. Will this be nothing but finite, mortal man?

BELLA. His eyes.

MADGE. Tongue.

PAMELA. Genitalia.

FRUMKAH. His liver.

WINKLEMAN. And his nerves.

MAX. And within the soft skull, a soft mass of white cells which will judge the world.

BELLA. O transfiguration!

ALL. He is being created.

GALLUPPO. Merely to jest? So that other animals may grin?

MAX. But there is no unmetaphysical calling.

PAMELA. And what is the mother doing? Does she go stately through the slums? Is her mind upon the gods? Does she understand what she is carrying?

MADGE. Not she. No thought, no prayer, no wine, no sacrifices. Only herring, potatoes, tea, cards, gossip, newspaper serials. How far is this Daughter of Man from authentic Being.

WINKLEMAN. The unborn Bummidge, afloat in Stygian darkness. (BUMMIDGE *floats like an embryo.*)

ALL. He's folding, unfolding, refolding. Now he's a fish. (BUMMIDGE *enacts the fish.*)

MAX. Dimly he beholds the geologic periods.

GALLUPPO and MADGE. The vacant lifeless seas.

BELLA and MAX. Things that crawl.

WINKLEMAN. The ferns.

FRUMKAH. The lumbering beasts.

MAX. From stone, from brine, sucking the seething power of the sun.

PAMELA. Now appears the backbone.

GALLUPPO. The gills.

WINKLEMAN. He's a reptile.

MADGE. A mammal. Higher. Up the vertebrate tree.

ALL. Up! Up! This thing is evolving into a man. (BUMMIDGE *stands.*)

FRUMKAH. Reason.

WINKLEMAN. Self-regard. Tragic apprehension. Comic knowledge.

BUMMIDGE (*Getting back on sofa*). It's great in here. I like it.

BELLA. Blind and dumb, the babe. Sheer happiness—Nirvana!

FRUMKAH. But it can't last. The pains are starting.

ALL. Contractions. (BUMMIDGE *sits up on sofa. The* CHORUS *makes a cloth billow behind him, by degrees more violently.*)

WINKLEMAN. Fifteen.

ALL. Ba-ba-ba-baboom!

WINKLEMAN. Ten.

ALL. Ba-ba-ba-baboom!

WINKLEMAN. Eight!

ALL. Ba-ba-ba-baboom!

WINKLEMAN. Four.

ALL. Ba-ba-ba-baboom!

WINKLEMAN. Two.

ALL. Ba-ba-ba-baboom!

BUMMIDGE. Oh, Mother! Our time has come. (*Knocks as if on a door.*) Mother! (*Stamps his foot.*) Mother! This bag is broken. (*Sharp cry.*) Help! I'm grounded in here. Oh, terror, rage, suffocation! This is expulsion. I hear screams. I'd scream, too, if I could breathe. Tante Frumkah has me by the head, dragging me. Take it easy, Tante—I'm choking. Choking. Air, air, give me air. Agony to my lungs! Oxygen! The light is scalding my eyes. (*Newborn with wrinkled blind face and clenched poor hand, he slaps himself on the behind and gives the feeble infant cry.*) Eh! . . . Ehh! (*He squalls like a newborn infant.*)

BELLA. It tears your heart to hear that cry.

MAX. A tyrant. Utterly helpless. Absolute from weakness.

PAMELA. They cut the cord. (BUMMIDGE *looks about.*)

WOMEN. So this is the world?

MEN. It is the Kingdom of Necessity.

ALL. Sein! Dasein! Bewusstsein! (IMOGEN *presses an inflated balloon to his mouth.*)

BELLA. The breast. She holds him in her arms.

ALL. Bliss.

BELLA. He breathes. He suckles.

ALL. Bliss.

BUMMIDGE. Where do I end, and where does the world begin? I must be the world myself. I'm it. It's me.

MAX. A little moment of omnipotence. (IMOGEN *pulls away the balloon, which is attached to a long string.*)

BUMMIDGE. So *that's* the way it is!

WINKLEMAN. Only the first lesson of reality.

BUMMIDGE (*Raging*). Give it back! (*The* CHORUS *now reads him a lesson.*)

MADGE. Strife.

PAMELA. Disappointment.

BELLA. Loss.

GALLUPPO. Law.

FRUMKAH. Thou shalt not.

MADGE. Thou shalt not covet.

PAMELA. Stifle those horrible needs.

MAX. Bow your head as all mankind must, and submit to your burden.

WINKLEMAN. The war has begun between the instincts of life and the instincts of death.

ALL. *Ave atque vale.* . . . (*With this incantation they go off to sides.*)

BUMMIDGE. As I took the first steps (*Rises.*) I heard the sins of history shouted in the street.

BERTRAM. Germany declares war.

AUFSCHNITT. Poison gas.

MOTT. Lenin in a sealed train. (*Sound of bells.*)

BUMMIDGE. Armistice Day, nineteen eighteen. From the abyss of blood, the sirens of peace. I have a vision of bandaged lepers screaming "Joy, joy!" Twenty million mummy bundles of the dead grin as the child, Philip Bummidge, intuits the condition of man and succumbs for the first time to Humanitis, that dread plague. Being human is too much for flesh and blood. . . . Excuse me, a fit of dizziness.

IMOGEN. He's having one of his attacks.

BUMMIDGE. No, no! I must continue. I became a buffoon in answer to this crisis. I amused terrible and sick audiences. I am the last great repository of old gags. (*He begins to parody old routines.*) "Do you file your fingernails?" "No, I throw them away."

MAX. He thinks he's back in burlesque.

BUMMIDGE. "Why did the chicken cross the road?" "That was no chicken, Jack, that was my life."

PAMELA. He's flipped.

MADGE. His mind was never strong.

BUMMIDGE. "What did the monkey say when he peed on the cash register?" "This is going to run into money. . . ." Farewell, old jokes. (*Waving arms.*) Fly away, flap-flap, like clumsy old chickens. I am sinking . . . sinking. . . . (*Backing up and stepping into laundry cart.* BELLA *comes forward, curious;* WINKLEMAN *follows.*)

BELLA. What's happening to him?

WINKLEMAN. He looks as if he's dying. . . . Is he?

PAMELA. I never could be sure of anything, with him.

BUMMIDGE (*Crawls into clothes basket*). The dark night of my soul has begun. Oh, Lazarus, we are brothers. I die of banality. Lay me in this mirthless tomb, and cover me with corn. Let me hear the laughter of evil for the last time. Oh, demons who murder while guffawing, I have succumbed. (*Reaches for lid of basket.*) Consummatum est. It is ended. (*Shuts the top of basket. He emerges seconds later from the back of the wicker clothes hamper.*) But I am Lazarus. I was sick unto death, died, and was buried. Now I await resurrection . . . the word, "Come forth, Lazarus. . . ." (*He waits.*) Will no one speak? (*Waits.*) No one? (*Faintly, appealing.*) Someone has got to speak!

IMOGEN (*Timidly raising her hand like a schoolgirl*). Come forth, Lazarus. (BUMMIDGE *rises slowly.*)

BERTRAM. He's being reborn.

BELLA (*Bossy, but stirred as well*). Come forth . . . okay already, come forth! (*They break into Handel's "Hallelujah Chorus" and modulate into the anthem "America, the Beautiful."*)

MOTT. Cut . . . time. Time. Cut.

IMOGEN. He's so full of soul, that marvelous man! He keeps talking about the Last Analysis. He is Freud's real successor with his revolutionary method to bring mental assistance to a misguided world, obsessed with horrible sex. Now I know what he meant. Mr. Bummidge. He's white, fainting. Help!

WINKLEMAN. I'll change and be back immediately.

MOTT. What sense of timing! Better than a clock. The broadcast is over.

PAMELA. I have to get out of this costume. Bert, lend me that dress. I've paid and paid and paid and paid for those diamonds. This experience was about the worst of all. Who has my anklet?

MAX (*Bending over him*). What's the matter, Pop, is it for real, or possum playing?

BELLA. No, he's out cold.

TECHNICIAN. Well, that's it. Save the lights. Wrap it up.

BERTRAM. Louie and I will put Bummidge to bed. (*They wheel* BUMMIDGE *out.* PAMELA *unbuttons* BERTRAM's *dress from back as he exits.*)

MAX (*Hurries to telephone*). I've got to see if my deal is still on. (WINKLEMAN *is changing into clothes and holding* MAX *off.*)

MADGE. No. We're waiting for Fiddleman to call. No call yet. (*Eyes fixed on the phone.*) Fifty-four seconds. This isn't like Fiddleman.

FRUMKAH. TV may be bad, but does it need this?

MADGE (*Staring at phone*). Fifty-eight, fifty-nine, sixty. I can't believe it. Fiddleman always has the phone in his hand as the lights go out.

WINKLEMAN. No ringing? (*Stands before the telephone expectantly.*) Not yet?

MADGE. Nothing.

PAMELA. Ring, damn it, ring.

MAX. My deal! Just one call.

MADGE (*Checking her watch*). This has never happened.

WINKLEMAN. Dead, dead silence—like a burial vault. Has he lost *all* his magic?

PAMELA. Recently he's been slipping in all departments.

(*Enter* MOTT. *They all look toward him.*)

MOTT. Boy—it looks as if they don't want any part of him.

IMOGEN. Why doesn't Professor Ratzenhofer call? He said he was interested.

PAMELA. A last bubble from sinking Bummy.

WINKLEMAN. I'll give Fiddleman five seconds more.

MADGE. He's always come through.

WINKLEMAN. One, two, three, four, five, six, seven, eight, nine, ten.

MOTT. He's out.

WINKLEMAN. Well, this is a Waterloo for me. First time in thirty years I was wrong about him.

FRUMKAH. Well, I'm going to blow this joint. I'm past these youthful anxieties.

GALLUPPO. I should have been in court fifteen minutes ago. (*Exits.*)

MAX. Winkleman, give me a lift downtown. (*Close elevator.*)

PAMELA. I'll be around tomorrow. I have loaned my diamonds, not given them.

MOTT. You want a ride downtown in our truck?

PAMELA. I've had all the anticlimax I want for a while. (*Exits lower door with* MOTT.)

BUMMIDGE (*Entering from study*). What's happening? How did it go? Where is everybody?—I heard telephones ringing. I woke up hearing telephones ringing. . . .

BELLA. Nobody called, Bummy.

BUMMIDGE. What do you mean nobody?

BELLA. Nobody.

BUMMIDGE. Imogen, hasn't Mr. Kalbfuss phoned?

IMOGEN. No, he hasn't been heard from.

BUMMIDGE. He seemed so sympathetic to my purpose. Such a kindly kraut. A butcher, a man of blood. But I spent days—days persuading him.

MADGE. I'm getting hives from this terrible letdown. I'd better go home and put on some ointment.

BUMMIDGE. But the phone was ringing. I got up when I heard it.

IMOGEN. Not one call.

BUMMIDGE. So? Dead silence? Experts are naturally cold to amateurs. Yet the greatest men of science were always amateurs. Newton, Einstein. They didn't belong to the professional racket. All right, I'll get the better of these professional bastards!

MADGE. Now you've turned into one of those goofy cranks that hang around the cafeteria and drink goat's milk, and tell you one of these days they're going to dial Atlantis on the telephone or that you're defending America from cosmic evil. I have to go home and put Harold to bed. What'll I tell him! (*Exits.*)

IMOGEN. It's cruel. They are all so cruel.

BUMMIDGE (*Wryly*). No revelation to me.

BELLA. Still, I won't abandon you. But you shouldn't have squandered all that money.

IMOGEN. He did that because he hated the way he earned it.

BUMMIDGE. I thought I could dash in from left field, Williamsburg, with the truth. Nobody else has got it. The professionals rejected me. They didn't want to give up their vested interests.

TECHNICIAN. Hey. Did you know your telephone was disconnected? The plug is out here.

BUMMIDGE (*Stunned*). What do you mean, disconnected! I disconnected it myself—I didn't want the ringing to interfere with the broadcast. (*He calls.*) Imogen. (*Wildly excited.*) Plug it in. My God, Bella, perhaps . . . (*He is sobbing with excitement.*) Do I get a reprieve? I take it back about those vested interests. (*Phone rings instantly.*)

IMOGEN. Hello . . .

BUMMIDGE. Kalbfuss? Dr. Ratzenhofer?

IMOGEN. Columbia Broadcasting System. He says he's been dialing frantically. Must see you at once.

BUMMIDGE. Oh, my heart is quaking. Like sneaky joy. . . . Hang up. He's not the one I want to hear from.

IMOGEN (*Hangs up*). He was babbling like he had brain fever. He's coming over, he says. (TECHNICIAN *is fondling her.*) Not now! Let go. (*Phone rings.*) Hello.

TECHNICIAN. How about supper tonight? Let's spread the wealth.

BUMMIDGE. Who? Who? Who? I'm about to burst. Who?

IMOGEN. American Broadcasting Company.

BELLA. Bummy, they want you back. I mean when two calls—CBS *AND* ABC . . .

BUMMIDGE. Hang up! Get him off the line. Tell him to call tomorrow. Kalbfuss hasn't got a chance with those guys, he can't get to the phone. (IMOGEN *hangs up. The* TECHNICIAN *continues to fondle her.*) Kalbfuss! Oh, Kalbfuss! Phone me.

IMOGEN. What's all the noise outside?

(FIDDLEMAN *enters, followed by* MADGE, MAX, PAMELA, WINKLEMAN, BERTRAM, *and* MOTT.)

BELLA. Sir Leslie Fiddleman.

FIDDLEMAN. Bummy! What a sensation! Your phone is out of whack, so I came with a squad-car escort. Emergency. This is the biggest thing I ever saw. . . .

MADGE. When I reached the streets and heard the sirens (*Enter* MESSENGER—*gives large pile of telegrams to* IMOGEN.) I thought it was an ambulance that had come for you, that you had had a heart attack or attempted suicide. Immediately I had a rush of pure old family feeling. I leaped back to you. I don't remember how I got up here. I just *rose* to be with you.

MAX. You've hit a new high. Our luck is back.

(*Enter* PAMELA.)

PAMELA. I was standing heartbroken in the street. So melancholy! I couldn't understand why your death and resurrection didn't overwhelm everybody as it overwhelmed me.

WINKLEMAN. I too have had an almost religious experience: Vindication! I was right, right about you. I've never been wrong on you yet.

BELLA. Why, you all left him flat on his ass.

MAX. Mother, Mr. Fiddleman wants to talk.

FIDDLEMAN (*A Napoleon but littler [Joseph Levine]*). You should have been at the Waldorf. Nothing compares with it except maybe Valentino's funeral. Or maybe the deck of the *Titanic* in *A Night to Remember*. People embraced. They roared. They crawled on the floor when you were born. Women cried and kissed the screen. They were yelling, "Meaning!" "Hope!" "Down with Encounter Groups, hurray for the Bummidge method." And then came the rush for the telephones.

BUMMIDGE. The busybodies, tough guys, and promoters grabbed the phones. Kalbfuss never had a chance. That mild dear ham-curing Westphalian.

MADGE. Mr. Fiddleman, tell him about the offers.

FIDDLEMAN. Spite Beverage Conglomerate was there. He wrote this check for a quarter of a million. Option money.

WINKLEMAN. Let's see.

MADGE. Tell him the rest.

FIDDLEMAN. Against a two-million-dollar contract.

PAMELA. Oh, my dear love. What a future lies before us.

WINKLEMAN. Of course we'll have to have time to study this proposition among others.

BUMMIDGE. Bertram, help her open the envelopes. Anything yet, Imogen?

IMOGEN. All commercial. . . .

MOTT. I've thought of several new angles, Bummy.

IMOGEN. Here, a wire from Dr. Waldemar Gumplovitch. (BUMMIDGE *snatches it.*)

BUMMIDGE. Oh, yes. (*Reads.*) Good, good. Ah! He thinks I may have hit on Scientific possibilities. Wants me to give a seminar at Cornell. Eight weeks.

WINKLEMAN. Does he name a figure?

MADGE. We must decide about Spite Beverage.

MAX. I was talking to an outfit that manufactures nail polish. I've got them outside.

WINKLEMAN. Two million is a nice sum, but we'll want to go slow.

(*Enter* KALBFUSS, *the butcher.*)

BUMMIDGE. It's Kalbfuss! Kalbfuss has come. Ernest! I've been waiting.

KALBFUSS. Bummovitch! Oh, you Bummovitch. (*Embraces* BUM-

MIDGE. *Kisses him on the head.*) You genius! I tried to call you. Here! My tribute! This aged steak, I was saving for my wedding anniversary. (*Unrolls a slab of meat.*)

BUMMIDGE. You saw the demonstration?

KALBFUSS. Saw it! (*He is choked up. Laughs. Sobs.*) Hold this. (*Gives meat to* PAMELA.) I'm still overcome. (*Covers his eyes with handkerchief.*) Anything you want, Bummovitch?

FIDDLEMAN. You see what he does to the public? You see?

MADGE. What does this big clunk want?

BUMMIDGE. Be quiet. He's affected—I moved him.

WINKLEMAN. We've got business here.

PAMELA (*Passing on the steak*). Here, hold this. Bummy, listen . . .

FIDDLEMAN. Spite Beverage says six shows a year. No outside writers needed. It's your show, Bummy. Write your own ticket. (*The steak is being passed around.*)

WINKLEMAN. The idea is, you do psychotherapy with important people. *Their* problems, *your* method. You act out the big events of their inner life. He wants to line up Jackie Onassis, J. Edgar Hoover, Martha Mitchell, Gore Vidal and Rex Reed together.

BUMMIDGE. Tell me more, Kalbfuss.

KALBFUSS. I never get downtown at all. I was never in the Waldorf before. I didn't have time today, and when the bus got stuck in the traffic I was angry I accepted your invitation. Then I saw all those important people. Then you were on the television. So beautiful. Every word. Such meaning!

BUMMIDGE. Now, Kalbfuss, terms. I give you this money. (*The valise.*) You give me the Old Trilby.

KALBFUSS. Yes, I am no more a butcher.

MAX. Is that the meaning of it . . . you want the old place back?

KALBFUSS. The man wants his theater back. He's going to have it. I am his disciple. I hate to think what I did to his shrine. I was so ignorant, blind. I remember moving in and putting the iceboxes on the stage. And all the ham, and all the sausage, and suet and the sauerkraut. Oh, Mr. Bummidge!

BUMMIDGE. What?

KALBFUSS. Change me. Change me. Killing always was against my nature. Handling dead flesh! Never again.

BUMMIDGE. Bless you, Kalbfuss, we shall work. You will be our first project.

FIDDLEMAN. What are we talking about?

KALBFUSS. We'll tear out the butcher shop ourselves, with crowbars.

BUMMIDGE. We must be careful of the beautiful paneling. The gilt! . . . A center, an academy, a conservatory.

MADGE. But you're a comedian.

BUMMIDGE. Yes. True. Certainly. Comedy will come back to us at the Trilby. We'll have people off the streets. Even the junkies and the freak-outs, the cripples, the desperadoes, drunks, queers, and rapists. My method will make them sane and whole. Forward from Freud.

MOTT. The sonofabitch is serious. He ought to have his head examined.

PAMELA. You're turning down millions.

BELLA. He wronged me, but this is a higher purpose. I'll run the business for him. We can charge a small entrance fee. I'll take over the box office.

WINKLEMAN. Yes, of course, we can make a thing of it.

MADGE. Yes! It can't go at random. I'll pick the talent off the street. Maybe some of our old people . . . it would be therapy for them.

WINKLEMAN. We can do better without the networks. I have a capital-gains brainstorm. Maybe a foundation, with us as the officers. Sorry, Leslie, when the Trilby opens, you'll be on the opening-night list.

MAX. I'll take the frozen-food concession. I can use Kalbfuss's cases for the lasagne.

BUMMIDGE. What? You'll all move in on me.

BELLA. I'll take care of you. Once and for all.

BUMMIDGE. Sure, you'd fix me fine. You'd put me in the Alcatraz of bliss in protective custody.

BERTRAM. She has a trapping instinct just like mine.

BUMMIDGE. They're back on me. Whither I go they go. I am their money, their magic, their thing. If they can't beat me, they're going to join me. Anything to force me to be their Bummy. But I'm not *your* Bummy. Finally, I am *my* Bummy— Tennis anyone? (*He makes imaginary tennis strokes and drives them all together.*) Oh, tennis is such a lovely game. Thwock! Pluck! Such lightness, such power, dance, fantasy! Where's the net? I'm playing. . . . (*A device above. They stare up.*)

BERTRAM. Right!

WINKLEMAN. A net! Duck! Look out!

BUMMIDGE (*Dancing with excitement*). Out, out! Bertram, out!

BELLA. You lunatic!

MADGE. They're going to kill us!

BUMMIDGE. Good-bye, good-bye to you all! Farewell. Oh, this is perfect.

FIDDLEMAN. I'll bring an action.

IMOGEN. Don't hurt them, Bertram.

BUMMIDGE. Kalbfuss, lend a hand. (*All are pushed in elevator in the net.* BUMMIDGE *dances with* IMOGEN.) A new life. A new man. I really am reborn. I baptize myself.

BERTRAM (*From above*). It worked. Technically perfect.

BUMMIDGE. I could vault over clouds. How happy I am. There's something insane in happiness. Except my heart is filled with love, and I know, I know what I'm doing.

KALBFUSS. I want to start too.

BUMMIDGE. Why, of course, Kalbfuss.

KALBFUSS. I suffer from awful headaches.

BUMMIDGE. I see. Is there any pattern?

KALBFUSS. It has something to do with pork sausage. The white kind.

BUMMIDGE. Now, Kalbfuss, spin on your heels as fast as you can. (KALBFUSS *spins.*) Now stop. Are you dizzy?

KALBFUSS. Dizzy, dizzy!

BUMMIDGE. Now shut your eyes and say the first thing that comes into your mind.

KALBFUSS. I am a sausage stuffed tight, a white pork sausage, and my head is bursting the skin!

BUMMIDGE. You have taken the first step.

KALBFUSS. I live in fear the customers will eat me! Master! I am overcome. I must lie down. (BUMMIDGE *leads him, trembling, to the barber chair.*)

BUMMIDGE. Oh, Imogen, we have so much to do. Help me arrange this toga. The BUMMIDGE INSTITUTE. We're going to do it in style. We'll have class.

IMOGEN. You ought to have a skyscraper of your own, like the United Nations.

BUMMIDGE. The poor, the bored, the neurotic of the earth will trust us better for beginning humbly. We will train people in the Method and send them as missionaries to Germany, even behind the Iron Curtain. All those bleak sadistic countries. My head is a-hum with all the possibilities. I am so moved! What a struggle! It took me so long to get through the brutal stage of life. When I was through with that, the mediocre stage was waiting. That lasted most of my life, but now it's done with, I am ready for the sublime. (*He raises his arms in a great gesture.*)

CURTAIN

ON
The Last
Analysis

Inherent in any spirited discussion of a "beautiful loser" is the un-voiced but underlying assumption that a sensitive and intelligently man-aged revival might yet transform it into a "beautiful winner." Saul Bellow's play, *The Last Analysis*, is unique among the selections in this book because it alone was offered a chance at vindication. The play was first performed on Broadway on October 1, 1964, and was hauled off after twenty-eight performances. Seven years later, on June 23, 1971, the play was revived off Broadway at the Circle in the Square, with Theodore Mann directing. With a touch of irony that is far truer to life and art than any contrived happy ending, the revival turned out to be as misconceived a production as the original. Although it survived through August 1, 1971, managing to generate a bit more enthusiasm with both the public and the professional theater community, it was scarcely a success. And because the production repeated fundamentally the same mistakes made by the original producing unit (besides com-pounding them with a few new ones), it had the adverse effect of con-firming, and indeed intensifying, the unfavorable critical judgments which greeted the play upon its initial New York appearance.

Although its off-Broadway revival failed to vindicate *The Last Analysis*, it achieved some measure of significance by illustrating both the flaws of the play and the weaknesses of the theatrical system under which it attempted to exist. The 1971 production established first of all that off Broadway is no more hospitable to the meritorious, imperfect, nonformula play than is Broadway. Whatever its place in theater history as a one-time artistic haven for the dramatically experimental, unusual, and esoteric, the off-Broadway theater of today is a sophisticated branch of mainstem theater beset by the same economic pressures and artistic restraints as its uptown counterpart. Therefore, an imperfectly wrought and catastrophically mishandled production like *The Last Analysis* can expect to fare no better off Broadway in 1971 than it could on Broadway in 1964.

Because it resurrected essentially the same production errors of the first production, the revival also indicated that the theater industry's misconceptions about play production tend to linger over the years. The inauspicious revival, in fact, actually underscored a key factor in the theater's continuing condition of perpetual crisis—its crucial need to create a more amenable working environment, if it hopes to attract our best writers and seduce them from other art forms.

The Last Analysis was the first play-writing effort of novelist Saul Bellow, a writer of such certain magnitude that he was once characterized in *The New York Times Book Review* as "the premier American novelist: the best writer we have in the literary form that has been dominant in the literature of the past hundred years." It takes no herculean mental effort to conclude that Bellow's is a talent it would well behoove the theater to court. One satisfactory stage experience might well mean a major new voice for the American theater. In analyzing *Analysis*, therefore, of primary consideration is whether Bellow's tentative interest in the theatrical form was effectively deflected by not one, but two disastrous stage experiences.

Bellow's early and tentative interest in the theater was encouraged by Lillian Hellman, who, he says, pressed him to write a play. *The Last Analysis* was the result, and when he later read it himself at Shirley Broughton's Theatre for Ideas, an informal Manhattan Symposium of artists and writers, he recalls that "it was received with gaiety and gratitude. Everyone laughed and had a wild time." To Bellow, working on a play was a surprisingly rewarding experience, precisely because the experience was unique to him, quite different from working on a novel. "I thought, well, this is very agreeable. One can write a play in the same language one would employ to write a novel. But it would be shared publicly by people who would understand and sympathize. It would be different because it would be immediate participation by many warm bodies."

The work with which Bellow entered a new art form bears subtle affinities with his novels, but in most respects is a marked departure in style and content from his books. Even within the stage idiom, the play is an oddity—a baroque grab-bag of elements ranging from burlesque humor to Greek satyr comedy. On its most accessible plot level, it is the saga of a burned-out Jewish comedian named Bummidge whose imagination has been ensnared by Freudian psychoanalytic theory. Obsessed with the idea of psychoanalyzing himself, he arranges to reenact his life over closed-circuit television, for the edification and delectation of the world's leading psychoanalytic authorities.

The play is additionally meaningful on several other levels. Besides the obvious satire on the theory, practice, and jargon of Freudian psychology, critics saw in the play a study of the nature of comedy; a serio-comic look at the Jewish intellectual; an analysis of contemporary civilization; a morality play; a confessional drama. Writing in *The New Republic*, Robert Brustein observed, "Bummy is apparently meant to be a representative of the artist in our time—his need to understand himself, to transcend his sense of futility, to achieve freedom, and to lead an austere life in the midst of American plenty." Seven years later, upon the occasion of the play's revival, John Simon offered this comprehensive analysis in *New York Magazine*: "*The Last Analysis* is many things: a satire on psychoanalysis, a critique of the pure unreason of Jewish family life, an indictment of the mass media, a lover's quarrel with America and its Bitch Goddess whose pursuit had botched so many lives, an allegory of the artist seen as a beleaguered public entertainer."

The play is crammed with ideas, one fairly tumbling over the next. Prior to the original production, Bellow offered a few insights in various newspaper interviews. To William Glover of the Associated Press he stated that "One of the ideas developed in the play is that there is a great speed with which original creative intentions are immediately utilized and made into commodities by industries that are standing by and which need to be fed continuously"—a statement which clearly indicates that the play is meant to be taken in part as a tragi-comic vision of how the technological society apprehends man, his mind and his talents, as an object.

"My play is about a comedian who has become a commodity," Bellow told Pete Hamill in the New York *Herald Tribune*. "It happens to all comedians. They are young and their attitude is one of joy and wonder, and from that attitude they create their humor. Then, if they are successful, the packagers move in. They grow more and more isolated from these things that gave them their wild young originality. . . . Suddenly, they're cut off. Even from themselves."

One reading suggested by the play is a metaphorical and parodistic treatment of the mythical birth, death, and resurrection of the archetypal hero. Philip Bummidge is a sublimely funny embodiment of the American character, and as such is a fitting hero. He is generous and good-natured to a fault, having let his family, friends, and business associates rob him for years. He is warm and compassionate and outgoing, having dedicated himself, in the role of a great American comic, to making an entire country find happiness in laughter. He is a typical product of American codes of value, a pursuer and achiever of success throughout his life.

Bellow consciously intended this character relationship between Bummidge and modern America. "Bummidge wants to create a kind of psychiatry for everybody—a psychiatry of which he would be the leader," he says. "America is a society filled with people like that, who teach one another about the truth and about reality. They're all full of love, full of heart, full of good will, and very crude and amateurish and funny. This is a side of American life that very few writers do anything with."

Although he disclaimed, initially, any affinities between Bummidge and the characters of his novels, Bellow does acknowledge that "the idea of having a man bigger than life was already established in *Henderson, the Rain King*." According to the author, "Henderson blowing up the frog pond in an effort to do good is a perfect image" of the same comic do-good urge which propels Bummidge to set up his own system of psychiatry for the weal of humankind.

Fanatically driven by the need to be loved; fascinated by the world of the intellect which he cannot really comprehend; pathetically eager to cleanse the world through noble and selfless deeds, and still absurd in his inadequate attempts at heroism; trapped by his own intrinsic character weaknesses and almost paralyzed with guilt at his own success, Bummy is a caricature of the American Everyman embodied in the figure of the tragic clown. The clown as buffoon-hero is an ancient tradition, and Bummidge the baggy-pants comedian is as wonderfully at home in the tradition as are the fools of Shakespeare, the tramps of Beckett, or the circus clowns of Fellini.

As the all-American Everyman hero *in extremis*, Bummy reaches heroic proportions by sacrificing himself for the sake of mankind, which he represents. As Harold Clurman astutely pointed out, in his review of the 1964 Broadway production for *The Nation*, the paramount theme of the play is regeneration and renewal. Analyzing Bummidge, Clurman stressed that the character "senses his corruption and acknowledges his guilt. He is besmirched by the slime of success and knows that he has both invited it and wallowed in it. He yearns to recover his proper being." In Clurman's view, the clown's public confession and contemplation of it will lead, he hopes, both him and his fellow men "to greater understanding, and to the path of self-renewal."

Comic stand-in for Christ, Apollo, Orestes, Orpheus, and other spiritual brothers of the mythic past, Bummidge the clown first assumes the burden of embodying in himself all the flaws and strengths inherent in the nature of mankind. "Being human is too much for flesh and blood," Bummy says, explaining how he suffers from "Humanitis," the soul-deep pain of the human condition. In clown guise, he thus becomes the perfect symbol of man—absurd, tragic, hilarious, selfless, petty, greedy, gross, foolish, noble, and, above all, simply human.

Since Bellow has created Bummy as a contemporary comic savior-victim, the human sacrifice is accomplished on the same terms. The sacrificial rite takes place on television, in an absurd burlesque parody of the death-and-rebirth ritual of religious and mythic tradition. Since science is our contemporary religion, Bummy's sacrifice is accomplished symbolically, as an epic scientific self-analysis in which he returns to the womb to be reborn. In a madly comic dramatic conclusion, the play ends with Bummy analyzed and, by extension, all mankind cleansed and purged of the sheer pain of the human condition.

The concept of *The Last Analysis* is ambitious, brilliant, and daring, and to Bellow's honor, he tried to fashion its dramatic treatment on the same uncompromising terms. The form of the play is outrageously wacky, a free-floating mishmash of comic elements borrowed from Restoration comedy, commedia dell'arte, burlesque, high farce, television variety shows, vaudeville, comedy of manners, and Yiddish theater. But for all its cocky bravery, the conglomerate style fails to realize more than a portion of the comic genius inherent in the play's concept. The essential flaw in its structure is Bellow's weakness in imposing a unified comic style on all his flashes of brilliant *schtick*. Too much is left for the imagination to fill in, and far too much is left for the director to interpret in stage terms.

With his novelist's sensibilities, Bellow has structured a play in terms that are far too literary, static, and linguistically dense for its own good. His basic difficulty has been in translating his comic insights into visual comedy workable on the living stage, and much of the humor remains unrealized. We hear much of Bummy's comic genius, for example, but Bellow has given the character insufficient chance to illustrate that great comedy skill. On the page, Bummy's tragicomic humanness is conveyed as clear as a bell, but the sheer zany nuttiness of his comic soul must depend on the skill of a great actor/comedian to articulate and illustrate it on stage. "The play requires an out-of-this-world comic, a Rabelaisian monster," Clurman wrote. What Bellow lacked was the kind of "partner" Bert Lahr was to S. J. Perelman during the evolution of *The Beauty Part*. Such a collaboration might have transformed the character of Bummidge by infusing into the literary creation a comic vitality contributed by the living person.

Jackie Gleason could have accomplished the co-creation of Bummidge—and so could have Milton Berle, Sid Caesar, Danny Kaye, or Red Skelton. These are the comedians of whom Bellow was thinking when he wrote the play. Each one is a kind of King Grotesque, a giant clown so much larger than the dimensions of mere mortal men that he is strong enough to represent all mankind in its awful and wonderful absurdity.

"There was a series in the New York *Post* about Sid Caesar's psychoanalysis," Bellow recalls, which served as a spur to his play-writing venture. "I had already listened to Artie Shaw's ecstasies over Freud, and then, with this *Post* series, I was tickled pink to see how serious Sid Caesar was about his unconscious, and about repression, and so forth." In an article which he wrote for *The New York Times* in 1964, just prior to the play's Broadway opening, Bellow further analyzed the origins of Bummidge. "I am attracted to auto-didacts, to those brave souls who rise to encounter ideas," he wrote. "I have been especially stirred by jazz musicians, prizefighters, and television comics who put on the philosopher's mantle. I find them peculiarly touching. In the tumult of Birdland they are thinking of Kierkegaard. . . . The self-absorption of people who never tire of exploring their depths is the source of our comedy."

There was a note in the March 19, 1964, issue of *The New York Times* to the effect that Milton Berle might do the show, "his first," the story pointed out, "since the *Ziegfeld Follies* of 1943." In the opinion of Roger L. Stevens, the producer of *The Last Analysis*, "The best performance of that play was done by Milton Berle. One day, in his office, he did practically the whole play for me, and I remember saying that it was the best performance of the play. But then he was afraid to try it on Broadway."

Not only was Stevens unable to persuade Berle to play the role; no other comedian of Berle's stature and talent was lured to undertake the enormously challenging characterization of Philip Bummidge—and therein lies a tale of one of the principal reasons why *The Last Analysis* never came alive in production. Both Stevens and the play's first director, Joseph Anthony, acknowledge the crucial importance of filling the Bummidge role with a talent as outsized as Bummy's own gargantuan dimensions. "The play was written for a great personality," Stevens says. "And without that personality—the *right* personality—you're in trouble. We never really had the personality that was believable . . . it's as simple as that."

In Anthony's opinion, the entire production hinged on the casting of the lead. "The play is filled with heroic juxtapositions," Anthony says. "A man in torment as a comic figure inhabits a world of both brilliance and near-insanity. And the play is so dependent upon the man playing Bummidge that if you don't have an inspired genius of a clown *in extremis*, to convey that kind of miserable magnificence—you're killed."

The director's choice for the role had been Zero Mostel, and for a while indications were that Mostel would indeed take on Bummidge. In a cliffhanger decision, Mostel finally turned down the Bellow play and opened instead in *Fiddler on the Roof* on September 22, 1964. It is Anthony's opinion that Mostel was ultimately dissuaded from the part by its enormous demands—physical, intellectual, and, especially, verbal. "I think that Zero felt the verbal load was so huge that he himself would drown in the role," Anthony says. "I think Zero's theater sense told him he would have to carry it all on his back. And that's a thing that Saul never took into account—the vast load that this character has to carry. Even in *Lear* there are subplots to take over."

There were other observers, however, who were less willing to grant Zero Mostel artistic reasons for declining the part. Writing in the October 24, 1964, issue of *The New Republic*, Robert Brustein offered this unyielding interpretation of the actor's motives: "There is only one actor in our theater capable of realizing the intricacies of [the] central character, and that is Zero Mostel—but he has elected to entertain the Hadassah ladies in *Fiddler on the Roof*." Eight years later that opinion still persists in some quarters. Certainly it was echoed in John Simon's review of the play's 1971 revival, when he wrote: "The obvious, the only choice in 1964 was Zero Mostel, who was interested in doing the part, but then found the bigger money in *Fiddler on the Roof* more to his interest."

If some critics were contemptuous of Mostel's motives in turning down the role, their evaluation of the actor who eventually played Bummidge on Broadway—Sam Levene—bordered on outright ridicule. "Sam Levene, who inherited the role by default, apparently did not understand one word of it, and to hide his bafflement, he plays this one too as if it were written for the Hadassah ladies," snarled Brustein. Simon disinterred this analysis in 1971, when he wrote, "So the role devolved on Sam Levene, who understood only a fraction of it, and often spouted lines without the semblance of comprehension."

Most critical comment, however, was less savage, generally confining itself to the observation that Levene simply lacked the comic dimension demanded by the extraordinary personage of Bummidge, whom Brustein pronounced "among the most flamboyant comic characters ever written for the American stage."

It was Joseph Anthony's directorial decision to go with Levene in the part and to stick with him in the belief that he would eventually grow into the role. "I sensed that Sam was in a climactic period of his life—some kind of emotional danger area," Anthony says. "And I thought that because he is a comedian, this part of him would *feed into* the part of Bummidge. It was one of those hunches. And it *might* have happened if Sam hadn't become intimidated by the role and lost faith in himself. I kept believing that with each week of rehearsal he would overcome this almost traumatic fear of the role. It was really a *bad* defeat that there wasn't a way that I could find to help Sam realize his talent in this part. It might have been a remarkable performance. But it didn't come. I didn't succeed."

What Anthony terms "that damned intimidation process" still has its echoes in a statement made by Levene in 1971. "Maybe I was wrong for the part," the actor concedes. "Yeah, I think maybe Zero Mostel would have been better. Maybe if Zero had played it, maybe it would have been a big success. But who knows? I don't know—there's no way for me to tell because he *didn't* play it."

In the opinion of Toby Cole, who, at the time of the production, was the agent of both Mostel and Bellow, "Mostel is the real culprit in this situation. Mostel was going to do this play. And if Mostel had done this play it would have come out all right, simply by virtue of his presence. Once Mostel dropped out of the picture, everything was wrong.

"When I represented him in *Ulysses in Nighttown* and *Rhinoceros*, Zero Mostel gave all the evidence of promise that he was on his way to becoming one of the country's leading actors, maybe one of the world's greatest actors," Miss Cole goes on. "But once Zero got caught up in that whole commercial scene, earning the kind of money he

earned, he was absolutely lost." And although there are theater professionals who would dispute her contention that "History will show that
Zero Mostel, who had enormous talent as a dramatic actor, went on to
become an extraordinary hack," it is hard to deny Miss Cole's argument
that *The Last Analysis* marked a turning point in several people's ca-
reers, including the career of Zero Mostel, who never acted in the play.

Playing the role in the 1971 Circle in the Square revival, Joseph
Wiseman received kinder critical comments. Indeed, Clive Barnes, in
The New York Times, found his turn "an acting tour de force." But
for all the emotional intensity and technical skill which Wiseman
poured into his portrayal, the essential Bummidge was beyond him. As
Jerry Tallmer observed, in his review for the New York *Post*, "Mr. Wiseman is a bravura actor giving a bravura performance in a bravura role—
but you can never believe him to have been a comedian." Precisely.
Joseph Wiseman is a marvelous actor and quite capable of convincing
an audience of his believability in any number of roles. But in type he
is essentially an aristocrat, from the beautiful lines of his fine-boned
face to his exquisite enunciation. He is impressive; he is stirring; but he
ain't funny—or, as John Lahr wrote in the *Village Voice*, "He doesn't
suffer with the comedian's ecstasy."

Time and again, when the script called for him to hop about in
confusion, or pace the floor in anticipation, Wiseman complied with
the studied gestures of a technically proficient actor, but gestures that
were awkward and unnatural for the spontaneous, *naturally* funny
Bummy. Bert Lahr would have hopped an audience into hilarity;
Groucho would have paced us into convulsions, but being neither nat-
ural-born clown nor sublimely mad buffoon, Wiseman moved us to
admiration for his technical virtuosity, but not at all to laughter.

Ironically, even his wonderful enunciation worked against his characterization. Although his verbal eloquence respected Bellow's elegant
prose, it tended also to invest the content of the language with far too
much seriousness. Audiences responded to Wiseman's speeches as to
Divine Writ, or at least as to the *actual* words of Freud—missing completely the point that Bummy's psychological pronouncements were
his own corrupted, garbled, half-digested, and absurdly comic interpretations of Freudian theory. Imagine Bert Lahr skipping blithely through
the thick verbal underbrush of Bellow's satire, mangling the lines and
glaring dumbfoundedly at those who dared to laugh at his new intellectual discoveries!

Because Wiseman is not and never has been a fanatically beloved popular comedian, he failed to convey the dark, often bedeviled personality tones which edge the characters of so many of the great clowns. Chaplin, Keaton, Harold Lloyd, and Stan Laurel notwithstanding, the majority of America's clown geniuses, and certainly our contemporary ones, combine with their lovability a sharp undertone of danger, of sinister unspoken motives. A clear-eyed scrutiny at the routines of circus clowns, vaudeville bananas, and the *schtick* of present-day comics from Red Skelton to Jerry Lewis to the most obvious example, Don Rickles, reveals a wide streak of semicruelty which is an integral part of their humor and which, indeed, gives it depth.

Clowns of the stature of Gleason and Berle invariably suggest that this Iago-faced side of their performing *personae* plagues them in private as well. The comic of which Bummidge is meant to be a prototype is almost grotesque. He is a man whose private personality is so shaped by his clown calling that he seems in thrall to it. Obsessed with comedy; a compulsive laugh-glutton who will starve if he cannot evoke mirth; paralyzed by fears of silence, of "dying" before an audience; fanatically dependent on success; a virtual slave to his public; a helpless host dependent on the parasites who feed off his talent; a public exhibitionist with no private retreat—the portrait of Bummidge is the picture of a *tragic* comic. Certainly it describes many of our great American clowns of past and present. And only one of them, one of the superclowns, could have done justice to this role.

Without Kaye, Berle, Caesar, Mostel, or Gleason, the director attempting to bring *The Last Analysis* alive on the stage must rely totally on his own ingenuity. The style of his production must flirt with genius on one side and madness on the other to bring the comedy to fruition. The basic flaw in Joseph Anthony's production was the same weakness he espied in Sam Levene—intimidation.

Deliberately haphazard in structure, its architecture a mongrel conglomeration of some half-dozen comedy styles, the play was clearly written in a mood of whimsy, and, by Bellow's own admission, was meant to be performed in the same spirit.

"This is a comedy written in the manner of Aristophanes," he says. "And not in the manner of a nineteenth-century well-made French comedy. It is thematic, with points made by a chorus, and plotless, in the sense that not much attention is given the finished plot patterns. I thought if you were going to do it, you should really have a healthy swing at this thing . . . do it very loosely."

In a self-interview written in 1971, at the time of the revival, and intended for publication in the Arts and Leisure section of the Sunday edition of *The New York Times,* Bellow further pronounced the style of the play as "shaggy, but stirring. It looked unprofessional but that was precisely the point of the thing. I had diagnosed the trouble with contemporary play-writing as excessive professionalism, and I wanted the homemade Fulton's Folly look. My early drafts were .bombastic, helter-skelter, improbable, but something mysteriously effective was there."

The staging approach for such a free-form larky comedy could take any direction, as long as it was bold and free and aggressively imaginative. According to Joseph Anthony, this was indeed his original intention.

"The original play that I read was really meant to be free. The characters came and went as in commedia dell'arte and in Restoration comedy . . . they just came and went without reason, with no sense of a before-entrance or an after-entrance. And that had a certain charm to it and suited Bellow's form, because this was not even a free-form play, but a *scrambled* free-form play. My feeling was that it was really an experimental play."

If Saul Bellow saw the play as experimental, and if Joseph Anthony saw the play as experimental, one might well ask why the Broadway production turned out so conventional. By Anthony's admission, it was his own fear that Broadway, with its rigid conceptions of what constitutes a good (read "successful") comedy, would not accommodate in 1964 a free-wheeling experimental staging approach. "I don't mean that Broadway couldn't bear a new form," Anthony says, after acknowledging that, in 1964, Broadway had already favorably received such unconventionally mounted plays as *J.B.* and *Stop the World . . . I Want to Get Off.* "But this play was a *mixture* of forms, some brilliant, some bad. It is that mixture which is most inviting to critical denunciations, because it does not *all* come off. We don't like things that don't *all* come off. We like things that *work,* and this play I don't think will ever 'work' because it's a great play with major flaws. That people discard great but flawed material for things that work is indicative of the kind of cultural suicide that we seem to be exacting. I think it's lousy, but that's the way we like our theater."

Having decided that Broadway would not be receptive to an experimental production of *The Last Analysis,* Anthony chose to adapt the play into a production form more familiar and "more palatable" to audiences used to conventional comedies treated in conventional terms. As he was to observe seven years later of that decision to "Broadway-ize" the play, it was a concession to the Broadway system rather than an artistic measure for realizing the play's dramatic virtues. "I would go along with an experimental approach if we were in a different kind of theater," he says. "But when a play has got to become a hit, you do everything possible to calculate what will help it make its way well. And sometimes you *mis*calculate."

In conceptual terms, to "Broadway-ize" a play is to literalize its meaning; to make its content accessible to the garden-variety playgoer by removing or toning down its unfamiliar imaginative flights; to conventionalize what is unconventional; to make it "palatable." Specifically, what Anthony did to *The Last Analysis* was to make it conform to the standardized pattern of the well-made Broadway comedy, to formula-ize it in an attempt to make it "work."

"Since we were not armed with Zero Mostel, I felt that for Broadway the play would become most palatable if it were more rooted in a continuing atmosphere—a place—and so I put it in a loft. . . . And as I worked with Saul on the play, I tried to make more of it logical."

No one is as severe a critic of Anthony's directorial choices as Anthony himself, or so perceptive in pinpointing the misconceptions in his staging of the play. "I think it was a miscalculation," he says of his decision not to give the play an experimental production. "I think that if we had gone totally into a very imaginative production of this play we would perhaps have done better. I think the play *should* have been done much more daringly, freely, imaginatively, than we did it. I think my hunch that the play needed 'rooting' actually disturbed it, took it out of its milieu and made it less of the kind of experimental play it should have been.

"That literal orientation that took place once I set the play in a specific place, a New York loft, proceeded then to invite a continuity of behavior, of realistic business, that ultimately hampered the inspirational quality of the play. It should have taken advantage of its original intended form, which is in the style and period of Molière, where you needn't follow the well-made play necessities of literal time and place. I tried to make the play more logical, and that was wrong. It should have had its own justification—not the justification of the well-made play. It should have been much freer."

Bellow himself never made a secret of his displeasure with the Broadway production of his play, which he called a "mongrel." In the preface which he wrote for the revised version published by Viking, he called the production "cluttered and inconsequential" and filled with "pointless noises and distracting bits of business." It was his contention that "the Broadway version neglected the 'mental' comedy." Although his reaction to the 1971 revival was not exactly one of unbounded enthusiasm, he did consider it an improvement over the original production for the specific reason that it seemed more faithful to the basic spirit of the play and his own original intentions.

"The Bleecker Street production at least communicated some of the original qualities of the play," he says. "At least, there was enough coming through to show audiences what was originally intended. And at least Ted Mann was eager to find out what I thought; he *consulted* me. But I was never able to explain myself fully there, either, and so my tendency was to make the best of it, since I had an *improvement*. I think the critics who saw that half a loaf was better than none had the right attitude. At least the thing was beginning to show itself."

With all due deference to Bellow's prodigious talent as a writer, his evaluation of theatrical production values is unsophisticated. While Ted Mann's production was, indeed, more accurate in conception than the play's earlier treatment, it was rife with misjudgments no less debilitating to the play. On the most obvious physical level, Mann failed to adapt his semi-arena stage to the peculiar needs of Bellow's script. Whereas the play's eccentric form demanded the imposition of a taut style full of farcical invention and burlesque zaniness, Mann's approach was loose and indulgent. Characters' entrances and exits—usually a fount of fun in the farce form—were haphazardly made, by actors wandering from one side of the large, sparsely set stage to the other.

Although an overreliance on hokey gimmickry was one of the vitiating factors in the original production, the revival swung to the other extreme, to become visually trite, almost totally lacking in comic business. Little was made, for example, of the actual televising of Bummidge's self-analysis, a climactic scene which should have been made pointed and hilarious with such props as yards of cable, mobile cameras, intrusive monitors, and blindingly bright lights, all mixing into comic pandemonium as Bummidge bares his psyche to the assembled headshrinkers gazing on from the ballroom of the Waldorf-Astoria.

As serious a flaw as was the paucity of comic ingenuity on a visual level, the production's lack of a strong and coherent directorial style was far more damaging. Beginning with Wiseman's overintellectualized portrayal of Bummy, most of the supporting cast offered the bland kind of capable-but-uninspired performance that is generally the telltale sign of an underdirected play.

Although the directorial approach of neither Anthony nor Mann brought *The Last Analysis* to stage fulfillment, the collaborative nature of theater production makes it imperative to look beyond the director's contribution. In the case of the Broadway production, the collaborative process appears to have functioned at a remarkably low level of efficiency. "I thought I was about to learn something about theater," Bellow wrote to one critic after his initial experience. "And what I 'learned' is that here, as elsewhere, the professionals simply don't know what they're doing."

Bellow was a theatrical neophyte at the time of his Broadway baptism. While he acknowledges the degree of pleasure which he felt in the process, he has hardly forgotten the drubbing he took from the critics or the ordeal of collaborating with theater professionals who didn't share his vision of his play. "It would have been different had I been a regular member of the trade," he now maintains. "I felt that the trade attitude was very strong that the theater is a kind of guild, and that if you were a novelist, or some other kind of person, you were considered an amateur."

Bellow also notes that his first theater experience was "all the more difficult" because it came so quickly on the heels of the publication of his novel *Herzog*. "I was extremely tired," he recalls. "I had exhausted myself in writing *Herzog*, which was just then coming out. While the reviews of the book were just beginning to come out, I was already at work at the Belasco Theatre."

The first discovery Bellow made about the theater was its marked difference from the novel as an art form, and how profoundly that difference affects the writer's professional sovereignty. In the 1964 article which he wrote for the *Times*, he said, "What I am aware of now is the limit placed on the authority of the writer by the theater. It intrigues and amuses me to recognize how independent the habits of a novelist are. Alone with his page, between four walls, he is compensated for his solitude by a high degree of autonomy. In the theater, he discovers the happiness of collaboration. . . . In the theater you see living faces, you feel yourself a part of a company. . . . The price of all this delight is a reduction in one's exclusive powers."

Because the theater itself was such a fresh experience for Bellow, his first few weeks of active participation in the production were spent in adjusting to the peculiar creative process that takes place in theatrical production. "At the beginning," he recalls, "it was not clear to me what was happening—not until the actors actually began to *speak* the lines. The first few weeks or so were spent just in working out actions and positions—where everyone was going to stand and how people were going to enter and make their exits. All of that seemed to be phenomenally important—to everybody else; not to me."

Although he came to realize later that he had definite artistic differences with Anthony's directorial decisions, from his casting choices to his basic comedic conceptions, it took Bellow quite some time to realize and articulate these differences. "When you start this kind of thing it is very exciting and has a great deal of glamour. It takes you a while to see the quality of the people that you're dealing with. It's the novelty of it which blinds you for a while, until things are well underway."

When the play actually began to take shape for Bellow in rehearsal, his initial baffled interest gave way to critical comprehension. "This is my own personality pattern," he says. "At first I was shocked. But then, when I saw that the play wasn't going to get anywhere, anyhow—by that time it was just a mongrel—I began to treat the whole thing as a joke."

While his own inexperience in the ways of the theater was responsible for Bellow's initial slowness to apprehend production flaws and to realize that he had the right to register his reservations with some degree of force, it was the nature of the Broadway system of production which frustrated his eventual belated attempts to salvage the play. There simply wasn't the luxury of time, within the structure of a Broadway production timetable, to reroute the play and begin afresh. Toby Cole, who represents many other playwrights besides Saul Bellow, observes of the production process, "It's a machinery. Once you set a production in motion, there's no going back. Once an author signs his name on one of those contracts, he's signed away his own life and the life of his play."

By the time the playwright actually rebelled against the direction in which his play was headed, the only tangible result was the unconstructive one of a personal rift between author and director. "At first, during the early period of rehearsal, Saul was very patient and trusting," Anthony recalls. "He was new; this was his first play. I was the one supposedly in the position of knowing. Saul is a very warm and kindly person, and during the early stages of work he was very supportive, very patient. It was as if he said, 'Joe, you *know*. Do it *your* way.' In casting, for example, he was quite casual about approving the actors; he felt we *knew*. And if he had uncertainties, we assured him, and he bought our assurances. He was very generous in the beginning—overly so.

"It was when Saul sensed that we had made wrong judgments that the conflict occurred. There's a bad side to Saul's nature, and once he sensed that the production wasn't going to work, he was quite capable of ruthless indifference to human values around the theater. He certainly was an unfriendly author when he sensed that the show was not going to work—to the point where I had to prevent him from working with us in the theater."

The picture which Anthony draws of *The Last Analysis* is one of tragic misunderstanding, fear, lack of communication, and pure hysterical anxiety—on everyone's part.

"I think I probably became stubborn, too, somewhere along the way," he says. "I knew that the management, as well as Saul, was 'agin' me in a sense. They also knew that the show was going down the drain. I just stubbornly refused to see that something heroic had to be done, or the show *would* go down the drain. I just kept crawling to the altar, I guess."

The "heroic" action of which Anthony spoke might have been the dismissal of Sam Levene—a measure which Bellow had strongly urged. But by this time, Anthony had become almost obsessional about making Levene "work" in the role—or vice versa.

"I was concerned with building Sam's confidence," Anthony says, "almost more than I was with figuring out how to make the whole thing work." Although Bellow came to him about ten days before the first preview and suggested that the play would never succeed with Levene in the lead, the director was intransigent. "Number one, I hate firing actors. Number two, I felt that Sam, at that moment in his life, was in an uncertain condition as a performing artist and a man—which may or may not be true, but that's what I felt—and I believed that a blow of this sort would be badly damaging to him. Number three, I had no alternative in mind to play that extraordinarily complex role. And that made numbers one and two irrelevant."

By his own admission, the director plunged ahead, trying to make Levene comfortable in the part. "I think I tried to compensate for Sam's lack of verbal virtuosity by inhabiting the play with *schtick* that I thought would give him confidence," Anthony says in reference to his directorial inventions subsequently scorned by the author as "clutter."

The playwright's differences with his director seem to have hinged on two specific areas of dispute: the play's ideas, and the language in which they were couched. "My own strongest feelings about the play had to do with the *ideas* in it," Bellow says. "The ideas were the least understood. I really couldn't get Joe Anthony to grasp the importance of the ideas to me." In Bellow's view, the Broadway production's failure to realize the play's intellectual content led directly to a perversion of the play's humor.

"It was pious," he says of the production, putting his finger on its most debilitating flaw. "They treated the thing piously because they're not used to language and they're not used to thought. They're used to mumbling a few scraps of language while doing their thing on stage. Their technique is in stage *business*, and so they're overwhelmed by unfamiliar elements in the play and begin to take them very seriously. It was not my idea that the play should be high-serious; my idea was that it should be *low*-serious."

To Bellow, the play's ideas are inextricably bound up with the language with which they're expressed. But "it was over the language that we had our worst fights," the writer recalls. "The language was elegant," he says in dispassionate appraisal. "Nevertheless, I really consider the play a failure as a literary work because I couldn't get anyone to accept the language on its own terms.

"I was amused, but at the same time appalled, to see how very important to these people was the technique of putting a play on stage. They don't really think about language. They don't really *know* anything about language. I don't think American actors—most of them—can speak these lines."

Whichever American actor Bellow was exempting from his condemnation, Sam Levene was not one of them. "Sam Levene is a dear man, but he found it hard to speak a sentence with a subordinate clause," is the playwright's recent terse evalution of his star, but one which he was unable to make at the time of production until the third week of rehearsal. "But by that time," as Bellow notes, "it was too late to ask to replace Sam and bring in somebody else."

In summing up his differences with Anthony, Bellow has this to say: "I just couldn't get through to Joe. We don't speak the same language."

With author and director at loggerheads, and a star whose work was undoubtedly suffering for his being the bone of their contention, one might well ask where in hell the show's producer was during all the *Sturm und Drang.* Not only is the producer a key partner in the collaborative creation of professional theater, but he frequently is also the arbiter of artistic disputes which arise during the course of a show's production.

Despite his enormously crucial central position in every theatrical enterprise, the producer is a shadowy figure simply because he wields his power completely behind the scenes. Essentially, his role is to package the product: he raises the money to mount it; he arranges every business detail from securing the theater to arranging for the truckers to come and cart off the scenery on closing night; he hires, and he has the right to fire, every person involved in the production, be he artist, craftsman, or non-entity. He weds these various talents by selecting the proper director for each production and then overseeing his choices for actors, designers, staff, and crew. He decides when a play must close, although, of course, the public gives him a big tip first.

The producer's personal degree of involvement within this framework of responsibility varies considerably from individual to individual, but many of these professional showmen consider themselves "creative producers," a term which may bring snickers at a Dramatists' Guild *kaffeklatsch* but which in reality translates into managerial assistance on an active artistic level: work with the playwright on revisions and with the director in mapping out the staging blueprint.

A producer who fully exercises his rights in all the areas of a play's production, both business and artistic, is said to be the "muscle" of that production—the "muscle" being the person who exerts the most influence and wields the most genuine power in the course of a production. Although this "muscle" man is often the producer, the muscle of some shows may be the director, the star, or, in the case of a few highly successful and theater-wise playwrights like Neil Simon or Arthur Miller, it can be the author.

The Last Analysis on Broadway was a classic case of displaced muscle. Its producer, Roger L. Stevens, is a man who is not, and does not care to be, the muscle behind his shows. Its author was a newcomer to the theater and ill-equipped to take the strong position. Its director, the "muscle apparent," was having such severe artistic tribulations with his leading actor that he was unable to handle the power that fell to him by default.

A producer who has always preferred the multi-project approach to producing, Stevens was especially busy during the period that Saul Bellow's comedy was in production. "This particular play came along just as I was going with the government," he says. (Stevens assumed the chairmanship of the National Council on the Arts in the spring of 1965.) "I unfortunately did not spend anywhere near as much time as I normally would on the play. I already had made my commitments to the government, and was also involved at the time with the Kennedy Center for the Performing Arts in Washington."

Two years earlier, in its issue of October 10, 1962, *Variety* ran a feature on the "umpteen" projects being undertaken at that time by the producer, who had come to the Broadway theater after a fabulously successful real-estate career which included buying *and* selling the Empire State Building. The trade publication noted with some awe that Stevens, as chairman of the board of the National Cultural Center in Washington, was in the middle of a hot campaign to raise thirty million dollars for the Center. In another capacity, that of general administrator of the Actors Studio Theater, Stevens was also trying to raise two million dollars for the Studio's New York operations. After referring to his several Broadway, off Broadway, and touring productions, *Variety* then went on to list *seventeen* other projects with which Stevens was then involved, or which were contemplated for the near future.

It would be inaccurate, however, to imply that Roger Stevens was simply "too busy" during the summer of 1964 to oversee his floundering production. By his own choice, Stevens had always been an "absentee" producer. Since it is an integral tenet of his managerial philosophy that a producer's function is to set the gears in motion and then leave the art to the artists, his hands-off policy during the production of *The Last Analysis* cannot be viewed as deviationist behavior.

"I think the key to a good producer is to take a good work, pick the director, and then let it go. The whole thing is setting up the right elements and then depending on the people. I think a producer always fails if he hires the wrong people. To make plays work, you just have to be lucky and blend the various personalities together, and it comes out okay. It doesn't mean that I always agree with what they're doing, but I would always let the director have the final say.

"If you've made a mistake, you've made a mistake—that's all. I know a lot of plays messed up because too many people have put their fingers in them. Producers who have nothing to do overproduce themselves. They sit around at all the rehearsals because they don't have anything else to do. If I could direct, I'd direct. If I could write a play, I'd write a play. If I could act, I'd act."

Roger Stevens has personally worked out this philosophy of producing, and for him it has proved viable, since he has functioned successfully for many years on Broadway. If his view is not always shared by other producers, it is at least respected within the theater community. As Sam Levene expresses it, "Each man has his own way of working, and you can't criticize it if that's the way he wants to work. There's no formula, no way of putting it down on paper. If Mr. Stevens has faith in Mr. Anthony and says: 'Here's the money—go ahead,' well, I don't see anything wrong in that."

There is room for criticism only when a producer's personal work ethic appears to be doing a disservice to the project at hand; and, when, in spite of evidence to this effect, he fails to adapt that code in an effort to salvage the play. It is Stevens' contention that he was indeed involved with his show, at least "enough so that I came around and kept it open for a few more weeks, hoping it would catch on."

But that doesn't seem to be the kind of involvement that *The Last Analysis* needed: better the warm authoritative body of the producer during the early stages of the show's production. Stevens himself begs the question.

"Whether my having spent more time on it would have made any difference, I don't know," he says. Others involved in the show don't think it would have mattered, since Stevens' absence from work sessions was itself a kind of commitment to a position—namely, the decision to override Saul Bellow's objections and to tacitly support Anthony in his casting choices and his directorial scheme.

"Roger Stevens is an absentee producer," says Bellow's agent, Toby Cole. "But what would be the point if he weren't? It wouldn't have mattered if he had been there, because when he was, and when Saul and I talked with him, it was clear that our positions about the production were totally reversed.

"Saul and I had a meeting with Stevens, and I begged him to stop the play. I said to him, 'Mr. Stevens, if you want to rescue this play and save some of your money for another situation, close it down—now. Don't open it.' But it's a question of how different people view the same thing. I saw the production as dreadful, and the producers saw it as wonderful—and what can you do about that? I couldn't stop them. I was called a Cassandra, for predicting that things would be terrible."

Although Stevens is quite accurate in his estimation of rambunctious producers who "mess up" their productions by becoming overly involved in the creative decisions better left to the artists, the irony of *The Last Analysis* is that it could have used a bit of this "meddling." It actually needed the authoritative voice of its producer to bail it out. Even today, Stevens is extremely reticent about discussing the show at all, and absolutely fearful about making any statement the least bit critical about anyone involved artistically in the production. Such behavior might be construed as gentlemanly fastidiousness by some, but in 1964, when a play's artistic fate was at stake, it must have seemed frustratingly isolationist.

To give Stevens his due, he did leave an associate, Lyn Austin, in titular charge of the production, but Miss Austin reports that it was diffi-cult for her to feel "close" to the show, since at the time she was involved in a number of other projects for Stevens. Although she now says she thought the venture "a very ill-conceived production," at the time of its casting she was in Europe on other business. Once she became actively involved, she says she felt that the show—and all its problems—was almost a *fait accompli*.

Plagued as it was by a number of internal and external problems, *The Last Analysis* was an almost certain failure on the perfection-demanding Broadway market. Failure is something all theater people are equipped to deal with, so nobody involved in the play actually collapsed from grief when the show folded. Although Stevens expressed admiration for his project, it was, after all, only one of many. In Sam Levene's caustic view, "Roger Stevens is a very rich man. He lost a few thousand dollars, but he can afford it. And that's the end of it." Levene's own reaction is philosophically stoic, like most theater pros. "Nobody wants to have a failure. But I have been a professional actor for forty-five years, and failure is part of my career. You accept failure, you accept success, and you go on. I do the best I can, and if it doesn't always work out, it's not because I didn't try. It's not because I didn't understand. It's not because I wanted it to fail. I don't go into a play so that it will fail. I'd like for it to run, so that I can live. But if people can't accept failure, that's unfortunate."

Joseph Anthony took it harder, and is still quick to shoulder the responsibility for the play's fate. "It's not modesty," he insists. "I'm really quite able to view my work in true objectivity. I have never enjoyed kidding myself; it gives me no pleasure at all to deceive myself. . . . In the theater, we take our failures very seriously."

But certainly the person most adversely affected was Saul Bellow. It was his first play, and perhaps his hopes were unrealistically lofty. But having been toughened by his active involvement in the production, he was prepared for failure. For failure, perhaps, but not for ignominy—and ignominy was what the reviews heaped on him. Allowing for all the flaws of the play and all the problems of its inadequate presentation, *The Last Analysis* is a play of distinction and deserving of critical respect. For whatever complex personal reasons, the majority of reviewers seemed psychologically unequipped to view the play with much objectivity. Bellow feels they jumped on him and savaged him as a presumptuous interloper on sacred grounds. And from all the evidence, he seems to be justified in his opinion.

"I was surprised by the quantity of spittle," he noted in his self-interview. "You would have thought from the intensity of their fury and contempt that the theater was a thriving institution, not a faltering one. These writers were its custodians; they had made their contributions to its decline, and they now denounced my suggestions for its improvement with the greatest hatred."

Bellow's champions included Robert Brustein, writing in *The New Republic*, and Harold Clurman, of *The Nation*. Clurman served the play and its author by writing a review that was uncompromising in its criticism of the play's flaws, but which perceived the merits of the work and the extraordinary talent of its author. Unlike most of his colleagues, who dismissed the play as an infectious disease and the playwright as its scabrous carrier, Clurman gave the play its most insightful analytic review.

Brustein, on the other hand, went for the throats of the other reviewers. He saw in the brief encounter of Saul Bellow and Broadway "the head-on collision of a gifted writer with the crassness and incompetence of the whole commercial theater system." Brustein was scornful of the play's production, as indicative of Broadway's inability to treat a serious comedy with subtlety, or in any but the most hackneyed conventional terms. But when he spoke of "crassness and incompetence," he was really raging at "the theater reviewers, who, exposing that awful gap that exists between the theatrical and literary worlds, dismissed Mr. Bellow as if he were simply another hack writer of the Broadway school. From the tone of some of their reviews, this response was partly motivated by a desire for revenge against those who have kept them in an abject state of inferiority. The next time these men begin asking, 'Where are the playwrights?', let them look at the corpses they have buried under their own reviews."

Not all the critics, of course, went after Bellow with the hatchet-tongued criticism which so aroused Brustein's fury. But an alarmingly large lot of them did indeed deliver diatribes which were unprofessional and personally vindictive, and the effect on Bellow was tantamount to an attack of artistic vandalism.

"Some critics felt that there was no place in the theater for novelists," Bellow wrote in his unpublished self-interview. "Others, less tolerant, behaved as though I had been trying to muscle my way into the racket. In their reviews they protected the profession itself and concentrated their fire on me, the outsider. I had no desire to muscle in. My view of the matter was different. I thought of my play as an offering laid on the altar. I should have known better—the first recorded murder took place before an altar. In any case, my offering was taken to be an aggression in disguise and elicited an unusual amount of hatred."

Bellow wasn't alone in feeling wounded and testy at the tone of the critical reception which greeted the play. His agent, Toby Cole, had some harshly critical opinions about the Broadway reviewers and, by extension, about the theater system that sustains them.

"I think Saul Bellow could have been an extraordinary playwright," she says. "But I fear he never will be because on his first attempt he was literally spat upon. He was told to get the hell out of the theater.

"The theater is very inhospitable. Its critics are, for the most part, philistine; they don't really know what the theater is about. The theater has driven a good many people away; there is a whole host of superior writers who will never write for the theater."

Bellow contends that after years of being "utterly turned off" by his experience, he was sufficiently heartened by the more temperate response to his play's revival to consider writing again for the theater. "I now have mixed feelings about it," he says. "But if I felt terribly moved to write a play, I'd write it. It wouldn't make any difference; the hell with those guys."

One of the more sensitive reactions came from Joseph Anthony, who considers his own role in the production to be very culpable. "Look at Saul," he says. "There's a man with a large theater appetite. He's an important writer and a man of great productivity. He could have given us a new play every year since that play opened. Instead, he has given us three short pieces that were put on for a handful of people in a downtown loft. And that's the total output of Saul Bellow to the American theater.

"Why should Saul's first play have been a winner? Do children climb out of the womb, suddenly running races? They've got to crawl first, and sometimes the movement of crawling is more beautiful than the fact that we end up walking, running, and even flying."

Writing in the October 30, 1964, issue of *Life*, Tom Prideaux devoted a long article to the question of the theater's inhospitable reception to "outsiders" from other writing disciplines. "It's an odd fact," Prideaux observed, "that whereas many English and European men of letters include play-writing as part of their profession, their American counterparts give it one or two tries and then wash their hands of it. Hemingway, Fitzgerald, Faulkner, O'Hara, Sinclair Lewis, Edmund Wilson, and Robert Penn Warren have all sidled up to Broadway, and then retreated with disappointment and disdain."

Prideaux declined to see the hostility as one-sided, advancing the opinion that some authors among the literati are snobbish about the stage, scorning it as too lowbrow for their talents, testy about collaborating with "inferiors," and altogether unwilling to recognize the nature of the job of play-writing. "American theater is poorer because more talented authors don't write for it, and the authors themselves are missing a fascinating medium of expression. Saul Bellow can certainly be forgiven for not writing a good play, but I can never forgive him if he doesn't try it again."

The insensitive reviews alone didn't "kill" Saul Bellow's first play. Nor did its poorly conceived production and the many errors in human judgment which contributed to it. As Brustein observed, "The major cause of the accident was the complex and ambitious nature of the work itself." One wonders if this eccentric play, whose flagrant flaws somehow seem intrinsic to its total character, would ever work in our commercial theater system.

XMAS IN LAS VEGAS

by Jack Richardson

CAST OF CHARACTERS

EDWARD T. WELLSPOT

LIONEL WELLSPOT

EMILY WELLSPOT

ELEANOR WELLSPOT

MICHEL WELLSPOT

MRS. EDNA SIMON

WILLY

SPIROS OLYMPUS

Act One

SCENE I

Darkness. A rock and roll version of "O Little Town of Beth-lehem" is heard and, as it fades away, the lights come up on EDWARD T. WELLSPOT *on his knees in front of the curtain. He is a heavy, assured man in his early fifties. He shakes a pair of dice furiously, and when he speaks, he sends most of his words heavenwards.*

The curtain behind him is black, except for the following designs in thin white lines: the outline of a roulette wheel, a blackjack table, and a dice table. The lines should interweave so that it is not clear exactly where one game leaves off and the other begins.

EDWARD. All right, fates, this is no stranger calling on you. This is Edward T. Wellspot, an old friend and flagealee of yours. I've taken every one of your punches without whimpering any more than a man should. Give me a toothsome smile now. (EDWARD *tosses the dice offstage and follows their roll intensely.*)

VOICE OFFSTAGE. Snake eyes—craps—a loser. (*The dice are pushed back on stage with a long croupier's stick.*)

EDWARD (*Picks up the dice and speaks in a nervous tone*). Now that wasn't nice. You don't have any quarrel with me. I wash every day, I had a Good Conduct Medal and two Purple Hearts in the last war, I donate to the Red Cross, I haven't cheated on my wife in four years, and I'm as superstitious as you could want. I'm no amateur human be-ing. So as one professional to another . . . (*He tosses the dice offstage again.*)

VOICE OFFSTAGE. Five—the point is five.

EDWARD. Oh, I need more encouragement than a point like five. I want to be someone special to you. Someone like Caesar, Shakespeare, Rembrandt or Nick the Greek. I want my luck to change the world.

(*The dice come back.*) You know I'm open-minded. No prejudices or hang-ups in any way. If you turn out to be men or women, disposed to saints or a bloody sacrifice or two, whipping grandmothers or deflowering little boys—that's your business. I am a liberal. (*He rolls again.*)

VOICE OFFSTAGE. Seven. A loser.

EDWARD (*Just barely controlling his anger*). Testing old Edward T's loyalty, are you? Well, you still have it. Look at this faithful face. Ah, there's something impressive about a man on his knees having the cheek to call you into a low-stake crap game. But I'm doing it with my vertebrae lined up proud and perpendicular. Admit I'm impressive! (EDWARD *sends the dice out again.*)

VOICE OFFSTAGE. Twelve. Boxcars. Craps. A loser.

EDWARD (*Standing up, furious*). You won't be inveigled or conned, will you? Well, I'm through asking nicely. The next time you take a peek at this planet, you're going to see Edward T. Wellspot standing on top of it. And don't come whining to me, saying I was always your favorite little gambler in the world. Fates, you had your chance to get with a winning human being and blew it.

BLACKOUT

SCENE II

The curtain goes up on a living room in a Las Vegas hotel suite. The room is packed with gambling apparatuses: two slot machines flank the door leading to the bedrooms; a roulette wheel and table stand at coffee-table level in front of the sofa sporting dice cages at each of its ends. French windows open out onto a balcony at L. There is a well-furnished bar against the back wall next to a large radio and television set. Bright morning sunshine lights up the imitation Louis Quinze furniture.

LIONEL WELLSPOT, *a tense, slender young man in his late twenties, sits on the sofa behind the roulette wheel. He has a pencil and a pad of paper in his hands, with which he calculates furiously as he spins the wheel, tilts the dice cages and starts the slot machines whirring. As the roulette wheel comes to a stop he goes back to the sofa, checks the roulette wheel and gives it another spin just as* EMILY WELLSPOT *enters. She*

*is nearly thirty, almost pretty, with an open, eager face. Her
hair is askew and she wears a crumpled bathrobe with pajamas
underneath.*

EMILY. Oh, Lionel, Lionel! I need some coffee, some strong black
coffee.

LIONEL (*Still at his calculations*). Not another bad dream?

EMILY. Oh that's too anemic a word. Wait till you hear it.

LIONEL (*Shrinking visibly*). Please, I'm trying to balance my slot
machine equations. I want to finish them before Father gets back from
the casino.

EMILY (*Sitting next to him on the sofa*). I'll tell it to you very
quickly. You'll enjoy this one.

LIONEL (*Painfully resigned*). Was it sexual?

EMILY (*Nods*). Uh-hum. But well disguised. It won't offend you.

LIONEL. All your dreams offend me.

EMILY. Just take a clinical attitude about it, Lionel, and listen. Now,
remember the summer house we used to go to in New Hampshire before Daddy lost it in a gin rummy game?

LIONEL. Edward T. Wellspot's first disaster and it had the only
playroom I ever liked, and I'm sure it was the first room he lost.

EMILY. Now listen, Lionel. I was in the back yard, and everything
was very bright around me. The sun seemed just ten feet over my head.
And then, suddenly, it was dark. I became frightened, looked up, and
saw—flapping the largest pair of wings in the world—this sad-looking
bird staring down at me. His eyes were bloodshot and his beak twitched
suggestively. Then anyway, he swooped down, picked me up in his
talons, and started to fly off. He even spoke to me. He said, "Emily
Wellspot, I'll be making you grow feathers and take care of me nest."

LIONEL. Why the Irish accent?

EMILY. He was that kind of bird—strange, unpredictable. When
we got to his nest, it was full of eggs and straw. I set to tidying up,
placing the straw in bundles and the eggs in pyramid piles. All the time
he watched me, pecking at himself happily. But when I finished, it
happened.

LIONEL (*Stiffening*). He flapped his wings and ravaged you. The
same old dream. (*He goes back to pencil and paper.*)

EMILY. He didn't touch me, Lionel. He just began to molt. Right
in front of me.

LIONEL. And that frightened you?

EMILY. It would you too, because when the feathers dropped off, that bird turned out to be my second husband, Sydney.

LIONEL. Which one was that?

EMILY. The one who took me parachuting on my honeymoon.

LIONEL. But he didn't have an Irish accent. He was Jewish.

EMILY. But everything else fits. I wish my dreams were more complicated. What am I going to do with the rest of the day?

LIONEL. Go back to sleep.

EMILY. I would, but Daddy'll be coming back soon, and he gets so angry when he sees me napping. He wants us to be bright for the holidays.

LIONEL. The family Christmas gathering. Why do we let Father bully us each year into coming out here? Every December first, back into our lives he thumps, bellowing that the next card will put everything into place. Just when you're ready after four husbands to doze off and take your chance with dreams, just when I'm adjusted to a graduate school dormitory, one suit and a Korean exchange student for my only friend, back we come for another Christmas to this maniac's dream of a town to gather around a plastic pine tree and lose.

EMILY. Maybe this year we won't.

LIONEL. Believe your brother who's had nine fellowships in as many years, we will.

EMILY. You always were gloomy, Lionel. I remember when you were a little boy the way you'd sit in the closet and make up lists of incurable diseases.

LIONEL. Even as an adolescent I had the right instincts about the world, and right now they tell me father's finally going to be wiped out.

EMILY. How do you know?

LIONEL. I've been calculating, that's how. I should have taken an interest in his gambling before. It's as if the universe wanted to sneak its secrets into us through all the chances we make up for ourselves. Mathematics, Emily, the music of the planets is a sad song, and in gambling it's an outright dirge. Each time you roll, each day you live, in the long run of the most compassionate probability theory, you come closer to being broke and broken. If there's any sign in the heavens it should be "You can't beat the house."

EMILY. Lionel, you remind me of Sydney after he molted. Did I ever tell you what happened when we jumped out of that plane together on our honeymoon?

LIONEL. Emily, I haven't even had breakfast yet. Don't drag me through your honeymoons.

EMILY. It was going to be so romantic, Lionel. We flew over a quiet forest in Vermont and parachuted down to consummate our marriage in a little lakeside hotel. (*Reminiscing.*) Sydney's mother was at the controls. She wished us happiness, and said life was long and love must be stretched thin to cover it. Then we jumped—I in my wedding dress and Sydney clutching one suitcase for the two of us. It was my first time, but we began descending perfectly—a few seconds' free-fall hand in hand, a moment's parting while we modestly opened our chutes, then back together for the soft glide downwards. For a second, we both turned cartwheels in the air. And then we hit a cloud formation. Sydney floated close to me and there in the midst of a cumulus cloud kissed me so intensely that we tangled our chutes. We started to fall—down, down, faster and faster. When we came out of the fog, there was Vermont racing up at us—all green and soft. I noticed what was happening first, but I didn't care. With Sydney biting on my ear, I was ready to sink with him into New England forever.

LIONEL. I hate romantic deaths.

EMILY. I don't think they exist anymore. With only half a mile left to go, Sydney pulled away to breathe and noticed what was happening.

LIONEL. And he didn't want to splatter over Vermont?

EMILY. He tried to push me away and loosen our chutes. And when I clung to him and told him it could never be better than this at thirty-two feet per second, he called me over-sexed and pulled the emergency cord. The second chute opened, and we started floating again. But it just wasn't the same. When we reached the ground I knew our best time as man and wife was past. Sitting on the ground, I looked back up at the sky and saw written in white smoke, "Have a good honeymoon, Sydney. Be careful. Don't tire yourself." His mother had taken an adult course in skywriting. That was our mark in the heavens, "Don't tire yourself!"

LIONEL (*After a pause*). The honeymoon over?

EMILY. I wonder if I'll ever find a husband who won't disappoint me?

LIONEL. Olympus has proposed for the last three years, hasn't he?

EMILY. Mr. Olympus would be afraid to jump out of a plane with me.

LIONEL. But he's going to break Father this time. I know it.

EMILY (*Sleepily*). He has little hands and bloodshot eyes.

LIONEL. He may not drop out of the sky, but he has enough money to provide you with a comfortable bed, velvet sleeping masks and as much unconsciousness as you want.

EMILY. Maybe marriage should be two people sleeping in shifts and turning each other into exciting dreams.

LIONEL. You should know, Emily. Better than anybody else.

EMILY. Oh, poor Daddy would be disappointed.

LIONEL. Don't pity him. A straight flush in Florida may have sent you to Europe for a year and eight passes in a row got me through my first year at Harvard, but he never did get the money to have your tonsils out. Remember that!

EMILY (*Sitting up*). I'd forgotten. He went to the race track and won just enough for my adenoids, but never enough for my tonsils. When I have sore throats I really hate him. (ELEANOR WELLSPOT *comes quickly into the room through the main door. She is round of figure with an abstracted air about her, as though she is constantly trying to make up her mind about some important problem and is not certain just what the problem is. She searches furiously in her purse as she begins speaking, which is immediately on entrance.*)

ELEANOR. Lionel, give me some silver dollars quick. I'm out of change and I want to play the slot machine.

LIONEL. The machine belongs to the hotel, Mother. You don't get the dollars back.

ELEANOR. I know that. But if there's no risk, there's no test. I'm not playing for fun.

EMILY. Now what test are you talking about?

ELEANOR (*In a conspirator's voice*). I saw them again. As plain as day, as plain as day.

LIONEL. Not the angels?

ELEANOR. They were fluttering over the entrance to the Golden Nugget.

LIONEL. These are the same angels you told me you saw in Schrafft's last year?

ELEANOR. I've seen them often, Lionel. And this time I'm sure it's a sign. They were so much clearer than they've ever been.

EMILY. What kind of sign, Mother?

ELEANOR. Well, I could tell, from how pink and white they were, that they must be Episcopal angels, and it was an Episcopal God I left behind in Boston when I married your father. Maybe he's forgiven the fact that I've come so far west and is ready to help us win.

LIONEL. You know better than that, Mother.

ELEANOR. What do I know better than, young man? I know that your father and I have been moving further and further west every year and losing more and more of the time. These Episcopal angels are a little touch of Boston that might just bring us luck. The silver dollars, Lionel.

LIONEL (*Giving* ELEANOR *some change*). Well, better sexless angels than trusting Father.

ELEANOR. Oh, they weren't sexless. They had tiny private parts—so cute.

LIONEL. Oh God! Couldn't my own mother have a better vision than pornographic angels?

ELEANOR. If they weren't naked, Lionel, how would I recognize them as angels? They'd look like big moths if they wore suits.

LIONEL. Forget theology and try the machine.

ELEANOR. Oh, one jackpot as a sign. I've never had one in my life and Edward would be so proud of me.

LIONEL. The odds are about 8000 to 3 against you on a dollar machine.

ELEANOR. What should the odds be to count for a miracle?

LIONEL. 8000 to 3 seems enough. Give it a try, Mother. (ELEANOR *puts a dollar in the machine and takes hold of the handle. Her eyes are closed.*)

ELEANOR. Well, here we go. It's been a long time since Boston. (ELEANOR *pulls the handle. The three watch silently until the spinning slots come to rest.*)

EMILY. Two plums and a cherry. What does that mean, Lionel?

LIONEL. Absolutely nothing.

ELEANOR. Maybe I just need a little more faith. (ELEANOR *inserts another dollar and sets the slots in motion. They again stop silently.*)

EMILY. A plum and two oranges?

LIONEL. Unmiraculous fruit.

ELEANOR. One dollar left. If they were going to work a miracle it wouldn't take them three chances to do it.

EMILY. You'll be happier if you let them take the last dollar.

ELEANOR. It is Christmas. You'd think that would count for something. (*Again* ELEANOR *closes her eyes and spins the machine. This time there is the ring of a pay-off when the slots stop spinning. Not daring to look.*)

EMILY. Oh, oh—what was it, Lionel?

LIONEL. You won three dollars. No miracle, but you break even.

ELEANOR. Oh, well, I guess he hasn't come from Boston for me. I can't blame him. I ran off without even saying good-bye panting for your father.

LIONEL. All right, Mother, you don't have to confess everything in front of the slot machine.

ELEANOR. You're such a delicate boy, Lionel.

LIONEL. The thought of my mother panting upsets me, that's all.

EMILY. Oh, I'd like to know what your dreams are like.

LIONEL. I dream like a philosopher. Syllogistic phantoms and synthetic a priori monsters never seen by man. But they don't molt or go panting after one another.

ELEANOR. All right, Lionel, calm down. Is your father back yet?

EMILY. No. Still out from last night.

LIONEL. What does he do in the casinos all this time?

ELEANOR. He shuffles about, trying to find the right time, the right rhythm for him to move to. I don't know what he'll do when I tell him about the angels. Edward lost five thousand dollars, when I saw them for the first time at the Kentucky Derby. Still, they are lovely to look at—white-feather wings and round, red bottoms.

LIONEL. Mother, please!

ELEANOR. Yes, you are delicate, Lionel. That's nice, but it means you'll never see a naked angel. (ELEANOR *exits through the bedroom door*.)

EMILY. It would have been nice if she'd had a jackpot.

LIONEL. People have dreamed up some very peculiar gods, but not one ever fixed slot machines. (*Offstage, there is the sound of* ELEANOR'S *voice, high-pitched and shocked*.)

ELEANOR (*Offstage*). Michel, for heaven's sake!

MICHEL (*Offstage*). What's the matter? I'm beautiful! Damned beautiful! (ELEANOR *comes back into the living room, closing the door behind her*.)

LIONEL. What's the matter?

ELEANOR. Naked angels are one thing, but your uncle is quite another. I wish he'd wear a bathrobe when he wanders back and forth from the shower. (MICHEL WELLSPOT *enters from the bedroom door. He is in his fifties, but so thin and wasted that he looks the result of at least a dozen vices. He is dressed only in a bathrobe*.)

MICHEL (*Angrily*). How dare you, Eleanor? How dare you?

ELEANOR. How dare I what?

MICHEL. Look at me without clothes on, scream, and make a face like you did! Have you forgotten that this body of mine has been loved by over two hundred women?

LIONEL (*Collapses on the sofa, hands over his eyes*). Oh God!

MICHEL. Over two hundred, Eleanor. And not one of them made a face.

ELEANOR. Well, they were prepared for it.

MICHEL. Prepared? (*He coughs violently.*) Who has to be prepared to see a sunset or a perfect rose?

ELEANOR. All right, Michel, I apologize.

MICHEL. Sorry's not enough. (*He coughs again.*) I'm deeply hurt.

ELEANOR. I was just startled, Michel. A man's body can do that.

MICHEL (*Peeking beneath his robe*). Do you think my appendix scar's ugly? I've thought of plastic surgery.

ELEANOR. Oh no, I thought it was very forcefully designed.

MICHEL (*He goes to the bar and pours himself a drink*). I don't know. Perhaps I'm not the man I was. Perhaps you had a right to jump back.

EMILY. A drink this early, Uncle Michel?

MICHEL. I was insulted this early, wasn't I? Ah, you're too young to remember what I used to be. You think your father has style? He was an old tennis ball compared to me. When I left home, a hot trombone player with bright red hair parted in the middle and played in a band that wore checkered vests and tight sharkskin suits, I glowed. Admit that, Eleanor. Admit I glowed!

ELEANOR. Your uncle did cut quite a figure.

MICHEL (*After draining his glass*). And so many women loved me; and the best part of it, I loved them back, every blessed one of them. (*He coughs.*) Oh, and when I'd slip out of that phosphorescent suit, vest, monogrammed shirt, and silk underwear, how gratefully they looked at me.

LIONEL. What about your socks and shoes?

MICHEL. I used to let the ladies take them off for me. They loved it. (*He starts to laugh, but it turns into a cough.*)

ELEANOR. You shouldn't drink that way. You promised Edward you wouldn't.

MICHEL. Your husband, my brother, deserves no promises kept. You know what he had the nerve to say to me? He said if I needed female companionship he'd fix me up. Like a bellboy to a scared conventioneer. (*He pours himself another drink.*) Fix me up! Why, I had more going for me in my playpen than he's had in his whole life.

ELEANOR. Well, thank you, Michel!

MICHEL.. Sorry, Eleanor. I just meant general experience, not quality. (*He toasts with his glass.*) Here's to those two hundred general experiences.

LIONEL. Don't tell me you remember them all.

MICHEL. When I'm sober, they all mix together. But after a little of this, I can close my eyes and a pair of particular legs comes out clearly and I sniff a special scent that reminds me—reminds me . . . Wait a moment, here comes the rest of the body— Oh, yes! Ah, ah—nice! A little plump, but still firm. And the face—long, gentle, sad, with large tired eyes. And the name. (*Eyes still closed, he gulps the rest of his glass.*) Ah, red hair. Red hair, as though she's surrounded by fire. It shouldn't be hard—there weren't so many with red hair.

LIONEL. The wages of second-class sin isn't death, just befuddlement.

MICHEL (*Eyes still closed*). Be quiet, you philosophic virgin. By God! Her front tooth is cracked! A cracked front tooth??! Margaret— Margaret Reilly! She took me and my trombone to meet her mother. And when the old lady went to sleep! Oh, that tooth cut my upper lip to ribbons. It was wonderful! Wonderful. (MICHEL *drops into a violent coughing fit.*)

ELEANOR. Quick, he's having an attack. (ELEANOR *and* LIONEL *take him, bend him over the back of a chair, and begin slapping his back.*)

LIONEL. What a horrible sound.

EMILY. He shouldn't have memories so early in the morning.

MICHEL (*Between wheezes*). That tooth was like a buzz saw. Beautiful! (MICHEL *wheezes violently.*)

EMILY. All this really makes me very sleepy. I could take a little nap right now. (EMILY *lies down on the sofa just as* EDWARD WELLSPOT *enters. He is wearing dark glasses which he takes off to watch the scene for a moment, shaking his head sadly.*)

EDWARD. Has he been reminiscing again?

ELEANOR. He was remembering this red-headed woman named Miss Reilly who . . .

EDWARD (*Lifting* MICHEL *up from the chair and massaging his back.* MICHEL *keeps trying to say something, but can only wheeze.* EDWARD, *disappointed*). Still only potent in the past, eh? Well, don't let it worry you, Michel. There's a bevy of girls in the casino downstairs— long-stemmed chorines we used to call them, eh?

MICHEL (*Breaking free and gulping a large breath of air*). And I'll line up my own women.

EDWARD. I just thought you might have been a little out of practice, living in a hotel for retired jazz musicians and playing old choruses of "Frenesi" with a lady bass player.

MICHEL. Ah, what do you know anyway? (*To* EMILY *and* LIONEL.) When we were young, it was your old uncle that had the glamour. Why Father used to say that I swaggered in my crib like a sailor on shore leave, while Edward, two years older, lay in bed like a lump.

EDWARD. I was just pacing myself. And how's the rest of my family this morning?

EMILY. I had a dream about my second husband, Sydney, that made me very tired.

EDWARD. Sydney? Good, I liked him. But wasn't he the third?

EMILY. No, the third was Boris, who got hepatitis on our wedding day.

EDWARD. Oh, yes. The golden son-in-law.

ELEANOR. Don't be angry, Edward, but I saw those angels again.

EDWARD. How much did it cost this time?

ELEANOR. I broke even on the slot machine.

EDWARD. Well, that's better than their usual cut. Now no more of them till we leave Las Vegas.

LIONEL (*Spinning the roulette wheel*). You're going to need something, Father. Calculus is closing in on you.

EDWARD. Well, well—I feel a certain lack of confidence in the old breadwinner in this room. Does one of you think this *is* going to be the first Noel when we leave Vegas loaded with presents, the Wellspot losing streak broken? (*Silence.*) Not one of you thinks Edward T. has it in him to take Olympus on the blackjack table this year?

EMILY. We've been losing for a long time, Daddy. Why should it change now?

EDWARD. Because we haven't packed it in yet, that's why. (*He picks up the miniature Christmas tree.*) We're still here, around the tree, every Christmas, aren't we? We're overdue for a good hand.

LIONEL. That, in mathematics, is known as the gambler's fallacy. We are never due anything.

EDWARD. Don't be certain, Lionel. (*He goes to the front door, peeks out and gestures to someone to wait.*)

LIONEL. Who's out there?

EDWARD. Something you can't figure out with mathematics, Lionel. Let me tell you what happened last night in the casino. There was just the usual crowd at first: the losing ladies on the slot machines with gloves on their pulling hands to keep away telltale calluses; the cool, dry, short-stop professionals defending discreet stacks of five-dollar chips in silence; and the high-living drunks and tourists not knowing what a dangerous cave they'd picked for their two-week vacation. Oh, it was lively with sights and sounds that'd undo a monthly bingo player. But I stood back and didn't play. Why? Because for the first time in my life I was tired. I kept seeing your laws everywhere, Lionel, and I realized that I'd fought too many battles on the crap table when I was outnumbered; too many of my courageous charges across the green blackjack board had been cut to ribbons by the dealer's heavy artillery; too many patrols . . .

LIONEL. You're dragging the metaphor around the street, Father. What happened?

EDWARD. All right, critic, I'll show you. (EDWARD *goes to and opens the front door.*) Mrs. Simon, come in and dazzle these skeptics. (MRS. SIMON *comes into the room. She is a small, pleasant-looking lady in her late fifties, dressed in a print dress and flowered hat.*) Excuse me for making you wait in the hall, but I didn't want my family to be unprepared for the shock of seeing you.

MRS. SIMON (*Nervously*). You're sure you're not having a family quarrel?

ELEANOR. Edward, who is this?

EDWARD. This is what every gambler needs. A lucky charm, a talisman, an amulet to beat the house. This is Mrs. Edna Simon, recently of New Rochelle, New York, and recently a widow.

MRS. SIMON. My husband, Stanly Simon, had a respiratory affliction. Whoever was wheezing in here while I was in the hall sounded just like him during the last month. It made me cry a little. Are my eyes red?

EDWARD. You look perfect, Mrs. Simon. And let me introduce you to the man who made you weep. My brother, Michel Wellspot.

MRS. SIMON. Poor man. Do you have trouble breathing in or breathing out?

MICHEL (*Surly*). Both.

MRS. SIMON. With Stanly, it was exhaling that gave him all the trouble. It was called inverted asthma. He could get all the air into him he wanted, but it was the devil's own time to squeeze it out. Sometimes he'd swell up like a balloon and I'd have to sit on his stomach to deflate him.

MICHEL. I just think I'll have another drink.

EDWARD. How bravely you must have borne it all, Mrs. Simon. But come, meet the rest of my family. My daughter, Emily, not yet thirty, but has already chalked up four marriages that have just worn her out. The trick now is to keep her conscious, since, with her experience, she can sleep twenty hours a day and feel she's missed nothing.

MRS. SIMON (*Shaking* EMILY's *hand*). What with raising two sons and Stanly's rattling at night, I don't think I ever got enough sleep myself.

EMILY. Well, it's really the dreams that count.

MRS. SIMON. I can imagine. Do you dream in color?

EMILY. All the time.

MRS. SIMON. There you are. In our house we all dreamed in black-and-white, and that's not much to look forward to.

EDWARD. And now, my wife, Eleanor. A woman whose soft figure points up her aversion to anything jagged or extreme—whose favorite time comes at dusk, when the harsh angles of the world blur and soften, and even a hustler's heart imagines peace tucked somewhere in the safe, middle-class dimness of twilight before a more difficult darkness falls. How's that for an introduction, Eleanor?

ELEANOR (*Coolly*). You *have* described me. That middle-class dimness—that *is* me.

MRS. SIMON. Men never know what to say. Stanly used to call me his little squash. Honestly, that turned my stomach, but he was so sincere that I took it for thirty-five years. The last words he said were, "Remember me, Squash." Isn't that an awful vegetable to be compared to? (*To* MICHEL, *as she goes to the bar*.) I'll have a teeny splash of that too, if you don't mind. (MICHEL *pours and hands her a drink*.)

EDWARD. Eleanor's losing faith in me and my compliments. But finally, my son, Lionel. Unmarried, a sour student of political history, with no practical occupation but a semiannual attempt at suicide.

MRS. SIMON. You look like such a nice boy, Lionel. You shouldn't kill yourself every year.

EDWARD. He only tries, Mrs. Simon. Kissing people with head colds during a flu epidemic—there's something wishy-washy about that as self-destruction, isn't there?

LIONEL. There was a lot of pneumonia that year. And I took long walks in the rain without a hat or rubbers on.

EDWARD. And that, Mrs. Simon, is my family, gathered here in Las Vegas for the Christmas season while I try to kick the new year off with a winning streak for them all.

LIONEL. And for fifteen years we've lost.

EDWARD. True enough. And what's happened to me on this patch of desert between Advent and the First of January has set the tone for the whole year. I've become a losing gambler, Mrs. Simon, as I told you downstairs. And a losing gambler is an albatross to everyone around him. He doesn't get those warm glowing smiles from his family. In a crap game he leaves the dice so damp with defeat that the stick man pushes them clinically to one side as though they were infected. No matter how jauntily he steps up to place a bet, a hundred grinning hustlers move to lay down against him. He has no style to fit him except the put-upon comedian, and he finds it harder and harder to laugh at himself. The odd friend he might still have can only tell him to give it up, pack it in—get a job. (MRS. SIMON *shakes her head sympathetically and hands her glass to* MICHEL *to be refilled.*)

LIONEL. And why doesn't he? That's the way it has to end.

EDWARD. Because he knows his luck will change, and suddenly he finds a Mrs. Simon, come west from New Rochelle, shooting dice like a goddess on the casino crap table.

ELEANOR. Why is *she* your lucky charm, Edward?

EDWARD. Did I hear a twitch of jealousy in your voice, Eleanor? (*To* MRS. SIMON.) See what a formidable woman you are?

MRS. SIMON. It must be the hat. Stanly always said I was a walking aphrodisiac in a summer hat.

EDWARD. Well, Eleanor, this lovely lady in her passionate hat, made nineteen straight passes with a bona fide pair of casino dice last night. Nineteen straight passes.

LIONEL. And then lost on the twentieth roll.

EDWARD. No, she quit to go to the bathroom.

MRS. SIMON. I was on my way when I stopped to play. I just had one silver dollar to lose and I had to stay at the table for over an hour. I thought I was going to die.

EDWARD. You should have seen it. She only bet a dollar each time, but there were twenty heavy bettors riding her roll. They denied that a ladies' room existed anywhere in Las Vegas.

MRS. SIMON. They would have made me roll the dice forever if your father hadn't stepped in. He was the only gentleman there.

EDWARD. I told you, it wasn't just good manners, Mrs. Simon. Unlike those other greedy clots, I wasn't going to waste you with a few side bets. You're a graced gambler, and one goes all the way on that. You're going to spend Christmas with the Wellspots and then be backed in a head-to-head game with the owner of the casino himself.

MRS. SIMON. Oh, that's exciting. Especially about Christmas. It was going to be the first time in my life I spent the holidays alone.

LIONEL. Father, you must be desperate. In the long run, she'll lose as much as anyone else.

EDWARD. The long run is for midnight prophets, Lionel. Here and now, in a sunny Christmas season in Las Vegas, she's going to win.

ELEANOR. Well, I don't see anything very special about her that's going to beat Mr. Olympus.

MICHEL (*A little drunk*). Even in the sexy hat. It doesn't do much for me.

EDWARD. Don't listen to them. They're talking like fifteen-year losers.

LIONEL. She'll face the odds like anyone else. I've got it all down on paper. All down in ballpoint pen.

EDWARD. Well, let's just see if we can shake up your equations a bit. Widow Simon, do you think you're up to pulling the handle on that little machine on the wall?

MRS. SIMON (*Now a little wobbly herself*). Alrighty.

EDWARD (*Taking a silver dollar from his pocket, he flips it in the air and then displays it*). Notice, one ordinary silver dollar bearing the rather butch profile of Lady Liberty, symbol of our great country. In her presence, there can be no shady maneuvers. Come, Mrs. Simon, to the pretty little machine.

ELEANOR. You're just trying to make my angels look small.

EDWARD. Send those hard-luck cherubs back to Boston, Eleanor. (*Mrs. Simon hooks her left arm around the machine's handle so that she has her back to the machine.*)

EMILY. She'll break her arm that way.

MRS. SIMON. Am I doing it wrong?

EDWARD. Approach your fate any way you like. (*He puts the dollar in the machine carefully.*) Now start those lemons, bars, and plums rolling.

MRS. SIMON. What's supposed to happen?

EDWARD. A lunar eclipse, a talking unicorn, a freak of nature—a jackpot!

LIONEL. Shall we make a private bet on it?

EDWARD. I wouldn't take your money, Lionel. You must have spent all your savings up for that suit. (*To* MRS. SIMON). All right, retired widow and mother of two, touch your hat for luck and pull.

MRS. SIMON. Well, here goes. (*One hand holding her hat,* MRS. SIMON *pulls down on the handle and holds onto it.*)

MICHEL. Maybe she's a witch.

EDWARD. One bar . . . two . . . (*The machine jackpots. Lights flash, bells ring, and dollars flush out onto the floor.*) Three golden bars! She did it! Merry Christmas! She did it! Left-handed and without looking to boot! (*Taking in his family.*) Well? Well? Where are all the Christmas smiles?

EMILY. The lights were very exciting.

LIONEL (*Somewhat shaken*). That was an inconclusive experiment, Father. But it might just help with this equation. (*On his way out.*) You're an interesting piece of data, Mrs. Simon. (LIONEL *exits.*)

EDWARD. Eleanor . . . ?

ELEANOR (*Heading for the bedroom, perplexed*). Given a little time my angels could have done the same. And Mr. Olympus doesn't have a little handle to pull.

MICHEL. Come on, Eleanor. I'll show you the scar Maggie Reilly left on me. It was a pretty jackpot, Edward. But I've seen a hundred of them before. (MICHEL *and* ELEANOR *exit.*)

MRS. SIMON (*Looking down at* EMILY *on the sofa, who has fallen asleep after the jackpot*). Your daughter doesn't seem very impressed either.

EDWARD (*Looking down at his daughter*). What does one have to do to wake up the world?

BLACKOUT

SCENE III

The office of Mr. Olympus.

OLYMPUS, *a fat, heavy man somewhere over forty, is in a leather reclining chair beneath a sun lamp. He wears only a terrycloth bathrobe and dark glasses.* WILLY, *who moves nervously about* MR. OLYMPUS *all through the scene, is thin and rodential.*

WILLY. So like I said, I didn't know what to do. Everybody's riding with the old lady, and she can't do nothin' but make passes. She tosses the dice up in the air like this— (*He makes an awkward, ladylike gesture.*) —and even when they bounce off the table they come up on the point or on the natural.

OLYMPUS (*Calmly, not moving*). What time is it, Willy?

WILLY. Four-thirty, p.m.

OLYMPUS. Adjust the lamp to late afternoon intensity, will you?

WILLY (*He adjusts the lamp*). And then she goes off with Wellspot, and later I hear she taps the slot machine out in his room left-handed.

OLYMPUS. That's fine, Willy. It feels like the beginning of sunset on my forehead.

WILLY. Tell me, Mr. Olympus, was I wrong to keep the table open so long?

OLYMPUS. You couldn't know, Willy. The old lady was one of the freaks. Every casino gets them now and then.

WILLY. She wasn't no freak. Just a normal lady from New Rochelle, I think.

OLYMPUS. I don't mean giants or midgets, Willy. Once, when I was starting, I was almost ruined by the most beautiful eight-months-old baby boy you could imagine. His mother, a nice little housewife, brought him to the casino and everyone, dealers, croupiers, customers thought him adorable. And how cute when his mother put him on her lap at the roulette table, and wasn't it a warm feeling the way she'd bet whatever number he'd happen to put a sticky finger on.

WILLY. Yeah, it sounds sweet, Mr. Olympus.

OLYMPUS. It was, except the little bastard never lost. If he put a jam-covered thumb on twenty-eight, up it would come, at thirty-five to one, Willy. He dribbled on red, two thousand in bets covered his saliva, and red turned up. The whole room was betting with that baby. And finally, the tension got to him. He threw up, neatly, on numbers one to twelve. Twenty-five thousand dollars followed the regurgitated baby mush, and that was all I could stand. I closed the table. That hustling housewife smiled at me, burped her kid, and left with everyone cheering and counting their money. It was horrible. But since then I've learned how to handle lucky old ladies and gifted babies.

WILLY. How's that, Mr. Olympus?

OLYMPUS. That's my secret, Willy. Besides you wouldn't understand if I told you.

WILLY. You underrate me, Mr. Olympus. I move pretty good.

OLYMPUS. Anyone can move well in a gambling room, Willy. It takes a well-developed sense of self-preservation, which most people have. Unfortunately, they also have a concomitant bent in the opposite direction, which puts them in that room in the first place. But now, tell me about Wellspot. He's prepared to back this old lady, is he?

WILLY. I suppose so. He always comes with a bundle every Christmas and he's got her all to himself.

OLYMPUS. Poor Edward. This is his last stand. The rumors that fil- tered out here are true. He's playing on borrowed money. And the men who lent it to him are intolerant and impatient sorts. This time he's in too deep and I can break him once and for all.

WILLY. He's not just another customer to you, is he?

OLYMPUS (*Taking off his glasses*). Why, Willy, I may *have* underes- timated you. No he's not. I should have outgrown personal involvement when it comes to my patrons, but Edward can still make my stomach tighten when he plays against me. I don't know why. He's one of the worst gamblers I've ever met: always takes the wrong odds, mumbles to the cards as though he could convert them, smiles like a cretin when he's holding a good hand and pouts when the cards are bad. He's never beaten the casino for a nickel and yet he makes me nervous when he comes in to play. If I were sentimental, I'd say I envied his stubbornness, his dry throat, his wet hands—all the palpable signs of life you lose when you're the house, when the odds are with you, and you grind down the Well- spots in a well-mannered, orderly way.

WILLY. But you're not sentimental, Mr. Olympus.

OLYMPUS. Perhaps I'm becoming so, Willy. What if I told you I might get married? To Wellspot's daughter?

WILLY. What? The one who never leaves her room? The one who sleeps all the time? Ah, you can do better than that, Mr. Olympus. Why, you can have your choice of any shill in the casino. At a hundred a pop, you could afford two a night.

OLYMPUS. I'm trying to be sentimental, Willy. I don't want simply to pop, as you put it. In fact, I have never wanted to pop.

WILLY. Never?

OLYMPUS. A matter of choice, Willy. Or partly a matter of choice. When I was a boy and the time for mating came, I was always left un- paired. I was fat, and on a poor block in Chicago, physical beauty was all that was negotiable.

WILLY. No appreciation of soul, huh?

OLYMPUS. That's right, Willy. No appreciation of soul. And then this girl moved next door whom nobody wanted.

WILLY. She was fat too?

OLYMPUS. No, quite attractive. But a tragic case of scarlet fever had left her bald. Oh, she had her glabrous head hid with a wig, but in ghettos secrets become open gossip in hours. I knew it, when I took her to the coal bin in our basement, I knew that everything I felt would shrivel up when the wig came off—and it would, no doubt about that, Willy. Yet, like a gambler with his nose open, I sent good money after bad, stroked and fondled her, spoke the short sentences I'd heard in movies, snapped her garters, and waited for the wig to fall.

WILLY. Hey, this is a real exciting story, Mr. Olympus. Did you slip it off?

OLYMPUS. No, she did. She knew we were a pair of losers in that coal bin as well as I, but we played the game anyway. I pretended I didn't care, she said she'd understand if I left. I protested, kissed her, and it turned out to be a noise of pity in the darkness. A terrible sound, pity. A terrible sound. She saved the day by leaving first, and I sat, a weeping fat boy, on lumps of bituminous coal by myself.

WILLY. That was hard luck, Mr. Olympus.

OLYMPUS. Anyway, I've never played that game again.

WILLY. But all women ain't bald, Mr. Olympus.

OLYMPUS. The ones that aren't were never interested in me, and for a long while I never missed them. But now there's something I want, and Emily Wellspot is available. We seem admirably suited. She wants to sleep, and I'm ready to finance peignoirs and pajamas for the rest of her life.

WILLY. I don't know, Mr. Olympus. Getting married scares me. I mean, it's hard enough makin' it on your own, against everybody out to con you. Your only edge, if you understand me clearly, Mr. Olympus, is that no one knows what you're really like—if you're a high roller or play scared, if you go for the inside straight or hold for a long, tight game. But as soon as you've got a wife, I mean a broad that you really flipped for at least at one time, it tells a lot of secrets about you. I mean, you're sort of saying, this is how I swing, and anyone can get the message for nothing. Getting married's like opening up your mind to the world, and who needs that?

OLYMPUS. True, Willy, if there's some real preference involved. But assuming that's rather romantic of you. In my case, I've found that being with the house, always on the solitary side of the table, has become lonely and cold. I need someone, even if it's only a sleeping body with a temperature of ninety-eight point six degrees Fahrenheit, to give me a little warmth.

WILLY. Now you sound like your old self, Mr. Olympus. And you think you'll get this sleeping beauty if you tap Wellspot out?

OLYMPUS. If I can keep him from backing her quest for a fifth husband, I think she might just give in to my charms, rather than leave Las Vegas without a bed to sleep in. Yes, we have to break him, Willy. It's head-to-head blackjack. That's the game he likes to try me with. I'll let you deal for me.

WILLY. Gee, I don't know. Against the old lady?

OLYMPUS. I'll handle her.

WILLY. Any movin' with the cards?

OLYMPUS. No, Willy, I want him beat in an honest game, if that's the word for it. You'll have the edge, Willy, and my money behind you. We won't lose. Now, what time is it?

WILLY. Five-fifteen.

OLYMPUS. Turn off the lamp, Willy, it's sunset.

WILLY. I'd love a lamp like this. The only way I can get a tan is to go outside during the day. And who needs that?

OLYMPUS. Well, Willy, I know what your Christmas present will be now.

WILLY. Mr. Olympus, you're the greatest Greek around.

OLYMPUS. And one of the loneliest. Now, switch off the lamp, Willy, I don't want to blister. (WILLY *does so, and the stage darkens.*)

SCENE IV

The lights come up quickly on the Wellspot suite. EDWARD, *carrying a pile of Christmas presents, dashes into the room, dropping several of the packages. He then places his knee against the half-open door and begins tugging on the arm of* MRS. SIMON *that is only half-visible past the door. There is the sound of a mob of voices along with* MRS. SIMON's *frightened cries.*

EDWARD. Come on, let go of her. Let go of her, you small-time con man, let go. (MRS. SIMON *is now half in the room, holding her hat with one hand.*)

MRS. SIMON. Oh, they're going to tear me in two.

EDWARD (*Dragging her into the room*). This is my horse, dammit! Stop mauling her. (*To* MRS. SIMON.) Here, help lean against the door. (MRS. SIMON *and* EDWARD *lean against the door and gradually manage to close it.*)

MRS. SIMON. What'll happen if they get in?

EDWARD. They won't. Those two-dollar bettors wanting to get you to blow on their dice. Like using champagne for a mouthwash. (*They finally close the door and* EDWARD *quickly locks it. There is still the sound of voices.* EDWARD *runs to the balcony. Addressing a crowd over the balcony.*) All right. The lady plays for Edward T. Wellspot. Pack it out of here and try your old prayers. (*The sound dies down in disappointment.*)

MRS. SIMON. I thought they were going to tear the clothes right off me.

EDWARD. Those low-action players will look for anything to bring them luck.

MRS. SIMON. One of them tried to bite my finger.

EDWARD. He probably wanted to nip it right off and take it to the crap table with him.

MRS. SIMON (*Cringing*). Ohh!

EDWARD. You see, it's a good thing you're with me. Someone who has a little perspective on things. But I should have known better than to have taken you out Christmas shopping with me. From now on you go from here to your room and nowhere else. (*He begins picking up the packages.*) I'll just put these away.

MRS. SIMON. Oh, what a time. That crowd made me remember what New York Christmas shopping was like. Since my sons grew up, I just bought for Stanly, and last year all he wanted was an atomizer for his asthma. It didn't give off much of a holiday feeling sitting on his night table. (*Sits down on sofa and jumps up when something moves.*) Wha? Well, look at this. It's your daughter. She slept through all of that.

EDWARD (*Walks over, looks at* EMILY, *and shakes his head sadly*). Mrs. Simon, you'd better go put something on that finger. I know the owner of those teeth that sunk into you—capable of instant gangrene.

MRS. SIMON. I can see you want to have a little heart-to-heart talk with your daughter. I'll just lie down in the next room for a minute. Being bitten is very flattering, but it can wear a woman out. (MRS. SIMON *exits.*)

EDWARD (*Sitting on the sofa and gently shaking* EMILY). Emily? Emily? (EMILY *starts awake with a little cry.*) What kind of dream was it?

EMILY (*Shaking the sleep from her*). Oh, I'm sorry, Daddy. I tried to stay awake. I kept thinking of the jackpot, put my bathing suit on to go out, came in to look at the slot machine to really freshen me up—and I still dropped off.

EDWARD (*Smiling and leaning back to reminisce*). Emily, do you know that when you were a little girl, you were a real insomniac. You were always looking forward to some adventure the next day that kept you doing acrobatics in your bed the whole night. And even when you did drop off, I'd slip in to look at you and you were coiled like a spring waiting to pop up at the first sign of light. Just looking at that little curve of female energy made me want to do a hundred push-ups or run around the block a dozen times. Make you be unconscious for a few minutes a day—well, that was the worst punishment you could have had.

EMILY. Well, Daddy, as you said, I was looking forward to things. Maybe I've had too many disappointing mornings.

EDWARD. Disappointments in me, for losing so long?

EMILY. Daddy, I'm just frightened. It's all going by so quickly, and there've been so many men beside the four legitimate ones. The way Uncle Michel talked about his women, that's the way I'm beginning to feel now. A girl can just let herself be seduced so many times before she gives up the idea of finding something to wake up for and stays with the exciting dreams that at least pass time.

EDWARD. There never was a man stretched out next to you you wanted to wake up for—if just to see how much his beard had grown during the night?

EMILY (*Grudgingly*). Sometimes—but when I'd take a hard, clear, early-morning look at him, and watch his stomach moving up and down, up and down, I'd be terrified that that would be the only rhythm I'd know for the rest of my life. Oh men look so promising in blue suits, white shirts and firm little neckties, and then . . .

EDWARD. Then they disrobe and you find that they're all stomach.

EMILY. And they breathe so evenly! After making love to me at night, they have the nerve to breathe evenly.

EDWARD (*Getting up from the sofa*). Well now, it couldn't be that bad. Your mother's looked at old Edward T's paunch for a long time, and, every now and then, she even pokes it playfully before breakfast.

EMILY. Maybe you have something special, Daddy.

EDWARD. Me???! Oh, now, sweetheart, Uncle Michel's right there! I'm just a normal hand for a woman to play. And your mother's found that out. I forget her favorite color, give her rump a good-night pat when she wants long, soft caresses, doze off now and then while making love, and reach so quickly afterwards for a cigarette that she's cried sometimes. But, you know, Emily, any amateur can win with aces. It takes a player to come out ahead when the cards aren't really running for him. He has to twist, turn, think, bluff, squeeze, and slip on through.

EMILY. But that's just work, Daddy.

EDWARD. Well, what else does a lady, stepping into her thirties, with no particular talents have to do except make that stomach next to her an exciting piece of geology. It's hard action, and you may even have to cheat a little bit now and then, but that's the only way to make it outside of those dreams of yours.

EMILY. Then why give up the dreams?

EDWARD. Now come on, little girl. You're not the only one that can get something cooking in her head at night. Why I've broken more casinos during afternoon naps than you've had husbands, and I know that one five-dollar win in the real world is worth all those chips at made-up Monte Carlos. And you do too. You keep looking, Emily. With what I'm going to win, you'll have the whole world to choose from. Trust me, and don't let Olympus put you to sleep forever. No one would blame you for not waking up with him breathing next to you.

EMILY (*Gets up*). All right, Daddy. I'll keep looking. And I'll stay wide awake.

EDWARD. Go on downstairs and cruise the pool for a while. Start getting yourself back in circulation.

EMILY. Oh, Daddy, I hope you win this time. We all need it so.

EDWARD. How can I lose with Mrs. Simon? We'll have enough for as many husbands as you need until you find the right one. And just try not to be quite so demanding, because they're all going to have stomachs and breathe evenly.

EMILY (*Smiling*). Well, if Mother can put up with yours every morning, I guess I'll be able to master it.

EDWARD (*Patting his stomach*). Actually I sleep on it, and get up on the dim side of the bed at night. I try to spare her as much as possible.

EMILY (*Smiling*). You are clever, Daddy. I'm sure you are going to win. (EMILY *exits.*)

EDWARD (*He stands for a moment silently, then looks up and makes a fist*). This time. Let me make it this time for all of them, and I'll never bother you again. (MRS. SIMON *enters.*)

MRS. SIMON. I'm so worked up I couldn't think of napping. Did you have a good talk?

EDWARD. I hope so. Oh, it's hard work being a father, Mrs. Simon. You start off telling your children stories with happy endings, playing blind man's bluff and making their eyes pop open with card tricks. It's all happy and simple at first. Then one day you look around and find you've got a daughter that won't wake up and a son who's half-heartedly suicidal. Then you have to start pumping life into them all over again.

MRS. SIMON. I know about children, Mr. Wellspot. I've seen two sons callously turn me into a grandmother and send me west to a town for senior citizens.

his eighth birthday he celebrated by swallowing a dozen mothballs, and he's clouded every holiday since then. (*To* LIONEL.) And now, when our luck is changing, you crawl out into the desert.

LIONEL. Our luck can't change, but you'll never understand why.

EDWARD. Try me. Lionel, I'm not an oyster. I've been through a depression and a war. I've seen people open their veins and blow off their only head over the wrong card, the wrong woman, or a bad cup of coffee. I can understand that. But you, why are you sharking me with gila monsters just when things look good?

LIONEL. One vulgar jackpot and everything looks good!

EDWARD. What is it, Lionel? Do you want me to lose? Why? When I was flush I bought you chemistry sets and sailor suits and had your teeth filled every time a cavity showed up. And you had a hell of a lot of cavities, Lionel.

LIONEL. I never wanted paternal affection.

EDWARD. Oh, I know that. (*To* MRS. SIMON.) I sent him to Paris when he was eighteen on money I'd actually saved from a good poker streak a long time ago. You know how hard it is for a gambler to keep his hands off money when it's lying around? But I did, because I wanted the kid to have a little fling before he started college. So what does he do? He throws himself in the Seine at the height of the tourist season as soon as he gets there. I heard about it during a weekend stud game in Baltimore, left losing, and dashed off a ten-page letter listing all the reasons I'd stayed out of rivers for forty years. And he . . . he sends it back with the spelling mistakes corrected in the margin.

LIONEL. It was such a firmly written overpunctuated letter. Trying to persuade me with misspelled words! I was supposed to take comfort in little epigrams like, "If you're holding a losing hand, at least look at how pretty the cards are!" And there I was in Paris with the terror of history all around me.

EDWARD. The terror of what?

LIONEL. Of history. Something you don't find out in Las Vegas.

EDWARD. Now you've made me mad. You can insult me, but don't talk about the weight of history. No one jumps into a river over that. You can be terrified you'll make an ass of yourself in front of the girls, or saunter into a party with your fly open, or never once get your name in the papers. Any one of these can push a man in, but don't bloat yourself up with history as if you're the only man left on this planet.

LIONEL. You see, you can only understand little, tiny things. Bring the family together at Christmas, and everything's all right as long as there are presents under the tree. And you still lose, and never learn what I've known since I swallowed the mothballs.

EDWARD. Well, what's your secret about this world, Lionel? Are you sure it's not just a question of an underweight young man with thick glasses who never drove a sports car or made a woman laugh in the morning?

LIONEL (*Wounded*). No, that's not true.

EDWARD. I think it is, Lionel. You'd like to wrap the whole world in that forty-dollar suit of yours, but then along comes a jackpot and for a minute you think maybe even you have a chance. And that's upsetting when you've already got the down payment on the gravestone.

LIONEL. I don't. This afternoon in the desert . . .

EDWARD. This afternoon, if I calculate correctly, was your thirty-second unsuccessful suicide.

LIONEL. I tried. Look at this sunburn. I've got water blisters already.

EDWARD. You tried? Then just how did that helicopter know where you were? Out of the whole damned Mojave Desert they spot Lionel Wellspot and his reluctant gila monster.

LIONEL. Well, I did stop at the police station downtown to ask the directions to the closest wasteland. But I didn't know which way to go.

EDWARD. And the reptile you were swatting—are you certain it was really a gila monster?

LIONEL. It was the largest lizard around, damn it.

EDWARD. And the cactus.

LIONEL. Small but evil-looking.

EDWARD. With soft needles.

LIONEL. Are you implying that I lack conviction?

EDWARD. I'm implying that you don't want to pack in the game any more than I do. The type of gambler that hangs around the tables holding on to his room rent. Can't bear to leave, but can't lay it on the table either.

MRS. SIMON. Just like Stanly. Always moaning that he couldn't stand his asthma any more, but never missing a pill time.

LIONEL (*Backing out onto the balcony*). All right! I'll show you both that I can leave the game to suckers.

EDWARD. Come on back in here, Lionel.

LIONEL (*At the balcony's edge, his hands on the rail*). Now I want you to notice that I'm *not* hysterical like someone with his fly open after a squalid love affair. I have the control of a man who knows the fate of his species.

MRS. SIMON. Oh, my Lord, I can't watch.

EDWARD. Watch what? Him come skulking back into the room? Turn around and look down, Lionel. (LIONEL *does so.*) There's eight floors of air between you and the ground. No Desert Patrol's going to get to you this time. You'll be locked up all the way down.

LIONEL (*A little shaken*). I don't care. It's what I want.

EDWARD. Just think what you'll be missing, Lionel, if we do break Olympus this time.

LIONEL. What would I miss?

EDWARD. Take your choice: a colored television set with private channels; a pistachio-colored foreign car; a pair of eighteen-year-old brown Brazilian twins; karate lessons; an opera box; caps for your teeth; contact lenses made of Belgian glass; a nymphomaniacal movie star; a trip to Japan, a hundred elevator shoes, a perfect nose.

MRS. SIMON. It's every dream I ever had.

LIONEL. It's vulgar! Offering me trinkets as if I were some illiterate savage. (LIONEL *gets up onto the balcony ledge and struggles for a moment to keep his balance.*)

EDWARD. Steady, Lionel! Servants to put down, two wines with dinner, a sympathetic listener, a satin-wood stereophonic set, a . . . a . . . help me, Mrs. Simon!

MRS. SIMON. Lifetime laundry service; a winter cruise for two; a musical vacuum cleaner.

EDWARD. Sweet breath, a sense of humor, a faithful dog.

LIONEL. That's enough! To think I'd tie my life to any of those things! (ELEANOR, MICHEL, *and* EMILY *enter. All are in bathing suits.*)

ELEANOR. What's going on? Ah, it *is* you up there, Lionel.

MICHEL. I told you. Who else?

EDWARD. We're trying to coax him back with Christmas presents.

EMILY. The whole pool emptied out when they saw him teetering over it.

LIONEL. You saw me from the ground and rushed up, did you, Mother?

ELEANOR. I thought it was one of my angels, and it's just you showing off. Oh, I need glasses.

LIONEL. I'm sorry you're disappointed.

EDWARD. Don't scold him, Eleanor. If he wants to stand outside with his nose pressed to the window while we celebrate a warm Christmas, let him. Michel, how about making us all a drink? (MICHEL *starts to do so.*)

LIONEL. Did you say it was eight floors down?

EDWARD. About ninety feet. And with history weighting you down, it'll be over in a second.

MRS. SIMON. Oh, don't say that.

EDWARD. He's had his chance. Let him mope out there while we take in a little festive liquor. (MICHEL *hands out drinks to everyone.*)

EMILY. Daddy, I think I found a good potential for number five in the swimming instructor. He can hold his breath under water for two and a half minutes without even making his eyes red.

EDWARD. Go get him, Emily. (*Raising his glass.*) There now, I formally inaugurate the Wellspot Christmas celebration. Here, gathered around the roulette wheel, all the family members—except one—to pay honor to this lucky time of year.

LIONEL. Er . . . is it concrete where I'll land?

ELEANOR. You'll probably hit by the swimming pool, Lionel, and the ground there's very hard for someone as delicate as you.

EMILY. Just don't hit my swimming instructor. *That* would give a fine impression of the family, wouldn't it?

MICHEL. I remember a little girl in Memphis threatened to drink a whole bottle of iodine if I left her. I had to stay over an extra day and let her keep the mouthpiece to my trombone for a souvenir.

EDWARD. All right, let's get our bets on the happier side of the table. (*Raises his glass.*) To my wife, who this Christmas gets a winning husband back; to Emily, and a sleepless, subaqueous future; to my brother, a rundown little rake, new conquests; and to our Christmas guest, Mrs. Edna Simon, the Lady Bountiful who's stuffed our stockings, gratitude and good wishes.

LIONEL. If I fall at the proper rate of gravity I'd make a terrible mess of the pool.

EDWARD (*Aware of* LIONEL, *but not showing it to him*). Ah, I feel possibility everywhere. (*He spins the roulette wheel.*) Until the last turn of the wheel.

LIONEL. But it would be a logically valid mess.

EDWARD. We should have some music. Michel, can you lead us in a little family wassailing?

MICHEL. You're all tone-deaf.

EDWARD. Just lead and we'll follow. (MICHEL *begins to sing "Deck the Halls with Boughs of Holly," and, one by one, tentatively, the others join in.*)

LIONEL (*Over the music*). I did get a bad sunburn. That shows *some* strength of purpose.

EDWARD (*Almost sotto voce to* LIONEL, *as he still keeps time to the music with his hand*). Golden golf clubs, pressed duck, your own lady softball team. (EDWARD *quickly rejoins the singing. They all continue singing as* LIONEL *steps down from the balcony into the room.*)

LIONEL. All right. Perhaps I'm not infallible. While I'm peeling in the next fews days, I'll just take some time for a final check. (*The singing stops.*)

MRS. SIMON. Thank heavens. With fresh skin, everything'll look different.

EDWARD (*Taking a coin from his pocket*). Show him he's not wrong, Mrs. Simon. (*He flips the coin, catches it in his hand, slaps it to his wrist, hidden.*) Call.

MRS. SIMON. Heads.

EDWARD. Heads it is. (*He repeats the process.*) Call.

MRS. SIMON. Heads.

EDWARD. Heads again. Brilliant.

LIONEL. Let it hit the floor the next time, Father.

EDWARD (*Flipping the coin toward* LIONEL *so that it lands on the floor behind the sofa*). Call it again. (*Pause.*) Well?

MRS. SIMON. I have a feeling it landed straight up on its edge.

EDWARD. On its edge? (EDWARD *starts to laugh until he notices* LIONEL *staring dumbfounded at where the coin landed behind the sofa.*) Don't tell me! (LIONEL *tries to speak, but can only indicate that the coin is on its edge.*) We could win the whole world matching pennies. (ED-WARD *starts to sing.*) "Joy to the world . . ."

CURTAIN

Act Two

SCENE I

The lights come up on a card table with chairs on either side.
WILLY, *wearing glasses, is placing out decks of cards, humming to himself while admiring the arrangement.* OLYMPUS *enters, and stands for a second before* WILLY *notices him and twitches nervously.*

WILLY. Hello, Mr. Olympus. Just fixin' things up.

OLYMPUS. I see, Willy, it looks very nice. (*He starts examining the cards on the table.*)

WILLY (*Quickly, trying to divert* OLYMPUS' *attention*). Well, you got a big game comin' up. I wanted everything to be proper, you know. Nice and proper.

OLYMPUS (*Sadly wagging his head as he holds two cards from the same pack up for examination*). Willy, I didn't know you were fond of asymmetry.

WILLY. Asymmetry? Well, uh, everyone gets their kicks the way they can, Mr. Olympus.

OLYMPUS. And so you get yours by doodling on the backs of cards so that no two are alike. Not the best marking I've ever seen, but it gives you just a little advantage over the lady you're going to play, doesn't it?

WILLY (*Petulantly*). All right! I know you said no movin'. But the old lady spooks me. She may not even be human.

OLYMPUS. Then put some wolf bane around your neck, Willy. But Wellspot gets an honest game.

WILLY (*Smiling, overeager*). O.K. No funny cards. You can check the other decks. They're clean.

OLYMPUS. And the glasses, Willy?

WILLY. The glasses? You know what light does to my eyes when I'm dealin'. I begin to squint and look suspicious to the customers.

OLYMPUS (*Takes the glasses off* WILLY, *picks up a card from the fresh*

295

deck, and examines it through one of the lenses.) Ah, magic glasses. Bad, bad, Willy.

WILLY (*Hurt and angry*). I can't help it. I got a drive in me to win. I hate losing. I hate it! I hate it!

OLYMPUS. Calm down, Willy.

WILLY. I was just doin' it for you. I mean, like you said you hadn't had a broad since that coal bin in Chicago. And then Wellspot's daughter with that human fish down at the pool.

OLYMPUS. I can be patient, Willy, and so should you. (*He pushes up* WILLY'S *sleeve and finds an arm booster. He starts to unfasten it as* WILLY *hangs his head ashamed.*) You know, Willy, this reminds me of the story of Tallahassee Slim. Do you know that one?

WILLY (*Sadly*). No.

OLYMPUS (*Motioning* WILLY *to put his foot up on a chair and lift up his trouser leg.* WILLY *does, and reveals a leg booster*). Well, old Tallahassee was a pool hustler who couldn't run twenty balls on his best night. Oh, he was always moving, but he had a con that a nun could see through, in fact one of them beat him in a nineball game in Miami for half a hundred once. No matter how he fretted, he just couldn't score. (*He takes the leg booster off and motions* WILLY *to put up the other foot. He does, the trouser comes up, and a similar apparatus is uncovered.* WILLY *takes this one off.*) And then one day, Willy, just as he was about to take a realistic estimate of himself and get a job, he met a pair of first-rate dice hustlers who were hatching a little plan for a quick score in Chicago. (*As* WILLY *hands him the booster, he takes* WILLY'S *wrist and looks at the cufflinks.*) Mirrors in cufflinks! (*He smiles sadly and takes them off.*) Now, since Tallahassee wasn't known as a dice man, they decided to bring him in as a cover for ten percent off the top. (WILLY *takes off his shoes during the following and cards fall out of each one.*) All Tallahassee had to do was come up with enough money to get to Chicago, no easy task for him, but fortunately his mother died and he got enough money from the insurance for bus fare. They had planned the old Canadian switch, Willy. He would be the shooter, while his two friends, creating a momentary absence of mind in the housemen by the introduction of some thousand dollar bills on the table, would on his roll, switch a pair of marker dice into the game—dice that you neither crap out nor roll a seven on. Coat, Willy. (WILLY *takes off his dinner jacket, hands it to* OLYMPUS, *who, shaking it as he talks, dislodges four or five aces.*) Dream dice, eh, Willy? Dream dice.

WILLY. They sure are.

OLYMPUS. And like dreams, they don't last too long. Unlike loads or flats you've got two, three rolls at the most before someone spots the numbers just don't match on the little cubes. But now remember that Tallahassee was a stone loser. Pants, Willy! (WILLY *takes off his pants, hands them to* OLYMPUS. OLYMPUS *goes on talking and finds cards pinned to the inside seam and hidden in the cuffs.*) So now when he hits this hard-type action room in Chicago and Slim finds himself up at the table getting a reassuring sign from his well-dressed confederates, he must have felt, for the first time in his life, that he was really on top of it. (*He tosses the pants and jacket back to* WILLY.) All right now; his friends make the switch, Slim has the con dice in his hand, he rolls, makes one pass, rolls again, makes another, again, and another—and now his colleagues lower their eyes modestly and signal him to send the dice down their side of the table for the re-switch. But . . . Willy . . . listen carefully, Tallahassee sends the dice back down the center of the board out of their skillful reach.

WILLY (*Enthralled*). Yeah, I know. He's hungry, right?

OLYMPUS. A nonplayer might say he was just greedy, Willy, but you know it's more than that. He'd never had anyone locked up before, and now he was a cold-ass winner, and he just couldn't let that roomful of players off the hook. Just one more pass, and one more after that, and suddenly instead of the agreed upon three passes he'd pushed up to seven. The other players are doubling up, starting to heat with highline action, and, finally, Tallahassee snaps out of it and glances over at his friends and discovers, Willy, that in the frenzy of the play they . . . had . . . left. Split, cut out, gone. His bridge to safety had been burned.

WILLY (*Sadly, softly*). Oh shit.

OLYMPUS. He can't switch by himself, sullen voices are calling for him to roll, if he quits in the middle of a streak everyone'll know the story. What can he do, but close his eyes, pray, and keep on rolling, winning more and more each time while that room in Chicago gets smaller and smaller until it squashes him altogether.

WILLY. Is that what happened?

OLYMPUS. No one knows, or at least no one has ever talked about Tallahassee's fate. He took his winning streak with him into oblivion.

WILLY. He was a hard-luck player, that's all.

OLYMPUS. So are we all, Willy. And even the percentage men like me are in a room that gets smaller and smaller until a hairy paw reaches out, checks the dice, and takes our edge away from us for good. So don't work so hard, Willy. Get the best odds you can, stretch the game out, but don't try to force something from it you'll never get.

WILLY. All right, Wellspot gets a fair game. You got my word for it.

OLYMPUS. Why, Willy, your eyes are red. Are you crying?

WILLY (*Nervously putting on his trousers*). Well, that was a sad story about Tallahassee. It choked me up.

OLYMPUS (*Examining his eyes closely*). Willy, you wouldn't weep at the end of the world. (*He slaps the back of* WILLY's *head sharply twice catching the contact lenses as they pop from his eyes. He holds a card up underneath one of the lenses.*) Can't believe it. I'd heard of these, but never seen them. Contact lenses. You certainly are up to date, Willy.

WILLY (*Crushed*). You got every one of my moves. I gotta play honest, now.

OLYMPUS. Don't fret so. We have the edge. You'll get a nice commission, Wellspot will be broken, and I'll have a wife. For whatever it's worth, like Tallahassee, we'll go out winners. Now get dressed, knot your bow tie neatly, and get ready to play cards. (OLYMPUS *exits.*)

WILLY (*Throws his clothes to the floor, sits down, and starts fingering the cards*). Play cards! (*Shouts after* OLYMPUS.) I still wanna win! (*He picks up a deck of cards, fans them and does a Niagara shuffle.*) And I'll pull every move to do it. (*Softer.*) It makes me happy to win. Get it while you can. (*Still softer.*) I ain't in any goddam room. I ain't in any goddam room I can't get out of.

BLACKOUT

SCENE II

The Wellspot suite. Christmas decorations festoon the roulette wheels, slot machines, dice cages, etc. . . . There is a rather wasted Christmas tree by the bar which LIONEL *is trimming while he hums. He is dressed in a dinner jacket. After a few seconds,* EMILY, *in a bathing suit covered by a terrycloth robe, enters.*

EMILY. My God. What are you doing?

LIONEL (*A little huffily*). What does it look like? I'm decorating.

EMILY. When did the tree come?

LIONEL. This afternoon. All the way from the Sierra Nevada mountains. It lost a third of its needles coming through Death Valley, but I've glued most of them back on. What do you think of it?

EMILY. Well, the *tree* looks a little worn out, but what you've done with it is beautiful.

LIONEL. I've tried to space the bulbs so that the colors are balanced. God, it's funny the way little problems can absorb you. First, there were too many blues sagging on the left; then I found the greens had crept insidiously into the center. But now I think *all colors* have an equal chance!

EMILY. It's a perfect tree, Lionel. A good and thoughtful job.

LIONEL (*Pleased*). Well, to tell you the truth, I just did it to keep my mind busy. I've got such a problem. . . .

EMILY. You weren't tiptoeing around the balcony again?

LIONEL. Oh, no. (*Musing.*) I've come to think that violent suicides are too egotistical anyway. (*Coming back.*) No, it's just that—well, with all the excitement over Mrs. Simon's jackpots, Christmas Eve and the chance that Father might just beat Olympus this time, I let myself be inveigled into going out on a double date with Uncle Michel tonight.

EMILY. Well, Merry Christmas, Lionel.

LIONEL. It was Father's present to me along with the dinner jacket. I don't want to dampen everything again by turning it down—but God, a chorus girl—and with Michel wheezing at the same table. . . .

EMILY. It will be marvelous for you. As a matter of fact, I'm going to take a little turn myself this night before Christmas with the swimming instructor. He's really a nice steady man who does the regulation breast stroke beautifully. Just right for a fifth husband to settle down with.

LIONEL. Well, this is an old game for you. But I'm a thinker, dammit. I've watched women bent over books in library cubicles or crossing their legs in a phenomenology class, and I knew what was there. I'd read all the sad sonnets and the keening ballads and I realized the world was divided into two tragic camps: one suffering from postcoital depression, the other, from post-Copernican. And to me the latter had a little more stature and greater scope. And so I just watched the ladies in black knee socks reading Baudelaire and Kierkegaard, and I put them and my little lusts aside. And I never . . . never. Oh, one should ooze into life slowly. A semi-illiterate chorus girl, bought by my father on Christmas Eve, who would never understand the agony of the naturalistic fallacy or a transcendental leap, might be too much for me.

EMILY. You mean this chorus girl will really be the first time, Lionel?

LIONEL (*Smiling in reminiscence*). Once in Central Park, while I was reading the obituary notices in *The New York Times*, the dog of a beautiful woman rubbed up against me in a very suggestive manner. I suppose it set a tone to the encounter and, since she was older than I was (the lady, that is), I accepted an invitation to come to her apartment to listen to recordings of Elizabethan lute solos, which, we discovered during our park talk, we both liked. Oh, now, don't look at me that way, Emily. I wasn't completely taken in. I knew something was afoot. But she was attractive, none of the deaths that day in the *Times* was particularly depressing, and I was more than just a little interested. Well, we got to her apartment, she put on a Julian Bream L.P., and humming counter-tenor improvisations we began fondling each other. My feelings were ambiguous, but not unpleasant, and then, just as things got serious, she jumped up, ran to the closet, and brought out a German World War I uniform, complete with gas mask, and asked me to put it on before making love to her.

EMILY. Oh boy. I can understand that.

LIONEL. I did. Even though I could hardly breathe and the puttees were cutting off circulation from the knees down.

EMILY. Nothing is alien to love. Go on!

LIONEL. It was like trying to solve a problem in calculus without knowing the multiplication tables. I was over my head, and she found me out.

EMILY. How, Lionel?

LIONEL. She wanted me to tie her up with my canteen belt.

EMILY. God, if only something romantic like that would ever happen to me.

LIONEL. But it stopped the whole thing, Emily.

EMILY. Why?

LIONEL. I just didn't know any knots. I mean I was never a Boy Scout, or anything. Oh, I could tie a bow, but it wasn't firm enough for her. Besides, she had to hold the knot with her finger while I made the loops. It just ruined everything. She made me get back in civilian clothes and leave. And I never went to anyone's apartment again. (MICHEL *enters. He, too, is dressed in a dinner jacket. Underneath is a checkered vest.*)

MICHEL. Hey! Well, Lionel, you old virgin, you look pretty spiffy.

EMILY. Now, don't be nasty, Uncle Michel.

MICHEL (*Going for a drink*). Don't worry, I've carried dead weight along before. Oh, Lionel, your father pointed out our dates to me at the pool. Big women. Looked like Mt. Rushmore on the move when they walked together.

LIONEL. I hope I won't be crushed, Uncle Michel.

MICHEL. Just follow my lead: if I slap mine on the rump, you do the same. If I tell a little joke, you tell a little joke. If I say something a—erratic—something to throw them off guard and make them think you're a bit of a dreamer, a little special—something like, let's go to Mexico City, eat ice cream and listen to guitar music—if I say something like that, Lionel, and give you a wink, you come up with a wild line yourself.

LIONEL. Why all the planning? I thought Father had arranged and paid. . . .

MICHEL. You don't think a man with my experience is going to pay a woman to make love to him, do you? Granted, I'm a little out of practice. I needed something to break the ice with. But when I'm finished with these hookers, they're going to be happy to give the money back, Lionel. And don't be surprised if *they* do a little late Christmas shopping for the two of us. (EDWARD *and* ELEANOR, *both in evening dress, enter.*)

EDWARD. Well, now this looks like a Christmas family.

EMILY. You look lovely, Mother.

ELEANOR. I spent hours getting ready, and now Edward tells me I can't come with him.

EDWARD. I'd love to spend every second of Xmas eve with you. But there's protocol in a high stake game that says you don't bring your wife to it, no matter how beautiful she looks.

ELEANOR. But you don't mind that Mrs. Simon coming.

EDWARD. She's part of the ammunition, that's all. A four-leaf hand grenade.

ELEANOR. What do you think I want to be?

MICHEL. The married couple. Be happy on Mt. Rushmore with me, Lionel.

EDWARD. What do you know, you imitation goat? Do you know how many hotel rooms this woman's been in? How many times she's gone back to a strange bed alone after giving me a good-luck kiss—right here on the tip of the nose, and how many times she's watched me drag myself back, the lipstick still there to remind her that she lost at the table with me.

EMILY. A brave woman to keep kissing your nose, Daddy.

EDWARD. Damn right she is. She's come a long way with me. Why, we started, on our honeymoon, in a hotel room in Atlantic City—there was good gin rummy action there in those days.

ELEANOR. The balcony looked out over the ocean.

EDWARD. And there were little crumbling cupids on top of each of the bedposts. God! It was a tasteless bridal suite.

ELEANOR. But the waves weren't. They were coming in like Roman legions right up against the wharf and breaking against the sea wall.

LIONEL. Mother, I have enough difficulties ahead of me in the next few hours. Don't go into your wedding night.

ELEANOR. Oh, be still, Lionel. This whole family really began on that night. Do you remember how a nice Boston bride shocked you, Edward?

EDWARD. It was something about the wedding. I was going to the bathroom to brush my teeth, and I remember it startled me and I dropped the toothpaste on the floor.

ELEANOR. I told you that in that Boston church, while the minister droned on, I said a polite good-bye to God and all the nice manners that went along with Him. You and your wildness were going to take His place for me.

EDWARD. No wonder I dropped the toothpaste.

ELEANOR. I stood on that balcony with the Atlantic breeze whipping in through the open windows, stripped off my clothes, and headed for you, making what I thought were pagan noises.

EDWARD. You don't know how you surprised me, Eleanor.

ELEANOR. Oh, Edward, you were young, with new decks of cards, and I thought you would never lose. And you were going to take me with you. That night I wanted you to be a human typhoon, a flood—all the chancy, wild natural things.

EDWARD. It was hard in an Atlantic City hotel.

ELEANOR. But you'd showed me you could do it, Edward. Remember what I asked *you* to remember then?

EDWARD. I'm trying, Eleanor.

ELEANOR. I said: "Remember the time I let you feel my breasts in Bridgeport?"

LIONEL (*Sits mourning*). What a beginning!

EDWARD (*Now involved in the tone of the memory*). In the front seat of a Pontiac. The smell of fresh leather around us.

ELEANOR. You fumbled with my clothes like an animal, Edward.

EDWARD. Well, I was in love, and I'd just beaten your father for a hundred dollars in pinochle.

ELEANOR. Oh, you were a winner. And on that honeymoon night, when we loved each other I thought you were going to fill every straight, and pick the right number on a thousand wheels. With God out of the house, and you in it, everything was possible.

EDWARD. And it still is. Look at the tree, Eleanor. Look at the Wellspots around it. Emily, restless and·beautiful; and Michel with the dash of a twenty-year-old degenerate. Mother would have been proud of him. And Lionel, my son and heir, looks like an Italian prince. God, I've waited for this picture a long time! And it's just the beginning. No more holiday hotel rooms. Next year I'm going to rent a real house for us where there's snow, crisp air, and a million pine trees to choose ours from. And Emily, Lionel, see if you can bring me some fat grandchildren that I can spoil. We'll wrap them in satin bunting embroidered with natural blackjacks. Tonight we found the Wellspot Dynasty! (MRS. SIMON *enters in evening dress and the same hat.*)

MRS. SIMON. Hi! Forgive me for not knocking, but I wanted to surprise you with the dress. I've never worn one like it before.

EDWARD (*After a pause*). You look perfect, like a riverboat queen.

MICHEL. Are you going to keep the hat on?

MRS. SIMON. I thought it might be lucky.

EDWARD. Don't you worry about luck. You don't need that.

MICHEL. All right. Let's get going, Lionel. We're already a few minutes late. Just enough to make them a little anxious but not enough to make them surly.

LIONEL. Well, Father, we'll see if we can beat the odds.

EDWARD. Have a good time. And if you like the lady you're with, wrap her up and put her under the tree.

LIONEL (*To room in general*). Do you know, I feel, really feel excited.

MICHEL. He's turning into a sex maniac. Come on!

EMILY. Good luck, Lionel. I wish I were starting for the first time. (LIONEL *and* MICHEL *exit.*) Oh, the dreams he'll be having.

EDWARD. No dreams. This is all going to be real. How do you feel, Mrs. Simon? Ready to go?

MRS. SIMON. I guess so. But shouldn't you tell me something about the game I'm going to play?

EDWARD. No need of that. You just draw the cards and I'll pull in the money. Eleanor, I'll be back soon and we'll have a Christmas without angels that'll make you forget about dinner parties and start thinking about five-day banquets. And you, sweetheart, are you wide awake?

EMILY. Insomnia.

EDWARD. Eleanor, this is for us. For all of us. All right then, Mrs. Simon, keep that New Rochelle hat on and let's go play cards.

MRS. SIMON. Oh, this is living. I should have let Stanly swell up and pop years ago. (*They exit.*)

ELEANOR (*Going to the balcony*). I hope he wins. Oh, I hope he wins.

EMILY. I really feel he will, Mother. This Christmas is different from any other I remember. He really has a chance.

ELEANOR. Look out, over the lights, into the desert. Think of people crossing it for the first time. Women walking straight as trees next to their men. But they had to wait, too, while their husbands fought or hunted without them. Pioneer American women, Emily, how hard it's always been for us.

DARKEN

SCENE III

The blackjack table. As the lights come up, MR. OLYMPUS *is seated in one of the players' seats reading a book—*Psycho-Sexual Hurdles of Modern Marriage. *After a moment,* WILLY *enters.*

WILLY. Hey, Mr. Olympus, they're comin'.

OLYMPUS. Wellspot and his lucky lady?

WILLY. They're all dressed up and walking big across the casino like they were winners already. And all the small-action customers are steppin' aside and touchin' the old lady's hat like it was something religious.

OLYMPUS. Well, Willy, get ready to deal.

WILLY. Can't I have the contact lenses at least? (OLYMPUS *shakes his head.*) Just one for the left eye.

OLYMPUS. Now, Willy, I thought you had faith in *me*.

WILLY. I do, Mr. Olympus, I do. But tell me, like do you have *anything* goin' for you except a percentage? Some real, clever behind-the-back move you're gonna pull?

OLYMPUS. Just knowledge, Willy.

WILLY. Knowledge? What's to know in blackjack? Wellspot knows the right move and he can count down with the best.

OLYMPUS. And he's always lost. Besides, it's the lady you're worried about, not Wellspot.

WILLY. But he'll tell her how to bet—when to pull and stay. I don't get it. I just don't get it.

OLYMPUS (*Looking up for the first time from his book*). Count yourself ahead that you don't. Being curious can sometimes take the bloom off things. Take this book, Willy, *Psycho-Sexual Hurdles of Modern Marriage*. Things have certainly changed since I went through puberty in the Chicago slums. Coeducational courses in sex hygiene, paragraphs on formal positions for maximum pleasure, clip-out reminder charts of erogenous zones. Well, it's a good thing I just want companionship.

WILLY. Already boning up on marriage. It's not right to be so certain.

OLYMPUS (*Snapping the book shut*). I just don't have a˙ choice, Willy. I have to be. (EDWARD *and* MRS. SIMON *enter arm in arm.*)

EDWARD. Ah, well, here they are. All dressed up and scrubbed, pink, and vulnerable.

OLYMPUS. Good evening, Edward. Welcome back.

EDWARD (*Smiling*). Welcome? Full of seasonal spirit, are you? (*He looks around him.*) How well I remember this room. Fifteen times I've crawled out of it on Christmas Eve, feeling like I'd been squeezed to jelly between its walls. But it's good to be back tonight.

OLYMPUS. And this is the famous Mrs. Simon?

MRS. SIMON. I guess I am.

OLYMPUS. A pleasure to meet you.

WILLY. Do I get introduced?

OLYMPUS. Of course. This is my dealer Willy. I hope you get along.

EDWARD. We will. Now I'm ready to play cards if you are.

OLYMPUS. Such confidence, eh, Willy? It's making me choke a little. Shall we put it all on one hand, Edward?

EDWARD. One hand? Oh, no. Not that easy. I want it to be slow so I can roll every minute of winning around in my mouth half a dozen times. Not quick and painless for you, Spiros. The death of a thousand cuts!

OLYMPUS. A cruel gambler, isn't he, Mrs. Simon?

MRS. SIMON. I think he just has a healthy winning spirit.

EDWARD. You bet I do, Widow Simon. (*He sits* MRS. SIMON *down in the chair.*) Now just sit down here, a big kiss on that hat for luck, a thousand dollars in chips please, and we're ready for the first hand. History's going to be made in this room.

WILLY. Well, Mr. Olympus?

OLYMPUS. Go ahead, Willy, the table's open.

WILLY. Okay. One thousand in chips for the lady and the first hand coming out. (*He begins to shuffle.*) Let's make our bets.

EDWARD. Five hundred, Willy.

WILLY. Covered.

MRS. SIMON. Do I have to do anything?

EDWARD. Look at me, Olympus. Look at the old fish of yours. Can you see me growing? Do you see the spine straightening, the shoulders squaring back? (*He struts over to* OLYMPUS *and pats him gently on the head.*) Winners don't slump in their chair, Spiros.

WILLY. Hey now, just a second.

OLYMPUS (*Straightening his hair*). That's all right, Willy.

WILLY. But he patted you on the head, Mr. Olympus. That's undignified.

EDWARD. He's done the same to me. (*Softly.*) God, Spiros, I enjoy beating you so much. It's been such a long time coming.

OLYMPUS. It's your party, Edward. (*To* MRS. SIMON.) It's wonderful to be able to make someone that happy, isn't it?

MRS. SIMON. Well, I'm glad to do it. Especially at Christmas.

OLYMPUS. And you never played cards before?

MRS. SIMON. Just hearts with my late husband Stanly.

EDWARD. And you beat him every time. Poor Stanly!

MRS. SIMON. Oh no, Stanly couldn't bear to lose. He'd crawl under his covers and sulk for hours.

EDWARD. Sweet wife that you were, you let him win.

MRS. SIMON. The least you can do for someone who can't exhale is to let him win a game of hearts now and then.

EDWARD. Well, we show no mercy here, Mrs. Simon. The bet stands. Deal the cards, Willy. Keep them whirling in the air like butterflies. (*To* OLYMPUS.) And I'll try to win with a little more dignity.

WILLY (*Dealing*). Comin' out.

EDWARD (*In wonder*). For the first time in my life I can watch cards sailing toward me without trembling. Now I wish I'd brought the family with me. They'd be so proud of me. They're going to be able to scoop the cream from the top of the world now.

WILLY. An eight up for the dealer.

MRS. SIMON. Can I look this time?

EDWARD. Just pass them back to me, Mrs. Simon. I'd like to be the first to see them. Oh—oh—no, I'm sorry. I can't take it calmly. Another natural. Absolute power in my hands. (*He starts stamping on the floor.*) I could step on every gambling man who ever took me. Just step on them all. Pop! Pop! Pop! (*He pulls himself together.*) But no—with winning, I don't even have to hate you any more, Olympus. I'm not cruel, I'm a good winner. That's nice to find out. I could pinch you. I could even pinch Willy there. They're like Picassos. (EDWARD *sits in a chair, leans back, closes his eyes, and smiles.*)

OLYMPUS (*Studying* EDWARD's *face*). You've made him a happy gambler, Mrs. Simon. I don't see many expressions like that in my casino.

MRS. SIMON (*Staring at* EDWARD). It makes you feel so warm inside having done something charitable.

OLYMPUS. And at no small risks. With all the odds that professional minds have created against you.

MRS. SIMON. Against me? I don't even know what odds are.

OLYMPUS (*Looks at* EDWARD, *who is still in a beatific daze, and in a conspirator's voice to* MRS. SIMON). Ah, Mrs. Simon, it would be nice if there were nothing but even chances out here. But it just can't be. There's a conspiracy of a few percentage points against little ladies like you. The whole city—the free-form hotels, the artificial golf courses, the oversized martinis, the air-conditioned rooms stuffed with Louis Quinze reproductions, the singers, dancers, comedians shipped here from every country in the world—all of this created in a desert wasteland on the principle that there's a little headstart on you when you put your money on a number or a card.

EDWARD (*Starting out of his reverie*). I can't relax a moment with you, Spiros, can I?

MRS. SIMON (*Flattered*). Did you know that the whole city was built all against me? All against me!

EDWARD. Don't worry, Mrs. Simon. When you're through, they'll name this town after you. Deal the cards, Willy. The bet is two thousand.

MRS. SIMON. Are you sure you should bet that much? You know they've got odds against me. We should be careful.

EDWARD (*Closing and opening his eyes as if in pain for a moment*). What do you know about odds? Just touch the cards as they come by.

WILLY. Nine up for the dealer.

EDWARD (*Snatching the cards from* MRS. SIMON *when she starts to peek at them*). Oh? What's this?

MRS. SIMON. Is it bad?

EDWARD. It's not a blackjack. Just a normal, everyday good hand.

WILLY. You want another card, Mr. Wellspot?

EDWARD (*Still confident*). No, we'll play these.

MRS. SIMON (*Mindless question*). Why not take another card if he's willing to give us one?

EDWARD. Please, Mrs. Simon? Here, let me straighten your hat.

WILLY (*Flipping his hole card over*). Nineteen. Pay twenty.

EDWARD (*A long sigh of relief*). It was just a little relapse. Pay the number.

MRS. SIMON. We won?

EDWARD (*Patting* MRS. SIMON's *cheek*). Just teasing old Edward, eh? Just want to keep him on his toes.

MRS. SIMON. But why didn't you take the other card? You could have beaten him by even more?

OLYMPUS. The object of the game is to get as close to twenty-one as possible *without* going over it.

MRS. SIMON (*Her eyes wide now*). Oh my. I didn't know that.

EDWARD. All right. This isn't a course in the fine points of blackjack. Bet four thousand.

MRS. SIMON. Oh my. I hope we don't go over. Even the golf course against me! (WILLY *starts to shuffle.*)

EDWARD (*Imploring*). Please stop thinking, Mrs. Simon. My God, you're perspiring. (*Takes out his handkerchief and begins wiping* MRS. SIMON's *brow.*) With the air-conditioning on, you're perspiring.

OLYMPUS (*To* MRS. SIMON). There's more excitement in gambling when you know the dangers, isn't there, Mrs. Simon?

MRS. SIMON. Well, I'm not a thrill-seeker, really.

EDWARD. Willy, will you deal the cards?

WILLY. Comin' out. (*He deals quickly.*)

OLYMPUS. This is even beginning to get to me.

WILLY. Ten up for the dealer.

OLYMPUS. Now, that's a bad sign for you, Mrs. Simon.

MRS. SIMON (*Slapping her hands over the cards and freezing*). Is it?

EDWARD. Olympus, are you trying to shark a grandmother?

OLYMPUS. Edward, I just want to point out to her that with a ten up we may have a blackjack.

EDWARD. What presumption!

OLYMPUS. How about it, Willy?

WILLY (*Glances quickly at his hole card*). Not this time.

EDWARD. Our cards, Mrs. Simon.

MRS. SIMON (*Still frozen, with her hand over the cards*). Just let me swallow for a moment. Something's caught in my throat.

OLYMPUS. That's known as the apple. Every real gambler chokes on it now and then, don't they, Edward?

EDWARD (*To* MRS. SIMON). Don't listen to that. Just look at old, honest Edward's face. See the confident smile? (MRS. SIMON *remains motionless and* EDWARD *tries to pry her fingers off the cards.*) Now let's win another hand.

MRS. SIMON. I'm not really a gambler.

OLYMPUS. And here you are a man's lucky piece. That takes courage.

MRS. SIMON. It does?

EDWARD. Can you lift your thumb up, Mrs. Simon, so we can see the cards?!

MRS. SIMON. Don't snatch, Mr. Wellspot. Can't you see Willy has a ten showing. I wouldn't be so anxious to see what we have.

EDWARD. Mrs. Simon. Your forehead's all pinched and furrowed. Just sit back and think of thousands of summer hats.

OLYMPUS. It's hard to do that when you're a man's lucky piece. All that pressure on those grandmother shoulders of yours.

EDWARD (*For a moment he stops trying to wrench the cards from* MRS. SIMON, *he massages her shoulders*). Just relax then, Mrs. Simon. Don't let them knot up. Stay loose.

OLYMPUS. Think of it, Mrs. Simon. If you don't perform the miracle, the disappointment and anger of someone who put his faith in you.

MRS. SIMON (*Looking back at* EDWARD). You wouldn't snap at me if we lost, would you?

OLYMPUS. Our hotel toilets are stuffed up every day with rabbits' feet that didn't work for their owners.

EDWARD. Damn it, Olympus, are you saying I'd throw her into a john if she doesn't win?

OLYMPUS. I'm sure she wouldn't blame you if you did.

MRS. SIMON. Well, I certainly would. I certainly would!

OLYMPUS (*Sharply and threateningly*). You would? When his whole style of action is staked on you? Look at him, Mrs. Simon, that's a gambler with his hands around your throat.

EDWARD (*Takes his hands away quickly as* MRS. SIMON *spins about anxiously*). A sweet gambler! A gentle gambler!

OLYMPUS. This is his case money, his case game. After coming on this strong, if you don't get him past the odds, he'd have every right in the world to pull the chain on you when you dog it.

EDWARD. Don't let him bluff you. Why, this is just a little sport for me. (*He snaps his fingers cavalierly.*) The money—a bagatelle. I couldn't be less involved.

MRS. SIMON. Now listen: I've had a long hard life in New Rochelle. There've been enough problems for me. I don't want any more. And certainly not yours.

EDWARD (*Snatching up the cards*). What problems? When we can't lose and stand to win the whole damned city?? (*His voice trails off as he looks at the cards.*)

MRS. SIMON. Well, what kind of cards do we have?

EDWARD (*Forcing a little ebullience into his voice*). They're fine. They'll do very nicely.

WILLY (*Flipping his hole card*). Twenty. Pay twenty-one.

EDWARD. You have twenty, do you?

MRS. SIMON. Well, what do *we* have?

EDWARD. Eighteen. We didn't quite make it that time.

MRS. SIMON. You look just the way Stanly used to when I let his atomizer run out. I hate that look.

EDWARD. I'm sorry. (*He smiles enormously.*) See? Bright and sassy again. It was just a little slip. (*He takes some money out of his wallet, and puts it on the table.*) Three thousand worth, Willy. And, Mrs. Simon, let's show them your unorthodox style, like with the slot machine. (*He turns her chair around so that her back is to* WILLY *across the table.*) Show them your backhand win.

MRS. SIMON. Really, Mr. Wellspot, I think I've had enough. I don't feel well.

OLYMPUS. You're a real gambler now, Mrs. Simon. I'm proud of you.

EDWARD. Shut up, Spiros! Deal, Willy!

WILLY (*Dealing*). Comin' out to the lady's back. (WILLY *guides them into* MRS. SIMON's *hands.*)

MRS. SIMON. They don't feel good to me.

EDWARD. Without looking, we stand. (*He strokes* MRS. SIMON's *hat.*) Just try to beat us.

WILLY (*Turns over his hole card*). A six to go with the five. (*He draws another card.*) And a ten to match it off. Twenty-one. The name of the game.

EDWARD (*He looks at his hand and then tosses them on table*). I can't understand. Eighteen passes in a row. Three jackpots. . . .

MRS. SIMON. I just felt they weren't going to be good cards.

EDWARD. You've let him get to you. Look at you. You've got that sharp frightened look of a hungry horse player. Well, he's not going to do that to you without a fight.

MRS. SIMON. Mr. Wellspot, I think I've had enough. I'd . . .

EDWARD. No, no. Listen! When were you as fresh and unmarked as you can remember?

OLYMPUS. Are you still playing, Edward?

EDWARD. I'm nowhere near out yet. Come on, Widow Simon. When didn't you know there was an angle in the world against you?

MRS. SIMON. Oh, I don't know. I guess it was *before* I had the first of my fat sons. And I feel now as though I'm pregnant again. I just can't calm down.

EDWARD. Can't I do something?

MRS. SIMON. Well, Stanly used to sing to me and hold my hand. Whenever I was queasy.

EDWARD (*Grabbing her hand*). What did he sing? What did he sing?

MRS. SIMON. Our favorite song was "Camptown Ladies"! You know, da dada dum dum, dum dum dum???

EDWARD (*Picking up the tune*). ". . . The Camptown Racetrack twelve miles long / Oh the dooda day." That it?

MRS. SIMON (*Not really pleased*). Well—Stanly had a tenor voice.

EDWARD (*His voice an inch from cracking, goes up an octave as he begins to rub*). "Gwin to run all night, Gwin to run all day / I bet my money on a bobtailed nag / Somebody bet on the bay.

MRS. SIMON (*Joins in*). "Gwin to run all night" . . . (*etc.*) (WILLY *gets up from the table as though frightened, and watches as they sing.*)

EDWARD (*As they come to a harmonizing end*). Well? Feel better?

MRS. SIMON. No. Stanly had a much better voice. I'm going to have to go lie down. I don't think I like to gamble. (MRS. SIMON *rises, and as she walks past* EDWARD, *he grabs her around the neck and behind her back.*)

EDWARD. I can't let you walk out on me. I'll practice singing.

MRS. SIMON. Let go of me.

EDWARD. No. You can't take it away, a touch like yours. Not when I was up so high.

MRS. SIMON. Help me!

OLYMPUS. I warned you, Mrs. Simon.

EDWARD (*Dragging her to the table*). Cards, Willy!

MRS. SIMON. If I see another card, I'll be sick right here.

WILLY. What's the bet?

EDWARD (*Throws billfold on table*). Everything.

OLYMPUS. Covered.

MRS. SIMON. Stanly never laid a hand on me in his life.

EDWARD. Then how did you have those two fat sons? Deal, Willy!

MRS. SIMON. That was affection!

EDWARD. And so is this! Dooda, dooda. (WILLY *deals gingerly, keeping out of* EDWARD's *range.*)

WILLY. Nine up for the dealer?

EDWARD (*Picking up his cards with one hand and freeing* MRS. SIMON's *arm*). Now kiss the cards for luck, Mrs. Simon.

MRS. SIMON. No! It's barbaric. It's not Christian.

EDWARD (*Tightening his grip around her neck*). Kiss them, and say that they're nice cards.

MRS. SIMON (*Kissing the cards*). Nice cards. Stanly, wherever you are, help me!

EDWARD (*Looking at the cards*). Oh God. I need another one, Willy.

WILLY (*Tosses a card across the table*). Ten.

EDWARD. We went over. We busted. (*Throws cards down on table.*) That kiss was insincere, Mrs. Simon. (MRS. SIMON *lashes back suddenly with her elbow, striking* EDWARD *in the stomach, doubling him over.*)

MRS. SIMON (*Jumping away from* EDWARD). Now you let go of me! You're all crazy. Kissing cards! Building cities to beat honest women like myself.

EDWARD (*Out of breath from the blow*). Please, Mrs. Simon. . . .

MRS. SIMON. Stay away from me! You're not stuffing me into a drain. I don't want your life in my hands. I don't need it. I've got social security and an allowance from my sons. I'm moving to an Arizona Ranchette for the affluent senior citizen—and I'm going to love it.

EDWARD. Please, I'll borrow another stake. I thought you had class, Mrs. Simon. I thought you had a one-in-a-million touch.

MRS. SIMON. I've got arthritis that I'm going to put in the desert sun, that's all.

EDWARD (*Still holding his side, he drops to his knees*). Please. I won't have any chance at all if you walk out. One more deal. With your eyes closed and my hands on that sexy hat for luck.

MRS. SIMON. Mr. Wellspot! What in the world could be worth a position like that? Even for air to breathe, Stanly never begged. (MRS. SIMON *exits.*)

EDWARD. I want more than just to breathe! I want more! Oh God! (EDWARD *cries, and there is a long pause.*)

OLYMPUS (*Walking over to* EDWARD). Can I help you up, Edward? (*Helping* EDWARD *up.*) You've got tear streaks down your face. That's not a good sight for business. (*He starts leading* EDWARD *off the stage.*) Let's go to the washroom. And don't fret, Edward. I haven't had a good Xmas in years myself.

EDWARD. Do you know, I feel cold. It's the air-conditioning. It's all wrong to have air-conditioning at Christmas. (OLYMPUS *leads* EDWARD *offstage.*)

WILLY. Willy, you've just seen the best move ever. Yeah, you're on a winnin' team. Just like you always wanted. On top of the action. So how come there's no kick? How come? That fat mother Olympus has done something. I feel choked up, like I suddenly got an eighty-dollar-a-week job and an ugly religious wife for the rest of my time. We took in the money, so why the hell should I feel like that? (*The light on* WILLY *goes out.*)

SCENE IV

The Wellspot suite. When the lights come up, EMILY, *in evening gown, is stretched out asleep on the sofa.* ELEANOR *enters!!!*

ELEANOR. Emily! Emily! (*She shakes* EMILY'S *shoulder.*) Emily, he's lost.

EMILY (*Sitting up quickly, she speaks hoarsely*). What??

ELEANOR. He's lost. Your father's lost everything!

EMILY. How do you know?

ELEANOR. Because of the angels. Edward was right. They've always doted on his losing.

EMILY. You saw them again?

ELEANOR. On television. I was watching Xmas eve at the White House and they were perched right over the vice-president's head.

EMILY. But Mother, that doesn't mean . . .

ELEANOR. Yes it does, those angels are a rebuke from the Episcopal church.

EMILY. But Mrs. Simon couldn't lose.

ELEANOR. Really? Then why were you asleep, Emily? All dressed up for your date with the swimming instructor, and you slept right through it.

EMILY (*Aware now of what it means*). My . . . my throat started to hurt. I just wanted to lie down and . . . (LIONEL *enters carrying* MICHEL *in his arms.*)

LIONEL. Off the sofa, Emily. Let me put him down.

ELEANOR. My God. He looks chalk-white.

EMILY. Is he dead?

LIONEL. No. He can still wheeze. But it's very faint.

EMILY. Well, what happened?

LIONEL. I think Mount Rushmore fell on him. God, Emily, the girl he was with must have been six-two—and huge. Once she got paid, she just didn't leave Michel alone—bounced him on her lap, tickled him, whistled in his ear. And he loved it. But when they went off together in the next room—well, something proved too much for him.

EMILY. Men! Always promises. But get them out of their locker-room dreams and then it's heart attacks and sluggish reflexes. A girl with any passion needs a first-aid kit next to her bed. (MICHEL *wheezes and tries to prop himself up.*)

LIONEL (*Holding him*). Don't upset him now. It was a very big woman.

ELEANOR (*Bringing the brandy which she puts to* MICHEL's *lips*). Here, this will help. (MICHEL *takes a sip and begins to sputter and wheeze.*)

EMILY. Yeeck! I can't look!

LIONEL. Why are you so sharp? Did your swimming instructor drown?

EMILY. I slept through the date and now I have a sore throat. (MICHEL *tries to get up from the sofa.*)

LIONEL. Here, Uncle Michel, don't try to move.

MICHEL (*Weakly*). I feel all right. I can sit up. I'm not dying.

ELEANOR. Shall we call a doctor?

MICHEL. No, no. I just need some rest. Something came to an end inside of me, and it makes a man a little tired. Lionel, go back and tell that giant hooker I'm all right.

LIONEL. Don't worry about her, Uncle Michel.

MICHEL (*Blankly rhetorical*). It's only fun if you care a little about them, Lionel. I've loved every one . . . every one.

EMILY (*Sarcastically*). Of course you did!

MICHEL. You're right to look at me that way. I tried to, even believed it at the time. But I was just a bottom-pinching clown, too scared to be anything more.

LIONEL. But you were a great help to me, Uncle Michel. (*To* ELEANOR.) You should have heard the snappy jokes, repartee, and double entendres he got off over dinner. He had the girls hysterical. They really liked us. I really think something developed between me and the . . .

MICHEL. Oh, get me to bed. The idiot's probably in love with that six-foot broad he was with. She had breasts that pointed in opposite directions. (MICHEL *begins laughing, quietly.*)

ELEANOR. Don't talk about it, Michel. You're still pale.

MICHEL. You all probably think the old heart gave out, that it exploded in protest. It wasn't that. It's just that I couldn't make myself believe it was fun anymore. It was like lying on top of my whole life—a lot of agitation and well-rehearsed moves, and it scared the hell out of me. I should have stuck with the memories. They were really kicks for me.

EMILY. If you'd married one of those memories you'd have someone to hold your hand when you get frightened on top of a woman.

LIONEL. Emily, shut up. What is it with you?

MICHEL. Your sister knows something, Lionel. She's been around. You know why I didn't, Emily. You know the search. Little hot pants, Emily.

EMILY (*Subdued*). Yes, I know.

ELEANOR. Will you please come to bed, Michel. It's Christmas Eve. You'll want to be up early tomorrow.

MICHEL (*Allowing himself to be led into the bedroom by* ELEANOR). Christmas! What the hell are we doing here on Christmas? I hope Edward gets busted out once and for all. No more of his hustling. Tomorrow I get my present and then back to my hotel in New York to swap innuendoes with a lady bass player who looks like she was never laid in her life.

ELEANOR. That's enough of that kind of talk, Michel.

MICHEL. Getting a little prim, aren't you, Eleanor? A bottom-pinching clown. A goddamned bottom-pinching clown. (*He and* EL-EANOR *exit.*)

LIONEL. You didn't have to say those things to him. He was a real sport tonight.

EMILY. I was saying them to myself too. He knew that.

LIONEL. What happened, Emily? Has Father come back from the game?

EMILY. Not yet. But Mother and I have a feeling. She saw those nudist angels on television and I fell asleep with a sore throat. Those are bad signs.

LIONEL. What kind of nonsense is that?

EMILY. It was your algebra, Lionel. Remember the long run.

LIONEL. But that was before Mrs. Simon. Oh, he can't lose now. Not after tonight.

EMILY. While your uncle was coughing up his whole life, you were having a good time.

LIONEL. That's right. I had a ball. It was fun. The food, the waiters all starched and subservient, the girls' impossible appetites, and the beautiful, clean, intricately designed underwear she had on.

EMILY. All bought and paid for.

LIONEL. I don't care if it was. I want more of it, and realistically speaking, I know I'm not beautiful, I've got no great talents, and I'm generally gloomy and unsociable. So I'll be happy to buy my way out for awhile.

EMILY. Well, if lace underwear can beat your philosophy, you've got a great future, Lionel. (ELEANOR *comes back into the room.*)

ELEANOR. Well, he's all right now. He told me a dirty joke, laughed and went to sleep.

EMILY. Forever and ever, amen, Uncle Michel. (EDWARD *comes in. He is wearing a Santa Claus suit and has a sack slung over his shoulder.*)

EDWARD. Ho ho ho—what a sweet Christian family gathered together on this special night.

EMILY. Daddy, what on earth . . . ?

EDWARD. How else should a man dress who's bringing presents and glad tidings to those who've stood behind for so many years?

LIONEL. You won? You came through?

EDWARD. Won? You better believe I won, Lionel. We all won tonight.

EMILY. How much?

EDWARD. How much? It can't be measured, Emily. Peace of mind and soul—you can't put a ruler next to them.

LIONEL. Something's wrong. You never said anything that nauseating before.

ELEANOR. Edward, did you win or not?

EDWARD (*He pauses, looks maliciously around the room*). Do you know it's after midnight? It's time for presents. It's time for real Christmas presents? (*He dips into the sack he's been carrying.*) Emily, my much-married little girl, here, first, neatly wrapped with a pleasant ribbon indicating the sender's good taste, is an invitation to Christmas brunch from Olympus, along with a pair of sleep shades, with your initials on them.

EMILY (*Taking the presents, sadly*). He's beaten you again.

EDWARD. You're disappointed with the present? It's so hard to know what children want. But for you, Lionel . . . I know I've got something you've dreamed about a long time.

LIONEL (*He takes the present and fingers it suspiciously*). What is it?

EDWARD (*Winking in confidence*). Something the house awards its good customers when they're heavy losers. And it won't play hard to get like that gila monster.

FRIEDMAN-ABELES

LIONEL (*Tossing the package on the sofa*). Oh no! Listen, I had a wonderful time tonight with that girl you arranged for me to meet. Yes, that's right, Lionel Wellspot really swinged, swang . . . swung or whatever it is—and he doesn't want a Christmas present from the house.

EDWARD (*He stares at* LIONEL *for a moment*). Well, Lionel, you never did have a sense of humor. And, Eleanor, old Santa hasn't forgotten you either. Here, two tickets, one way, back to Boston for both of us. A job for me, if your family still has a vice-presidency open, and after church, on Sunday, strolls through Beacon Hill, hand in hand, to look for your angels.

ELEANOR. It's been so long. Edward, I'm sorry.

EDWARD. Sorry? That a man's come out of a fever and can see clearly? Eleanor, when I saw my last dollar go into Olympus' pocket I danced for joy and shook his hand. Right there at the table I thanked him—yes, really thanked him for helping make me a reformed gambler. Now, Eleanor, we can put our lives in order, stop chasing aces, and sleep in separate beds to get as much rest as possible. We'll grow closer together than ever, and the Episcopal church will see us through the bad moments, when we hear dice rolling in the night or someone shuffling cards downstairs in the parlor.

ELEANOR. Well, I'd better call the family and tell them we'll be flying in tomorrow.

EDWARD. You do that, Eleanor. And when you pack leave all the loud Las Vegas clothes here.

ELEANOR. Edward, what happened with Mrs. Simon?

EDWARD. She was a false idol, Eleanor, and fell apart when just a little faith was needed.

ELEANOR. Well, I'd never say this if we were going on the road again, but I did find her a little coarse, Edward. A little lowbred and coarse.

EDWARD. You haven't said something like that for thirty years, Eleanor. And I've missed it. Well, Emily, what are you waiting for? Olympus is pacing downstairs in expectation. He really has quite a nice profile if you catch him with his head tilted the right way.

EMILY. You don't think there's something better? It'll mean an awful lot of sleep.

EDWARD (*For a moment dropping the forced geniality*). I can't help you any more, Emily. I'm as tired as you are. (*Brightening.*) But I even made him promise a tonsillectomy as a wedding present—and you can have all the ether you want with your Daddy's blessing.

EMILY (*Yawns*). Well, I'll meet him and see. Maybe it's time I did settle for a good, sensible stomach in a separate bed. I'll let you know, Daddy. Good night. (EMILY *exits.*)

EDWARD (*In almost a cry*). Ho ho ho—Merry Christmas.

LIONEL. You fraud!

EDWARD. Don't say it, Lionel.

LIONEL. You ho-ho-hoing Christmas fraud. You're not going to laugh at my gila monster, give me a taste of jackpot living, and then put that (*Pointing to the gun.*) in my Christmas stocking.

EDWARD. I was beaten, Lionel. I thought I could burn this city down with a deck of cards, and now there's no fire anywhere. But like you said, Lionel, there's nothing to win anyway, and there's not even the right odds for a chance at that nothing.

LIONEL. No, no, no! It could be, Father, you're just a poor loser.

EDWARD (*Sharply*). What?

LIONEL. You, Edward Wellspot, were unlucky, that's all. But *I* wasn't betting on your blackjack game.

EDWARD. What about your long-run, Lionel?

LIONEL. That was an invalid deduction based on my weak eyes, post-adolescent acne, and the incorrect notion that I was unlikable. But tonight . . . At twenty-seven I discovered that I like being slumped next to a champagne bucket. I caught a glimpse of myself in a mirror and thought I had possible dash in a dinner jacket and a pert black tie. And how restful a woman can be when you don't have to think.

EDWARD. Don't be a fool. Go back to graduate school, find a serious girl who never wears lipstick, and have a pair of high-IQ babies. Don't play for the stakes I did.

LIONEL. Not enough. I want everything you coaxed me off that balcony with, and the feeling that goes with them. Do you know what that girl did while she was nuzzling me in the restaurant? She stripped the skin from the back of my neck where I started to peel. Now that's significant, isn't it?

EDWARD. My son Lionel. Peel off one layer, and the next is just as dumb. All right. Run back to the casino. Go out and win a Christmas goose for yourself.

LIONEL. Who knows? I just might. No offense, Dad, but maybe you just tried too hard to be popular. I mean, now, I have a perspective you didn't when you started off. Yes, a little more conservative in dress and better educated, I might just get along fine. You know when you've stretched out in the desert or jumped into a famous river—well, it gives you a sense of irony about things. And I think whoever watches over gamblers likes irony.

EDWARD. It's ridiculous to say, but good luck, Lionel.

LIONEL. Don't look so glum. You tried as hard as you could.

ELEANOR. Lionel, you don't have the right to console your father.

LIONEL. Not yet, perhaps. But just wait. (*Going to the door.*) I think I'll start off at the crap table—that's where the best odds are. (*He strikes a crapshooter's pose.*) Do I look like a winning roller, Father?

EDWARD. You could be the new style, Lionel.

LIONEL (*Still shaking imaginary dice and speaking indirectly to* EDWARD *and* ELEANOR). I think it's time there was a little luck for people like me, a little myopic and serious minded. After all, I speak six languages, know I'm going to die, and I do have an ironic smile about the whole thing. (*Now directly to* ELEANOR *and* EDWARD.) Father, Mother—Merry Christmas. Have a happy retirement in Boston. And don't worry about me. The world's going to find every inch of Lionel Wellspot lovable. I know it. I know it. (LIONEL *exits.*)

EDWARD. Well, there he goes. Next up at the table. (*He goes to the balcony.*) Look at all those Christmas stars. I used to think I was something special to them, and they never gave a damn about me. They frighten me now. I wish they'd go out one by one.

ELEANOR. Don't you want to come to bed now?

EDWARD. On Christmas? Ho ho ho, Eleanor, we've got presents to open. (*He picks up the package on the sofa and unwraps the pistol.*) What do you suppose was wrong with me? Was I too crude? Did I dress too loudly? (*He shrugs.*) It doesn't matter now. (*Indicating with a sweep of his arms the gambling machines.*) Look at them all, Eleanor. So peaceful. So smug. As if they didn't know they just did Edward T. Wellspot in once and for all. They should be celebrating. Dammit, I thought I had it in my hand this time. (*To the roulette wheel.*) I was going to make you dance my tune. This was going to be the Christmas it all happened. Christmas! (*He looks at the pistol in his hand.*) Is there one reason, Eleanor, why I shouldn't play with my son's present? (*He holds the pistol to his temple, and closes his eyes.* ELEANOR *walks toward him.*) It's the traditional thing for a father to do on Christmas morning. No one would think I was being childish.

ELEANOR. Edward, won't going back to Boston accomplish the same thing? (EDWARD *smiles slowly, drops gun. Arm in arm they head for the bedroom as the curtain falls.*)

THE END

ON
Xmas In
Las Vegas

Each of the other plays in this collection has its vociferous claque of believers—drum-beaters and horn-tooters who predict its imminent revival and who plump for the vindication of its unsung merits. There is yet to be heard either tattoo or toot for Jack Richardson's *Xmas in Las Vegas*, which had a four-day Broadway lifespan, November 4–7, 1965, at the Ethel Barrymore Theatre. If the play does have its devotees, then the fan club must be holding its meetings in a phone booth in Secaucus, New Jersey, because the reactions I've picked up have ranged from scornful dismissal to vehement antagonism.

And yet, in some important ways, *Xmas in Las Vegas* is the most interesting play in this collection. Thematically, it's a bold attempt to dramatize a complex point of existentialist philosophy; namely, modern man's struggle "to be" or "to attain essence" through a calculated commitment to active involvement in the affairs of his world. Stylistically, the play is even more audacious, because it ventures to convey this theme through an inverted metaphor. Furthermore, the play's masterful use of language shows Jack Richardson to be a superb writer, arguably one of the most talented American dramatists to come to maturity in the 1960's.

Given the inventiveness of the play's theme and structure and the sheer scope and depth of its author's talent, the ignominious commercial failure of *Xmas* deserves close examination. There is indeed a fascinating behind-the-scenes story to this production, and it illustrates a good many of the classic flaws in the system of Broadway production.

Since *Xmas in Las Vegas* makes extended metaphorical use of gambling, it becomes an especially apt illustration of the commercial theater's dependence on chance. When asked to analyze the reasons for his play's disastrous showing on Broadway, Jack Richardson appropriately used a gambling metaphor. "In the theater, you never really know why you didn't roll a seven when you wanted to roll a seven," he says. "There's a certain serendipity involved in getting a play on. I don't want to sound like a Druid, but you do have a feeling sometimes that the times are right, the entrances seem to be good, or the signs propitious. As I get older and gamble more I think that there's a right time to roll, and if you pick it, you'll probably win."

Conversely, and more to the point in this study, is the fact that if the entrails *aren't* favorable, a perfectly fine play can be relegated to oblivion simply because its subject or treatment is ahead of its time, or because any number of other arbitrary factors converged to destroy the "serendipity" of which Richardson spoke.

Aside from being a most appropriate example of the Broadway theater's rather chilling dependence on the intangible and nonartistic element of luck, *Xmas in Las Vegas* also emerges as a classic illustration of the inexorability of the commercial system of play production. Once the machinery has been set into motion, it simply cannot be stopped, redirected, or recalled. Fred Coe, the producer and director of *Xmas*, likened the phenomenon to an army marching out to war, and the metaphor is stunningly appropriate. The creators of *Xmas* made some appalling errors of interpretation and judgment in mounting the play, but even when they confronted their own mistakes, the relentless mechanism of the Broadway producing system made it impossible to correct them.

Finally, making their own special contributions to the failure of the production were the additional factors of Jack Richardson's unorthodox relationship to the New York critical establishment; the singular difficulties posed by the play's black humor; structural flaws aggravated by a fatal distortion of the play's expressionistic style; and the inevitable and always unpredictable human component.

In considering the text itself, one must acknowledge at the outset a few pronounced artistic limitations; specifically, Richardson's observable difficulty in conveying the richness and complexity of his ideas in viable and popularly accessible dramatic terms. Attendant on this basic problem is the further obstacle of Richardson's language, which, although mostly sublime in the writing, can boggle an audience bred on less demanding stuff. One last, and less defensible, structural weakness in the work is its tentative and often disjointed application of the expressionist dramatic style.

Far outbalancing, though, any of these scriptual blemishes are the strength and impact of the ideas in the play and the singularly effective metaphor through which they are dramatized. Although the play is structured as a slightly eccentric variation of the conventional family comedy, it clearly must be interpreted as a kind of modern parable if it is to be apprehended on any but the most superficial level. Dealing first with surfaces, *Xmas in Las Vegas* introduces us to Edward T. Wellspot, a compulsive gambler and a born loser, and his singularly idiosyncratic family, composed of his son, Lionel, whose severe sense of detachment leads him to repeated and consistently unsuccessful suicide attempts; his daughter, Emily, whose similar state of detachment makes her a chronic sleeper; and his wife, Eleanor, who alone believes in the ineffectual head of the bizarre family unit. The Wellspots are Christmasing in Las Vegas, where Edward hopes to break his losing streak and infuse his emotionally anesthetized children with the invigorating excitement of gambling.

The vicissitudes of the Wellspots in Las Vegas are funny enough in themselves, but when they are interpreted as a parable of human existence in contemporary society, they become profound, as well. Clearly, Richardson intends gambling to be construed as a positive metaphor for human involvement and commitment in the arbitrary, chancey, even dirty, game of life.

Las Vegas thus becomes a perfect symbol for modern America. As sleazy and tawdry as it is, it has the throb of life. When Edward tries to coax his son out of yet another suicide attempt, he tempts him with visions of life's joys: "A colored television set with private channels; a pistachio-colored foreign car; a pair of eighteen-year-old brown Brazilian twins; karate lessons; an opera box; caps for your teeth; contact lenses made of Belgian glass; a nymphomaniacal movie star; a trip to Japan . . . etc." Lionel calls them vulgar, which of course they are, but within the play's symbolic structure they are not to be interpreted as images of satire but as metaphors for the dreams we dream. Son Lionel's spiritual resurrection—the point at which he recovers from his death wish—is in fact the moment when he is infected with the gambling urge, when he commits himself to fight for these same tacky symbols of life's gratifications.

Richardson does not for an instant defend contemporary American society. He sees it as a vulgar bazaar, but the alternatives he sees to man's commitment to living are infinitely more harrowing. One can commit suicide, as Lionel almost does, by broiling to death alone in the Nevada desert. One can escape into a perpetual somnambulistic state, as Emily does. One can even go so far as to move to Boston, to live in the bosom of one's family, as Edward and Eleanor Wellspot eventually do. Richardson describes that existence in this manner: "Now, Eleanor, we can put our lives in order, stop chasing aces, and sleep in separate beds to get as much rest as possible. We'll grow closer together than ever, and the Episcopal church will see us through the bad moments, when we hear dice rolling in the night or someone shuffling cards downstairs in the parlor." For a moment Edward seriously contemplates shooting himself, but Eleanor observes, in a devastating curtain line, "Won't going back to Boston accomplish the same thing?"

Each of these alternative, self-immured modes of existence is used by Richardson to convey a sense of noninvolvement, of lack of commitment, of extreme detachment in isolation. But as spiritually corrosive as are compulsive sleeping and literal suicide, more drastic still is the elder Wellspots' return to the bosom of Boston, which represents a capitulation to the regimentation of society's ordered, formalistic structure of "life." At the crux of Richardson's philosophy is the belief that the planned and placid existence of the normally structured life cripples human vitality and spiritual energy. In *Xmas in Las Vegas*, Las Vegas becomes the metaphorical antithesis of the formalistic deathly "peace" represented by Boston, and the act of gambling becomes a symbol for the life urge, for the chaos, turmoil, and pure agonizing joy of being alive.

Spiros Olympus, the owner of the gambling casino, fully understands the difference between order/death and chaos/life. Speaking as a member of an economic order as formalistically structured as Boston society, he observes of Wellspot: "He's never beaten the casino for a nickel and yet he makes me nervous when he comes in to play. If I were sentimental, I'd say I envied his stubbornness, his dry throat, his wet hands—all the palpable signs of life you lose when you're the house, when the odds are with you, and you grind down the Wellspots in a well-mannered, orderly way."

To play the life game takes courage, because the player is fully aware that it is always a losing gamble. "If there's any sign in the heavens, it should be 'You can't beat the house,' " Edward Wellspot ruefully observes. But he still acknowledges that life is, after all, the only game we've got. "If you're holding a losing hand, at least look at how pretty the cards are," he advises his son, in an attempt to convey the joys that visit the man who commits himself to the life/gamble, even though it is his destiny to lose.

What makes Wellspot a dignified, even a noble human being is his commitment to play the game and to play it without losing faith in his ability to "beat the house," that is, the system, and to win—common sense and the history of civilization to the contrary. Clutzy little Edward T. Wellspot, born patsy and inveterate failure, thus becomes a kind of heroic Everyman of the times, for having the temerity and the tenacity to play the game at all. In an attempt to articulate his sense of commitment to the bruising game he has chosen to play, he notes, "Any amateur can win with aces. It takes a player to come out ahead when the cards aren't really running for him. He has to twist, turn, think, bluff, squeeze, and slip on through." If that is not a felicitous description of what it's like to live in these times, then I'll eat my dice.

Richardson gives his dramatic thesis a further, subtle twist when he makes it clear that merely dipping in the life flux is insufficient for a man to attain character stature. The commitment must be total and unswerving if one is to reach heroic height. Through Wellspot, Richardson describes the man who half-commits himself, leaving himself an escape loophole, as "The type of gambler that hangs around the tables holding on to his room rent. Can't bear to leave, but can't lay it on the table, either."

The theme of man's achieving dignity through commitment to action is a venerable motif in literature, especially in the works of contemporary absurdist dramatists, in whose thematic tradition *Xmas in Las Vegas* very much belongs. Certainly there are parallels to be drawn between Edward T. Wellspot and Vladimir and Estragon of Samuel Beckett's *Waiting for Godot*. Beckett's suffering tramps commit themselves totally to the act of waiting—an act every bit as futile and absurd as Wellspot's act of gambling. The point, of course, is that the *commitment* to the act is the most noble piece of behavior of which man is capable, given the profoundly absurd nature of life.

Like Vladimir and Estragon, Edward T. Wellspot is fully, dynamically alive precisely when his commitment is most futile. These are the living. The dead are those who give up and retreat, laying their heads in the lap of such anti-life forces as laws, rules, social systems, formalized art, conventional orders of morality and ethics, and other rigid constructs governing human behavior, thought, and creation. To resist the false peace of such systematization, in favor of life with all its chaos, violence, dirt, pain, defeat, and sublime absurdity, is to be man at his most noble level.

In the Dostoevskian tradition, Richardson here chose gambling as the metaphor for the life/chaos. Given his own personal penchant for the gaming tables, it is a particularly rich metaphor, which he once explored in a magazine article called "Grace Through Gambling" (*Esquire*, April, 1967). "For over a year I had grown more inclined to do less and less that required decisive effort," he wrote. "While in semi-hibernation one thing began to snap me into a state of keen sensitivity over and over again. I had begun to gamble." The act of gambling was thus divested of its conventional associations of vice and character corruption and assumed instead the qualities of a virtue because of its power to lead him out of lethargic peace. "I admitted that all the chaos I was going into frightened me and that I knew I would someday grow numb even to the pleasures of gambling," he wrote of his decision to abandon his contentful life style. "I was going west in the morning so that the peace that was around me would never be my final end."

In earlier plays, Richardson has explored the same commitment-to-life theme through other metaphors. In *Lorenzo*, which is about an actor who refuses to involve himself in war, he employs art as the symbol for the escapist, isolationist state of retreat from the chaos of reality here symbolized by war. *The Prodigal*, Richardson's first play, retells the Orestes legend in modern terms, making Orestes a symbol of the contemporary intellectual who resists making a commitment to the political issues of his times, hiding from involvement through his deep cynicism. The theme of involvement in life is most explicitly treated in *Gallows Humor*, in which a prisoner condemned to death finds jail itself to be the ultimate haven of impregnable peace. "All my pieces are in their proper place, and I don't want them disarranged," the prisoner states, in explanation of why he is resisting the ministrations of a whore who tries to invade his numbing "peace" with sex—here an overt metaphor for the dizzying stimulants of the life throbbing outside his tidy cell. In his novel, *The Prison Life of Harris Filmore*, Richardson explores in still fuller detail his distrust of rigid, formalistic systems which offer a false sense of peace to men who are unwilling to cast themselves into the unpredictable disorder of life.

I have gone on at rather extended length about the philosophical content of *Xmas in Las Vegas* for a very specific reason—namely, to illustrate that Richardson's thematic concepts are not only presented with clarity in the play but are also unmistakably presaged in the body of his earlier writing. It seems especially important to establish these two facts about the play, because an overwhelming majority of the many newspaper and magazine reviewers writing in 1965 not only failed utterly to comprehend Richardson's dramatic intent, but actually took him to task for being obscure. Phrases such as "thick layers of obscurity," "elusive," "fidgety philosophy," "intellectual garbage," "vague in its point," riddle their reviews like so much grapeshot. Some critics claimed to discover no meaning in the play whatsoever, while those reviewers who did take a stab at analyzing the play's meaning came up with the most literal of interpretations.

To Richard Watts of the *New York Post*, the play was "a slender comedy on the manifestations and perversities of the gambling mania." Writing for the *Village Voice*, Julius Novick dismissed the plot as another "familiar" story "about the optimistic ne'er-do-well." To their credit, a few of the critics extended themselves to a greater degree, but their interpretations were just as wildly off the mark. The most thoughtful critique came from Walter Kerr, writing in the New York *Herald Tribune*. While failing, as did his critical colleagues, to see that Richardson was using gambling as a positive rather than a negative metaphor, he did sense that the hero "still has hope [that] the American dream persists," noting shrewdly that "All Americans have always been gamblers, sure that nerve and luck would see them through."

It was obvious that all the critics shared an unswerving tendency to interpret the central gambling metaphor in the most literal sense, as a negative vice. The critic of the critics might fall into the same temptation and view this as gross anti-intellectualism, were it not for the quite extraordinary antagonism—in some cases, actual fury—directed toward Richardson for having somehow "withheld" his meaning from them. Most of the reviews, in fact, simmered with a sense of frustration at being unable to fathom the less palpable meaning which they sensed was present in the play but placed tantalizingly just beyond their grasp.

But rather than simply being intellectually unequipped to penetrate Richardson's meaning, it would appear that the reviewers were actually *blocked* in some fashion. Something closed their minds to Richardson's inverted use of gambling as a positive life-force metaphor. Something stopped them from viewing the gambling act as anything deeper than a representation of the tacky, tawdry values of the false American Dream. That "something" was probably the powerful and rigid Judeo-Christian ethic which has long conditioned us to react on a reflexive level to gambling as a vice and to gamblers as virtueless, or at the least, as misguided persons caught up in the evil power of a "bad habit." Preconditioned by traditional codes of morals and ethics, the reviewers were effectively blinded by their own *moral outrage* to Richardson's meaning, specifically, to Richardson's *inversion* of the metaphor—to gambling as a symbol for an action both exemplary and desirable, one that could bring a man into what Richardson has termed "a state of grace."

Consequently, the reviewers misdirected their anger onto the offendingly unfathomable dramatic metaphor itself—dismissing it as a "frivolous" subject for a serious play—and onto the play's author, for insulting their intellects by tossing them this playful trifle, instead of the serious and important work they had anticipated. On the subject of the critical reaction to his play, Richardson is eloquently scornful. But he rejects the theory that the Judeo-Christian code predisposed the reviewers to misread the symbolism of his play. "I may have misjudged gambling's *power* over the imagination," he semi-concedes, "but it seemed to me a simple metaphor. You have all the elements of chance and all the elements of commitment in gambling. But to a lot of people gambling does seem to be a very trivial occupation, and certainly not something which should be used as a large metaphor. To those people for whom gambling had no meaning, the play seemed to have no substance. I found that unfortunate. But I thought that, in the same way that, say, *Moby Dick* hangs on whaling as a practical occupation, I thought that gambling could feed the larger ideas I had, which were very palpable, concrete items."

While professing a kind of cynical acceptance of the critics' superficial analyses of *Xmas in Las Vegas*, he was more intrigued by the sheer emotional intensity with which these "generally so phlegmatic" men damned his play. "I was really quite surprised to find them emotionally cogent in their outrage." He offers, "At least they *hated* it with a certain amount of fervor." In analyzing their response, he makes a keen distinction between two kinds of plays which he terms "inchoate" and "complex," respectively. "What I call the inchoate play is the play of innuendo," he explains. "In it, everything is obfuscated and every meaning is only hinted at, if indeed it has any meaning at all. But knowing that there is no absolute explicit meaning, the critics can always fall back on notions of mood, and supply their own trivial thoughts on what they think the play is about.

"But a play like mine," he continues, "palpably has meaning, and although that meaning is quite explicit, one must listen to it very carefully. The critics sense that I'm not trying to hide behind anything, but am presenting a thesis with a number of alternatives and colorations and difficulties to it. And I think *that* infuriates them more. They're antagonized not because I'm 'hiding' my meaning from them, but because I'm presenting them with something *complex*, and they don't really *want* to be presented with something complex. It's the very Philistine reaction of any third-rate mind when faced with anything that is demanding."

Given the cavalier fashion in which the reviewers either dismissed or misunderstood the serious and subtly presented thesis of his play, Richardson's attack on them is understandable and to a degree justified. It would be more defensible, however, had he not halfway seduced them into their false pronouncements by virtue of the play's misleading dramatic style. *Xmas in Las Vegas* is a bleak, really quite bitter, black comedy thoroughly in the modern tradition of absurdist humor—a dramatic form difficult to apprehend under the most favorable production conditions. The *Women's Wear Daily* critic, Martin Gottfried, seemed most uncowed by what he called the play's "surreal" comedy. "The play makes few pretenses to realism," he wrote; "Richardson plays it all in cool abstraction. His characters are consistently written as unreal-real."

The remainder of the critics were less unflappable. Although many of them noted the play's absurdist stylistic aspirations, this seemed merely to fan the fires of their antipathy. The consensus was that the stylistic "symbols," of which they were foggily aware, further obfuscated a theme about "the human condition" which God knows they were finding difficult enough to fathom even on its most superficial level.

In one respect, there was justification for their confusion. In an attempt to establish the concrete contemporary basis of his absurdist humor, Richardson had given his play a realistic substructure which frequently assumed a prominence that was intrusive and misleading. "It was not *all* critical misjudgment," Richardson acknowledges. "Obviously, there are debits on both sides of the ledger. There were a lot of elements in the play which were disjointed, and in part, I'm to blame."

Having been led astray by stylistic elements which seemed to indicate that the play was meant to be taken as a conventional family comedy-drama, the reviewers hastened to apply all their traditional critical criteria for that genre. Judged by these conventions, of course, *Xmas* is a disaster. All those stylistic niceties so familiar in the well-made play

—order, cohesiveness, thematic accessibility, logic—all fly out the window in the chaotic reality structure posited by comedy of the absurd. Nonplussed, the *Times*'s Howard Taubman was almost scandalized that Richardson had "neglected" such elements as "conflict, character development, and suspense."

In retrospect, Richardson acknowledges the stylistic inconsistencies of which he had been guilty. "My frailties in this are as culpable as anybody else's," he says. "People were confused by the fact that the play did present itself as a realistic play, and this confusion was partly my fault. I wanted to invest Las Vegas with as much reality as possible. I didn't want everything to be taking place in Limbo, or on a ramp, or in a garbage can. The empirical trappings of the play were realistic— a real set, contemporary people. It was a real family, and they had normal names; they were not called Erg or Bul. I wanted to prove to myself, too, that one need not put everything of importance outside the realm of four walls. I think human beings can behave in an extraordinary way within an ordinary environment. They don't have to be hanging in the cosmos or lying in a dustbin.

"Well, as usual in the theater, when you try to be too subtle you get hoisted by your own petard. All they saw on stage seemed to indicate a light Broadway family comedy, and there are certain rules which determine such a genre. After ten minutes, one knew that according to the theatrical regulations for a light family comedy, this play was a complete failure. People were talking too long, lines weren't snappy enough, speeches rambled on, the behavior was disjointed, and so forth. That was not only a critical confusion, but it also confused most of the audience."

If the critics' confusion about the play's basic stylistic ambiguities of realistic and absurdist humor is somewhat understandable, their evaluation of the play's linguistic structure is not. Even the most cursory reading of *Xmas in Las Vegas* reveals its author to be a writer of exceptional—perhaps extraordinary—talent and craftsmanship. Although not always reconciled to dramatic form, Richardson's language is always precise, metaphorically rich, and often not less than aesthetically dazzling. And yet, Howard Taubman carped that "its brightness often degenerates into the sophomoric and chichi. Its eloquence tends to be ostentatious fanciness. These are flaws of callowness . . . Mr. Richardson is infatuated with the sound of his own voice." "There are endless monologues from everybody, dreary soul-searching," wrote John Mc-Clain of Richardson's brilliant dialogue. *Variety* was especially appalled that Richardson was "unable to control his love of words." There is a very real problem here, and one which has helped to impede the modern theater's development—namely, a strong bias for "natural" theatrical language and a disinclination to allow this popular art form the "unnatural" linguistic intricacies of, say, poetry, or the novel.

Still more dismaying than the reviewers' aggressive insensitivity to Richardson's masterly use of language was their almost gleeful pronouncement that the fair-haired wonder-boy whom they had praised so lavishly for *Gallows Humor*, and especially for *The Prodigal*, had failed to live up to the great "promise" which they had decreed for his future career. The *Village Voice's* Julius Novick was more apoplectic than most, demanding, "What is there to say about a dramatist who started out as 'promising' and then got worse? On the evidence of *Xmas in Las Vegas*, there are two possible conclusions respecting Mr. Richardson: either his play-writing talent has been strangled . . . or else he had no play-writing talent to begin with."

There is interesting material for speculation in the phenomenon of critical overpraise and consequent abandonment of "promising" writers. Like a son, the favored playwright's early promise reflects, in a fashion, on the acumen of the parent-figure critic who "discovered" him; that is, just so long as the surrogate son follows the dramatic direction expected of him. But like any real son, the playwright runs the risk of being disowned, or at least severely chastised, the moment he chooses a road of individual development contrary to the elder's preconceived expectations. The analogy is especially apt when applied to the career of Jack Richardson. His earlier play, *The Prodigal*, was misinterpreted by his critical admirers as a conventional historical drama, rather than as a symbolic treatment of modern man in ideological conflict with himself over the necessity for commitment to the political issues of his day. Under the circumstances of their having similarly misinterpreted *Xmas*—judging it a "frivolous" family comedy—it is no wonder that the critics were outraged at his betrayal.

Recognizing the irony of the situation, Richardson notes, "There is a tendency, in American criticism, to overpraise an early work, and then to resent having done that, and then to snipe away for the rest of the writer's career. Every critic likes to "discover" someone, but he doesn't like to have to go on praising him all the time. When I wrote *The Prodigal*, people like Walter Kerr and Richard Watts thought they had another noble, uplifting, deep-thinking classicist. And that, of course, wasn't my style at all. It always amused me that the critics wrote such outsized eulogies about that play. Subsequently, my attitude and style of theater just seemed to drift further and further away from what they considered my teleological 'in'—what I was destined to be— which seemed to be a sort of spokesman for genteel philosophy on the stage, with a little bit of irony and a good sense of language."

Although there can be little serious question that the critics failed to penetrate Richardson's thematic metaphor in *Xmas in Las Vegas;* that they erred, too, in interpreting its stylistic construct; and that they greatly undervalued the sheer craftsmanship of the play; nevertheless, to "blame" them for these critical lapses is to shift attention from a rather more important point—the Broadway theater's traditional audiences wouldn't have liked the play much more than they did. The critics, after all, are a pretty fair bellwether group, and their miscomprehension of the play, just as much as their negative critical consensus, was sure to be reflected in the responses of the play's audiences. Rather, their reaction to *Xmas* should be read as indication that the play was beset by yet another set of problems—specifically, in terms of its production.

Jack Richardson is clearly a writer of intellectual complexity, and one quite incapable of churning out formula Broadway comedies. Ideally, his play should have been produced off Broadway, preferably by a producing operation like Ted Mann's Circle in the Square or Wynn Handman's American Place Theater, with their past history for sensitive productions of unusual works, and with their built-in minority audience of intellectually oriented theatergoers. This is not to say that the play couldn't have succeeded on Broadway as well, but under quite different circumstances. The basic and quite devastating flaw of the 1965 production was the fact that, instead of observing an integrity to the play's intrinsic oddities of style and substance, the producers chose instead to *bend* it into conformity with Broadway convention.

For their part, a good many of the critics were critical of the play's physical production. Some, like *Newsday's* George Oppenheimer, criticized director-producer Fred Coe for his "solemn direction" and "prosaic staging." A few agreed with Norman Nadel's judgment, stated in the *World-Telegram and Sun,* on the "prevailing inadequacy of the acting." And more than a few commented on the scenery, which, according to *Variety's* Hobe Morrison, was "architecturally illogical," as well as unfunctional. Most critics, however, while sensing the inadequacies of the physical production, chose to cast the blame at the writer's feet.

"They always attack the writer," Jack Richardson sanguinely observes. "I've never known a playwright to escape general condemnation, no matter how poorly his play is done. Critics never say, for example, 'This was a fine play ruined by an inept performance or by the incredibly poor direction,' because critics aren't aware of this. They've been watching theater all their lives, and they have no idea that there's a question of execution involved in the theater, the way there is in music."

Richardson's overstated, but still valid case against the critics should not distract from a central and crucial misconception in the play's production. This was the artistic decision to underscore the play's realistic and family-comedy elements (thereby hoping to make it pass muster with Broadway audiences in search of conventional comedy), while at the same time to underplay the play's darker, absurdist-humor elements (a bit too intellectual and "fruity" for popular consumption). What resulted was a production both intrinsically and physically schizophrenic, one partly expressionistic and partly realistic. "Neither fish nor fowl," producer-director Fred Coe admits.

A gentle, soft-spoken, and eminently likable man, with a quite decent track record (*Two for the Seesaw, The Miracle Worker, All the Way Home, A Thousand Clowns*), Fred Coe is a living refutation of the cliché image of the Broadway producer as a hard-as-nails cigar-chewer. The behind-the-scenes story he told of the *Xmas* debacle was a saga of mistakes and miscalculations, made within a system which doesn't allow for second chances. According to Coe, who now feels that the play "probably belonged more in some off Broadway experimental theater," the key decision at the time was to produce the play on Broadway and in accordance with Broadway production traditions, which decision necessitated, first of all, the engagement of a star. The "star syndrome" of Broadway producing states categorically that unless your play has been written by someone named Neil Simon or Arthur Miller, you'd better cast a "name" personality in the lead role if you expect to pull in an audience. Accordingly, Coe made overtures to his first choice for the part, Bob Hope, who wasn't interested.

If acquiescing to the tyranny of the star system was the first mistake made by Coe and his associates, engaging Tom Ewell for the lead was the second. "We spent a great deal of time and a great deal of energy twisting his arm and using all kinds of pressure to put the wrong man in the part," is the succinct way Fred Coe put it. "Tom resisted this role—he probably knew more about himself than we did. But I personally pressured him," he says. "Tom and I went back a long time, all the way to college, and he had a certain kind of faith in me. But I found that the worst thing you can do is to put somebody in a play where you've pressured him into doing it. It's already starting off on your left foot."

"I hadn't wanted to take the role," Tom Ewell says, recalling the concerted wooing campaign. "On first reading the script I didn't find it particularly interesting. And I didn't find the part interesting. And I didn't find the humor that Fred saw in the show. Fred would talk about the show and just *laugh*. And I didn't know what he was talking about, because I didn't think it was funny." What finally convinced Ewell to sit on his misgivings was a luncheon discussion with the late Harold Freedman, Jack Richardson's agent, who, according to Ewell, convinced him that *Xmas in Las Vegas* would be an important play and one that would usher in a new theatrical wave. "Well," recalls Ewell, "I thought to myself, I've been wrong a great many times in my life. And I want to try something new. If there's going to be a new wave, I want to be wafted in on it."

It is hardly discrediting to an actor's talent that he is simply unsuitable for certain roles. Today, each of the key figures involved in the *Xmas in Las Vegas* production acknowledges that Tom Ewell was the wrong actor in the wrong part—including Tom Ewell. But what is really under analysis here is not Ewell's talent, or even his suitability in the part of Edward T. Wellspot, but rather the effect his casting had upon the intrinsic nature of the play and consequently upon its production.

Primarily, it heightened the initial production mistake of emphasizing the play's realistic elements, to the detriment of its abstract qualities. From Ewell's own statements, it is apparent that he was ill-attuned intellectually to the play's meaning—a fact which nettled him very much—and emotionally not in empathy with its absurdist humor—something which unsettled him even more. Theater people are fond of quoting a Bert Lahr story to illustrate that a star need not always be on the same wavelength as his material. When asked how he could play Samuel Beckett's intellectually abstruse *Waiting for Godot*, Lahr reportedly replied, "That's easy. I just play: What is this crazy play all about?"

But Ewell is quite another case. Ewell was rankled that the play's "meaning" was eluding him. An intelligent man with an impulse to probe his material, he communicated on stage the confusion, frustration, and intellectual insecurity with which the play afflicted him.

"I never did completely understand the character," Ewell says, in tones suggesting frustration mixed with self-doubt. "I never really got to the core of him. There were times when something would happen, and out of somewhere would emerge this marvelous character. I wish I knew where he came from and how I got him." Ewell, Coe, and Richardson all agree that the star's main drawback was his tendency toward literal and concrete, rather than abstract and poetic, apprehension of the play and its central character. Ewell illustrated the problem by revealing a few specific reservations he had about the play. It disturbed him, for example, that in one of the scenes a character returns from the Nevada desert with sunburn and heat stroke. "Everyone who's been out there knows that in Vegas, at that time of the year, you never have that kind of weather," he says. "At Christmastime, it's really quite chilly there, out on the high desert." He was also unsettled by the fact that Edward T. Wellspot "talks a lot." "Gamblers don't talk," Ewell says. "I've observed gamblers in casinos around the world, and those people who gamble, they don't talk. Their minds are working on the odds. The people in this play talk and talk and talk and talk. That doesn't happen with real gamblers."

Ewell's concern for what was "real" consistently unnerved the director and author, who apparently failed to assuage his need for a realistic dramatic landscape. "As an actor, Tom is a highly literal person," Fred Coe says. "His acting technique is a very rational method. But this is the kind of play that defies rationalization. You have to go with it, give yourself to it. If you're always *fighting* it for literal explanation, then you can kill it, because the play often defies you on those terms."

The miscasting was especially ironic, because, in a sense, Ewell was exactly the kind of actor they wanted. He *is* a Broadway comedy star, and was certainly capable of supplying the light-family-comedy image the producers had deemed necessary for the success of the show. What Ewell couldn't resolve was the producers' own ambiguous attitude toward the play, their hope to reconcile a potentially lucrative "laff-riot" image for the play with its deeper and infinitely more complex reality as a black philosophical comedy.

If Ewell's central position in the play weighted the conventional and realistic aspect of its schizophrenic nature, it had an even more pronounced effect on the physical creation of the production. In what Richardson terms "a tawdry, sordid experience," there was the incident, during the Philadelphia tryout, of the replacement of the show's original director, George Sherman, because of an artistic conflict with Ewell. "I don't really feel that he understood the play," Ewell says.

"At least, if he did understand the play, he certainly didn't communicate it to me." To Jack Richardson, "It was a question of whether Sherman would go or whether Tom Ewell would go. We could function without Sherman, but there was no way we could function without Tom Ewell. We couldn't possibly bring in another lead actor at that point."

Richardson's evaluation of the trouble in Philadelphia raises a very important point about the rigid conventions of the Broadway producing system. Why, indeed, could not the play's artistic creators release the star or the director, or even both, if they saw that the production was not developing in the direction they desired? According to both Coe and Richardson, it had become clear to all at this point that the production had been misconceived in the conventional family-comedy vein, and that its darker and more dramatically significant side would have to be given the prominence it deserved if the play's original merit were to be rescued. Richardson answers the question best when he says, "It takes a long time before you can see what a play is—much longer than you generally have in the commercial theater." Up until the Philadelphia opening, he says, they were involved with immediate problems concerning specific technical areas, just trying to get the play's scenes to coalesce into a single unit. "Gradually, one did see that there were certain problems with the overall style, the total presentation," Richardson says, "but not until one had spent one's time working on the most obvious problems. Most of our work was concentrated on making the play as vital, as lively, and as un-moribund as possible, within the structure that we had decided on. An overall conceptual change would have demanded a complete rethinking of everything I'd written. If we had had another month—and perhaps another half-million dollars—we would have tried it."

The American commercial theater, as Richardson well knows, is not constructed on the "developing-creation" principle, whereby the creative talents involved have the luxury of redirecting the thrust of their continually evolving production. Outside of subsidized theaters, continually operating repertory companies, and experimental semiprofessional groups with special contracts with the crafts' and actors' unions —rare birds indeed, in this country—the commercial theater is structured on rigid timetables and large but unexpandable budgets, neither of which can be compromised for mere artistic considerations. "If a play starts to go off in the wrong direction," Jack Richardson says, from experience, "it can go off in the wrong direction for two weeks before you halt it. And it's a long and laborious process to bring it back in line, if you can ever do it." Broadway is indeed a machine, and one whose mechanism, once set into motion, moves ahead with an inexorable energy.

Like the play's script, like Ewell's performance, and like Coe's overall directorial concept, the scenic designs suffered from the same sense of schizophrenic ambiguity which plagued the production on its most basic level and made it subject to Broadway's "inexorable machine." The critics and the play's creators—from Coe and Richardson to the set designer himself, Robert Randolph—all agree that the scene in the gambling casino played best, struck the audience most potently, and had the most effective set. And yet, this scene was the most abstract one of the entire show, even to its set, which was, in Fred Coe's words, "an impressive set and an impressive scene. The set had the marvelous device of an overhanging mirror, so that the playing of the cards and the chips could be seen by the audience. The set and the entire scene had a marvelous feel to it." Tom Ewell, in fact, earned his best reviews for the "marvelous" scene which he played on this "impressive" set.

Yet, the play's other set, the Las Vegas hotel room of the Wellspots, was criticized by several reviewers, scorned by Richardson, and "hated" by Coe. While the word used most frequently to indicate approbation of the gambling-scene set was "impressionistic," the words applied to the hotel-room set were "lumbering," "awkward," and "literal"—which all indicate that the set, like the total production, was too earthbound, too grounded in the reality of the light comedy. Actually, this is not surprising, since Robert Randolph's specialty as a set designer is in the field of the Broadway musical. Randolph shows, through his work on such shows as *Golden Rainbow* and *Applause*, that his forte is elaborate production design, not expressionistic design.

Interestingly enough, Randolph reveals that his hotel-room set gradually became *more* realistic as the production progressed. "The thing originally had gambling devices all over the place," he says. "These were all eliminated, so that the hotel-room bar became just a bar, not one with all the gadgets around it. It became less of a zany place and more realistic, especially with the props."

Both the irony and the agony of what Fred Coe called a "debacle" of a production is that all its movers and shakers became aware of their specific mistakes, but were forced to watch their production blunder onward in the wrong direction because the mechanistic nature of the Broadway production system made it impossible for them to correct their errors. Once it became apparent that one of Randolph's sets was not what they had anticipated from his original sketch of it, the producers were unable to have the set redesigned and replaced. They had neither the money nor the time to do anything more than "doctor" the offending set, which emerged finally as more restrictively realistic than had been intended at the outset. Similarly, and on a more crucial level, once it was unavoidably obvious that Ewell was miscast in the lead, the only salvation Coe saw was to take over the direction himself and devote himself to working on Ewell's interpretation of the role. Since Coe had had such a difficult time casting the part to begin with, and since he would be compounding the risk if he brought in a new lead in mid-production, to replace Ewell entirely seemed to him foolhardy— if indeed it was possible at all. Most unlikely of all was the possibility of reevaluating and redirecting the production's first and most costly error, the misguided decision to "go Broadway" and emphasize the script's most accessible level of meaning, its elements of light family comedy. Inexorable. Once switched on, the Broadway machine is a remorselessly inexorable force.

Today, listening to Richardson talk about his intentions in *Xmas in Las Vegas* is to be swept by an almost painful desire to see the play revived—by a director like Alan Arkin, perhaps, who rescued from oblivion Jules Feiffer's black comedy, *Little Murders*—and cast with a mad crew of Second City stalwarts.

"There would be many alterations that I would make," Jack Richardson says. "I would certainly emphasize the extremities of the play, rather than the domesticity of it. I would not worry about the humor of the play, or worry about establishing a reality notion of the play. I'd let the play drift with a great deal more freedom than it did. I would look for a set that would give one the idea that *more* was taking place than a family's jaunt to Las Vegas—a set with a great deal more use of space, to emphasize the terror and mystery of the play, rather than the homeliness of the play. I would generally look for a much rougher production—something much more intense, to avoid the notion of calm at all, to impress upon an audience that *everyone* in the play should feel under threat of execution, of being snuffed out, of having their lives completely butchered."

To complete the ironic story of this unusual production, Tom Ewell had a flash of insight right in the middle of our interview, six years after the production of *Xmas*. "I think I understand the play now," he announced. "I suddenly realize that it should have been a nightmare. I suddenly realize that it should have been a nightmare about some very mad people. It was the *madness* that we failed to capture. And the *terror* that happens in a nightmare. Even when you experience nice things in a nightmare, there's always a sense of doom about it. That was the key to it, and I never captured it."

If this chapter illustrates anything about theater, it is that the theater, because it is a collaborative form of art, is in constant evolution, and individual productions go through a long and complex production before they can be said to "exist." But because the Broadway system of production does not acknowledge that process; because tradition and economics determine that a production must go through so many weeks of rehearsal, so many weeks of tryouts, so many weeks of previews, and then do or die in one night, many a play whose process of creation demands a longer period of evolution automatically becomes a "flop." As far as I am concerned, Jack Richardson's *Xmas in Las Vegas* is the farthest thing from a flop. It is a profound play still in the process of being created.

JOHNNY
NO-TRUMP

by Mary Mercier

CAST OF CHARACTERS

HARRY ARMSTRONG

MRS. FRANKLIN

JOHN EDWARDS

FLORENCE EDWARDS

ALEXANDER EDWARDS

BETTINA

NOTES

The time is February, 1965, and the first act takes place on a rainy Saturday. The second act on a cold, sunny Sunday.

The locale is Jefferson, a small town on Long Island.

The people are fifth-generation Americans, and with the exception of Bettina, in dress, hair style and general air, they are unvarnished.

The house they live in is old, and it shows the mark along with the mementos of several generations. The action takes place in the living room, which was originally "the parlor." The room therefore has a dual character—the original design of the parlor, and what has since been imposed upon it. A breakfast nook has been added D.L., because the family no longer eats out in the kitchen. When central heating came, the fireplace fell into disuse, and is now a place to pile up magazines. Many bookshelves along with cupboards have been built, U.L.C. The wallpaper has seen better days, and part of the furniture is solid. D.L. is a door that leads to the kitchen. The front door opens into a hallway at U.R., and under the landing, U.L.C. is a door leading to the basement. U.C. is a curbed staircase with a small landing part way up. This, and the upper landing leading to the bedrooms, are also acting areas.

NOTE FOR ACTORS

Nearly all of the people in this play love each other, and no matter what they ask of one another, it is all done in the name of love rather than anything else. In other words, I have not meant anyone to be singled out as a "villain." They are what they are, and I have tried to be fair to them, so hopefully actors will also be fair to the characters and leave it to the audience to decide who is right or wrong.

Act One

SCENE I

Prior to rise of curtain, the sound of heavy rain coming down in gusts, gradually petering off until it becomes a soft steady murmur.

The curtain rises on UNCLE HARRY, *a heavyset man somewhat on the short side. He sits at a table R. drinking coffee, totally absorbed in a tabloid. As he reads over various headlines and ads, he is given to grunting "Huh!" or "How about that!"*

After a while, MRS. FRANKLIN, *a neighbor, lets herself in through the front door. She wears a full apron and holds a raincoat up over her head. This, she shakes out, and hangs on a peg in hallway. As she carefully wipes her feet on the doormat, she surveys both the room and* HARRY, *who never looks up. She deliberately makes a noise taking cleaning equipment from a closet, while* HARRY *just as deliberately keeps her "tuned out."*

MRS. FRANKLIN (*Standing in hallway*). We-e-ell, I'm here. . . . (*No response.*) I got a full day. . . . (*No response.*) Saturday means work. . . . Mmmmmm. (*She now takes out more equipment from the closet. At this point* JOHN *emerges onto the upper landing from his bedroom. He wears old pajamas with an old robe, and is toweling his hair dry.* JOHN *is short, thin, wears glasses, and has an "odd" look to him. He is very much the opposite of an all-American boy. He dawdles downstairs, traces patterns on the carpet, and half-slides the banister—all of which makes his descent into a production.* JOHN *also sings snatches of songs which, together with* MRS. FRANKLIN's *noise, make* HARRY *squirm around in his seat.* MRS. FRANKLIN *meets* JOHN *on stairway as she goes up—puts out a warning hand.*) Stay outa trouble! (*She passes him, then looks back.*) Brighten the corner where you are! Remember that!

JOHN. Yes, ma'm. You get me that book?

MRS. FRANKLIN (*Goes on up*). You'll see tomorrow. And don't make noise. Your Nanna's asleep. And just you brighten the corner where you are. (*She exits into a bedroom.* JOHN *continues on downstairs. He looks over at* HARRY *when he reaches the bottom step.*)

HARRY (*Looks up for the first time*). You up?

JOHN (*Pauses*). No-o-o. . . . (*They stare at each other.*) I'm still in bed. (JOHN *has a dry humor, and when he and* HARRY *are together there is always a hint of danger.* JOHN *goes to desk, U.L.C., and sits in a swivel chair that creeks as he rocks. He takes binoculars out of desk drawer and regards* HARRY *through them.* HARRY *goes back to his paper.*) Wanna know where Mother went?

HARRY (*Turns a page*). You're gonna be late for school.

JOHN. On Saturday?

HARRY. This is Saturday? . . . (*He checks date on paper.*) Huh! Howdya like that? Another week gone. . . . Feels like a Friday to me. . . . Coulda sworn it was a Friday. . . . Feels like it should be pay-day. Always got paid of a Friday. Mmmmmm. . . . Get your breakfast then.

JOHN. Not hungry.

HARRY. Take yourself a walk then. Don't sit creakin' in that chair.

JOHN (*Continues to rock in chair*). Coming down cats and dogs.

HARRY (*Sitting in a window seat, is able to pull back a curtain*). Still? You're kiddin'. . . . Oh, my God, look at that! . . . Now that is rain . . . that is certainly rain! . . . Huh! . . . Can't even trust the weather—sun was up when I first come down. . . . We-e-ell, it's good for the ground, look on the bright side, good for the ground. (*Sits back in his place.*) Too bad. Ya couda pulled a few weeds for me today.

JOHN (*Still looking through binoculars*). Uncle Harry?

HARRY (*Puts out a warning hand*). I can see it comin'—the answer's no.

JOHN (*Ponders*). Do you . . . ?

HARRY (*Returns to his paper*). Do I what? No.

JOHN (*Starts to bait* HARRY). Do you believe in . . . ?

HARRY. Believe in nuthin', no. Macy got a sale I see.

JOHN. Do you . . . ?

HARRY (*Looks up*). Ya got a question, ask! Don't keep messin' with it. "Do you, do you?" Ask! The answer's no! Ya want dough? NO!

JOHN. You think there are actual *places* . . . I mean, do you believe in actual places . . . I mean, do you think heaven and hell are . . .

HARRY (*Returns to his paper*). Oh-h-h, don't be a pipsqueak.

JOHN. When you die, can you picture yourself lined up in front of a . . .

HARRY. I'm as strong as a horse, don't talk about me dying. Wanna depress me at nine o'clocka day?

JOHN. Ten o'clock. Do you ever get sorry for God?

HARRY. What ?

JOHN. Think He keeps office hours? Shows from nine to five, shuffles around His papers, groans and mutters to Himself, "My God, have I got some boobs down there"?

HARRY (*Points a finger*). This is gonna be . . . a quiet day. And I'm not foolin' with ya, so there. Ya take sides just to get arguments. And I got a personal God and it's nobody's business, so there. (*Attempts to read paper.*)

JOHN. A personal God? . . . Do you have a personal Devil then?

HARRY. NO!

JOHN (*Rocks in the chair*). Oh. . . . That's very lucky, isn't it?

HARRY. Discuss it to yourself, AND! You're gonna break that chair, which is a memory piece of your grandmother's! (*They stare at each other.*) And I got no personal Devil unless he's you.

JOHN (*Stands up*). Now, that's very interesting, Mr. Armstrong. Could my paper have your views? Because my paper's wondering how you manage to get a God without a Devil, seeing as how they're thought to travel in pairs.

HARRY. Aw! Sit down and go and get dressed! You're gettin' a fresh mouth worse than your old woman. This is gonna be . . . a quiet day! . . . Understand! . . . Not that carry-on from last week. And what you doin' with my towel? Happens that's offa my rack. Learn hygiene! Keep clean and ya go a distance, believe me. And cut your hair, it's halfway down your back. (JOHN *towels his hair.*) And do that in the bathroom. A time and a place. Learn that. A place and a time!

MRS. FRANKLIN (*Leans over banister*). Oh, shush! (*To* JOHN.) You eating yet?

JOHN. Yeah.

MRS. FRANKLIN (*Collects some laundry together on landing*). You are not! Get your juice! People should eat first thing or they get all kinds wrong. There'd be a lot less trouble around, and a few brighter corners, if everybody ate three squares a day, and took a good three-mile walk!

JOHN (*Wraps towel into a turban*). And slept with someone three times a week.

HARRY (*Slowly*). What . . . did you say?

JOHN (*Innocently*). Mrs. Franklin felt there'd be lots less trouble around if we all ate well, and exercised. And I agreed they should sleep well too. Just a remark.

MRS. FRANKLIN. I didn't mention nothin' private!

HARRY (*To* JOHN). I heard ya the first time, AND!! . . . Make no sex jokes around HERE!

JOHN. Yessir. Shhh. (*Points to ceiling.*) Nanna's asleep.

HARRY. This is a clean home!

JOHN. Yessir.

HARRY. A clean one!

JOHN. Yessir, I'll take your word for it.

HARRY. I am not a puritan but I believe in a clean mind!

JOHN. Right.

HARRY. YA HEAR?

JOHN (*In loud whisper*). It was only an observation. . . .

HARRY (*Points his finger—in loud whisper*). Because I'll tell your mother! And keep your opinions quiet! And be still, and find something to do! . . . Now then! . . . Huh! (*Returns to his paper.*) A little PEACE!

JOHN (*Shrugs to* MRS. FRANKLIN). I'm reading a book on it, that's all. . . .

HARRY (*Throws down paper*). BOOKS AND AGGRAVATION! That's all there is to this house! Ya sit with the paper and whaddya get? Irritation and nervousness. (*He glares at* JOHN.) Opinions! (*Slaps the newspaper.*) TOO MUCH FREEDOM! That's what they all got! These schnooky creepy kids! What happened yesterday right on the open streets of New York? An old man of seventy-nine, *seventy-nine* mind you, got beaten up and robbed of fifty-four cents. . . . *Fifty-four* cents. By eight-year-olds. . . . *Eight*-year-olds. Give 'em THE CHAIR . . . LENIENCE . . . TOO MUCH THEY GOT.

When I was a *child*, if I didn't listen to my *father*, he used to smack me from here to outside, WHOOSH!	JOHN (*Repeats with him*). When I was a *child*, if I didn't listen to my *father*, he used to smack me from here to outside, WHOOSH!

HARRY (*After a pause*). A backhander, that's what ya got, that's what came your way. Which meant ya got very familiar with the back of his hand! (*Demonstrates.*) WHOOSH! And ya learned you P's and Q's all right. Sat up and took notice good! WHOOSH! Are ya listenin'?

JOHN. Always.

HARRY. Yeah, yeah, always what?

JOHN (*Gets up and heads for kitchen*). Yeah, yeah, you always lis-

BERT ANDREWS

tened to your father. And he used to smash you from here to there BINGO! Because he didn't care for freedom, BINGO! Which naturally means that in the good old golden days all the kids were angels . . . which is very strange when you consider WHAT SOME OF THEM GREW UP TO BE! (*He disappears into kitchen.*)

HARRY. Oh, awright you, just go to your room. Get in your room and keep outa my path for the rest of the day.

JOHN (*Sings in the kitchen*). "In the good old golden days. . . ."

HARRY. One more squeak from you . . .

JOHN. I thought you promised me a quiet day!

HARRY. Well, that settles it! Boy, ya bin in a mean mood for a week, and I shoulda known by the way ya futzed around comin' down those stairs we was headed for trouble! And that settles it! I've a good mind not to give ya any birthday gift, and I got sometin' great for ya! Ya hear that? Ya missin' out on somethin' *great*! Ya got no respect, none! You're just loadin' yourself up with opinions and meanness. What the hell you'll wind up as is a good mystery story. Just another smartass, and I don't wanna hear another word. Not one more WORD! Ya hear me? Don't speak no more!

JOHN (*Enters, eating cold toast*). How about a . . .

HARRY. No!

JOHN. Or a little . . .

HARRY (*Points his finger*). RUSSIA! . . . That's the place for you . . . down the salt mines! With the REDS! . . . They'd make ya work for your keep. Everythin' ya got here! (JOHN *repeating with him.*) Meals on the table. Soft bed to sleep in. But there's no thanks. (*Pauses.*) We-e-ell, it's O.K. . . . I'm glad I'm not your father. No skin offa my nose how ya end up. (*Turns the pages of his paper.*) Old folks don't matter anymore. . . . Youth's taken over. . . . The women and kids took over. . . . That's all right . . . they know it all . . . THE SHIP IS HEADED FOR THE ROCKS! . . . Apart from that, we're gonna be fine! (*The phone rings.*) Who the hell's that? Tell 'em nobody's in! Some goddam salesman hawkin' encyclopedias we don't need thank ya very much!

JOHN (*Picks up phone*). We're not in.

HARRY. Who is it? Don't fool around.

JOHN (*Into phone*). Gee, no . . . no . . . no. . . . Our Uncle Harry passed away years ago. We were broken up. . . .

HARRY (*Jumps up*). Hey! Quit that kid stuff. (*Grabs phone.*) Speak up! Who are ya? . . . They've gone now! (*Replaces phone.*) Was that for me? Ya nitwit, who was it? . . . (*Tracks* JOHN *around desk and tries to whack at him with the newspaper.*)

JOHN (*Backs away and whispers loudly*). The Russians, and they've landed on Long Island. But it's O.K. I've got the code and I think I can break it. Gimme a second. (*Exaggerates thinking.*) Wait, wait, WAIT! . . . I hear voices . . . "John" . . . "fight the English" . . . "go to Lorraine."

HARRY (*Attempts another whack*). Did it occur to you somebody just wasted a whole hard-earned dime? Ya halfwit! And they gotta run around now lookin' for another coin to make the call again! . . . Ah-h-h. . . . (*Shuffles back to his place.*) School. Wish they'd keep you kids locked in seven days a week. Who was it? Sayin' I was dead. Wanna bring me bad luck? For God's sake do your homework.

JOHN. It's done. And could you up my allowance please, or else I'm gonna take payola for doing other guys' themes for them.

HARRY. Somebody just wasted their dime.

MRS. FRANKLIN (*Comes downstairs. Sees* JOHN *eating toast*). Is that your breakfast?

JOHN. Yeah.

MRS. FRANKLIN. Gonna get malnutrition. And ya woke the old lady up with your noise and nonsense. (*Exits into kitchen.*)

JOHN (*Looks toward kitchen*). Brighten the corner where you are! (*Takes a paperback from his pocket and reads at random.*) "Hold your tongue," said the Queen, turning purple. "I won't," said Alice. (*He flips some pages.*) The White Rabbit put on his spectacles. "Where shall I begin, please, Your Majesty?" "Begin at the beginning," the King said, very gravely, "and go on till you come to the end: then stop." There was dead silence in the court . . .

HARRY (*Looks at* JOHN *and shakes his head*). I tell you, it beats me. . . . Bet ya never give it a thought.

JOHN. What?

HARRY (*Attempts great understanding and patience*). Talk nice to me once, and answer me this—what the hell you gonna be? That's what I'd give dollars to find out. Ever give it consideration? Whatcha gonna do when it comes time to put on a shirt and collar and act responsible? Sometimes I try to picture you ten years from now . . . and my mind, well, a fog comes over it.

JOHN. It does? A fog?

HARRY. Yeah.

JOHN. Yeah? . . . A real fog, huh?

HARRY. Whatcha gonna make of yaself?

JOHN (*Takes a long pause, then faces away from* HARRY—*to an imaginary person*). Take a letter. . . . Mr. Harold Armstrong, 31 Jefferson Road, Jefferson, Long Island, New York. . . . Uh? . . . With regards to your kind inquiry, concerning the intentions of Mr. John Edwards, he begs me to inform you, that this matter has been given . . . a great deal of thought . . . time . . . attention . . . and emotional . . . investment. And he might consider discussing such . . . (*Walks over to* HARRY) if . . . underline that if . . . *if* . . . you do not let loose the cat from the bag . . . and tell his *mother*.

HARRY. Your *mother!* Who can say two words? I'd as soon face brick walls. Whadya plan? (JOHN *unwraps a piece of gum.*) Whatcha got cookin'?

JOHN. Huh?

HARRY. Huh? . . . Gonna join the Navy, let's hope.

JOHN. Yeah, well, forget it. Where's my origami set?

HARRY. There ya go. Force up a subject, then back out in a piggy mean fashion. "Forget it," he says.

JOHN (*Walks around*). You see those birds?

HARRY. Realize how mean it is . . .

JOHN. I'm not gonna be anything.

HARRY. And ya can say that several times. Huh!

JOHN. Not gonna be anything, not gonna be anything, huh!

HARRY. Huh!

JOHN (*Makes a Frankenstein face*). Huh!

HARRY. Awright, awright, enough. (JOHN *finds the origami set and snips away at a paper bird.*) Ya got no cards worth layin' on the table. (*Mutters as he reads his paper.*) Piggy mean. . . . Whole bunch of yas selfish . . . and your mother's as bad. . . . My right arm she's had one time or another . . . my two arms for that matter. . . . We-ee-ll ya get a paste in the puss from everybody, regardless what ya give 'em. . . . Even my own mother up there. "A fat stupid lummox" she called me yesterday . . . in front of a stranger . . . a fat lummox. . . .

JOHN. Aw, quit getting sorry for yourself. . . .

HARRY. I was a skinny kid, so I ate up, so's they wouldn't call me Scarecrow. So now I'm fat. Fat Harry. . . . And you don't love me either.

JOHN. Cut it out, will ya? . . . If you promise not to tell . . . a real promise, cross your heart and all, because I have to put it to mother at the right time. . . .

HARRY (*He crosses his heart indifferently*). Sure.

JOHN. Do it properly.

HARRY. What?

JOHN. Cross your heart. (HARRY *does so.*) And hope to die.

HARRY (*Makes a face*). Aw, ya keep on mentionin' death to an older person. BE SENSITIVE!

JOHN. Well, just cross your heart again then.

HARRY (*Does so with great exaggeration*). For God's sake, here! . . . So? . . . Yeah?

JOHN. See.

HARRY. Well?

JOHN. If I . . . ?

HARRY (*Pauses*). Yeah?

JOHN (*Pauses*). No, nothing. Forget it. (*He walks away.*)

HARRY. What no nothing?

JOHN (*Walks further away*). Nothing, no.

HARRY. What nothing no?

JOHN. Nothing! Nothing!

HARRY. WHAT? NOTHING NOTHING!

JOHN. NOTHING!

HARRY (*Pauses*). What grade you in?

JOHN. Forget it I said. You wouldn't understand.

HARRY. Don't tell me then, I don't wanna know. How come it's so hard to get out? Whatcha wanna be? A *fence* or something? A *bookie*?

JOHN. People make this thing into a joke that's all. I mentioned it to a few guys one time and all it got was a big laugh.

HARRY. Laugh! Gimme a laugh, I'll give ya two bucks. All you did today was carry on about a next world. Listen, be a dentist! See that bill I got over there? The lousy crooks, they're sockin' it away! And! . . . And! . . . You would mention to *guys* . . . just *guys* around . . . somethin' ya wouldn't tell me? Answer me if that's nice, when I'm your flesh and blood.

JOHN. Will you shut up if I tell ya? . . .

HARRY. Well, O.K. then . . .

JOHN. Well, all right then. . . .

HARRY. Don't tell me unless ya want to, so speak!

JOHN (*Pauses*). We-ell . . . first of all . . . I'm not saying I can *be* one . . . but I would like to *try* . . . have time to *try* . . . you understand. Because it involves . . . oh-h, things like . . . sitting . . . and staring.

HARRY (*Pauses*). Sitting and staring?

JOHN. Well, like staring at grass.

HARRY (*Pauses*). Staring at *grass*?

JOHN. And wondering and thinking, and taking time out to think, and loafing, and wandering around and looking . . . and trying to dig what's happening, and reading a lot, and it's not *easy* . . . in fact it's definitely *difficult* . . . and there's a lot to it . . . a *lot*, believe me, and I mean I do it all the time . . . but you don't blab about it, because a private . . . a privacy . . . is a private thing right? (*They stare at each other.*) And I keep it all quiet . . . well, it's not fashionable, it's not for the swingers or anything, in fact very few people ever give it the time of day, so it all gets very little attention, real attention you know.

HARRY. Is that so?

JOHN. And that's the joke, because the only word for it all, is beautiful. And as I said before, I'd just like to try it . . . have time to mess with it.

HARRY (*Pauses*). Mess with what?

JOHN. Oh. . . . Uh? . . . I'd like to be a poet.

HARRY (*Strains to hear the last word*). A pet? . . . Whose pet?

JOHN (*Clears his throat*). No-o, a poet. . . . A *poet*. . . . Po-et. . . . (HARRY *just stares.*) Poetry, write poems! . . . A poet! . . . Shakespeare!

HARRY. Shakes-speare? . . . You pullin' my leg? I was listenin' serious.

JOHN. On the level, it's serious.

HARRY. A POET! Who the hell buys poems for God's sake? And it sounds like one helluva lazy loafin'-about profession—starin' at grass! And all that stuff's for . . . well, never mind, who it's for. Get outa here! Get dressed!

JOHN. *I mean it.*

HARRY (*With barely a pause for breath*). For long-haired pretty puffballs! That's who all that stuff is for, and don't bring any of 'em around here! And maybe ya don't know what I mean, but it's like a MAFIA they're takin' over everyplace! Stay away from them *feminine kinda jobs!* And there's no money in it in the first place, and ya got no talent, so there! Never make a dime, and who's gonna support ya? Answer me that? When ya starve, and they all starve ya know—all on the bum for pennies, hangin' on for a meal. You just take a good gander at your old man, cos he went off his rocker too. Boy, oh, boy, everything ya got here. Food on the table. Soft place to bed down. You'll go to college, although what the hell good that does beats me, but they'll give ya some kinda trade. Maybe like your mother. Be a teacher! Even though she's nuts, at least she's got a trade. Be a doctor! They're saltin' it away, the lousy crooks! With their ten bucks for just lettin' ya walk in the door! Ya got it *easy*—no sloggin' like me. You'll wear a business suit. You'll find a wife someplace. But for God's sake find one that can do more than warm up frozen food, if there's any of 'em left—which I doubt. You'll have a coupla kids to bring joy to your old age, I don't think! Get a piece of ground. The old girl up there'll leave ya something. Ya got it made! Don't screw it up! A poet! Lemme tell ya somethin'—take me, me! Out on the go at *fourteen*. And who put that mother of yours through a fancy college? Joe Blow Sucker Me! And who wound up supporting that loser dimwit father of yours she brought home? Sucker Me again! While he sat around here splashin' out masterpieces and smellin' up the place with turpentine. And did he ever sell a piece of canvas! One a year! Your father, in the three years he lived in this house, earned two hundred and ten dollars and seventy-five cents! Believe it or not, two hundred and ten dollars and seventy-five cents in three years! And when he lit out, I said, "goooood riddance to baaaaad rubbish." . . . You takin' all this in?

JOHN (*Dryly*). Uncle Harold . . . if there's one thing that keeps me going, it's the pleasure of hearing you go on and on and on and on and on and on and on and on and on and on and on and on and on and on. AND ON AND ON AND ON AND ON . . . every day of my life.

HARRY (*Points his finger*). You don't understand the outside world.

JOHN (*Points his finger back*). WHEN YOU'RE OLD ENOUGH TO UNDERSTAND, and I'm old enough so's you'll believe I understand, then we'll both understand! UNTIL THEN? FORGET IT! . . . I'm sorry I told you. You never heard what I said. Wipe it from your mind!

MRS. FRANKLIN (*Enters from kitchen with tray*). I imagine the lungs would be the first part of both of you to collapse. (*To* JOHN.) Staying in night-clothes all day? Suppose you had a visitor? How'd it look? Ever consider that? (*She goes upstairs.*) I'm clearing here next, so park yourselves elsewhere.

JOHN (*To* MRS. FRANKLIN). Do you like my father? I mean, what do you think about him?

MRS. FRANKLIN (*Continues upstairs*). I don't think about him. I think about the work to be done. (*Looks back at* HARRY *from landing.*) But he had a surprisingly soft voice! (*She exits into bedroom.*)

HARRY (*Calls after her*). Yeah, from booze it went soft. From my booze his larynx went gin-soaked.

MRS. FRANKLIN (*Off*). Ya might call him a gentleman even! Several notches above certain people around here!

HARRY (*To* JOHN). Old bat! . . . Can't find a damn thing once she cleans up. Throws out my Sports Section for spite, that old tabby! And she took in another boarder, did ya know? Makes four old buzzards livin' next door now. (*Points upstairs.*) There's a woman that's got fifty cents of every dollar that ever came her way . . . (*Inhales deeply.*) and I wish I could say the same. And I'll bet dollars to doughnuts she voted for Goldwater.

JOHN. How do you know?

HARRY. Cos everybody that voted for that guy had a lousy thin mean mouth, that's how I know!

JOHN. Boy, you're too much. Your reasoning powers are two, three, four, five much!

HARRY (*Drinks some cold coffee*). Uugh! (*Pushes cup across table.*) Johnny, be a sweetheart, be a sweet potato pancake and see if she made fresh out there. Good and hot. Easy on the sugar. Gotta watch myself. (*JOHN goes into kitchen with the cup.*) Ah-h, what a life, what a carry-on . . . Saturday . . . Sunday follows Saturday. . . . Mmmmm. . . . (*Calls out.*) Guess whatcha gettin' for your birthday? Three guesses, come on. Somethin' great!

JOHN (*Off*). Unless it's the books I asked for, I don't care.

HARRY. Ya got enough books. Come on, guess. . . . Are ya guessin'? . . . Now don't start goin' silent on me.

JOHN (*Returns with* HARRY's *coffee and a Coke for himself*). Mmmmm. (*Gestures that he doesn't want to talk.*)

HARRY. Three guesses.

JOHN (*Walks away*). Mmmmmm.

HARRY. Aw, come on, I hate it when you go quiet. It's worse even than when ya yack.

JOHN. You tell me "Shut up" all the time. Make up your mind.

HARRY. That's where ya don't understand me. If I tell ya "Shut up," I only mean "Shut up." I don't mean shut up the store, close down the store, which is what you do, and what your mother does. Never close down the store. Just remember there's a lotta guys around who never made the mistake of opening their mouths. But if I tell you "Shut up" in an ordinary everyday kinda way, I still mean "Shut up."

JOHN. You realize one of us is headed for a mental home? Some days you can contradict yourself four times by using only three words.

HARRY. Yeah, yeah. Well, there's many a fool around, and I can often see one across the room from me. (*They fall silent.*)

JOHN. Well, take your pick, shall I talk or not talk?

HARRY. Guess what I got you for your birthday.

JOHN. I don't wanna know, goddammit!

HARRY. And no swearing. A kid shouldn't foul his mouth.

JOHN. You swear.

HARRY. I'm over sixty, for God's sake.

JOHN. Why's it different for you?

HARRY. Now there's a fool remark! A kid's gotta be guided right.

JOHN. Are you lighting my way?

HARRY. If that's SARCASM, which it is, go to your room then!

JOHN. Because I'll stay in the dark!

HARRY. Stay in the dark then, and see if I care! Wait till the ARMY grabs ya! Fifty push-ups instead of loafin' around in your pajamas.

JOHN. HOW ABOUT A QUIET RECITATION THEN? "FEBRUARY IS THE ROTTENEST MONTH."

HARRY. IF YOU HAD A HEAD, THAT'S WHAT YOU'D BE OFF OF. . . . Father and son, I see it comin'. . . . You'll be the same! Well, not a nickel support you're gettin' from me. I'm leavin' mine to a dogs' home.

JOHN (*Tiptoes dramatically around*). "A *rat* crept through the vegetation." . . . Could it be my Uncle Harry?

HARRY. Sticks and stone, kid, stick and stones . . . yeah, yeah, can break your head. But you don't worry me. Do I seem worried? I'm not! You'll get your come-uppance one of these days.

JOHN. So let's go silent then!

HARRY. Good!

JOHN (*Pauses*). Huh!

HARRY (*Pauses*). That means not even saying "Huh."

JOHN. So don't talk to me then.

HARRY. Who's talkin' to ya?

JOHN. You are!

HARRY. I'm not. I went silent til you said "Huh." (JOHN *walks around room. Takes a scrap of paper from his pocket, reads it, then tears it up. Wanders over to the window.*)

JOHN. You'll be happy to hear my father can't make it here tomorrow. Mother went to pick up a gift from him. He got me rock and roll records. I must have dropped ninety thousand hints about the books I want, so Mother buys me a suit, he gets me rock and roll, and you probably got me a baseball bat. Boy, I'd settle, if you just weren't all so positive you know what's good for me. If you'd just trust me once in a while, occasionally trust me, that I know what's good for myself.

HARRY. Anytime ya talk to me reasonable, I go along with ya, but many times you're plain crazy.

JOHN. Yeah. (JOHN *wanders across the room. Takes out another scrap of paper. Reads it, then tears it up.*) I had trouble with words this week, that's why I'm mean to you. Nothing sounds good to me. . . . You know . . . if I ever should happen to sell a poem . . . actually ever *sell* one, I'm hauling home the cash to lay at your feet . . . and if I ever even write one I like . . . (*He walks toward* HARRY). I might give you *twice* as much trouble, so feel good while you can. (*He sits at table with* HARRY.) So . . . You won't mention it to mother, huh?

HARRY (*Continues reading*). A man of my word, me. I never give you away yet. Who took the blame yesterday for the ink all over the sofa? Sucker Joe again. (JOHN *gets up and wanders the room again.* HARRY *watches him.*) Lemme put it to ya this way. . . . Can you open up a newspaper, like this; glance over the columns and see "Poets Wanted"? Apply such and such. . . . You can't, no? So what's a bright young man like yourself do? He argues around with hisself awhile, then he figures "Why spend time doin' what nobody wants." (*Points to the paper.*) There's a million opportunities here to work yourself into the nuthouse as it is. And that's even the great thing about this country—you can work yourself to death a million ways. Are you aware what a *bricklayer* earns? Hand over fist they're makin' it. We got the *best* here—this is the *best* country in the world. That Irishman guy next door. In America thirty years—all he does is sing out what's wrong with it. I think he's writin' a catalogue of the American Blues every day, "ah-h, the billboards, ah-h the traffic, ah-h the hours I'm workin', ah-h the heart attacks, nyah, nyah, nyah." Seven o'clock this mornin' I'm havin' an argument with him. "Whatcha come to this country for? You was lookin' for the best, right? Ya come with your mitts out already, gimme." He said, "I was a slave over the other side." I said, "So? . . . You're a slave here too, right?" Then he said, "We-ll, I'm my own slave . . . it's better." I told him, "You're goddam right it's better. You had nuthin' over there, a fat nuthin'. Here, ya got work." And in my time I seen guys on a line beggin' for jobs, for bread on the table! (*Slaps the newspaper.*) Here ya got everythin'. This is the best country in the world, so you appreciate it!

JOHN. All I said was, ALL I said was, I would like to try. . . .

HARRY (*Waves the paper*). But there ain't no poets in here, kid. And ya just get notions all the time anyway. Like Mississippi down the river, you was tryin' to get to last year. Boy, all you'd have to do is open your yack South of the Mason Dixon, and we'd be down there by this time diggin' you up from somebody's backyard. And you can't walk three blocks up North. But down South you could suddenly march miles?

JOHN. I probably could.

HARRY. But I'll say this for ya. Ya got ambition, and I like that. You always did reach for the more expensive candy. . . . As long as you don't get too big in the head. You're always on about great *works* of *Art*. You never care much about plain old ordinary fry . . . and if they don't matter to ya . . . we-ell, you come from common stock. And I wouldn't care even if you was Shakespeare. Him! I'd tell it to him even! Watch out for the common folk.

JOHN. You would tell Shakespeare, "Watch out for the common folk"?

HARRY. I certainly would. And anybody else! Who was at Armentiers? And Omaha Beach? With the mud and the blood.

JOHN. I like plain people! . . . If they don't eat me alive! Aw, you depress me. You're as bad as Mother.

HARRY. Thanks a heap.

JOHN. I felt good when I came down.

HARRY. Me depress you? It's you can depress me.

JOHN. I can't depress you nearly as much as you can me.

HARRY. That's what you say, because you can *really* depress me. (JOHN *makes a loud groan.* HARRY *makes a louder groan.* JOHN *makes a soft groan.*) Yeah, well, that's the way it goes. . . . Cheer up! Live in hopes! Like me! What else is there to do? Guess what?

JOHN. Oh, don't start those three guesses again.

HARRY. Read me one of your bits.

JOHN. My bits?

HARRY. Your writing pieces. I'll tell you if there's any talent . . .

JOHN. Oh-h-h, pppllleeeaaase.

HARRY. You chicky? Recite me nice now. Fair enough? I can spot good from bad. Don't I always point out on the television the crap from the real crap? They never kid me.

JOHN. Hang it up, Harry.

HARRY. *Uncle* Harry. I'll tell ya what's up to scratch.

JOHN. I tear it all up. None of it's ready for the open air.

HARRY. What use is that? A person goes around saying, "I AM A POET. . . ."

JOHN. Shush!

HARRY (*In a loud whisper*). Saying, "I am a poet," and not have samples. Even they sell brushes with samples, with the goddam doorbell goin' every second, with their goddam brushes nobody wants.

JOHN (*Goes to stairway*). I have to dress.

HARRY. Ah-ha. Suddenly have to clothe yaself? . . . Ya never lay your eggs on the table—why? Always back out. SPEAK UP! What's to be afraid of! I keep tellin' ya many a man's never made the mistake of openin' his mouth. I told ya that when you was six, and ya musta listened cos you haven't piped down since, except—except, when it comes to the real goods.

JOHN. What's the point? You'd just laugh.

HARRY. Ya promised me a laugh earlier on, and nearly gimme a stroke. If ya got laughs, I'd say go ahead. Jokes make money.

JOHN. Which makes one of us worth Fort Knox.

HARRY. Figure a potential customer is sittin' here, right? Do a good job. Handle yaself well, and ya go a distance.

JOHN. You wouldn't understand my poems!

HARRY. See, phony balony, I got you in a lie. Bet ya don't have one recitation piece to your name. All your dreams are up in your noggin. Where's the proof of the pudding? (JOHN *marches to his bookshelf, and takes out a copybook from behind his books.*)

JOHN. If you'll shut up, I'll read you the first one I ever wrote. I was thirteen, and it happens to be TERRIBLE, but there's an outside chance you'll understand it!

HARRY. Is it in English?

JOHN. I think so!

HARRY. Because with you, it might be in Chinese. O.K. then! Throw your shoulders back! And be a man!

JOHN. Now don't watch me. You're already narrowing your eyes down, and you're getting ready to CRITICIZE.

HARRY. My eyes are wide open, and I'm not gonna say a WORD!

JOHN. Well, don't watch me. (HARRY *turns away with great exaggeration.* JOHN *leafs through the copybook.*) See, I have a lot of half-baked, scratched over messy stuff here. . . .

HARRY. Lemme hear this great first one.

JOHN. It's not great. . . .

HARRY. Lemme hear this rotten first one then.

JOHN. See, I was thirteen.

HARRY. All right, O.K.

JOHN. Well, are you ready?

HARRY. My God in Heaven, I'm here a half hour. (JOHN *is very nervous. He shuffles the pages around, clears his throat, and takes some Coke.*)

JOHN. All right then. . . . It's called "Someday" . . . and it starts out . . . "Someday, when winds stop blowing." Oh! You don't wanna listen to this! (*Closes the book.*)

HARRY (*Turns to face him*). You'll be amazed I got every word. Understood the entire line. Yeah, what's next?

JOHN (*Pauses, looks up at ceiling, then recites from memory*).

> "Someday when winds stop blowing,
> Someday when snow stops snowing"

. . . see, I was thirteen. I'm not this sentimental anymore. . . .

HARRY. Lemme see, ya musta written this the winter of '61. . . .

JOHN. You want me to *finish?* . . .

> "Someday when time is resting
> Someday when life stops living,

(*He groans with embarrassment.*)

> When earthly cries turn to heavenly sighs,
> And confused darkness to clean bright light,
> Then maybe the whys I'm wondering
> Will be the knows I'm knowing."

. . . THERE!

HARRY (*Has listened as if hard of hearing*). What's that last line?

JOHN.

> "Will be the knows I'm knowing."

HARRY (*Touches his nose*). The *nose* you're knowing? That don't make sense.

JOHN. No-o-o! The knows! The knowledge, it means. Took me *days* to find a word to fit in.

HARRY (*Is now the expert*). Want an opinion? Listen here. First of all . . . (*He thinks.*) ya had too many "Somedays" in it . . . but ya know what else? And here's where I'm smart. (*Slowly points his finger at* JOHN.) You . . . could be . . . a songwriter . . . write words for the *top ten.* Those guys are . . .

JOHN. ARE SOCKIN' IT AWAY, I KNOW! And Someday I may sock you away!

HARRY (*Ignores this*). In fact ya could turn that there right into a tune. (*Makes up a melody.*) "Someday . . . chacha . . . winds stop blowing."

JOHN. Oh, sure! (*Helps him sing.*) "Snow stops snowing, oobi doobi." (*Starts dancing over to front door.*) "Someday, sock it away. Piece of change, sock it away." (*He stops near front door.*) Wait a minute! I could take the Constitution. (*Sings.*) "Someday, we the people, Someday, of the USA, chachacha."

HARRY. Aw, take a walk, joker.

JOHN. Aw, if I only could. (*He opens front door and exits into the rain. Belts out.*) "I'M SINGING IN THE RAIN, JUST SINGING IN THE RAIN. . . ."

HARRY. Where'dya go?

JOHN (*Off*). "WHAT A GLORIOUS FEELING. . . ."

HARRY (*Looks through window*). COME BACK HERE!

JOHN (*Skips in and out front door, already wet*). EVER SEE GENE KELLY DO THIS? GREAT.

HARRY (*Rushes to front door*). DON'T FLING YOUR PAJAMAS OVER MY PLANTS!

JOHN (*Off*). DA DEE DA DA DA. . . ." (HARRY *gets his raincoat from closet.*)

HARRY. Oh, my God. Why couldn't you be born pleasant and nice!

NANNA (*Appears at top of stairs with cane*). Harold! You're upsetting that baby! I'll take this to you!

HARRY (*Rushes to foot of stairs*). Mother, he's undressing, in the wide open of the street! (JOHN *suddenly swoops in door, very wet, holding his pajama top. He heads straight for his room upstairs.*)

JOHN. Mother's coming!

HARRY (*Throws a shoe after him*). Good, good, good! Hope she whacks ya! If you've torn up any bulbs! Boy, you've never seen me lose my temper, but it's coming, IT'S COMING.

FLORENCE (*Enters front door, holding the pajama top*). Harry? What are you doing?

HARRY (*Turns, almost in fright*). Who me? Nothing.

FLORENCE (*Calls upstairs*). Johnny? . . . Well?

JOHN (*Appears on landing*). Who me? Nothing . . . I was . . . taking a shower. (*The four of them look at each other.*)

FLORENCE. I see. Well, get dry then. (JOHN *exits into his bedroom, and* FLORENCE *puts some packages aside.*)

HARRY. Aren't ya gonna get after him? Go get him.

FLORENCE (*Goes toward kitchen*). Sit down, Harry. Just sit and relax and take things in stride in your old age.

HARRY (*Sits down in his raincoat*). In stride! And who the hell can relax? THERE'S TOO MUCH FREEDOM ABOUT! Relax! And why the hell didn't I stay on the job! What the hell did I wanna retire for! Forty-six years I'm workin', and now all I got is aggravation and nervousness! (*The curtain comes down on him muttering.*)

SCENE II

Curtain rises on the same scene 45 minutes later. HARRY *sits in exactly the same position. The table has been set for lunch.*

HARRY. And they're all the same. That smelly kid two blocks down. The one who's part-ape, always up in the trees. I said to her the other day about this woman who got herself *raped* and killed. Guess what she jokes back? "We-ell," she pipes up, "that's better than bein' *killed* then raped!" Where's she pick up ideas like that? Is that moral? Ask yourself? Is that moral?

FLORENCE (*Enters from kitchen*). Is that moral?

HARRY. Well, it isn't, so there!

FLORENCE (*Puts sandwiches down on table*). Eating in your coat?

HARRY (*Looks toward phone*). Surprised the neighbors didn't call up.

FLORENCE (*Sits at table*). Staying in your coat?

HARRY. Or the police.

FLORENCE (*Starts eating*). Then I guess you will be eating in your coat.

HARRY. Well, if your kid can take showers on the lawn, on top of my bulbs . . .

FLORENCE. I'm eating now, Harry.

HARRY. Then I can pick at a sandwich in my raincoat, yes! I'm gonna sit here in my coat!

FLORENCE. Gee! Goodness, I'm glad we settled that.

HARRY. That kid comin' down? Or is he dinin' on the roof?

FLORENCE. A *kid* is a young goat, Harold. Call him by his given name.

HARRY. A kid is a young goat! Well, young goats, kiddo, come from older goats!

FLORENCE. And you must be very familiar with them. Now, please.

No more about wasting dimes, or lack of respect for the old folks at home. It's my day off. Leave me be.

HARRY. And your young goat made a crack about sleepin' around three times a week! How about that?

FLORENCE. Which means?

HARRY. He's no innocent, lemme inform ya. Behind them glasses, yessir, trouble! Fools you, but not this one.

FLORENCE. Oh, *my* Johnny, *my* John sleeps with girls three times a week? *My* Johnny?

HARRY (*Makes a face*). Yes, *your* Johnny. And today, nothing would surprise me! Not for a second I wouldn't be surprised! At his age, when I once found myself, by *accident*, under a blanket with a girl, and she said, "Take me" . . . Believe it or not, Mrs. Ripley, I said, "Take you *where?*" . . . I thought she wanted to go see a SHOW! That was the trouble, we was babes in the woods, Florrie. They didn't tell us nuthin'. Today! God help us how much he knows! . . . He takes a lotta long bike rides. What's he do on 'em? Where's he goin'? Who's he meetin' up with? And he don't like Sports. (*Becomes confidential.*) And there's a suspicion. It's a very *feminine* kinda business not to go for a little rough and tumble. I watched him the other day. Who else but him would *skate* right over his own hands. Last year, he got up to bat . . . and who else but him, would run through the pitcher's mound, over to second, then back to first! Shoutin' at the players, "Forget it!" I tell ya straight, Florrie, there's many days it's hard to believe he's an American. He's so bass-ackwards.

FLORENCE. Are you through?

HARRY. No.

FLORENCE. When will you be through? Because you've managed to suggest he's carting girls by the bushel into the woods, but at the same time, watch out, he's feminine! Now make up your mind.

HARRY. What I'm really sayin' is he don't fit in right. Somethin' funny, and not funny ha-ha, funny peculiar about him. Ya best start straightenin' him out. Wise him up some. We all gotta fit the jigsaw puzzle ya know.

FLORENCE. On what points, wise him?

HARRY. And that's you all over! Stone-deaf-blind! Never see your nose for the trees! What points! He's a nice boy, a lovely boy, who's growin' into a smartness! "I'm not so sure there's a God" he tells me. And he's readin' Socialist crap in some of them books. Play with the other kids more, tell him. Tell him, be more *natural!* He better not wind up any further left than the Democratic party or I'm cuttin' his allowance! And he's got another brain-wave again. (*Puts out a warning hand.*) Don't ask me what it is. I promised him. But mark my words, he's gonna be Edwards all over again.

FLORENCE. Don't call his father "Edwards."

HARRY. Another Edwards for sure! There's Win, Place, and Show in life, and Edwards never even made Show. There's another nag that ran the wrong way—and if he's comin' here tomorrow, I'm goin' out for a few beers.

FLORENCE. You'll stay home on Johnny's birthday, and why'd you have such a sudden interest in his welfare?

HARRY. Cos I'm around the place now, and I *see*, and you're off out and ya come back tired and ya don't see!

FLORENCE (*Pushes aside her plate*). Out of a large family, that you and I should finish up together under the same roof! Well, I wish it amused me more. Harry, you're my very own North Star. Your ignorance is the one constant on this witless earth. Without fail, I can absolutely rely on you to come up with hopeless and aimless suggestions. . . .

HARRY. Ah-h, your sarcasm don't reach me. And too bad ya don't care for livin' under a roof that happens to be half mine. Also listen out one of my more aimless suggestions. (*Points upstairs.*) Watch where he's headed, cos give or take a coupla years, they're gonna call him a *Man*. Now what cards is he gonna play with? Answer me that! What cards? Number One . . . he's short! (*He throws up his arms.*) It's already a bust! The end! Finish! Good-bye Charlie! Number Two . . . he's homely . . . so comes the insult on top of the injury! And Number Three . . . he's a KOOK! . . . Well, happy days! Ya look at that hand and ya say NO TRUMPS! The kid's got no trumps! Number Three at least ya can do somethin' about—change him around in his ideas a little. The other two! Ya know the agony? . . . the *agony?* of every short, homely guy in this world? Who the hell ever gives 'em the real time of day, unless they got dough? And they all just happen to manage to want MISS RHEINGOLD, or MISS RHINESTONE, or what the hell she calls herself! The American Rose they all want! And she goes to the pretty ones. Because, Miss Teacher, the piece of cake always goes to the pretty guys. And I should know, cos nobody ever looked at me. And if I ever get born over again, and have to go through ALL THIS CRAP all over, PLEASE GOD, make me handsome and cute!

FLORENCE. You're through now? . . . The endless all-American tragedy is upon us then? Johnny won't be six foot in your land of giants? And no home runs or touchdowns? He reads, and picks up ideas . . . what a bore he must be to you, Harry, my poor short little son.

HARRY. Win, Place, and Show, Sissie. Teach him to play with the cards he's got, if ya can figure out what they are.

FLORENCE. Harold, you're my brother, and if you ever get sick, God forbid, I'll take care of you, but you are a fat ignoramus, and an old fart into the bargain! And I'm also past forty and too tired to be tolerant! You take up *space!* . . . You hear me? . . . An ignorant man in this world takes up *space!* and if you all dropped dead! . . . Well, I'm sorry, my dear, but for me, Christ would be risen at last!

HARRY (*Pauses*). You're quite sure it's me that's the one that takes up space, huh . . . Well, ya don't hurt my feelings, cos all of my sparks are kept way down . . . where they don't get damaged by *educated* people like yourself. And it's a real shame that all of your damn books and your education didn't teach ya allowance for a person's feelings and the way they are. Ya grew up into a tough old bird all right, and you was a sweet little thing. . . .

FLORENCE. And *down* you grew, *down!* Now please, go and look at some football game on the television, or nose around what the neighbors are up to, or whatever you fill your time with.

HARRY. SO? I'm an ordinary man, whatcha want from me? I'm fond of the kid like he's mine, that's all. I wanna see him go right.

FLORENCE. WELL, that's dandy fine, but keep your ordinary hands off him. What an insult! What trumps does he have! He's a straight A. He can be twelve feet by the side of your six-footers. A lot of ways to measure feet! . . . He can be anything he wants.

HARRY. Yeah?

FLORENCE. Yes. Can study anywhere. He can have the best and be the best!

HARRY. Yeah? . . . Well (*He picks up his untouched plate.*), I'm sorry to take up space here. I'll eat down the workshop, and listen to some stinky old American football game. The air up here is too rare for me. . . . (*He walks toward basement door.*) That's O.K. The women and kids know it all. The ship is headed for the rocks! (*He turns back.*) But I'll bet cheese and beer, old Johnny No-Trump up there, got a surprise in store for ya. One idea too many he's picked up, I'd say. He can be anything he wants, huh? Funny, how you've always given me the impression you'd like him to be a teacher. . . .

FLORENCE. He can be anything he wants. . . .

HARRY. So ya keep sayin'.

FLORENCE. He has the brains.

HARRY. I'll settle if he's got more kindness in him than his old woman. And one more thing strikes me funny. How my goin' out to work, me bein' so ignorant and all, and goin' out to slog, made it possible for you to get fancy, and not exactly walk alongside of us no more. Now there must be a joke there, if it would only come to me.

FLORENCE. Aw, cut it, Harry.

HARRY (*Turns back at basement door*). And ya can do anythin' with a dame, except talk with her! OLD FART YOURSELF! (*He exits and slams the door.*)

FLORENCE (*Pauses, attempts to eat her sandwich, then gives up. Calls out*). You want lunch? . . . Johnny? . . . You coming?

JOHN (*Off*). Who, me?

FLORENCE. You eat breakfast?

JOHN (*Off*). Yeah.

FLORENCE. Well, lunch is up.

JOHN (*Dressed in chinos and sweater, appears on landing. He starts his usual production of descending the stairs*). You mad? . . . You look like a teacher sitting there. . . . See, about the uh . . . see, we weren't eye to eye this morning. And when he sets his teeth in. . . .

FLORENCE. It's your own fault every time. You bait him.

JOHN. You're sitting funny. I feel like this is an interview.

FLORENCE. I'm sitting up straight. You want me slumped across the table?

JOHN. You look awful teachery to me.

FLORENCE. What do you really want out of this world, Johnny?

JOHN. Huh?

FLORENCE. I don't care how you word it, honey. What do you *really* want?

JOHN. Nothing. . . . Did he tell you!? Aw, Ma, he was on his *honor!* Whatcha worm it out of him for!?

FLORENCE. He never gives you away. . . . So?

JOHN. Nothing. I don't want anything—well, maybe a loose healthy immoral life like everybody else. I don't wanna be any different. (*He has reached the bottom step.*) I mean are you *really* asking?

FLORENCE. Yes.

JOHN. Oh. . . . Yeah? . . . You're *really* asking?

FLORENCE. *Really* for *really*.

JOHN (*Wanders across to her*). Oh. . . . Huh! . . . Fancy that. . . . Well, *really*. . . . You know when some guy in a movie wants to strike oil? . . . That's what I'd like. Have it all gush down on me and just, well, not smother me, but just gush down. . . . Life, I mean . . . strike life, like some guy strikes oil.

FLORENCE (*Smiles*). Strike life?

JOHN. Yeah.

FLORENCE. I see.

JOHN. Why are you smiling?

FLORENCE (*Shrugs*). Nothing.

JOHN. I mean it's probably hard, but that's what I'd like, since you're really interested. . . . Why are you smiling?

FLORENCE. Because you often remind me of me. And me just standing right where you are now, and facing my father—yelling at him because I wanted education, and he thought girls should stick to the kitchen. . . . I don't want you *ever* to have to scream at me for what you want . . . O.K.? . . . Fair enough?

JOHN (*Smiles*). It *sounds* good, but . . . (*He shrugs an expression of distrust.*)

FLORENCE. So, you enjoyed your shower out there?

JOHN. Uncle Harry didn't say anything, huh?

FLORENCE. Breathe easy, honey, whatever your secret is. You got good and clean this February ice-cold morning?

JOHN (*Picks up a package*). These the records you picked up? You-know-who isn't coming tomorrow?

FLORENCE. Your father isn't You-know-who, he's your father, and if he gets off work he'll be out. So, what's on your mind?

JOHN. Nothing. (*Imitates* HARRY.) "Do I look worried? I'm not! The ship is headed for the . . ."

FLORENCE. And *please*, do anything, but don't imitate Harry. And because I've never seen you undressing in the rain before today—it was silly of me, I know, but I thought, "Oh, something's on his mind."

JOHN. No-o-o, nothing. We swapped some jokes, and it got very hot in here, so I cooled off a few seconds in the rain. . . .

FLORENCE. Aw, lambchop, sit down and cut it, will you? And without any chitchat, wisechat, backchat, or any other kind of chat, what is it I'm not supposed to find out?

JOHN. Whadya mean? "Not supposed?" . . . It was all nothing!

FLORENCE. Johnny, I'm no Harry! There are still many days when I'm way ahead of you!

JOHN. What am I, on the carpet here!? (*Imitates* HARRY.) "The women took over, boy, the ship. . . ."

FLORENCE. I said don't copy him! You'll get speech problems as it is! You can wisecrack jokes O.K., but anything else comes out, "well, see, uh, well, look, see, see, uh, uh, huh."

JOHN. It's very hard to communicate. All the magazines say so.

FLORENCE. And you can come off that! Neither one of us is ego-centric enough, yet!, to have a communication problem. Just speak, then listen, then speak again, and if you don't forget to listen, you'll find that's communication!

JOHN (*Acts out an exaggerated response*). Gee! Mom! Gee Whizzo! My mother has the answer the whole country is waiting for!? You *speak*, then *listen*, that's *communication!?* AND ALL AMERICA'S HANG-ING ON, AND MY MOTHER KNOWS. . . .

FLORENCE. Aw, don't be such a smartass!

JOHN. No-o, see, well, uh? huh? see, look, I only have a problem with nouns, pronouns, adjectives, verbs, adverbs, prepositions, conjunc-tions and interjections, with teachers, mothers, uncles, fathers, strangers and very close friends! Anybody else—listen, it's a picnic.

FLORENCE. Yeah, yeah. . . .

JOHN. Yeah, yeah? Don't copy Harry, mother. "Yeah, yeah."

FLORENCE. Yeah, yeah, don't kid me. The cat isn't born that could get your tongue.

JOHN. Well, we're off to a good start, as usual.

FLORENCE. What's on your mind?

JOHN. Nothing! Noth—ing! No thing at all! I don't have a mind to have anything on!

FLORENCE. Oh, silly!

JOHN. We're off to a good start again!

FLORENCE. What's on your mind?

JOHN (*Gestures "nothing"—silently mouths "nothing"—gestures "nothing," then mouths it again. Pauses*). And it so happens . . . at the right time . . . well, you're not in the best kind of mood! In fact it's pretty clear, we're both in no mood, and this particular . . . well, it re-quires an excellent mood! I mean, I'd be willing to wait out the three months til we hit one of your better days . . . so we could work something out. . . . (*In a sudden rush.*) Well, I'd like to quit school so I can learn something, get a job, then write verse!

FLORENCE (*Pauses*). What was that last thing?

JOHN. Write verse.

FLORENCE. Before that.

JOHN. Quit school so that I can learn something, and before you ask me "What's that supposed to mean?", it means, quit school so that I can *learn* something . . . and then get a job.

FLORENCE. Quit at sixteen, and get a job! . . . Would you please get lost!

JOHN (*Gets agitated and moves around room*). They're not teaching me what I wanna be! It's Boresville every day! Apart from English, the rest is sit-and-stare time. It's killing me, and it's even killing them! Only one teacher down there looks less fed up than me! I hate, and detest, and I mean I hate, boy, all that math and science pukey stuff. What do I care if two and two are four! Let it make nine hundred! (*He hits parts of his body.*) Whole chunks of me are dropping dead! Feel that arm! It's going numb! Pretty soon all my entrails'll conk out. . . . And none of you remember it anyway. What's a half into a half?

FLORENCE. A half.

JOHN. Ha-ha, wrong! Is the change of momentum proportional to the force and the time during which it acts and in the same direction as force?

FLORENCE. My subject's history! Ask me about George Washington! And two and two is a fact, and certain facts . . .

JOHN. FACTS! Boy, those are the killers I hate the most! To me, a *fact* is worse than any girl—there's no room for—they're rigid—no room for discussion! Ah-h, forget it! Because I could be wrong! Maybe I just happen to have sat in on ten thousand crummy classes and missed all the great ones.

FLORENCE. Johnny? Can I ask you a personal question?

JOHN (*Stops in his tracks*). A *personal* one? . . . About my private life?

FLORENCE. If you wanna put it that way, yes.

JOHN. All right. . . . Let's not overstep the mark though.

FLORENCE. Have you ever slept with a girl? I mean, uh? . . . I meant, do you . . . sleep with them?

JOHN (*Removes his glasses, glances at himself in mirror*). Well, I always thought I looked pure.

FLORENCE. I only wondered, because Harry made a crack. . . .

JOHN. Aw, come on! "Harry made a crack. . . ." I was looking over one of your books on men and women, and it's all enough to put me off this whole entire intercourse, marital, sexual stuff. Putting girls at ease! No chapters for girls putting me at ease! Because I'm likely to faint clean away—pass out—crack my head open on some strange four poster bed. Couldn't you have given me Ovid to read? He's at least funny.

FLORENCE (*Gets up*). Well, everything'll straighten itself out. You're in a phase right now. Just ride it out. Eat your sandwich and take a . . .

JOHN. Mother, I'm very serious.

FLORENCE (*Crosses to her desk*). Children all get romantic ideas. I used to too, with verse and . . .

JOHN (*Follows her*). They're not teaching me what I want to know. They're *boring* me. Don't you care?

FLORENCE. Honey, I'm very familiar with boring teachers. You teach the same lesson over and over, yes, a person gets bored passing it on. I can't always hold the interest of my kids in class either. And if one of them doesn't like me, then he can't learn from me—and the strange part is, that you really only learn what you half-know already. If I say something to a child, and it touches off something in him, almost like a distant memory, then he grows. But otherwise very little happens. I'm very acquainted with sit-and-stare time, you don't have to tell me . . .

JOHN (*Shakes her arm*). Who do I tell then?

FLORENCE (*Removes his hand*). You're raising your voice.

JOHN (*Shakes her again*). Who do I raise it to then?

FLORENCE. Quit shaking me, and don't take a rude tone or I'll slap you.

JOHN (*Extends his face*). I'll take off my glasses, and could you please do it then. Make a fist and sock me, but after that, listen to me. You speak, right? Then you listen.

FLORENCE. Oh, silly-billy, I've never hit you. We've always had everything out man to man. . . .

JOHN. And maybe that's our trouble, because neither of us is a man yet! Although you're gonna make it quicker than me!

FLORENCE (*Grabs his sweater*). You're pushing me into corners, Johnny. Now easy with those cracks, or we'll both start up with lots we don't mean . . . and then not talk for days after. Harry's right, you're getting very fresh. (JOHN *groans and walks back to the table. He sits with his back to her and picks his sandwich apart.*) Eat your sandwich. Don't pick it. (*He keeps on picking and fashioning the bread into a shape.*) Johnny? . . . John? . . . Baby? . . . Let's not be this way. We used to be so close. . . . (*He doesn't respond.*) What makes you want to write verse?

JOHN (*Pauses*). Because.

FLORENCE. Of?

JOHN (*Shrugs*). Just because.

FLORENCE. Yes?

JOHN (*Remains with his back to her*). Oh-h, it's the only time, I'm not self-conscious . . . or mean. Deep-down mean, or bored. Well, I lose myself in it. I guess it makes me happy.

FLORENCE. You write often?

JOHN. And it's best when you get a feeling, and hear some words. They kinda whisper themselves, so you rush to put it down . . . and then later on . . . you wonder *about* it, and sort of *around* it. To see if you've really seen it—what the theme is, I mean. Well, I'm not putting it right, but it's the best feeling there is.

FLORENCE (*Is very gentle*). You write many?

JOHN. Yeah, but I'm in hot water with them always. I sling a lot out. The words and the sounds have to come just right ya know . . . and— (*Shrugs.*)

FLORENCE. Who's your favorite poet?

JOHN. All.

FLORENCE. No good, bad, in the middle?

JOHN. Yeah, but it's hard to pick out a favorite. They're all magic— for me, anyone who writes a poem . . . is a magic person . . . except yours truly. They're just . . . well, I'd give them anything. If I owned the whole world even, I'd give it to them.

FLORENCE. Why?

JOHN. What?

FLORENCE. Why the world?

JOHN (*Shrugs*). Because.

FLORENCE. Of?

JOHN. I dunno because of . . . maybe they'd all figure what to do with it.

FLORENCE (*Comes across to him*). John, John, John, sometimes you're very young, even for someone who's very young.

JOHN. Mmmmm.

FLORENCE. Cheer up then. Show me what you've done.

JOHN. Well, see, there's nothing really. A lot of scribble. . . .

FLORENCE. But show me. Scribble's all right.

JOHN. No. There's nothing worth seeing.

FLORENCE. Shall I mark papers instead then? . . . Shall I? (*She waits, then returns to the desk.* JOHN *gets up and fetches his red copybook.*)

JOHN. Are your hands clean? (*She checks and nods.*) Here then. (*She leafs through the book. John watches over her shoulder. They both make their comments, not listening to each other.*)

FLORENCE. I used to write poems . . . very similar to all this. . . . They must be up in the back room. . . . Course I was very sentimental then . . . always off on a cloud . . . used to fall in love with practically anything . . . trees and faces . . . strangers even.

JOHN. I'm redoing that one. . . . Couldn't find a rhyme there. . . . Well, that's all erased. . . . Turn over the page. . . . That word means owl. . . .   .

FLORENCE (*Smiles*). Oh, there's one on me. "Lines on My Assodynia Mother."

JOHN (*Attempts to turn the page*). It's scratched over.

FLORENCE (*Turns the page back*). What's it mean?

JOHN. I forget. It's a made-up word.

FLORENCE. Yes?

JOHN. It's lost to me now.

FLORENCE. Yes? . . . A whole literature is devoted to why forgetting means remembering.

JOHN. Oh, is there? . . . It was written on one of our off-days. . . . Odynia means "pain in" . . . so *ass*-odynia means . . . assodynia.

FLORENCE. I see. (*She puts the book down.*) It's all very sweet, Johnny, but do this alongside your education. . . .

JOHN (*Gets excited*). To be what? Education for what?

FLORENCE. Whatever you might want to be next *week*, or next *year*.

JOHN. But I've decided! It's set in me!

FLORENCE. Honey! It's very nice, it is, it's marvelous what you want! But this world no more belongs to the poets than the man in the moon! And it never will! (*Picks up the copybook.*) What you've scrawled on the cover here. (*She reads.*)

To a certain Big G, high in the sky, a plea.

Make me Big T—no small e, edwards for me.

Make me a Swanseatown Thomas.

Well, to want to be another Dylan Thomas is very ambitious, but you better come down to earth.

JOHN. Are you kidding? It's even worse, I wish I was Keats and Dante and everybody! (*He paces the room.*) And it's all gotta be more than a wish. I have to get going! Grow up and move! Cos they all die young! Nearly every poet takes one good look around and passes out!

Keats popped off at twenty-five. That could happen to me. Nine years to go! Think of it from that angle. Aw, lemme get a job.

FLORENCE. There's a long lifetime in you, baby.

JOHN. And could you cut the baby, lambchop, business?

FLORENCE. Nanna calls you baby.

JOHN. She's eighty, and we're in tune.

FLORENCE. Well, then, Mr. Edwards, what do you want? Me, to say, "*drop out*," be a messenger boy someplace, so you'll learn the ropes, and consequently be able to turn out a large book of verse? Forget it! Messenger boys learn only one thing—why one guy goes up, and the next one stays in the packing room!

JOHN. See, this sure isn't the right mood for all this. I could work down at Joe's Diner. "BLT down, heavy on the mayo!"

FLORENCE. I've got no moods for this one. You'll leave me armed to the teeth with whatever's necessary to make a life and a living. We got a toe-or-go world here, and there's a rhyme for you, toe or go. For any seat in the marketplace, the questionnaire reads, name, address, do you have a degree? And not, unfortunately not, name, address, are you charitable and friendly to your neighbors? Any place I've held a job, no one's ever asked me if I could smile. Now let's finish.

JOHN. Why don't you put it like Harry? "Be a dentist! THEY'RE SOCKIN' IT AWAY!" (*He grabs her arm.*) Mother, I'm inquisitive, nosy all the time. I'd learn anyway. It doesn't have to be in class. Every day I pick up things about people, and there's money put aside for me. Next year, please, couldn't I travel? Or at least, promise me no college.

FLORENCE. The answer's no!

JOHN. Well, I hope they start a sense of humor class down there! Cos that's what ya need to get out in one piece! In that GODDAM BITCH OF A . . .

FLORENCE. Don't swear!

JOHN. You swear!

FLORENCE. Hold your tongue!

JOHN (*Throws up his hands*). OH-H! IT'S NOT FAIR! ISN'T THERE SOME GOD YA COULD JUST WALK UP TO? AND TELL HIM "STRAIGHTEN EVERYBODY OUT"?

FLORENCE. Too bad, but there's only me around here. You haven't a clue inside your head what happens to the unskilled and untaught. And nobody really gives a damn *what* you've learnt, but they care *where*. Between what set of walls you've learnt it! And they want papers to show for it. You gotta ride it out.

JOHN. I won't!

FLORENCE. Yes, you will! THE ANSWER'S NO, NOW LEAVE THE ROOM!

JOHN. The answer's no, now leave the room? . . . Then I should start letting you in on *what* and *where* I learn . . . shouldn't I? Like, for instance, a book on the union of men and women . . . handed me four years too late. Because some kid in camp told me when I was nine. He said, "Guess how babies get born? A man sticks his thing in a woman's thing" . . . except he didn't say THING, he said, "A man sticks his peepee in a woman's CUT." . . . We all thought he said CUT! And the kids laughed and acted it out! They acted it out all over camp! And some kids cried because they didn't wanna believe it, but they all went on *laughing*, and *crying*, and *trying*, until they saw it was all *possible!* . . . So, if you care *what* and *where* I learn . . . then you're late, or asleep, or something! (*The width of the room is between them and a deep silence.*) Well, why don't you say something? . . . And I hope you're not crying over there.

FLORENCE (*Stares down at her desk*). No, I'm not.

JOHN. See, very little that means beans to me, well, it just doesn't. . . . I don't learn it at a desk. And that's a fact, same as two and two.

FLORENCE. I'm sorry . . . truly . . . I am sorry. I give you my word, I wanted . . . all that side of things . . . to be clean. And Harry chickened out on me once, when you were smaller, so I started to lay it out in proper fashion . . . but then you joked so, it made it difficult for me.

JOHN. You looked so embarrassed that day, I joked you so you wouldn't have to go through with it.

FLORENCE. Yes. . . . You're a nice boy, John.

JOHN. No, I'm not. I just do a lot to please you, like bring home A's so's you'll smile. Somehow a B only gets me half a smile. (*He moves toward stairs.*) But it's all starting not to please me.

FLORENCE. I don't know what to tell you. I'd almost give you the earth, just in return for the years together—for the company you've been—but it isn't possible to let you go your own way. I'm aware of more than you, I'm always aware of next week. . . .

JOHN. And next year, and next next. Or else last year. Couldn't we ever have *today* in the house? Can't we have a few here and nows? Why's it always tomorrow time?

FLORENCE. You see . . .

JOHN. I wish I was three again.

FLORENCE. So do I. But you're gonna be sixteen tomorrow, and

then soon twenty-one. And it's all numbers outside, baby. It's all how
to count. All hip, hop, hup two three four. That's how we name our
streets even—plain old 1234. There's no Byron Boulevards. We don't
tip our hats in that direction. And you may want an entirely different
life two years from now, and My God! you have to be born with it, you
really do! True poets have . . . (*She lifts her hands to indicate the divine.*) Your father got stuck with the desire to paint. He's in love with
a way of life, an Art, that just doesn't love him back. One of those million fringe people, kidding themselves they have talent. You want to
clean off tables in cafeterias like him? Or part-time bartending? I don't
want you in the Arts. For most of them, it's a lifetime of humiliation.

JOHN. Mother, I never feel special, ever. Not how I look, or dress
or sound. But one time a special *feeling* happened to me, and it never
goes away. Ya know how ya have to recite bits and pieces for class? Even
if it's all Greek they make ya learn them. Well . . . out of no-place once,
I'm going over and over some lines, and suddenly they made sense. I
mean I knew inside me what they meant. Like they were written for
me! And it was such a shock, that I raced around the house to let you
all in on it. But everybody was out, so I just kept putting down the book,
and picking it up again, and holding it way out . . . like a sparkler . . .
like it was alive. And I *had* to *tell* somebody . . . but the only person
. . . well, the picture in the front of his old book . . . I held it under
a light . . . and finally I said to William Shakespeare . . . "Do you *know*
who you *are?*" I was just so amazed to find this dead, well, friend really.
Dead friend. And after that, I'd read anybody called a poet. I mean,
they're better than me, and I wanted in. And if I play around with
rhymes and stuff now, it's because, it's the only part of me that's any
good. I mean, honestly, Mother, do I look like some swinger, that's
gonna wear a suit and all, and a tie, and snap my fingers and show 'em?
I'm a schlunk, a homely schlunk, and I've just been sent down here
too late, that's all. Why? WHY? couldn't I have been born tall and
brave and brilliantly talented back in the eighteenth century, when if ya
wanted to be a poet, they all said, "Go, man, go, it's the most!" Mother,
I'm a short coward in Nassau County, February, 1965, and couldn't
you be on my side? (*He checks his pulse.*) And I hope I don't have
high blood pressure because I'll never make the next week, next year,
you're so worried about.

FLORENCE. Johnny . . .

JOHN. And ya know, you could scare Jesus Christ! You'd advise
Him to get a teaching license and prepare for the future, for the BIG

WORLD out there! Listen, if it's all as bad as you make out, do me a favor and keep it. Don't hand me any *lemons*, cos I'm a *lemon* myself, and *enough* is *enough!*

FLORENCE. Johnny . . .

JOHN. Ya wanna fancy college for me? Is that it? I don't want it. Ma, pleeeaaase, when I'm seventeen, lemme go. I want out. Take a chance on me. Let me travel.

FLORENCE. Where to?!

JOHN. Rome and Greece. . . .

FLORENCE. Rome, Italy! At seventeen!

JOHN. I could see Shelley's grave. . . .

FLORENCE. You'll see my grave on Long Island soon. . . .

JOHN. I could see . . .

FLORENCE. This split second you're traveling and you're unaware of it! From here to there (*Indicates from room to front door.*) is about the longest journey on the map. Up to and through the door of any father's house!

JOHN. This is my mother's house! And ya know, you're worse than Uncle Harry. At least he's honest, he comes in on a straight line! You come in on a curve!

FLORENCE. Oh, do I?! Well, I'm sorry! You wanna go to the moon? No! Travel? No! And you'll quit school over my carcass!

JOHN. Can ya promise me the dead body'll be yours?! Instead of mine? (*Picks up his copybook.*) This is rubbish then?

FLORENCE. Of course not! But alongside school . . .

JOHN (*Waves the book*). Garbage should go!

FLORENCE. After homework, Johnny.

JOHN (*Goes toward front door*). You never trust me! Always telling me I can be the *best*, and have the *best*, but this is my lousy *best!* (*Waves the book.*) But it really belongs buried! In the garden! (*He exits out front door into rain.*)

FLORENCE. Oh, you idiot! . . . (*She runs to door.*) Where are you?

JOHN (*Off*). PLOUGH IT UNDER!

FLORENCE (*Runs to window, trying to see where he is*). Come in from the rain!

JOHN (*Off*). SO I'LL MAKE A HOLE!

FLORENCE. Why do you have to be such an either/or boy!

JOHN (*Off*). AND HAVE A FUNERAL!

FLORENCE (*Grabs a raincoat and goes outside*). CAN'T YOU EVER MEET ME HALFWAY?

JOHN (*Returns through kitchen entrance and looks at* FLORENCE *outside*). IT'S BURIED!

FLORENCE (*Off*). Well, you're gonna un-bury it!

JOHN. Yeah? Try and find it!

FLORENCE (*Returns to room*). Bring that book in!

JOHN. No!

FLORENCE. Are you gonna bring it in?

JOHN. No!

FLORENCE. I only want what's best for you!

JOHN (*Goes upstairs*). Yeah? But I ain't playin' no game where I don't like the ground rules! We just parted company, Ma! (*He exits into his room.*)

HARRY (*Opens the basement door and comes into room*). So, I'm the one that's honest, huh?

FLORENCE. Harry, ask him for me? He just put me down along with his book. . . .

HARRY (*Puts out a warning hand*). A fat ignoramus who takes up space is not a person to give out with favors. . . .

NANNA (*Appears on upper landing*). What a feckless lot of varmints you are! How come all my quiet children left home, and all we got left is your cackle? I missed out on the good part of a television story cos of yas. Your daddy would've shut yas up good . . . yessir. . . . (*She turns back to her room.*) Bobby Armstrong would've done it . . . and I'll be glad to get up there alongside him. Dry-eyed, I'll be leavin' your company . . . yessir . . . dry-eyed, I'll be rid of this world. . . . (*She enters her room.*)

JOHN (*Pops his head out of his room*). There's something about this life I don't go for either!

HARRY (*Walks back to basement door*). The ship . . . I tell ya . . . the ship is headed for the rocks. (NANNA *slams her door shut.* JOHN *slams his door shut.* HARRY *exits into basement and slams door shut.* FLORENCE *walks to front door and slams it shut.*)

CURTAIN

Act Two

JOHN *enters from bedroom with suitcase and crosses down stairs to desk.* HARRY *enters from the kitchen whipping some kind of stuff in a bowl.*

HARRY. Where's all the knives and forks? I can't find one. (HARRY *sees suitcase.*) What's that for?

JOHN. Have you seen my sleeping bag?

HARRY. Nope. The table look O.K.? Suit your style?

JOHN. Fine.

HARRY. Think I oughta wear a different shirt?

JOHN. No.

HARRY (HARRY *crosses to sofa which has birthday gifts on it, one of which is a new suit*). Change into your new suit then, let's see it.

JOHN. I hate the suit, tie, wallet, and the keychain.

HARRY. And my transoceanic A.M./F.M. what-not special radio? Ya hate that too, huh? Know what it set me back?

JOHN. Don't get nervous, I'll take it with me. (JOHN *crosses to desk, gets pencils, crosses back to suitcase and puts them inside.*)

HARRY. If I might make so bold, just why are you packing that case?

JOHN. I have to take some reference books along.

HARRY. Along where?

JOHN. Now don't get upset.

HARRY. No.

JOHN. Don't get a heart attack now.

HARRY. No.

JOHN. But . . . I'm leaving. . . . Just *zip*, out the door, off. (*Pause.*)

HARRY. And you've picked this very second to *zip*, out and off?

JOHN. Yep.

HARRY. I see. . . . So, I've just spent an hour makin' this Creamo Whippo for no reason. You won't be at the party?

JOHN (JOHN *crosses to window seat for books*). No, but think of this more as a gesture, it's not real defiance.

HARRY. So what's this gesture include?

JOHN. Well, I'll catch rides, like, and well, I'll head for maybe . . . Maine.

HARRY. Yeah?

JOHN. And then I can probably get another ride up to Canada, like northern Canada . . . and look around.

HARRY. Yeah?

JOHN. Then maybe I could turn back . . . head South.

HARRY. Why are you givin' the Arctic the gate? Something's wrong with the snowy wastes of the extreme Far North?

JOHN. Listen . . .

HARRY. And then what? Into the steaming jungles of the Amazon?

JOHN. I'll call you collect. You'll know exactly where I am. . . .

HARRY. You're absolutely right. Unpack that bag. (JOHN *exits into the basement.*)

JOHN. Where's my boots?

HARRY (HARRY *begins to toss books out of the suitcase*). What you got in here? My God, you've robbed us blind! WELL HELLO THERE! My knives . . . and . . . forks . . . were on their way where? And my dad's watch! Shakespeare! You're another Murf the Surf! Get out of that basement.

JOHN (JOHN *enters from basement with boots*). I think you oughta be proud of me. . . . This is the first time I'm taking *positive action* and *zip*, you know, forge ahead. (JOHN *crosses to fireplace for more books.*)

HARRY (HARRY *crosses to sideboard and replaces silverware*). You were plannin' to *hock* my personal possessions?

JOHN. Don't act like I'd robbed a garage.

HARRY. Better a garage than me! Take one step out of this house, I call the cops and they'll have your head. (HARRY *crosses to the phone.* NANNA *begins to come downstairs with* MRS. FRANKLIN.)

NANNA. Gee whiz, look at the carpet. Pattern's all goin' away. Place used to have such shine. Is there a young man down there to come fetch me? (JOHN *goes to his grandmother. She kisses him on the head.*) My, that's nice, ya smell of soap. Easy now, I'm no fresh chicken. Wanna ride with us? We're gonna look at the sea. Harold?

HARRY. No. Watch out the intersections.

NANNA. Who made the coffee today?

HARRY. Me. (JOHN *leads* NANNA *to door.*)

NANNA (*To* HARRY). Did all right. Just hit the spot. Your father used to say to me, "Fay, you're a great cook, but you can't make coffee." Just hit the spot, Harry.

HARRY. Thank you, Mother.

NANNA. I'm off then. What time I'm to be back?

HARRY. By four.

NANNA. I'll come back all festive. Goodness, if I was sixteen again, I'd dance and sing songs. Boys used to like me, ya know. I was an airy fairy piece—used to trip down the street, ribbons flyin' in the breeze. (*Nudges* JOHN.) You should take more after me, trippety-trip, ribbons flyin'.

HARRY. O.K., Ma. Take your ride.

NANNA. Where's my present to ye? Fetch 'em here. . . . (JOHN *gets two books from shelf.*) I best give 'em to ya once more. All your people are in this album, and I handwrote in all the names and dates and places, and you're to remember even if they don't look too bright, they're all your own kin, so regard 'em kindly. And your great Aunt Ada's in there . . . she's the one . . . *walked* to California, she did, didn't have wagon money, walked every step of the way. . . .

HARRY. You'll be in traffic, Ma, if you don't move. . . .

NANNA. Out through Indian country. The Comanches didn't set her back. . . .

HARRY. Quit with old Ada now. . . .

NANNA. Out she went, zip, up and out lookin' for the *best*. . . .

HARRY (*Opens the front door for her*). Be back by four, girlie. . . .

NANNA. Fought snakes in the desert, she did; looked coyotes straight in the eyes.

JOHN. Yes.

NANNA. *Courage*. Let nothin' set her back. . . .

JOHN. Great. Yes.

NANNA. Out she went lookin' for valleys, streams, soil . . . ribbons flyin'. . . .

HARRY (*Taps her on shoulder*). The sea, Ma, sea looks lovely to-day. . . .

NANNA (*Nudges* JOHN). She didn't associate with a pukey lot, know what I mean? *Determination!* And there's Bobby Armstrong's Bible, but as none as yas went to church today, I wouldn't bet a red cent you'll make the Pearly Gates. But anyways, I'm off. . . . Where'm I goin'?

HARRY. The sea.

NANNA. That's it then. Ya made the coffee good, Harold. Did I say that? Just hit the spot. (*Exits.* JOHN *goes back to closet and searches.*)

HARRY. Kid, forget right now old Ada and that walkin' bit. . . .

JOHN. Where's my sleeping bag? Could you pack me a few sandwiches?

HARRY. I could not!

JOHN. You're not being very nice on my birthday. (JOHN *crosses to suitcase.*)

HARRY (HARRY *crosses to table*). TO FIX THIS· CREAMO WHIPPO IS NOT BEIN' NICE! WHEN I COULDN'T GET THE DIRECTIONS RIGHT? AND IT'S ALL FLOPPED DOWN AND SHOULD BE STANDIN' UP? AND IT'S ALL FOR YOU? AND YOU WOULDN'T HAVE LEFT US WITH A SPOON TO EAT IT WITH? AND WE'D HAVE SAT AROUND LIKE FOOLS! I'M CALLIN' THE COPS.

JOHN. Oh, for Pete's sake, you're so hysterical over nothing.

HARRY. And you call a million dollar heist nothin'? How much dough you got?

JOHN. Never you mind.

HARRY. No-o, I'd get the bills you run up in the Amazon, right?

JOHN. I'm not off to the Amazon. . . . That's more like for next year. . . .

HARRY. Hope ya starve to death before you hit Mineola!

JOHN. I'll cut a piece of the cake, there. (JOHN *crosses to cake on table.*)

HARRY (HARRY *stops* JOHN *from cutting the cake*). And leave that alone!

JOHN. Boy, to get your own piece of cake, you gotta know how to chisel and have STRENGTH, and just zip out the door!

HARRY. You cut that cake! I'll split you open with an ax!

JOHN. I dreamt about you last night. I killed you with a fork. . . . You just lay there bleeding. . . .

HARRY. And apparently you've had my flatware on the brain for some time. . . . (HARRY *crosses to the suitcase.*) What else is in here? (HARRY *roots around in the suitcase, throwing stuff out. A ring at the door.*) Who's that?

JOHN (JOHN *crosses to the fireplace*). How should I know?

HARRY. Get the door.

JOHN. You get the door.

HARRY. Will you get the door! (ALEC *enters the front door.*)

ALEC (*Sings*). Merry Christmas and Happy New Year. Happy Birthday to you. (HARRY *hides bottle in sideboard.*)

HARRY. Oh-ho-ho-ho, well, you're just in time to see your son light out for the Old Burma Road! (HARRY *crosses to the landing.*)

JOHN. I'm only going to Maine. . . .

HARRY. But not, I might add, with the family silver. (ALEC *comes further down and looks at* HARRY.)

ALEC. And how's the one and only Harold?

HARRY (*Growls*). Yeah.

ALEC. Yeah?

HARRY. Mmmmmm.

ALEC. As good as that, huh?

HARRY. What are ya? Lit? (ALEC *crosses U. and shakes* JOHN'S *hand.*)

ALEC. In a mild state of celebration. Harry, prepare yourself—you're going to be proud of me.

HARRY (HARRY *crosses to* ALEC). I am? It's good you're warnin' me, in case I should fall over. Didja improve yourself yet?

ALEC. God forbid.

HARRY. Ya look awful. Your cuffs are frayed.

ALEC (*Smiles*). Thank you.

HARRY. Ya look a wreck. (*To* JOHN.) Put the coffee on. (JOHN *exits into the kitchen.*)

ALEC (*Smiles*). Me, a wreck? Thanks again. Let's hope you never lose that endearing capacity of yours for direct statement and attack.

HARRY. Yeah.

ALEC. Yeah. Harry, my old war-horse. I gotta one-man show coming up. Are you proud? Tell me you're proud.

HARRY. I'm proud! . . . Try not to screw it up. Don't worry, you'll screw it up. (JOHN *returns and continues to search, find, and pack books.*)

ALEC. Seeing as how we've established our usual rapport, how about hauling the good stuff and offering your old pal a snort?

HARRY. In some faraway pig's left ear, my boy. You're not swillin' down my licker. And if ya root round for the bottle, it's *marked.*

ALEC. Ever my cautious Harry. And still wearing suspenders with a belt. Venture forth, you're still too careful.

HARRY. Take me once, shame on you. Take me twice, shame on me. That's my motto and thought for the day.

ALEC (*Looks at* JOHN). Happy Birthday. . . . (JOHN *nods.*) I came early so's we could chat, I mean your mother would like us to chat. (*To* HARRY.) You're supposed to be off on a Sunday drive with Nanna and the dame next door. (JOHN *crosses to hall tree for coat and* HARRY *crosses to sofa.*)

HARRY. They're already gone. They're down the ocean smellin' the air. Who the hell can drive any more of a Sunday? With all them city people out clutterin' up the highways, and throwin' their orange peel all over the roads. You wanna chat? I won't open my mouth. Chat!

JOHN (*To* ALEC). You put on weight.

HARRY. He's thinner. He don't eat right, same as you don't.

JOHN. No, he's heavier.

HARRY. He's thinner.

ALEC. For the record, I'm exactly the same. And I'm eating fine.

HARRY. Ya look thinner. Coulda fooled me.

ALEC. But then you're so easily fooled.

HARRY. Yeah?

JOHN. So what do you eat then?

ALEC. Huh?

JOHN. You said you were eating fine. What do you eat?

ALEC. Oh-h. . . . Food.

HARRY. They're all hangin' on the ropes for a meal, these artist starvin' painter people.

JOHN. Well what did you have for breakfast?

ALEC. Well now I fried two eggs, over easy . . . slipped them out onto the middle of a regular sized plate. Put some toast on the side. Usually to the left side, because that's my habit. And my coffee was on the right side. Black, with one sugar. Then I sat down . . . on a chair . . . at a table . . . and proceeded to eat and drink just like you all. (*To* HARRY.) Shall I take you through lunch?

HARRY. Be honest! Ya wanna sandwich?

ALEC (*Crosses to armchair and sits*). No.

HARRY (*To* JOHN). See if we still got that roast beef in the icebox. (JOHN *exits into the kitchen.*) And listen here, if ya got a show comin' up, protect yaself, and paint a few pretty pictures to sell. That's my advice. People got too much problems. Ya open a newspaper and you're sick before ya get to page two! Forget the concentration camp pictures ya used to do, with women's heads hangin' off. People don't want that starin' from walls. Give 'em pretty flowers, so's they'll feel good.

ALEC. Right you are, Harry.

HARRY. Life today . . .

ALEC. Don't give me any run-down on life today. . . . (JOHN *has re-entered from the kitchen and continues to pack bag, including clock from over fireplace.*)

HARRY. And your profession. . . .

ALEC (*Crosses to coat on hall tree and takes drawing from pocket*).

Before we argue over something you know nothing about, let me give you this right now. Because once we argue I couldn't give you anything less than a black eye. So with all good wishes. . . . From me to you. (ALEC *puts drawing in front of* HARRY *as* JOHN *crosses behind sofa.*)

HARRY. What's that?

ALEC. Find out. (HARRY *unrolls the drawing . . . is amazed, touched, and embarrassed.*)

HARRY. This is for me? . . . You're kidding? . . . You drew me a picture? (*To* JOHN.) See here . . . some hands . . . a pair of hands. . . . It's very . . . well, that very uh . . . ?

JOHN. Nice of you, thank you.

HARRY. Yeah, nice of you, thank you.

ALEC. You're very welcome.

JOHN. Hands hold your interest, huh?

ALEC. Mmmmm.

JOHN (*Examines his own hands*). What do you like best about them?

ALEC. Everything. (*Looks at his own hands.*)

HARRY (*Begins looking at his own hands*). Well, mine are shot, that's for sure.

JOHN (*Measures his against* HARRY'S.) Mine aren't too hot either.

HARRY. I always did like clean fingernails and shined up shoes on a person. (*The gift influences* HARRY. *He reveals a much softer and more sentimental side. To* ALEC.) It's cos of my father, right?

ALEC. What?

HARRY. Ya gimme a picture of hands cos of my father . . . and there's a coincidence for ya—even this morning, I was mullin' over how my whole life was changed because of a pair of hands. (*To* JOHN.) Somebody can say one word to ya, or make one silly nothin' kind of gesture, and you just detour down a different road. Like when my old man was around here, workin' hisself into the ground, runnin' day and night with two jobs, and sometimes he'd even do odd jobs as well for folks. Like washin' down walls. . . . And I see him once . . . puttin' his hands in and out a pail of cold, dirty water. And his fingers had gone all arthritic, all knobbly. . . . So that's why I went to work young . . . cos his hands upset me in a paila water. . . . Ah me, I'm gettin' like my mother. Oftentimes I don't wanna remember last week, but long ago comes in clear as clear. . . . (*He stands up.*) I better get the coffee. Mother said I made it good today. (*To* ALEC.) Ya wanna sandwich? Be honest. (ALEC *shakes his head.*) Ya get a sandwich. . . . And thank ya. (*He goes into kitchen.*)

ALEC. Is your mother in good temper?

JOHN. O.K. She oughta be psychoanalyzed, but she's all right.

ALEC. Analyzed?

JOHN. Something's wrong with her. She doesn't even read anymore. I think she's shrinking.

ALEC. Yeah, well that's the way it goes. (HARRY *bursts into song in the kitchen. "If you were the only girl in the world. . . ."*)

JOHN. You made his day.

ALEC. It was really for you—the drawing. To make up for those damn records I got you. Your mother gave me hell for those things, but I'll change them for you. But Harry always responds to a little something you give him, and it shuts his mouth for a while.

HARRY (*Off, sings*). "And I was the only boy . . ."

ALEC. God, he's off and running. Got a cigarette around?

JOHN. Oh, sure.

ALEC. I've really stopped. (JOHN *pulls out a number of half-opened packs from behind his books. He gives them to* ALEC.) Are you this much of a smoker?

JOHN. No, it's bad for you. I quit last year. I'm now a hypochondriac.

ALEC. Oh, you are? Well how are you this year?

JOHN (JOHN *crosses upstairs to bedroom*). Fine, fine. . . . I'm terrible, but I'm O.K. . . . I mean I'm still on my feet. . . . I feel like a Russian novel, but it'll all work out . . . so they keep telling me. . . . (JOHN *enters bedroom.*) Ugh! terrible, I'm terrible.

ALEC (*Coughs from the staleness of the cigarette*). Terrible, huh?

JOHN (*He comes out of bedroom and down stairs*). Yes.

ALEC. I'm sorry to hear it.

JOHN. Yes. . . . So am I. (HARRY *comes out of kitchen with coffee and sandwiches and places them on table. Also brings drawing pinned on breadboard and places it on table.*)

ALEC (*He sees sandwiches . . . sits at table*). Harry, I don't need this. Fix me a drink. (JOHN *crosses to table and takes cup of coffee.*)

HARRY. Eat while there's a chance. . . .

JOHN (*He tastes his coffee*). You *always* put sugar in mine!

HARRY. Fatten you up. Skinnamalink.

JOHN. But you have to like sweet coffee to want sugar!

HARRY. What you do is don't stir it up . . . that way ya get the goodness while you're not really knowin' it.

JOHN (*He crosses to desk and typewriter*). O-h-h, I will absolutely never, ever, forget you.

HARRY. I should hope to tell ya no. I'm the best sucker you ever met up with, what with expensive radios and all. Show your old man what I give ya. . . . (HARRY *is tacking the drawing to the breadboard with thumbtacks.*) See, he don't want it. Two hundred bucks! (HARRY *nods toward radio.*)

ALEC. Two hundred for that!

HARRY. We-e-ell, that old bat next door cornered me. "What that set ya? What that set ya?" so I told her two hundred—but it was really a hundred and forty-nine. Why should she know what price I pay? But he played with it ten minutes, then finish.

JOHN. I love it.

HARRY. Nah, ya don't. When you love somethin', ya go hide it, and ya don't want no one to touch it.

JOHN (*He crosses to table, takes radio, and sets it beside stairway near suitcase*). I love it. I'm taking it with me. (*He crosses back to typewriter.*)

HARRY. Figures he's about to go someplace. (*To* JOHN.) Travel to the basement and bring me up a few party chairs.

JOHN. Like to find out about human nature.

HARRY (*Rises*). People are a pile of Italian salami with a lotta baloney thrown in and by the time ya find that out, ya wish ya'd never bothered. Will ya get me them chairs? (HARRY *places the picture on sideboard.*)

JOHN. I'm typing.

HARRY (*He goes toward basement*). And there's gratitude with the pains I've got that go from here to there, and there to all over.

ALEC. So how's school?

HARRY. Oh God, don't start him on that! (HARRY *exits into basement.*)

JOHN. It's worse than a blind date. . . . Always want an answer, never get it through their fat heads there's two answers, theirs and mine, but just give 'em theirs, that's all they want. Guess what the creep for geography said to me Friday? "John Edwards, you're not participating, tell the class, are you merely very *shy* or very *conceited?*" Well, there was a long pause, during which I nearly dropped dead, *then*, he said, "Well, perhaps I should rephrase that, perhaps you're simply *living* from *within*." Boy, I shoulda cracked right back, "Listen, Buster! Just watch that phrasing and rephrasing stuff!" . . . They never tell you anything's beautiful, like it's some secret you're not supposed to know. (HARRY *enters from basement with chair.*) And I've only got one good teacher

. . . name's Walker. I call her Georgia because she's a peach . . . AND SHE'S WIRED EASY. SHE'S COOL AS A TEACHER AND AS A WOMAN!

HARRY. BRING HER HOME THEN. IF SHE CAN COOK I'LL MARRY HER.

JOHN. She smiles slow and she reaches me.

HARRY. She's even reaching me.

JOHN. But she's the only one. . . . Anyway, I've quit, as of today.

ALEC. WHAT?

JOHN (*He sits by his father at the table*). Look, if you really want to help, drop a remark to Ma that I look horrible—that's why I need to get away. Say I seem despondent. That's a neat word. And dejected. Disheartened. Despoiled! Desperate! In a state of deterioration! (HARRY *crosses behind* JOHN.)

ALEC. You reading the dictionary?

JOHN. Yes. I'm up to D. Nah, forget despondent. She'll figure that came from me, and a short word's best, but add feeling. "He looks baa-a-ad." Are you with me? Lemme hear ya say "Ba-aa-ad."

ALEC. Bad.

JOHN. No, frown with it. BAD.

ALEC. Ba-d. (HARRY *leans between them.*)

HARRY. BAAAAAD!

JOHN. That's it. Otherwise, I'm ZIP out the door and off. (*He rises and crosses to desk.*)

ALEC. I see, well, well, well. Don't be a cheapskate, Harry. Let's have a drink here. Be a host!

HARRY. Eat your sandwich. Waste not, want not.

ALEC. Quit huh? (*To* HARRY.) Did you know he'd quit?

HARRY. The old man here's the one that's about to quit. You two just fetch me up chairs. . . . (*He exits into kitchen with dishes.*)

ALEC (*Rises*). Now listen, Johnny. I came early because I'm supposed to ask you about the copybook. Your mother was on the phone to me. You have poems buried in the garden, is that right?

JOHN. And I'm not digging them up! The answer's no. They're staying down there. (*A ring at the door.* HARRY *reenters at kitchen door.*)

HARRY. Will you get the door? (JOHN *crosses to front door.*)

JOHN. It's Betty Barracuda. (BETTINA *enters and crosses in front of window seat.*)

BETTINA. Hi! Hi! I'm Bettina.

JOHN. Cake's at four. This is two-thirty.

BETTINA. I can tell time, stupid.

HARRY. All right, watch it. No rudeness of a Sunday. Ya wanna sit with us?

BETTINA. Oh, okay, although sitting's bad for my figure. (*She throws coat on* HARRY's *chair and sits on foot stool.*)

ALEC (*He crosses to* BETTINA). Hello, I'm Johnny's . . . I'm Mr. Edwards. (*They shake hands . . .* HARRY *exits into the kitchen with dishes . . .* ALEC *sits on sofa.*)

BETTINA. Ye-eas, I know. I watched you drive up in an old Ford. Are you all right?

ALEC. All right? Ye-s. Keeping my end up.

BETTINA. You wouldn't remember, but we began an association four years ago today, but I had braids then and was terribly young.

ALEC. Well, splendid. You look splendid.

BETTINA. Oh, thank you, that's a pretty compliment. (*She touches her perfect hairdo.*) My hair was done yesterday, but it's any which way today.

JOHN (*Mimics*). Any which way today. (HARRY *enters from kitchen with hats, napkins, noise-makers.*)

BETTINA. And my first daddy, my real daddy's AA so I understand how important it is to be sympathetic and open about drinking. That's why I asked if you were all right.

ALEC. Oh really? . . . How thoughtful.

JOHN (*Mimics*). How thoughtful. (HARRY *sits at table and folds napkins.*)

ALEC. Uh? You study, Bettina?

BETTINA. Oh, sure! I'm planning to continue on to the University of Paris—in France. This dress was copied from a Paris, France, style.

ALEC. Marvelous.

BETTINA (*She rises and displays dress*). It's my newest.

ALEC. Well, I meant the idea of Paris.

BETTINA. Oh, yeah. I'm going to take sculpture and painting and fashion.

JOHN (*Mimics*). Fashion.

BETTINA. . . . And all of the arts mostly, although I really have to light on one because my doctor advises me not to spread out that much, so I'll definitely pick fashion design as that's my pet. And I figure, failing all that, I could always go into modeling—

JOHN (*Mimics*). Modeling.

BETTINA. . . . And if that doesn't work, there's always acting. And after that, I'll get married.

JOHN. HUH!

BETTINA. I'm going with a boy now. (*She shows ring.*) I was going with two. . . . (*She shows other ring on other hand.*) But I ditched one. He had his mother send me a Valentine. Imagine! His mother! "Good grief," I told him, "that's no way to get ahead." You like this dress?

JOHN (*With his back to her*). No.

BETTINA. Who asked you? (*She rises and crosses C.*)

HARRY. Looks tight. Can ya move your arms?

BETTINA (*She models the dress*). Oh, the top is designed this way, and the skirt full, see? And there's two pockets, and here's a kerchief to match. Notice how many panels this skirt has? And the seams? Seams are very important. Isn't it fabulous?

JOHN (*Mimics*). Fabulous.

BETTINA. I've got 32 outfits, not counting draggy stuff for around the house, so it takes ages to choose every morning. Accessories and everything. But I get up early enough.

ALEC. Amazing. . . . All that material. (JOHN *hums,* "Get out of town, before it's too late, my love.")

BETTINA. And it's great for dancing! I'd love to be a ballet dancer as well. Wanna try a new step? (*She demonstrates a step and hums louder than* JOHN.)

ALEC. John, you dance.

JOHN (*Remains facing away*). I happen to have many broken legs.

BETTINA (*With her back to* JOHN). Scared to chicky! You're no dancer!

JOHN. Those steps are nothing! That's either the Mashed Potato or the Fried Chicken or the Frug You! (HARRY *hits* JOHN's *arm.*) Anything a fifteen year old teen-ager can do couldn't possibly take talent!

BETTINA (*Continues step*). Ho ho de ho! The Mashed Potatoes was ninety years ago! (*Swings around to face him*). Bet ya! Show me a single step!

JOHN (*Swivels round to face her*). No, stupid!

HARRY. PEACE!

BETTINA (*Moves toward* JOHN). Stupid yourself, rat!

JOHN (*Rises and crosses to* BETTINA). Stupid girl, snake!

ALEC. Listen now . . .

BETTINA (*Advances on* JOHN). Stupid boy! (*She hits* JOHN *and runs behind* HARRY.)

HARRY (*He stands up*). I told yas be pleasant! (JOHN *and* BETTINA *circle each other.*)

JOHN. GIRL!

BETTINA. BOY!

ALEC. Hey, fellas . . . don't tangle physically.

JOHN. Studying art in Paris!

HARRY. Shut up, you rats.

BETTINA (*She punches* JOHN *in ribs and crosses between sofa and* HARRY's *chair*). Your daddy's a big improvement over you. You're for the birds and I doubt if they'd have you! (ALEC *grabs for* JOHN.)

FLORENCE (*Offstage*). Quiet!

BETTINA. And you've got wheels missing and it's not the small ones either! (*She crosses to stairs.*)

ALEC. Harry, batten down this guest.

BETTINA. I wouldn't come to your old party.

JOHN. Who asked you! (JOHN *crosses to* BETTINA *and pushes her.*)

FLORENCE (*Offstage*). Do you hear me?

BETTINA. Wouldn't look at your old radio either.

HARRY. Florrie! Get down here! How many baths can ya take? (ALEC *is holding* BETTINA *back.*)

JOHN. What she say?

HARRY. Whadja say?

FLORENCE (*Offstage*). I said, "Cool it!"

HARRY. She said, "Cool it." (*He takes* JOHN *and sits him down at table.*)

JOHN. Ma, we got a guest who's ninety minutes early.

BETTINA (*She crosses in front of sofa*). Gracious, hostile, hostile! So troglo—dytaish!

JOHN. Troglo-dytaish!

HARRY. Keep still. That's just a girl-way of showing she likes you!

JOHN. Likes me! I've got two broken ribs!

BETTINA. Listen, Edgar Guest! (JOHN *crosses over sofa after* BETTINA *and* ALEC *stops him.*)

JOHN. Oh, I'll kill her, gimme a gun. . . .

HARRY. FLORRIE!

ALEC. MAYBE THE FOUR OF US COULD PLAY CARDS. . . .

BETTINA (*She crosses to stairs*). My grandma says you wanna be a poet! Wowee! (FLORENCE *comes downstairs and* BETTINA *crosses behind her.*)

JOHN (*He crosses to stairs*). You blab that over town, I'll . . .

FLORENCE. That's enough, now apologize!

JOHN. No.

FLORENCE. I said, make your apologies. . . .

JOHN. She called me "stupid" first. . . .

FLORENCE. Tell her "sorry" first, then let it go at that. . . . (*Pause . . .* BETTINA *leans on landing post.*)

JOHN. Sorry. (*He sits in chair at table.* BETTINA *crosses down stairs in front of* FLORENCE.)

FLORENCE. Can you come later?

BETTINA (*She crosses to* ALEC, *who has her coat*). Oh, sure. (*To* ALEC.) It was a pleasure meeting up with you again. (*To* FLORENCE.) I think your husband has a marvelous sort of savoir faire.

FLORENCE (*She opens the front door*). Yes, he certainly does.

BETTINA (*She crosses to door . . . turns*). I only dropped by to be friendly. (*She exits.*)

FLORENCE. Come back at four o'clock, Betty. (*She closes door . . . turns to* JOHN.) Now I won't have you be rude. . . . (*She crosses above sofa.*)

JOHN. Let's forget what you want. . . .

FLORENCE. You could have aked her to play a game. . . .

JOHN. She cheats! And she's coconuts!

FLORENCE. She's just a scatterbrain! (*She sits on windowseat.*)

JOHN. Her brain! It's her ass she scatters, not her brain. . . .

FLORENCE. You quit showing off to your father. . . .

JOHN (*He rises and crosses to* FLORENCE). She once wanted to throw it my way, but it had to be done in her *Mother's bed!* Get that one! Can you picture that big ox she's got for a mother, suddenly breathing down my neck!

FLORENCE. She *throws* because she's got three stepfathers and no friends! Glossy dead little girl who pretends she's got a date every Saturday night!

JOHN. How dare you understand a stranger and not me! (*Pause.*)

FLORENCE. I'd like to speak with your father. Go to the store please. We need bread.

JOHN. And the guys needn't get too optimistic about what Bettina's got up top either. She's all foam and pads. No wonder there's forty million faggots.

FLORENCE. I said, "Go to the store. . . ."

JOHN. You want white bread? White enriched bread? Cracked wheat? Whole wheat? Stone ground whole wheat? Pumpernickel? Romany rye? Westphalian rye? Westphalian pumpernickel? Westchester rye? Whole grain? Protein? Gluten? Italian? French? . . . Jewish rye? . . .

Catholic? . . . Protestant? . . . Nondenominational . . . Quaker oats? . . . Did you speak? (FLORENCE *waits him out.*)

HARRY. We need E-Z Opened Sliced Thin Round!

FLORENCE. Just do what I ask, Johnny. (*She crosses to* JOHN.)

JOHN. No.

FLORENCE. Are you going?

JOHN. I said, "NO!"

FLORENCE. Nobody likes a smartass, Johnny.

JOHN. Then we're both gonna have to change our style! (FLORENCE *slaps* JOHN *across the face.* JOHN *takes off glasses.*) If you wanna hurt me, do that again! (FLORENCE *slaps him again.*) And again! (FLORENCE *slaps* JOHN *again.*)

HARRY. Sissie, please, he's a kid.

FLORENCE. Is that enough? (JOHN *crosses to stairs and sits on steps.* . . . FLORENCE *sinks to arm of sofa.* . . .) I don't know how to cope anymore . . . never seem to do what's right. (*She sees the gifts on the sofa.*) These can go back . . . no point to spend money for things he doesn't want. . . . (*She crosses to* JOHN.) I wonder, if you ever did go away, what you'd say about us. Something like, "Oh, I'm from one of those hopelessly middle-class families, very dull, trivial type people, always carping on about bills. You wouldn't care for them much, they're so ordinary. Always a fight over this and that—not much style to them, no manners, no affection, no tenderness, not particularly honest. Never done anything fine or beautiful in their whole lives. And guess what? They tried figuring out how to give me everything and they really came up with a fast nothing." . . . Well, tell them for me that I wish I knew how to be happy . . . and wish I'd never loved anyone, then no one could do a single thing to reach me. I'd be free as the breeze, easy come, easy go. . . . Anyway, leave us if that's what you want—find somebody else who can make human footsteps for you. Lots of kids leave home, so you're bound to meet up with company. . . . Well, we need bread. (*She crosses to hall tree for coat.*)

ALEC (*He rises*). Listen, I'll go. . . .

HARRY (*He rises*). I could easily go. . . .

FLORENCE. No, you three visit awhile. (*She crosses down a step with the coat.*) I'm sorry I hit you, baby. . . . I'll never do it again. (FLORENCE *exits . . . pause.*)

JOHN. I do love my mother . . . it's just that you'd never know it. Can't even tell her, though. I can write in a book, "You are the eye and the sky of my heart," but I can't just walk across the room and say, "I love you . . . even if I have to let you down." Why's a for-real feeling always come out like corn? Why's it hard to be honest—even with a pal? (*He rises.*) Whydya get so ashamed of how you feel that you write it down and hide it away? (*He crosses to* HARRY.) You see, I meant to tell Mother yesterday that I'd get into line, if I *could.* Do everything she wants, if I *could.* I'd be so all-American, if I *could,* but I can't *swing* any way but *mine.* (*He walks near the bookshelves.*) And guess who did me in? WALT WHITMAN AND BOOKS! Walt Whitman! Son of a Long Island Gun! "Resist much, obey little" he tells you! Girls have got it made—all they have to do is walk around cutesy! But a boy! Ya gotta hide all the soft parts, cos I guess everyone gets scared you're not gonna finish up a man! Hope you guys all know what a MAN is, cos if you don't, and I don't . . . ha ha ha. (*He sits at table. Pause.*)

ALEC. "The eye and sky of my heart." . . . Like that line, Harry?

JOHN. Uncle Harry doesn't understand poetry. . . .

HARRY (*He stands up*). GODDAMIT! That's where ya sell me short, ya pipsqueak! It so happens I like that line! It's not logical English —A HEART don't have A SKY in it—but it sounds O.K. to me, yeah! I can figure a meanin'. (*To* JOHN.) I know ya don't respect me, but no matter how much I nag . . . when I see a young person flounder around not knowin' his ass from his elbow, and all he sees is an obstacle course up ahead—ya think it don't hurt me? Make me sad? . . . I would cry . . . if I *could.* I understand your dreams, and that's right, a boy's life is harder. A man's gotta earn bacon for the rest. And be responsible for. And how do ya fit it all in?

ALEC (*To* JOHN). Johnny, not a soul in this room can tell you what a man is.

HARRY (*He crosses C.*). Well, I'm over twenty-one.

ALEC. Jesus! I hope you don't find that too lonely. I thought we were all kids together.

HARRY (*He crosses to sofa*). Over twenty-one, and got a few answers for him.

ALEC (*He crosses to sofa*). You got any questions for yourself?

HARRY. I ain't no intellectual, thank you! I'm an ordinary man. . . .

ALEC. No, you're an extraordinary man, and I'll give you credit . . .

HARRY. Keep it! Who needs credit from you! Ya wanna fight me?! Take back your lousy drawing!

ALEC. Well, you're about to get credit! (*To* JOHN.) See, when I was a young pain in the poop around here, your uncle would approach his customers—perfect strangers—right in his cab. "I got this so-and-so livin' offa me, wanna buy a painting cheap?" So Harry smiled at me, in his own offensive fashion. However, a smile is a smile, and in the Arts it's worth a lotta bookkeeping or philosophy. Now it happens I could give you a smile—encourage you like crazy.

HARRY. Oh, and I couldn't?

ALEC. No, you couldn't! Cos you and your sister are so damned scared he could be another me—I can just hear you making bargains with God. "Dear God, if You promise us John will never be *less* than average, not a bum like his dad, then we'll settle if he *is* average."

HARRY. I wouldn't encourage him?

ALEC. Let me finish.

JOHN. Why do you drink?

ALEC (*Surprised*). I like liquor.

JOHN. O.K. Go on.

ALEC. Now that man came through the depression and that's why he knows the price of everything and that's about all. How'd you keep a roof over your head? Is there enough in the house to eat? Is the insurance paid up? Can I get a job? When's pay day? But he's forgotten that he once wanted to be Caruso. Heard him on a record and said My God! That's a sound, huh? Wish I could do that. Stand up and sing. Yeah, old Harry once saw himself big and beautiful with the arias. Not the cheap stuff, the real goods he wanted. (*To* HARRY.) What happened to the dream?

HARRY (*Aggressively*). You get pushed around in that line of work.

ALEC (*He rises and crosses to* HARRY). Yeah? What can you do where you don't get pushed around? Even when you owned your own cab there was always some dame in back with the orders, "Go right, turn left, no I said straight ahead."

JOHN. Why'd you marry my mother?

ALEC. That's a long story.

JOHN. But you kissed her off, so why'd you marry her?

ALEC. Well. . . . (*He crosses to* JOHN.) I married your mother because of long hair that she could sit on and eyes and a sweet mouth that all reached me like Miss Walker reaches you. She used to have a very delicate, a richer mind than me. And a better spirit. And I truly loved her. She could have been a very complete woman. That's what she wanted, you know. (*He crosses above table.*) That was her dream. I would like to be complete, Alec, she told me. And that's why I signed the papers with her, because I'm always taken with such desires when someone wants to be full and rich and human and beautiful. (*He sits at the table.*)

JOHN. But you didn't want me, did you? You wanted her to get rid of me. Uncle Harry let it slip once.

ALEC. Yeah, she never forgave me for that, but I had no way of supportin' you. And I couldn't leave my work. I'd have gone mad. Always the same story. "Get yourself a *real* job," they told me. But no one's ever come between me and my canvas, and I'm ashamed, I am, but I'll never change. And while I loved her, it wasn't enough. You have to demand from and develop all someone has inside them. But I paid the real attention to my work, and so she closed off. And the bickering began and I wound up handing her a lot of fears. I was always the only man for her. She probably died the day I walked. But I truly didn't set out to be a bad father or husband, because nobody does. And if you really want to know, I drink because my feel disappears. I need the booze to bring back my senses. The everyday grind robs me of my birthright. My touch and my imagination go flying out the window. Sometimes I walk down a street and feel nothing, numb. I pass someone by and not give a damn who he is. What's he to me? And the fight is always on—to stay human. I still try to reach out to myself and I still can't figure out why it's hard to do, let alone do it. Listen, you want a life in the arts, I hope you're crossed with Joe Lewis, but I'll give you a motto: "Never let the bastards get you down"—which sounds better in Latin. (*Pause.*) Anyway I'm sorry. I regret that we're not father and son.

JOHN. My father, my dad is Uncle Harry and could never be anybody else.

ALEC. Yes, now where's that book of poems?

JOHN. Oh, forget it.

ALEC. No, I don't want to forget it. You just point out the spot marked "X" and I'll go dig up the book. (*He crosses above table.*)

JOHN. I said forget it.

ALEC. You care to dare me to dig up the entire front yard? (*He crosses to sofa.*)

HARRY. Leave my garden alone. I know where your book is. (*He crosses to* JOHN.)

JOHN. No you don't.

HARRY (*In style of door-to-door salesman*). You want to fool me, you'd better not get out of bed the same day. Get up a week ahead of time. I seen from the basement window where the book went. It ain't in no ground. He stuck it up his sweater. Alexander, you see this kid sitting here. You would never guess in a million years. This kid sittin' here, who always looks like he don't know what's comin' off, and who spends hours starin' into space, and arguin' with me, that kid sitting there is a FANTASTIC talent.

JOHN (*He groans and covers his ears*). Uncle Harrrrry.

ALEC. He is?

HARRY. Yes! And where he gets it from God only knows because it certainly ain't you or me. But yesterday, he musta read me out twenty or thirty of his poems, and IN . . . CREDIBLE they were! And he had lovely thoughts—not like he sounds off in a room—and he had all the end words rhymin' together like ya never heard! BLOWIN', SNOWIN', GROWIN', SHOWING, KNOWING. . . . Fantastic! Ya got five bucks? Get out your money! (*To* JOHN.) You! Get that poem from yesterday! (*To* ALEC *as he reaches for his wallet.*) And imagine this. . . . (*He takes money from* ALEC.) Now here's what you'll be gettin' . . . a white piece of paper with beautiful words comin' at you. . . . "The snoooow was snoooowin' . . . the wiiind was bloooowin' . . . and eeeeeaaarthly criiiieees become heeeeaaavenly siiiiighs." Sound good? It's got a religious tone to it, this poem. (*To* JOHN.) You! Don't fool around coverin' up your ears! Get out that poem! YOU'RE MAKIN' YOUR FIRST SALE! AND WHETHER YOU GUYS LIKE IT OR NOT, THAT'S AMERICA, CASH ON THE LINE! THERE! FIVE SMACKEROOS. (*He crosses to* JOHN *and puts the money on the table.*) AND THAT'S HOW YA SELL A POEM! (JOHN *starts to say something.*) Ya wanna write poetry and stare at grass?! That's what you'll do then! Cos if ya listen to your mother, you'll wind up in pressed pants, and you'll be dancin' to a lot of other people's music. So you do what's inside, and meant for you to do! And that's my final word! (*He crosses C.*) And I may be sorry in two minutes from now that I said all this. (*He crosses to* JOHN.) But I'm sayin' it, and that's that! I'm puttin' my money on ya, kid! (*He takes out money and puts it on the table.*) My two-dollar bet is down! AND, I could even think up RHYMES FOR YA! Churnin', Yearnin', Burnin', . . . Moanin' . . . Phonin' . . . Loanin' . . . Groanin'. . . .

ALEC (*He is leaning on back of sofa*). As a matter of fact, I was about to ask you for a loan. . . .

HARRY. Of what?

ALEC. Fifty bucks.

HARRY (*To* JOHN). Fifty he wants! Ya wanna be an artist? Right off, a problem with the bills!

JOHN. Uncle Harry, the sale is just great. . . . But I think . . . I've changed my mind.

HARRY. You've what?

JOHN. Changed my mind.

HARRY. Say that again. I mean, I dare you to have the *neck* to say it again.

JOHN. Changed my mind. See, poetry is very hard, and yesterday I wrote down thirty lines, and this morning, there they were—yelling to be cut to the bone. Well, I finished up with two lines! So there obviously wasn't any bone! And it's always like that! (*He rises, crosses to* ALEC, HARRY *follows*.) And my mother's right—you have to be born with it . . . and be sensitive . . . and . . . I'm really just another crawly kid.

HARRY (*He grabs and hauls* JOHN *over to the window*). Look out the window. Ya see that tree out there?

JOHN. Yeah.

HARRY. What's that tree do to you?

JOHN. I dunno.

HARRY (*He considers*). Well, to me . . . a Wintertime tree . . . looks like . . . it's bound up with arthritis. . . . (ALEC *crosses to table and sits*.) But there must be fancier ways of seein' it than that. (HARRY *and* JOHN *cross to back of sofa*.) And I've already put my bet on you to find the ways. Now for your birthday—ya don't want my radio, so I'm gonna gamble recklessly and offer you my trust. Answer me this. If I turn back the radio—get $149 . . . ya want the money? . . . Or my faith?

JOHN. Huh?

HARRY. $149. . . . Ya can pay off your library bills. Fill up the room with a thousand more books . . . or ya want the other?

JOHN. $149 in hard cash, or the other?

HARRY. Yeah.

JOHN. Yeah? . . . No way I can get both, is there?

HARRY. Absolutely not.

JOHN. What kind of trust would you be giving me?

HARRY. Trust is trust.

JOHN. Well if I take it—would you put the money aside so I can claim it next Wednesday when you'll have lost all your trust in me?

HARRY. No, no. Gotta trust me, that I'll trust you, long beyond Wednesday. So which one is it to be?

JOHN (*To* ALEC). Which one is the bargain? . . . What would you do?

ALEC (*He shrugs*). My rent's due, and I'm too old to trust anybody.

JOHN (*To* HARRY). What would you do?

HARRY. I'm askin' you.

JOHN. But if you were me, what?

HARRY. Do ya know me sixteen years?

JOHN. Yeah, you'd take the cash. (*He crosses to armchair.*)

HARRY. That's the way I am. But how about you?

JOHN (*He crosses above armchair*). Boy, you're makin' me need a cigarette. You'd both take the cash? Of course, the trouble is, I don't know if I trust your trust, that's the trouble. Course I need a little trust—that's what I'm always asking for, but at the same time $149 is $149. I better take the dough.

ALEC (*He shakes his head*). No-o. Do the opposite of us—you might come out ahead.

JOHN. That's right! I'll take your trust! . . . Hope that works out!

HARRY. Come here.

JOHN (*He walks over to* HARRY, *who puts his arm around him.*) Shake on it.

ALEC. All right, let's hear them then.

JOHN. What?

ALEC. The two lines. The poems.

JOHN (*He walks away*). Weeee-ll . . .

ALEC. Come on.

JOHN. Uh . . .

HARRY. Stand up proud now! (*Follows* JOHN.) See, in a funny odd, peculiar, strange way, it won't really bother me if ya wanna be a grease monkey or a dish washer, but I gotta see ya stand up straight with it. How'm I gonna be on your side, if you're bent up double and ashamed and all? All my life, I said right out, "I'm a hackie, and if ya don't like it, lump it!" So, come on now, brush your hair back and give us a show.

JOHN (*He smoothes his hair, and goes into his coughing, shuffling routine*). Now . . . if I laugh, it's only from nerves. . . .

HARRY (*He crosses to* ALEC *at the table*). Gimme a dollar.

ALEC. What for?

HARRY. We don't give no free shows here.

ALEC (*He takes out his wallet*). You wouldn't care to become my manager, would you? I think I could use you.

HARRY. Well, poetry's supposed to make ya happy, and ya don't get happy for free—O.K. Start the movie. (ALEC *and* HARRY *sit at table.*)

JOHN. Could you stay standing? It seems like an audience if you sit. And don't interrupt me. (HARRY *and* ALEC *rise.*)

HARRY. He's blushing. We have to turn away. It helps him. (*They face away from* JOHN.)

ALEC. The two of you are gonna make a swell Greenwich Village group.

HARRY. O.K.!

JOHN. Well, this doesn't have a title, but it's to my mother.

ALEC. When I have my show, maybe if people don't actually look at my work and face the other way, I'll sell like hotcakes.

HARRY. Are ya throwin' your shoulders back?

JOHN. Yeah, yeah. Did I tell you this was to my mother? (*He takes a deep breath, looks at the ceiling.*)

> "If the sun shines not,
>   Would you dawn the day for me?
> If the moon rides not,
>   Will you light the night?
> Or honor the spark, in the dark that hides
> Inside your son, who shines not, nor rides."

Well I had fifteen lines before, but that's all I've got left on that one. . . . You don't have to like it. I mean, did you hate it?

ALEC. No. No. (*He turns to* JOHN.)

HARRY (*He slaps* ALEC *on the shoulder*). What I tell ya? (*He grabs money from the table.*) Wanna buy another? (*He crosses to* JOHN *and gives him the money.*) We're gonna recite 'em all. I think we hooked a sucker! (*To* ALEC.) Is he Shakespeare or is he Shakespeare!

JOHN. None of it's easy.

HARRY. Don't run yourself down! I feel good! Ya made your first sale and Harold feels good. And we'll get out the bottle and have a little drink—and get out the cigars and have a little smoke. I'm treatin' everybody. Let's have a private party. Let's cut the cake. (*As* HARRY *mentions the bottle and cigars he takes them from sideboard and puts them on table along with matches. . . .* ALEC *gets glasses off the sideboard for the booze.*)

JOHN. I'll get the knife. (*He gets the cake knife off the sideboard.*)

HARRY. The hell with 'em. We'll greet the guests at the door. "Go home! We done ate the cake!" (HARRY *lights cigars.* ALEC *lights candles on the cake.*) Stand back, cos I'm gonna give yas a song. (HARRY *bursts into song.* ALEC *and* JOHN *pick up his mood and join in. Sings.*)

> They called her frivolous Sal,
> A peculiar sort of a gal,

ALEC (*Does a little tap-dance. Sings*).
> Gal, gal, gal.

HARRY.

> With a heart that was mellow,
> An all 'round good fellow . . .

ALEC.

> Was my old pal.

JOHN.

> Pal, pal, pal . . .

HARRY and ALEC.

> Your troubles, sorrow and care,
> She was always willing to share
> A wild sort of devil,
> But dead on the level,
> Was my gal Sal.

(*They continue singing the song for as much time as they need to light the candles and the cigars, put on paper hats, bring out the bottle of liquor, lay paper plates, etc.*)

ALEC (*Pouring drinks*). You're sure we aren't afraid to cut that cake?

HARRY (*He stands over cake poised with the knife*). We absolutely are! But what the hell, here goes!

JOHN. Hey, we could slice off the entire bottom. That way no one will see anything's missing.

HARRY (*He begins to cut the cake*). You're a born crook kid, but this is right in the open.

JOHN. We're gonna see the inside of a doghouse. We oughta chisel off the bottom. That's why I pretended to bury my book . . . because if you want anything . . . want to get your own way . . . or even your own piece of cake . . . ya gotta know how to chisel and fool people. (*To* ALEC.) Can I get loaded?

HARRY. Give him one little drink. (ALEC *gets glass off sideboard.*)

JOHN. Yeah? Say, things are pickin' up here. (*They all are sitting at the table now.* JOHN *sings.*)

"They called her frivolous Sal . . ."

BERT ANDREWS

Ya know, in case you're interested. . . . If I ever get married . . . which is an extreeeeeeeeeeemely remote possibility (*He lights his cigar.*), but if I ever get cornered, I'm going over every inch of my bride with a microscope. She's gonna be no Bettina with steel traps and foam pads, and all that stuff to kid you they're Marilyn Monroe when they're really Ma Kettle.

HARRY. I wouldn't even marry Elizabeth Taylor. She could beg on her knees. *Or* Ingrid Bergman, and she was my favorite till she upset the nation. (*He passes out napkins.*) All right. We got the cake. We got the drinks.

ALEC (*He rises to toast* JOHN). Here's to sixteen, which ain't sweet —but when you feel brave enough to change the world. (*They all drink.*)

HARRY (*He rises*). Yeah, yeah, and here's to forty-one. (HARRY *pours booze and* JOHN *puts his glass out for a refill.*) Get out of here. (HARRY *pours booze for* ALEC, *and* JOHN *again sticks his glass out for a drink.*) And here's to fifty-six. (*To* JOHN.) Get out of here. . . . When ya figure that foolhardiness is here to stay, and what can ya do about it anyway.

ALEC. But mostly—to sixteen. (*All are now sitting at the table.*)

JOHN. Hey, this is swell! My two father images and me woopin' it up. If you keep up the good work, I'll grade you A. Say! Could you stand another?

ALEC. Drink?

JOHN. No, poem. I have one called "The Student" which is not for sale. It's for my tombstone. Can you bear it?

HARRY. It's not sad, is it?

JOHN. Nah, only for me, not for you. O.K.? (JOHN *rises and stands behind chair.*) "The Student" it's called. And steel yourselves—maybe you shouldn't be encouraging me. If you gimme an inch, I always take three miles. (*He clears his throat.*) O.K.? (HARRY *and* ALEC *both clear their throats with him.*)

HARRY. Shall we face away?

JOHN. No. (*He looks at the ceiling.*)

"The cat in back sits tight upon his blues.
He stares at time—then blinks.
His hands dry, his mind sweats out the spleen of Teen
Agement . . . Cagement . . . Ragement.
A raft of hours more, and endless more,
He worries at the wood, and scratches out,
And glares without, an inward shout, screaming out, FOR

THOSE . . . WHO'VE . . . DIED . . . IN . . . VAIN,
WAITING FOR THE BELL TO RING."

AND THAT'S DEDICATED TO EVERYBODY UNDER EIGH-
TEEN!

HARRY (*He has listened intently*). What's that, "He worries at the
wood"?

JOHN. The guy's writing, ya know, scribbling on the desk. (*Demon-strates.*) Worrying away at the wood.

HARRY. I get it! (*To* ALEC.) Didja get it? The guy's worrying away
at the wood. (*He demonstrates.*)

ALEC. Thank you. I picked it up.

JOHN (*To* HARRY). I've got one to give you . . . if you don't want
it explained. Is it a deal?

HARRY. You're gonna give *me* a poem?

JOHN. Yeah—can you believe it? I've just changed some words
around in my mind—so now it's for you.

"You are the eye and the sky of my heart,
    And I will love you a thousand years, perhaps less,
    But at least until I step away from you—
    Old man of the straight gaze and kindly hand.
    And then we will remember fair, a thousand tears, perhaps
        more,
    Until who owns your heart comes back, and through a door,
        and up a step. . . ."

BETTINA (*Offstage*). Johnny . . . Johnny. . . .

JOHN. Aw! (BETTINA *enters front door and crosses C.*)

HARRY (*Sings*).
    There she is, Miss America.

ALEC. Come over here and hear a real artist at work.

BETTINA (*To* JOHN). Some kid's taking your bike apart down the
block.

JOHN. My bike!

HARRY and ALEC. Huh? What?

BETTINA. Some kid's taking your bike apart down the block.

HARRY. Go get him.

JOHN. I'll be right back. Hold the party. (*He goes.*)

HARRY. Sit down and have a piece of cake. (BETTINA *looks from*

HARRY *to* ALEC *and back to* HARRY. *She is badly frightened and holds a crumpled kerchief close to her.*)

BETTINA. Mister Harry? (*She sits in chair by table.*) Mister Harry, please. Don't get scared.

HARRY. Calm yourself. What's wrong?

BETTINA. I had to come, I just saw it, so I had to come . . . don't be . . . please don't be upset with me, but I just . . . she had blood on her hair, so I had to. . . .

HARRY. Oh, my God. Who?

BETTINA. Johnny's mother. But there wasn't any painful part . . . honestly, I wouldn't lie about a thing like that, and I wanted you to know so that you couldn't . . . so that you needn't say anything because it's his birthday, and so it could wait for tomorrow, or maybe until after the party, and also you know the way, well like, they'll call you up now from the hospital, and that's the way it is on television, they call and you'll have to go down there and a doctor explains it all, but in a nice way, except that he couldn't know how it was all so fast, and that must be the best way, and there was even this little smile around her mouth, and the truck driver was crying, and I never saw a man shake like that—that was a surprise, but the blood . . . I got rid of the blood . . . (*Pause.*) Oh . . . I shouldn't have come. . . . Bet I worded that all wrong. (*Pause; to* ALEC.) Shall I go tell the others we won't have the party?

ALEC. Yes. (BETTINA *rises and crosses* C.)

BETTINA. Would you rather have heard it more formal . . . from the doctor?

HARRY. No . . . but it's enough now.

BETTINA (*She crosses to hall*). Can I come back later?

ALEC. Sure.

BETTINA. Yes. . . . Don't be upset. (*She exits.*)

HARRY (*Pause*). My sissie's dead. . . . Is that what she said? (ALEC *goes to the desk looking for a phone book.* HARRY *crosses bottom of stairs.*) Right outta the blue she said Florrie's gone? That couldn't be true—she was just standin' there—she just went for bread, that's all. And we just bin sittin' here . . . jokin' around . . . and . . . we gotta call 'em up. (*The phone rings, and they stare at it, until finally* ALEC *picks it up.*)

ALEC. Hello? . . . Yes, he's here. . . . (*He holds phone out to* HARRY.)

HARRY (*He shakes his head*). You speak.

ALEC (*Into the phone*). I'm Mr. Edwards, I'm the husband, I'll come on down. . . . No, no, we already heard. . . . You can tell me now. . . . (*He listens.*) Yes. . . . Mmmmmmmm. . . . Thank you. (*He replaces phone and sits down at desk. He automatically straightens things out on desk.*) "Mrs. Florence Edwards . . . of 31 Jefferson Road . . . was brought in . . ."

HARRY. Oh, Jesus God in Heaven, it's all true. (*He crosses himself.*) How'm I gonna break it to my Ma, she's an old woman. And it's his birthday. Sixteen years ago he got born upstairs to Florrie, and we was down here, just like this, you and me.

ALEC. One of us has to go down there.

HARRY. I'll go.

ALEC. No, you stay and take care of your kid. (*He crosses, gets coat, goes to door, and meets* JOHN *coming in door.*)

JOHN. There wasn't anyone with my bike. Where ya goin'? We're in the middle of our private party.

ALEC. I have an errand. I won't be long. (*He exits.*)

JOHN. No, wait! Boy, I feel great, and when I feel great, great is what I feel. So I toast, and you can laugh if you want, but I toast Mr. Keats, Mr. Shelley, Mr. Auden, and all the rest of the guys that I call Mister. (*He crosses to fireplace for streamers for decoration.*) Come on, let's decorate. (*He throws a streamer over top rail of banister.*) We could make the place all colors. Come on, Uncle Harry. (*He throws another streamer.*) What's the matter? You coming down with a sickness? Want any of my pills? Wanna hear a joke? I'll cheer you up.

HARRY. John, your mother's dead. Wish I had a real gift of the gab, and could put it to you exactly right and proper, and it wouldn't come out blunt. And if it came out that way, then I mean for it to be different. (*Pause.*)

JOHN. My mother's . . . ?

HARRY. Yes.

JOHN. No! A person can get older and not be so outgoing and they kind of die and that's the way it is. They just get older and afraid.

HARRY (*He crosses to armchair*). She met up with an accident on the street. And we have to go down and look. But there wasn't any pain. The little girl said it was all quick. She went real fast. (*He sits in armchair.*)

JOHN. Oh. . . . I should have gone for the bread. Gone for the bread. She was just in the room. She was there. Right there. (*He crosses to jacket on sofa.*) I was going to put it on, honest. I'm putting it on. Look. She'll see me in the suit. And the tie. The tie is pretty. I'll do what she wants. Everything she wants. I'll do what you all want.

HARRY. Sit by me.

JOHN (*He takes copybook from sweater*). I'll tear it up. It's kid stuff. She didn't really want it.

HARRY. Gimme that.

JOHN. I'll be good.

HARRY. Gimme the book. Trust me.

JOHN. Why don't I cry?

HARRY. Come sit by me, please, just this once.

JOHN. Why aren't I crying? I don't feel anything.

HARRY. Now tell me the joke. See if you can make me smile.

JOHN. Yeah, that's right. (*He sits on ottoman.*) You mustn't get upset, you hear. You worry too much. That's all you do. You sit around and worry. Nothing's wrong. We're gonna be all right. Nothing! Nothing's wrong! NOTHING! NOTHING! NOTHING!

CURTAIN

ON

Johnny
No-Trump

Johnny No-Trump has become almost a generic term for the flop *célèbre*. The first produced work of an unknown playwright, a reserved, sometime-actress named Mary Mercier, the play opened October 8, 1967, at the Cort Theatre. Its small cast, which was headed by Pat Hingle, Don Scardino, and Sada Thompson, had been directed by Joseph Hardy. Its producers, Richard Barr and Charles Woodward, Jr., closed the play the next morning.

Sic transit show biz, one might conclude. And yet, five years later, fast-flopping shows are still said to be "pulling a *Johnny No-Trump*." A casual mention of the play at a soporifically dull Drama Desk meeting can ignite a nasty exchange of invective among usually clubby critics. In his acerbic best-selling book of 1969, *The Season*, William Goldman used *Johnny No-Trump*, which he called "the best new American play of the season," to launch the book's most controversial chapter, a free-floating diatribe against the entire critical establishment of the Broadway theater. Susan Jacobs, a Midwestern writer in the children's literature field, wrote a book, *On Stage*, about the production to acquaint a future generation of theatergoers with the vagaries of the commercial theater. And even today, an offhand remark about the play can still set off New York *Times* drama critic Clive Barnes on a rousing recounting of his touchy, if now-buried, feud with producer Richard Barr. Occasionally a rumor of an imminent revival goes the Shubert Alley rounds and manages to stir up a few antagonisms before being squelched. For a one-night quickie, the play has made louder rumbles in the theater community than any number of now-forgotten hits.

Johnny No-Trump is a fine, honest family drama. Its dramatic goals are modest—the character delineation of the members of a middle-class family and the analysis of their interrelationships—but it attains them admirably, with a good deal of emotional power and a superb depth of sensitivity. Its dramatic structure is a wobbly affair, but the sheer force of its compassion, the superior quality of its writing, and the flesh-and-blood dimensions of its characters easily compensate for its sketchy plot mechanics.

Its action is almost completely internalized, concentrated as it is in the probing of its characters—a sensitive teen-ager, his rough-edged uncle, and his disillusioned mother. The play's action moves forward with each tentative emotional contact or withdrawal made between these people, as they struggle to understand and communicate with one another. What makes the play rewarding are its characters, who are substantial human beings. Miss Mercier has given them psychological complexity and an unlimited supply of warmly funny and sympathetic dialogue.

Harry, the loud-mouthed uncle, is an especially successful creation. He is a vivid dramatic embodiment of Richard Nixon's "silent majority," which finds itself displaced and superfluous in a world of changing values it can neither understand nor accept, but to which it reacts with envy, hostility, and grudging admiration. For all of Harry's braying criticism of his "arty" and educated sister and nephew, he has a deep love for them which he can't articulate. So he barks—and continues to push his own workingman's values, even though he suspects that the Great American Dream standards may not be quite adequate anymore.

Johnny is also a fascinating character. Despite his obvious affinities with the young heroes of a number of other plays and novels, he is a complete individual in his own right, and no mere spokesman for the younger generation in revolt against its elders, no clichéd caricature of the sensitive young plant kicking up its soil. Johnny is an exceptionally intelligent boy, which sets him apart from his own generation as much as from his family's generation. He uses that intelligence, just as Harry wields his rough-and-gruff anti-intellectualism, as a defensive weapon to preserve the separateness of his identity. Extremely articulate, he is always sparring verbally—jabbing and clipping with sharp jokes, witty digs, snide criticisms—with those he'd really rather reach and touch with affection. Johnny is caught up in conflicting values and at this point in his life doesn't know who he is or where he's going, but he's on the verge of asserting his identity, if he can just get it all together.

The mother's character is secondary, but she too has her points and is a most sympathetic figure. Disillusioned by her unhappy marriage and disappointed by her teaching experiences (this second point was made clearer in a scene which Miss Mercier cut from the final performed version of the play), she seems to have lost her dreams and hopes for herself, and now derives her happiness from her son and from her visions for his future. Like Harry, she is proud of Johnny's artistic urges, but feels bound to protect him from them because she has learned from her own life to associate young dreams with old failures.

Johnny No-Trump, then, seems to be the sum of its characters, whose dimensions far override the play's structural flaws. "I wanted to write a play about middle-class Americana," Mary Mercier says of her play, "about the way in which these people's love is expressed through continual carping and fighting. And about the way in which they attempt to control each other's lives to an extreme degree—all in the name of love. Love is never really mentioned between them, but they do love each other, this family.

"I somehow wanted to make the point, also, that whatever affection or feeling they have for each other is the one thing that they never express. And yet, that feeling is in them. If these people had to expose their real feelings, they would show themselves to be so *vulnerable*."

Although *Johnny No-Trump* is successful on its own artistic terms, it does have one serious internal flaw—its dramatically arbitrary ending, which has the mother killed offstage in a melodramatic accident. It throws the entire play out of gear, shifts its thematic emphasis disastrously, and alters the sensitive tone established and sustained by Miss Mercier up to this moment.

The critics all pounced on the flaw like marauding hawks sighting a wounded fieldmouse. But although they were justified in knocking the ending, they placed undue importance on it, allowing it to discolor their judgment about the rest of the play. It was as if their discovery of the flaw gave them justification for dismissing the entire play.

The ending figured prominently in the failure of *Johnny No-Trump* in one other significant way. It revealed the single major point of artistic disharmony which existed among the creative staff. The ending, in fact, had been the cause of serious disagreement between the writer, director, and producers.

When, during an interview with *The New York Times*'s critic, Clive Barnes, I asked him to comment further on the play's ending, which he had called "absolutely ridiculous," he started to suggest that "perhaps a better producer, or a more engaged producer" might have exerted more influence on the writer and had the ending revised. Placing some of the responsibility with the director as well, he said, "Although I think Hardy did a good job, a more experienced director—that is, 'experienced' in the ways of Broadway—would have got some rewriting done."

Mary Mercier liked and still likes her ending, and implied that it would have worked on the stage had it been directed differently. "It depends on how the ending is performed," she says. "That final scene, if it's performed at the timing that I meant—which is actually a very slow ending—would not be sentimental. . . . The director somehow found the characters to be somewhat more sentimental than they really are."

Joseph Hardy disagrees with Miss Mercier's assessment of his direction, insisting that it had been, on the contrary, very "clean." "I didn't feel there was any sentimentality in my direction," he says. "In fact, I directed *away* from it." However, Hardy did *not* like the play's ending, and he admits attempting to influence the playwright to change it. "It was too abrupt," he says. "But we did not change it, because Mary absolutely refused to. We did talk about alternatives; we discussed them. We came up with solutions to the ending. Mary was adamant; she absolutely refused; she would not accept them."

Producer Richard Barr agrees with his director. "If we had exercised a kind of dictatorial power that I disapprove of," he says, "it is possible we could have *forced* Mary to sit down and rewrite that ending. But we did not insist, because of our attitude that the author is boss."

But Mary Mercier doesn't seem to feel that she was treated as deferentially as Barr implies. "There is no question that both the director and producer were far stronger than I was—stronger in the sense that if I said something, it was not listened to," she says, about the rewrites, character eliminations, scene omissions, and other script changes. "Now, I can't deal with people on those terms. When someone behaves like that, I don't know what to do. I can't take hold of a producer's arm and say: 'Now, you put that line in, or else.' I don't think that to be the playwright is to be in any position of power at all. The playwright has very little control."

This is a common complaint among playwrights, and is usually a justifiable one. But in this particular case, the play would certainly have been improved if Barr and Hardy had pulled their weight a little and convinced Mary Mercier to scuttle that awkward ending.

Flawed and all, *Johnny No-Trump* is a fine play, with the case for it resting on its human, *reachable* characters; its pungent and richly comic dialogue; and its compassionate but honest portrayal of middle-class American life. It is not a great play, neither in subject nor in dramatic technique, but it is the kind of play we need desperately on our stages—a play that can appeal to the largest segment of the middle-class theatergoing public without insulting their intelligence or duping them with a romanticized, dishonest picture of their way of life.

Writing in the October 22, 1967, issue of the Sunday *New York Times*, Walter Kerr said that: "the damage done by the sudden closing . . . is enormous. Beyond doubt, author Mary Mercier's confidence has been damaged. . . . She is at this moment a failure rather than a discovery. . . . Yet she *is*—or should have been—a discovery. . . . Her structural gaucheries were almost unimportant; she has a voice."

So, if *Johnny No-Trump* was indeed such a lovely play, written by such a promising new writer, why did it flop in a single night?

The usual shotgun response is that the stupid, insensitive critics didn't respond to its modest merits and therefore "killed" it, and this is more or less what the play's producers claim. There was indeed some appalling insensitivity, on the part of a few critics, to the quality of the play. One critic claimed Miss Mercier had "no sense of real-people kind of conversation"—which is simply dense in the face of the play's exceptionally vital language. He further stated that "the play is dated in both style and attitude and is unprofessionally written to, as it is said, boot" —which itself is such a gruesome piece of bad writing that one wonders how he has the gall to pass judgment on subway graffiti, let alone on Miss Mercier's manifestly verisimilitudinous dialogue.

Another of my compatriots wrote: "During the course of her labored caper . . . Miss Mercier manages to create not a single believable character or credible situation"—which is so obtuse a response to the play that it might be considered downright irresponsible.

Most of the reviewers, however, delivered what co-producer Charles Woodward, Jr., called "kind" notices. A few, including Walter Kerr of the *Times*, Brendan Gill of *The New Yorker*, George Oppenheimer of *Newsday*, Hobe Morrison of *Variety*, voiced even stronger approval. In fact, rather than Bronx-cheer dismissals, the critics registered quite a bit of favorable reaction.

What was really surprising about the critical responses was a bewildering display of almost unanimous misinterpretation of the play's *subject*. Practically all the critics interpreted the theme as the coming-of-age of a young boy in the throes of generation-gap traumas. Period.

Review after review turned up phrases like: "16-year-old misfit at odds with his parents and the world" . . . "about the coming of age of a young man" . . . "mixed-up boy unmixed" . . . "the misunderstanding between the generations" . . . "pitfalls of misunderstanding which separate parent and offspring" . . . "about life with a late-model American boy" . . . "about a youth in revolt," etc.

Certainly Johnny's *Sturm-und-Drang* adolescence is an element in the play, but to interpret it as the focal issue, and to undervalue or ignore totally the love relationships between all four members of the family—which, in their ambiguous complexities constitute the real *core* of the play—is to misinterpret Miss Mercier's very straightforward dramatic statement.

Ironically, many critics seemed to sense the inadequacy of this interpretation, but chose to fault the play rather than to reexamine their own limited appraisal of it. They saw it as a generation-gap comedy-drama, and by God, that's what it was going to be.

The tendency of the critical community to seize upon this superficial bromide can be understood, although not forgiven, by the fact that the entire nation, and certainly the American theater, was at the time utterly gripped by the first strong wave of the "generation-gap" syndrome. The country was being pricked on all tender sides by "Don't Trust Anyone Over 30" buttons. The going movies were youth-cult specimens like *The Trip, Privilege, Blow-Up, The Family Way,* and *How I Won the War.* In October, the month that *Johnny No-Trump* opened on Broadway, the Sunday *New York Times* entertainment section carried youth-oriented articles with a vengeance: Robert Brustein wrote a major feature on how the theater was failing its young people; the art page had a story entitled "The Generation Gap"; the music section ran a piece called "To Understand Our Children," discussing the "drastic cultural change" which rock music was then effecting.

Most telling of all, on the day of *Johnny No-Trump*'s opening, the front-page article in the Sunday *Times* drama section was titled "The Generations War on Broadway." In it, Lewis Funke wrote that "by January's thaw, at least ten productions on the situation—mostly comedies—will have been displayed." Funke followed up that report by listing the ten shows, which included *Johnny No-Trump* right up front. Under the circumstances, the casual "generation-gap" reading given the play by the majority of New York critics seems understandable. Preconditioned by the deluge of "youth speaks and their elders tremble" phenomena abroad in the land, the critics were simply not in the mood to give proper attention to the psychological subtleties of Mary Mercier's play. As director Joseph Hardy said, with the most economical simplicity: "They were all up to their ears with it."

What was particularly devastating for *Johnny No-Trump*'s cause was the fact that the youth explosion, with its attendant glut of publicity, had also made the critics strongly (if unconsciously) resentful of youth-oriented plays. One review, that of the late Whitney Bolton, which appeared in the *Morning Telegraph*, expressed that antagonism most openly: "It arouses resentments toward brassy young," Bolton said of *Johnny No-Trump*. "I am angry at that young fellow . . . the brat irritated me from the start and the irritation never abated . . . infuriating adolescent." Bolton went on to use the play review as an occasion for an outburst against the entire "up youth" temper of the time, stating that he couldn't rouse in himself "the compassion one is supposed to bring to the problems of the young today, no matter how brash, how arrogant, how mannerless and defiant the young may be. It is difficult to look dispassionately upon a young character who richly deserves a swat across the fundament instead of the placations and gropings for understanding through which his surrounding adults have to pass in order to reach his flinty, self-satisfied, rebellious core."

The tragedy, of course, about Mary Mercier's play was that it wasn't at all about the generation gap. It simply happened to have been standing in the direct line of fire as the first of the season's rash of plays dealing solidly or peripherally with any subject remotely resembling a young kid's problems with his parents. By the end of the season, when *Hair* and *Your Own Thing* had opened, the critics had mellowed somewhat. By that time Mary Mercier was out looking for acting jobs.

The critics, however, do not kill a show—maim it, scar it, perhaps, but kill it they don't. They *can't*. The producer is the final arbiter. It is his decision, and his only, that determines the fate of a theatrical property. So-called "audience shows," loathsome to critics on artistic grounds, are always kept merrily running by producers. And when a producer's personal vanity is involved, he will even support a show that the audience itself doesn't like and won't attend.

The producers of *Johnny No-Trump* chose to close the show the night it opened. This judgment was made, they said, primarily on the basis of *The New York Times*'s notice. After mourning briefly the warm and lukewarm reviews of all the other critical sources, Richard Barr focused his ire on the *Times* reviewer, then-newcomer Clive Barnes. He fired off to him an irate telegram which Barr recalls as having said:

"I too am very angry. Here is a new play by a new playwright which certainly requires a good deal more attention than you paid it, and a good deal more encouragement than was indicated in your review." Barr followed up his telegram with a letter to Barnes, "much more amenable than my angry wire," according to Barr, "in which I explained to him the finances of the theater."

Barr took this retaliatory action—which is considered rather a daring measure for a producer, even in the theater's emotionally impulsive climate—out of what can only be construed as intense frustration at not having been fairly treated by the critical community's dean. Barr's anger transcended the simple, unadorned fury of a producer whose financial investment had gone down the hopper. His charge that Barnes "did not give us credit for trying to put on Broadway a young, new playwright with a very, very possible play" is a far more serious charge because of its implication that the critic did not treat the play with the respect due it as a piece of dramatic literature.

Barr was justified in his assessment of Barnes's review. Except for some enthusiastic words for the production, the notice was unfavorable. Certainly Barnes can't be criticized for writing an unfavorable review, but what seems slightly scandalous is the fact that he brushed off the play with the dismissive tones critics usually reserve for utter unadulterated trash.

THEATER: MISFIT AT ODDS WITH WORLD
'*Johnny No-Trump*' in Premiere at Cort

BY CLIVE BARNES

The critic's life would be greatly simplified if there were only two kinds of play—the good and the bad. But in fact plays stubbornly refuse to admit such a categorization, and only people with a "hit-or-miss" mentality are foolish enough to impose on themselves and us what can never be natural. Plays are not to be dismissed as either a hit or miss—and producers should possibly ponder over this a little.

Mary Mercier's *Johnny No-Trump*, which came to the Cort Theater last night cannot be characterized as either good or bad. In fact if I had to summarize it with one word I'd be tempted to call it schizophrenic. For there are times when the characters (it is beautifully acted, incidentally) seem to be talking with absolute truthfulness, but the moment passes, and within seconds the play has changed gear and is offering what, especially by comparison, is nothing more than slick gibberish.

Miss Mercier (it is a first play, by the way) has taken a cliché, and now and again embroidered it with truth. The latter does not forgive the former, but it certainly helps.

First for the cliché: this is the 16-year-old misfit at odds with his parents and the world. Here he is a fresh kid who wants to become a drop-out and a poet. Brought up by a wise-cracking yet school marmish mother and a reactionary lump of an uncle, the boy appears to be going to take after his divorced father—a painter, wastrel and alcoholic.

The strains of hearts and flowers are never far away from this orchestra pit, and when the author solves her problem of a suitable ending with a death far too melodramatic for the theater (only real life normally can get away with such random coups de théâtre) she lost a certain amount of my sympathy.

Miss Mercier's difficulty seems to be that while she knows how people really speak, she is unable to heighten dialogue consistently for the theater. Usually she went too far so that her people sounded like any other synthetic theatricals. Something of her own realization of this emerged toward the end, when one of the characters said: "Why does a for-real feeling always come out as corn?" This is a problem for Miss Mercier's next play.

Where the play did succeed, unequivocally I thought, was in its staging and acting. Joseph Hardy, a distinguished refugee from Off Broadway on his first Broadway assignment, does wonders, not only in giving a fundamentally mechanical play a genuine air of spontaneity, but also in finding the rare but special passages when the characters sound as if from life rather than romantic fiction, and gently underscoring them.

Pat Hingle is the kind of actor who can wring out the truth from the blandest commonplace, and given a role that demanded nothing more than gruff lovability, he played it as if it had the dimensions of a role by Ibsen. Almost as good (although her role did not have the same temptations for crass syrup as did Mr. Hingle's) was Sada Thompson as the boy's mother, a portrayal that suggested a depth of reality and pain far beyond the conventional sweet and sour writing of the dialogue.

As the boy, Don Scardino had the difficulty of an uncon-vincing role, seeming both surprisingly mature and unbeliev-ably unsophisticated often in the same speech. For this fresh kid with an antic disposition and a tongue that sounded as if it had been plucked out of a stand-up comic's scriptwriter, could have been unsympathetic, and Mr. Scardino played him with charm and aplomb. James Broderick was also happily efficient as the painter-father, slightly drunk, completely weak, but not altogether unendearing.

So there it is. A cliché play at heart, yet one with good enough passages and strong enough (if rickety) architecture to support a sextet of good players. I personally would have preferred to have written it than, say, "Cactus Flower," but that does not mean it will run as long.

The New York Times
Monday, October 9, 1967

In discussing the review recently, Barnes said: "I would stand by my assessment of this play completely. Actually, I did not consider that it was a killing notice. I thought it was an encouraging notice. . . . I would have liked this play to have run because (a) it was very well acted, and (b) I think it would have given quite a bit of pleasure to some people, if the people could find it. It was the kind of respectable play that makes up the respectable theater—the kind of honorable failure.

"When I say that I would have preferred to have written it than, say, *Cactus Flower*, that was a genuine remark. I really meant that. I meant that there's something very sick with our theater in which a play like *Cactus Flower* can run for three years and this can only run for one night."

If Barnes had said this five years ago, in his review—as he evidently thinks he did say—*Johnny No-Trump* would probably have had a de-cent run, one that would have given a lot of people the chance to gain that "pleasure" which he mentions. His critical position, as stated here, in his words and five years later, is both honorable and well considered —but it wasn't in his original review.

What is so intriguing about it all is that Barnes still insists that he wrote an "encouraging" notice when it was, in fact, a bomb-blast. The play's other producer, Charles Woodward, Jr., sounded more than a little bewildered when he said recently, "Clive Barnes, even after he had reviewed the show, said that he liked the show very much and that he thought he had written a better review than he had." His partner, Richard Barr, says pretty much the same thing: "He did not admit that he'd made an error; he thought that he'd written a better notice than he had."

Like that childhood game of "Whisper Me a Secret," this tale gets quite a little muddled in the retelling. Witness Mary Mercier's statement: "I was told by someone that one month later Barnes said that if he had the thing to do over again he would write a better review." It would seem as if the "someone" to whom she was referring might have been director Joseph Hardy, who had earlier launched into a fascinating recounting of a meeting between him and Barnes a month or so after *Johnny No-Trump* had closed. "Barnes was just falling all over me with apologies," Hardy claims, "saying that if he had known that the review would have done what it did, he would have written it differently. . . . I respect him for that. I think it's very nice of him to say, 'I made a mistake.' "

According to Barnes, however, that conversation would have appeared to have taken place ten percent in reality and ninety percent in Hardy's fantasy. "I probably apologized," Barnes says, "in the sense that I was sorry that the play came off. I'd felt that it *shouldn't* have come off. I'd felt that it deserved a modest run. Perhaps I'd said that it was a pity that I *couldn't* have written the notice in a different way. I *could* have said something like that."

According to Hardy's remembrances of his five-year-old conversation with Barnes, he went on to criticize the *Times*'s reviewer to his face for his construction of his notice, pointing out that it began in a strongly downbeat fashion, and that it was not until the middle of his review that Barnes got around to mentioning what he had liked about the play. Hardy claims also to have given the critic a friendly lecture on how he *should* have constructed and phrased his notice. "And Barnes said to me, 'I know exactly what you mean,' " says Hardy, continuing his story; "Barnes said that had he known, he would have done it differently. He would have written about the good things first. And you notice that he does it that way now. He always puts the good things first."

Although Hardy's tone is both presumptuous and condescending to the *Times*'s critic (who calls Hardy's recollections "nonsense"), the man is an excellent director. Prior to *Johnny No-Trump*, he directed *You're a Good Man, Charlie Brown* off Broadway, which won him the Vernon Rice-Drama Desk Award, the Outer Critics Circle Award, and the Lola D'Annunzio Award. In subsequent seasons, he directed Woody Allen's *Play It Again, Sam,* both in New York and London, and won the 1969–70 Tony for his direction of *Child's Play.* He staged Joe Orton's black farce, *What the Butler Saw,* which won an Obie Award, and in 1970 directed the successful Broadway comedy *Bob and Ray— The Two and Only.*

Besides being a fine director, Hardy has a sharp analytical mind. His assessment of Barnes's review is most astute. The notice *was* badly constructed, and it communicated not at all the thoughtful judgment which Barnes later stated as his critical opinion.

But there is one additional factor which made this particular notice something quite out of the ordinary. Barnes had just taken over the function of theater critic for the *Times,* and *Johnny No-Trump* was, in fact, the first original American drama of this season of his initiation. (He had reviewed only four Broadway plays at this point: *The Home-coming,* which was the only successful entry; plus two comedies—*Keep It in the Family* and *Song of the Grasshopper*—and a melodrama, *Dr. Cook's Garden,* which were all instant flops.) *Johnny No-Trump* was at the same time the first *flawed* American drama to greet newcomer Barnes, who said that he wanted this particular review to make it clear to the theatrical community at large that he had no intention of pandering to imperfection.

"This was the first play where I had to face head-on the problem of a play that was neither good nor bad," Barnes recalls. "I think previously that season all the plays had been comfortably bad. [My review] was, to an extent, a kind of *manifesto,* an indication of intent, that just because a play was half-good, I wasn't going to say it was all good. And that if Broadway chooses to treat this as a death sentence, then too bad."

When Barnes, who has now been the *Times's* critic for five seasons, was asked whether he felt that he had now come to terms with the problem of the flawed play, the subject of that long-ago "manifesto," he began with the positive statement: "I think I personally have acquired in these years perhaps a better technique for handling this kind of situation." But he then went on to qualify the statement, and then, on further consideration, to reverse it completely, with the downbeat pronouncement: "I think it's probably not true."

Barnes's initial reaction seems most accurate; he has indeed devised a workable formula for communicating the peculiarly schizophrenic neither-hit-nor-miss quality of some plays in such a way that the reader can decide for himself whether the play's merits outweigh its flaws. If *Johnny No-Trump* were to open tomorrow, Clive Barnes would probably write quite a different review of the play. Its critical opinion would probably not be altered, but certainly it would be advanced in such a way that the play's merits would be more forcefully acknowledged.

So the flaw with Barnes's "manifesto" is not the principle of it, but that at that time he hadn't yet learned how to live up to it. It would appear that, in making his statement of principles so conscientiously, Barnes was led by the solemnity of the occasion to an overly scrupulous attitude toward this, his "guinea pig" show. It was simply *Johnny No-Trump*'s hard luck that it happened to be the first of its kind to confront the neophyte theater critic, and it went down as a sort of sacrificial offering.

Anyone personally uninvolved with the production can afford to analyze the *Times*'s unfavorable review and then dismiss it philosophically without bleeding. Producer Richard Barr, however, had the proverbial kittens and hit the proverbial roof when news of Barnes's pan reached him. And when every other reason for the play's failure has been hashed over, this emotional factor of rage remains to be considered.

Quickie closings are part of the dismal facts of life about the theater, but an opening-night swan song is rather an extreme measure, even for the most jaded old cynics in the business. And Richard Barr is neither jaded, old, nor cynical. Barr is, in fact, the epitome of the new younger breed of theater producers in whose hands lies the industry's major hope of survival, revitalization, and future growth. The theater community is well aware that Barr has supplied a good deal of the impetus and brain-power behind many of the projects of the League of New York Theatres, the loosely organized unit of Broadway producers of which he is president.

Among the ventures of his own multifaceted producing organization is the respected Theatre 1972, which was begun as Theatre 1960 and has produced in those twelve years a fine body of work, from plays by Edward Albee, Samuel Beckett, and Eugene Ionesco to works by a number of talented unknowns. Together with playwright Edward Albee and then-co-producer Clinton Wilder, Barr has been the organizer of the Playwrights Unit, a workshop where a young writer can practice his craft without the usual pressures of commercial production. LeRoi Jones's *Dutchman* came out of the Playwrights Unit, as did Mart

Crowley's *The Boys in the Band.* Judging from his record, Barr is well deserving of his reputation in the trade as a smart, sensitive, enterprising producer.

Although appearing too shrewd a man to erupt into temper rages, Barr has yet been known to have strongly emotional public responses when certain of his shows get bombed. Barr took great umbrage, for example, at the critical reception to his productions of *Lovey* (March, 1965) and *Party on Greenwich Avenue* (May, 1967), and shuttered both shows almost immediately after opening them. (In the matter of *Lovey*, Barr's outrage is mystifying, since the play received an excellent set of notices.)

Howard Atlee, who handled the publicity for *Johnny No-Trump*, recalls Barr's frame of mind as "determined" when he announced his intention to close that play. "Nobody objected" to Barr's decision, Atlee says. "Richard is rather prepossessing when he makes a decision. You don't stand up to him, and you don't talk back to him. Richard tried to make it all seem very light—this is what you do in the professional theater when you don't get out-and-out rave notices that are going to send people rushing in droves to the box office. He was being very practical, and he refused to have any sentiment or to give anybody else the chance. It's a whole school of producing."

A more unsettling recollection of Barr's decision to close *Johnny No-Trump* comes from Mary Mercier. "The next day," she recalls, "I had to meet the producer and director at the place where they were preparing the advertising for the show. It was over in the Sardi Building. It was there that Richard Barr just walked in and said that he was closing the show. He would not run it even a second night.

"There was nothing that I could do to make him fight for the show. The director didn't even vote. He didn't say: 'I think you should fight for it' or anything like that. He remained silent about the situation. There was no one who worked for Richard Barr who was going to oppose his opinion. I said to him, 'I think that you should fight for the show.' But he was, in fact, so angry that he was incapable of making a business decision.

"I don't know *who* Barr thought he was spiting. His anger was directed very much at Barnes, because of the *Times*'s notice. But I felt that Barr should have gambled, really. The play already had good word-of-mouth from the preview audiences. Amongst the reviews he had enough good ones to help him. He had some good radio and TV notices, too.

"But Barr was not in a state to listen, really, to anything that I had to say, or to any reasonable argument that I might have given. He was just very angry and adamant about closing. And that was that.

"I don't know why Barr didn't listen. He himself was someone, it seemed to me, who *did* appreciate the play. So why he didn't choose to fight for a play that he claimed to love—well, that's something to do with his character."

To Miss Mercier's account, one might reasonably advance the position that theatrical producing is still a business venture. In substance, this is Richard Barr's position. "Indeed, I was emotional," he says. "I was mad as hell. Sure, there was a lot of emotion mixed up in it—no question about that. But I would never take out an emotion to jeopardize a property if I thought it had a fighting chance. It wasn't an emotional decision; it was a sheer dollars-and-cents decision."

But here, too, *Johnny No-Trump* was in an unusual situation. Although the producing unit of Albee-Barr-Wilder had seen a lot of theatrical action, this was the first venture for the *new* producing entente of Richard Barr and Charles Woodward. Barr certainly must have been concerned about the feelings of his new partner and wary about hazarding his investment by plowing what was left of it into a gamble that *Johnny No-Trump* would pay off.

It is the opinion of publicist Howard Atlee that Barr was actually overly wary of the reactions of his new partner and his investors. "He was concerned about the investors," Atlee states. "Barr was *always* concerned about the investors and has always protected whatever dollar he could. After all, he's in the business of producing plays, and he wants to get his investors back next time. But I don't know why, in this case, he didn't canvass his investors to see if they *wanted* to spend the rest of their money, letting the show run out whatever money it had left. I don't think it would have cost them that much."

As for the actual figures involved, Barr says, "We were financed for $100,000. The show actually cost $84,000 to produce." Barr also gives $20,000 a week as the figure which it would take to keep the show running. Elementary mathematics would seem to indicate that *Johnny No-Trump* couldn't have run more than a few days, even if Barr hadn't decided to fold it. But the higher mathematics of the theater world alter the picture somewhat.

Let's start with that $20,000 a week operating-expenses figure. It is not unusual procedure, when a show is fighting for its life, for the creative personnel to take cuts in their returns. When asked about that possibility, director Joseph Hardy said, "They could have cut every-body's royalties, cut back the salaries. Every actor in that cast would have been happy to do so. Of course, I would have, too—immediately." Questioned about that point, Barr conceded, "$20,000 would be an exaggeration. But let's assume we *could* have gotten cuts from the author and so forth. It would still have cost us $10,000 or $12,000 a week to run it."

The figure for the play's investment is also misleading. "Actually, the show did not cost $84,000," co-producer Charles Woodward admits. "It cost $84,000 because we had to close after one performance. So we threw in all our closing expenses. And we had theater guarantees, advances to the author, and everything else." So it turns out that the actual *actual* amount of the $100,000 investment that it took to open (*not* open *and close*) *Johnny No-Trump* was $67,000—or, in Woodward's words: "If the play had run, for example, for a month, our actual costs, as of opening night, would have been $67,000." Which would have left $33,000 plus the next week's advance, which Woodward said was $1,000, to operate a show whose realistic weekly expenses, after royalty and salary cuts, would have been between $10,000 and $12,000 a week. And this is still assuming, by the way, that not a blessed soul turned up at the box office.

It was Joseph Hardy who put the financial angle in its clearest perspective in relation to a producer's duty to his property. "I think the producers are at fault," he says. "My guess is that they were nervous about their investors. I think they ran absolutely scared, and rather than spend another $25–$40,000 to keep it open a week or two, they decided to protect their investors and close it immediately. That, I think, was unfair."

As Hardy and Howard Atlee both point out, it *is* the producer's prerogative to protect the investment of his backers. But he also has a duty to his theatrical property and to his creative staff—who have also "invested" something of themselves and their talent with him. Even the most ardent aesthete of theater art would hardly claim that the business-man-producer should function as a philanthropist. But neither is he in business in the same way that, say, a wholesale meat distributor is. His product is a piece of living art, not a piece of dead meat, and he has a duty to it.

It was to this responsibility that Clive Barnes was referring when he fired off a curt retaliatory telegram to Richard Barr, after the producer had rapped him for his review of *Johnny No-Trump*. "I too am very angry," the critic wired. "No play worth one performance in the view of any producer should not be worth a month's run. Have more faith in your product."

Although a full month's run might indeed be economically unfeasible, as Barr pointed out to Barnes in his answering letter, the *Times's* critic still has a justifiable principle. Regardless of reviews or public response, the producer should be prepared to see his production through the minimum of a two-week run. This commitment should be included in the original investment, and investors should be fully apprised of it. Anything less than this full two-week commitment should be considered an underfinanced show and, as such, a purely self-serving business investment on the part of a producer who would serve the theater better by limiting his economic investments to oil-well speculation in Kuwait.

That the specific producer under discussion here should be Richard Barr is very ironic, since Barr is far more aware than most, of the responsibility a producer bears to his productions. On more than one occasion he has even taken financial losses to support plays in whose artistic merits he believed. It would seem that, in the case of *Johnny No-Trump*, Barr simply lost his head and in closing the play so abruptly acted rashly out of anger. (This rather charitable concession to Barr's motives could be made more convincingly had I not learned from one of the cast that Barr had the closing notice posted before the play had even opened!)

Clive Barnes is less charitable. It is his judgment that Barr deliberately underproduced the play, relying on a good press. The critic implies that Barr closed it out of sheer pique with himself, when he discovered his own "miscalculation." In Barnes's words: "Producers never say that they were wrong; it's always the critics who were wrong. I'm sure that they believed in the play. But how *much* did they believe in the play? The entire thing was done modestly, obviously on the cheap. Nothing wrong about that, but at the first breath of criticism Barr pulls it out.

"I think that both he and Hardy decided that this was a play that was going to get rave notices. It's often occurred to me whether they were affected by the success of Frank Gilroy's *The Subject Was Roses* a couple of seasons earlier. That was a sort of sleeper success, and perhaps they thought they had the same kind of play."

This last observation is certainly a very sharp insight. The ironic contrast between the reception for Gilroy's play—a decent but certainly artistically mediocre little family drama that was overrated to the tune of a Pulitzer Prize and the Drama Critics Circle Award—and the yawning response paid *Johnny No-Trump*, a similarly themed play which in many respects had it all over *Roses*, must have made Barr livid.

The case of *Johnny No-Trump* illustrates one other facet of the producer's responsibility to his properties, and that is the special duty demanded by the serious drama, the form of theater which is always the least likely candidate for success on the commercial marketplace. Under any circumstances, Mary Mercier's play—with a cast of fine, but relative no-name actors, with a debuting director, and a totally unknown playwright—would have had a rough time on Broadway, even with more enthusiastic notices. Many professional theater people, including Clive Barnes, feel that there is no Broadway audience for the serious drama. It is my contention that it *does* exist, but that this particular audience responds warily and carefully. The buildup for a drama is a much slower process than the gangbusters explosion of audience response which greets musicals and comedies. So in undertaking the production of a drama, producers must always consider the very special nature of this audience. In letting his emotions scramble his usual intelligence and theatrical acumen, Richard Barr never gave this audience the chance to find *Johnny No-Trump*. He was, as Hardy said, "unfair."

It does seem, then, as if Mary Mercier's play wins some kind of booby prize for having suffered such incredible rotten luck. Rather than being "just one of those things" in the touch-and-go-broke business of Broadway, the play's fast flop was the combination of a truly impressive number of converging phenomena, from the playwright's hard-headedness and the producer's petulance to the reviewers' misreadings and the jitters of the *Times*'s neophyte critic. And when all the "ifs" are put aside (*If* Walter Kerr were still the daily *Times* critic; *if* the ending had been changed; *if* the play were done in some other, less "generation-gap"-oriented season . . .), what remains is the fact that a good many people were deprived of the pleasure of experiencing a lovely play.